# Teacher Leadership

# Studies in the
# Postmodern Theory of Education

Shirley R. Steinberg
*General Editor*

Vol. 408

PETER LANG
New York • Washington, D.C./Baltimore • Bern
Frankfurt • Berlin • Brussels • Vienna • Oxford

# Teacher Leadership

## The "New" Foundations of Teacher Education
### A READER

EDITED BY ELEANOR BLAIR HILTY

PETER LANG
New York • Washington, D.C./Baltimore • Bern
Frankfurt • Berlin • Brussels • Vienna • Oxford

Library of Congress Cataloging-in-Publication Data

Teacher leadership: the "new" foundations of teacher education:
a reader / edited by Eleanor Blair Hilty.
p. cm. — (Counterpoints: studies in the postmodern theory
of education; v. 408)
Includes bibliographical references.
1. Teachers—Professional relationships. 2. Teacher participation in administration.
3. Educational leadership. 4. Professional learning communities.
I. Hilty, Eleanor Blair. II. Title. III. Series.
LB1775.T4165    371.2'011—dc22    2011009006
ISBN 978-1-4331-1292-8 (hardcover)
ISBN 978-1-4331-1291-1 (paperback)
ISSN 1058-1634


Bibliographic information published by **Die Deutsche Nationalbibliothek**.
**Die Deutsche Nationalbibliothek** lists this publication in the "Deutsche
Nationalbibliografie"; detailed bibliographic data is available
on the Internet at http://dnb.d-nb.de/.

The paper in this book meets the guidelines for permanence and durability
of the Committee on Production Guidelines for Book Longevity
of the Council of Library Resources.

Printed in the United States of America

To the many thousands of teacher leaders that I have encountered in both Jamaica and the United States: Your valiant efforts to be leaders in classrooms, schools and communities are seldom recognized or granted status, and yet, it would be frightening to consider where education might be without you.

And, to Ms. Ruth Ann Harrison Bearden—
You are an important part of my memories of school in
Memphis, Tennessee…I consider you both a role model and friend.

And

Ms. Angie Lovedahl—
Thank you for being an extraordinary teacher…the children
whose lives have been touched by you are very lucky indeed.

# Contents

## Section Three: Teacher Leaders and Student Learning

## Section Four: Teacher Leadership and Professional Learning Communities

## Section Five: Teacher Leadership: The New Foundations of Education

## Section Six: Teacher Leadership in the 21st Century

# Acknowledgments

The present book presents a collection of essays, several of which have been previously published. We gratefully acknowledge the permission to reprint from the respective copyright holder.

Angelle, P. (2007). Teachers as Leaders: Collaborative Leadership for Learning Communities. *Middle School Journal, 38*(3). (Chapter 23). Reprinted with permission from National Middle School Association.

Barth, R. S. (2001, February). Teacher leader. *Phi Delta Kappan, 82*(6), 443–449. (Chapter 2).

Cambron-McCabe, N., & McCarthy, M. M. (2005, January/March). Educating school leaders for social justice. *Educational Policy, 19*(1), 201–222. (Chapter 20).

Conley, S., & Muncey, D. E. (1999, Winter). Teachers talk about teaming and leadership in their work. *Theory into Practice, 38*(1), 46–55. (Chapter 13). Reprinted by permission of Taylor & Francis Ltd.

Coyle, M. (1997, May/June). Teacher leadership vs. school management: Flatten the hierarchies. *The Clearing House, 70*, 236–239. (Chapter 5). Reprinted by permission of Taylor & Francis Ltd.

"Turning Good Teachers into Great Leaders," by Terry Knecht Dozier, 2007, *Educational Leadership 65*(1), pp. 54–58. (Chapter 17).© 2007 by ASCD. Reprinted with permission. Learn more about ASCD at *www.ascd.org*.

DuFour, R. (2007). Professional learning communities: A bandwagon, an idea worth considering or our best hope for high levels of learning? *Middle School Journal, 29*(11), 4–8. (Chapter 15). Reprinted with permission from National Middle School Association.

Heller, M. G., & Firestone, W. A. (1994). Heroes, teams and teachers: A study of leadership for change. Washington, DC: ERIC. (ERIC Document Reproduction Service No. ED 386 784). (Chapter 8).

"Overcoming Obstacles to Leadership," by Susan Moore Johnson & Morgaen L. Donaldson, 2007,

*Educational Leadership* 65(1), pp. 8–13. (Chapter 21). © 2007 by ASCD. Reprinted with permission. Learn more about ASCD at *www.ascd.org*.

Kahne, J., & Westheimer, J. (2000). A pedagogy of collective action and reflection: Preparing teachers for collective school leadership. *Journal of Teacher Education, 51*(5), 372–383. (Chapter 14).

Katzenmeyer, M., & Moller, G. (2009). Understanding teacher leadership. In M. Katzenmeyer and G. Moller, *Awakening the Sleeping Giant: Helping Teachers Develop as Leaders* (3rd ed.). Thousand Oaks, CA: Corwin Press, Inc. (Chapter 1).

"What Does Leadership Capacity Really Mean" by Linda Lambert, JSD, Spring 2005. (Chapter 3). Reprinted with permission of the National Staff Development Council, *www.nsdc.org*. All rights reserved.

Leadership for Student Learning: Redefining the Teacher as Leader. School Leadership for the 21st Century Initiative: A Report of the Task Force on Teacher Leadership. (2001, April). Institute for Educational Leadership, Inc., pp. 1–27. (Chapter 9).

"Teachers, Learners, Leaders," by Ann Lieberman, 2010, *Educational Leadership* 67(9), Online. (Chapter 10). © 2010 by ASCD. Reprinted with permission. Learn more about ASCD at *www.ascd.org*.

Peterson, K. D., & Deal, T. E. (1998). How leaders influence the culture of schools. *Educational Leadership, 56*(1), 28–30. (Chapter 6).

"On the Frontier of School Reform with Trailblazers, Pioneers, and Settlers" by Phillip Schlechty, JSD, Fall 1993. (Chapter 4). Reprinted with permission of the National Staff Development Council, *www.nsdc.org*. All rights reserved.

Searby, L., & Shaddix, L. (2008, Spring). Growing teacher leaders in a culture of excellence. *Professional Educator, 32*(1), 35–43. (Chapter 7).

Sherrill, J. A. (1999). Preparing teachers for leadership roles in the 21st century. *Theory into Practice, 38*, 56–61. (Chapter 22). Reprinted by permission of Taylor & Francis Ltd.

Smylie, M. A., Conley, S., & Marks, H. M. (2003). Exploring new approaches to teacher leadership for school improvement. In J. Murphy (Ed.), *The Educational Leadership Challenge: Redefining Leadership for the 21st Century* (pp. 162–188). Chicago, IL: University of Chicago Press. (Chapter 25).

Teacher Leadership in High Schools: How Principals Encourage It, How Teachers Practice It. (2008). Institute for Educational Leadership, Inc., pp. 1–23. (Chapter 12).

"The Search for Teacher Leaders," by Meena Wilson, 1993, *Educational Leadership* 50(6), pp. 24–27. (Chapter 18) © 1993 by ASCD. Reprinted with permission. Learn more about ASCD at *www.ascd.org*.

# Foreword

DAVID GABBARD

I WANT TO BEGIN BY THANKING DR. HILTY FOR THE OPPORTUNITY TO WRITE THE FOREWORD to this important collection of readings. Our conversations on teacher leadership date back many years to the time when we first began teaching courses in the social foundations of education at our respective institutions in the University of North Carolina system. From the very beginning, those conversations on teacher leadership have intersected with our shared concern for the future of our field and its place in teacher education. While we lament the erosion that we have witnessed over the past fifteen years in social foundations' place in teacher education here in North Carolina (and nationally), we believe the ascension of "teacher leadership" as a primary focus of contemporary reforms can offer us a measure of hope.

On the one hand, "teacher leadership" provides social foundations educators with a new frame through which to understand and, most importantly, to communicate the importance of social foundations course content for pre-service and in-service teacher education programs. This concept applies to how we communicate to our students about what significance our interdisciplinary field of study carries for their future lives of service to their students and the communities where they live, to their school and their colleagues, to their broader profession and the broader society, and to the highest ideals of what it means to be an educated person. It also applies to how we communicate with our colleagues outside of social foundations, as well as policy makers, about the importance of our field for the professional preparation and development of teachers. We need to understand how the work of teacher educators outside of foundations, because it focuses so heavily on what teachers do in the day-to-day instructional environment of the classroom, can limit their perspective on what teachers need to know and be able to do. The notion of teacher leadership can help us remind them that, while teaching will and should always remain the most important work that teachers do, teachers' work entails much more than teaching.

On the other hand, precisely because it broadens our perspective on the scope and the multiple contexts of teachers' work beyond the traditional limits of the classroom, teacher leadership can also function as a new frame for helping social foundations educators, and teacher educators more generally, rethink the scope of our own work. In the first place, we need to begin thinking of ourselves more as teachers and teacher educators, though the reward structure of higher education and the culture of our field condition us to wrap our identities around our roles as critical researchers and scholars. More specifically, we need to view ourselves, first and foremost, as teachers of teachers. This role places us on more equal footing with our colleagues outside of the social foundations, reminding us—and them—that we are all part of the same enterprise. Though we may, at times, feel ourselves marginalized from the mainstream of the teacher education establishment, we can no longer afford the luxury of wallowing in that marginalization just to sustain our Quixotic identity as members of the noble opposition or the oppositional nobility. The days when we could count on accreditation standards to secure our courses a place in the required curriculum of teacher education programs across the United States have come to a close. Social foundations educators, then, need to do more than advocate teacher leadership; they need to practice it. Effective teacher leadership at any level demands relational as well as strategic thinking. Whether one teaches kindergarten or undergraduate social foundations courses, we are situated within a complex network of relationships that influence how we perceive and conduct our work. Social foundations educators form a subset of a larger community of teacher educators within their own local institutional context. Since there are no undergraduate degrees offered in the social foundations of education, the job security of social foundations educators has come to depend almost exclusively on the importance ascribed to social foundations coursework by that larger community of teacher educators. Strategically, then, leadership in the social foundations should recognize the paramount importance of sustaining and strengthening their colleagues' understanding of and appreciation for what their coursework contributes to the larger mission of preparing outstanding candidates for teaching certification and licensure.

The network of relationships in which social foundations and other teacher educators work, of course, extends far beyond the local context. They are part of a larger education/teacher education establishment that forms part of an even larger governance structure at the state level. Here in North Carolina, the teacher education establishment centers around the State Board of Education (SBE), which sets the requirements and accreditation standards for all teacher education programs, including those at private as well as public Institutions of Higher Education (IHEs). Those requirements begin with the regional standards set by the Southern Association of Colleges and Schools, as well as national standards. IHEs may choose national accreditation from either the National Council for Accreditation of Teacher Education (NCATE) or the Teacher Education Accreditation Council (TEAC). In addition to national and regional accreditation, IHEs must also comply with the SBE's own standards, as developed by the North Carolina Professional Teaching Standards Commission and approved by the SBE.

Of course, the SBE does not implement the North Carolina Teacher Education Program Approval Process itself but rather delegates that responsibility to the IHE Program Approval Section of the North Carolina Department of Public Instruction (NCDPI). Because none of the various sets of standards created by any of the above listed accreditation agencies explicitly requires any social foundations coursework, we find ourselves in a very precarious position. In fact, during the latest round of teacher education curriculum re-visioning here in our state, the Director of the IHE Program Approval Section was informally encouraging teacher education programs across the state to drop social foundations coursework from their curriculum entirely. Fortunately for us, the most recent iteration of the North Carolina Professional Teaching Standards requires all teacher education graduates to demonstrate an initial or "developing" degree of competency in teacher leadership. Though we teach social foundations courses on opposite ends of the state, our conversation on the linkages between social foundations and teacher leadership that dated back fifteen years and—in her case—an impressive record of scholarship on teachers' work, guided Dr. Hilty and me in our successful efforts to maintain social foundations coursework in the undergraduate teacher education curricula at our respective institutions by linking social foundations content to teacher leadership.

According to the North Carolina Professional Teaching Standards (NCPTS), there are five dimensions of teacher leadership. As explained in Standard I: Teachers demonstrate leadership:

1. Teachers lead in their classrooms.
2. Teachers demonstrate leadership in the school.
3. Teachers lead the teaching profession.
4. Teachers advocate for students and schools.
5. Teachers demonstrate high ethical standards.

Not only must teacher education programs require pre-service teachers to create products or outcomes demonstrating their developing leadership competencies, but teachers at all stages of their careers must be able to show "proficiency" in leadership and other elements of the NCPTS, as well. These standards are now being used by building principals in conducting their annual evaluations of teachers by means of a five-point rubric. Depending on teachers' degree of competency, they can receive a rating of either: Developing, Proficient, Accomplished, Distinguished, or Not Demonstrated. The use of this rubric, tied to NCPTS, creates opportunities for social foundations educators to infuse social foundations content into graduate as well as undergraduate courses in teacher leadership.

While providing specific guidance or recommendations on how we might tie social foundations coursework to the teacher leadership standard of the NCPTS and the discrete elements of the evaluation rubric currently in use in North Carolina schools lies beyond the scope of this brief foreword, there should be little doubt among social foundations educators that before we pronounce the death of our field, we should begin rethinking our arguments on why foundations matters to the professional preparation and development of teachers. As Parker Palmer (2007) explains in his call for the development of a "new professional":

> We must help our students uncover, examine, and debunk the myth that institutions are external to us and constrain us, as if they possessed autonomous powers that render us helpless—an assumption that is largely unconscious and entirely untrue.
>
> We professionals, who by any standard are among the most powerful people on the planet, have a bad habit of telling victim stories to excuse our unprofessional behavior [and I would add our complacency, cynicism, and fatalism]: 'The devil (boss, rules, pressures) made me do it.' We do this not only because it gives us a cheap ethical out but also because we are conditioned to think this way. (p. 205)

In our case, a focus on teacher leadership in the social foundations might help not only our students to become the "new professionals" called for by Palmer, but we might become "new professionals" ourselves.

## Reference

Palmer, P. (2007). *The courage to teach: Exploring the inner landscape of a teacher's life* (10th anniversary ed.). San Francisco, CA: Jossey-Bass.

# Introduction

ELEANOR BLAIR HILTY

---

> When the best leader's work is done, the people say, "We did it ourselves!"
> —LAO-TZU

THE CONCEPTS OF TEACHER LEADERS, TEACHER LEADERSHIP, AND LEADERSHIP CAPACITY building are not new in the field of education. These terms began to emerge in the mid-1990s as the importance of principals and teachers working together on school improvement began to be recognized (Katzenmeyer & Moller, 2009; Lambert, 2003). Today, however, these concepts are dominating discussions regarding the roles and responsibilities of teachers in educational reform. Sweeping across the country are teacher leader courses that have, in effect, become the "new" foundations of education in both the undergraduate and graduate teacher education programs. Teacher leader courses, as they are presently conceptualized, include the study of the social, historical, and philosophical foundations of education as well as curriculum studies and leadership theory. These courses appear, on the surface, to be a fairly benign rendering of foundational information within the context of an examination of teacher leadership. However, I believe that the concept of teacher leaders is a radical notion that has the potential to profoundly impact the growth of a stronger, more resilient teaching profession.

Teachers, today, are committed professionals who are better educated than ever before, and yet, they often enter a profession where their talents and enthusiasm are marginalized in the pursuit of higher test scores. Teachers know how to teach, and most have an understanding of student learning and classroom dynamics that far exceeds the knowledge base of the politicians, lobbyists, and even the administrators who seem intent on dictating the processes and procedures that will shape the daily lives of children and teachers. If teachers can be prepared to enter schools and embrace new opportunities to lead and collaborate with individuals both within and beyond the classroom, the possibilities for increased student learning are endless, and the reform of schools will simultaneously include a much overdue reform of the teaching profession.

Any discussion of teacher leadership must acknowledge the historical foundations of the profession of teaching. As Warren (1985), poignantly argued, "To call teaching a career in the nineteenth century would be misleading….for most, it was a part-time job taken up temporarily. School terms could be measured in weeks and those who taught tended to move on to other occupations or to marriage after a few years" (Finkelstein, 1970, qtd. in Warren, 1985, p. 6). In the twentieth century, the educational requirements for teachers increased, but the profession was seen, nevertheless, as a semi-profession (Lortie, 2002). Teacher salaries were notoriously low, and the status and autonomy granted to teachers were limited. In most schools, the teachers were primarily women and the administrators were male. These gender differences were often accompanied by differentiated roles and responsibilities for teachers and administrators: administrators had power and authority over entire schools; teachers had *very limited* power and authority in their classrooms. This phenomenon led Tyack (1974) to refer to schools as "pedagogical harems" where male administrators ruled and teachers unquestioningly performed the tasks assigned to them. Within this context, teacher leadership was seen by many teachers as a noble term used to assign many mundane and decidedly "unnoble" duties to teachers in order to "free" the administrators to "lead" the schools. In these settings, teacher hostility often led to petty acts of rebellion that tended to reinforce the patriarchal role of administrators and the childlike dependency of female teachers. Teaching would never be a "real" profession as long as teachers were not granted the same respect and autonomy that other professionals routinely expect and enjoy. Indeed, herein lies the problem with teacher leadership: it is often misunderstood by teachers and administrators, and thus, teachers are reluctant to seek out leadership roles and administrators prefer to retain all of the power and authority that they presently have in schools. Instead of seeing teaching and leadership as "two sides of the same coin," these skills are seen as separate and distinct entities that seldom exist in one individual. As one teacher recently asked, "Can I teach kindergarten and still be seen as a competent leader of both adults and children of all ages?" The answer should be yes, but the response to this question is usually accompanied by numerous caveats suggesting that a love of small children is not consistent with our ideas about whom we will allow to lead us.

Teacher leaders, as discussed by contemporary writers in the field of education, are defined quite differently. Katzenmeyer and Moller (2009) define teacher leaders as those who "lead within and beyond the classroom; identify with and contribute to a community of teacher learners and leaders; influence others toward improved educational practice; and accept responsibility for achieving the outcomes of their leadership" (p. 6). Lambert (2003) takes expands this definition by elaborating upon the idea of "leadership capacity" as a cornerstone of teacher leadership that involves "broad-based, skillful participation in the work of leadership" (p. 4). Taken together these two concepts set the parameters for a "new" kind of teaching profession where "professional development is as much about *adult* learning as student learning."…and "teacher leadership does not replace, but rather augments, principal leadership" (Lieberman, 2003, p. viii). Thinking about teaching is these ways represents a re-visioning of the teaching profession as a place where teachers can begin to confront the obstacles that have impeded the growth of the teaching profession. "Some of these obstacles are related to gender bias, but others are more personal, related to narrow definitions of leadership roles and responsibilities within schools and communities" (Hilty, 1999, p. 167). If teacher leaders and leadership capacity building were seriously embraced by schools and communities across the nation, our ability to work thoughtfully and collaboratively to reform the schools would be radically enhanced. The voices of all major stakeholders, teachers, administrators, parents, and students would be a part of the conversation, and the effort, to change schools today. Rather than piecemeal, disconnected efforts to reform the schools, teachers would "step up" and lead efforts that are based on the knowledge and skills of experienced teachers and reflect the needs and desires of our most important constituents: parents and students.

This book represents a sampling of some of the best-known writings on teacher leadership from the past twenty years. The authors included in this book are regularly cited in the literature, and their ideas are a reflection of the best thinking on the changing roles and responsibilities of teacher leaders and the potential of teacher leadership to transform the teaching profession as well as the quality of teaching and learning in schools across America. It is hoped that the reading of these essays will be accompanied by a lively, and critical, discussion of the roles and responsibilities of teacher leaders in the transforming 21$^{st}$ century schools in America.

# References

Finkelstein, B. J. (1970). *Governing the young: Teacher behavior in American primary schools, 1820–1880* (Unpublished doctoral dissertation, Teachers College, Columbia University).

Hilty, E. B. (1999). Southern schools, southern teachers: Redefining leadership in rural communities. In D. Chalker (Ed.). *Leadership for rural schools: Lessons for all educators:* Lancaster, PA: Technomic Publishing Company.

Katzenmeyer, M., & Moller, G. (2009). *Awakening the sleeping giant* (3rd ed.). Thousand Oaks, CA: Corwin.

Lambert, L. (2003). *Leadership capacity for lasting school improvement*. Alexandria, VA: Association for Supervision and Curriculum Development.

Lieberman, A. (2003). Foreword. In L. Lambert *Leadership capacity for lasting school improvement*. Alexandria, VA: Association for Supervision and Curriculum Development.

Lortie, D. (2002). *Schoolteacher* (2nd ed.). Chicago, IL: The University of Chicago Press.

Tyack, D. (1974). *The one best system: A history of American urban education*. Cambridge, MA: Harvard University Press.

Warren, D. (1985). Learning from experience: History and teacher education. *Educational Researcher, 14*(10), 5–12.

# SECTION ONE

# Teacher Leadership Defined

# CHAPTER ONE

# Understanding Teacher Leadership

MARILYN KATZENMEYER & GAYLE MOLLER

> Being a teacher leader means sharing and representing relevant and key ideas of our work as teachers in contexts beyond our individual classrooms so as to improve the education of our students and our ability to provide it for them.
> —ARIEL SACKS, EIGHTH GRADE TEACHER LEADER

HARDWORKING EDUCATORS STRUGGLE EVERY DAY WITHIN A SYSTEM THAT WAS NOT DESIGNED FOR the needs of today's students. In spite of the skepticism of the public and the ensuing policy reports that reveal failures within our educational system, most teachers are committed to searching for answers to improve student outcomes, although other demands compete for their attention. The unending need to find social services for students and their families, competitive challenges from advocates of charter schools and school vouchers, and the dwindling numbers of capable individuals who want to become teachers and school administrators create distractions from the challenge committed educators face in improving student learning.

Over the last 25 years, the massive number of reports on how to improve schools influenced policymakers to pass legislation placing pressure on educators to provide quality education for all students. Few would disagree with this goal. Many would argue, though, that the goal cannot be accomplished by simply raising standards, creating and implementing more outcome measures, and holding students, teachers, and administrators ever more accountable for test scores. Research on the impact of the accountability movement (Darling Hammond & Prince, 2007; Wechsler et al., 2007) has helped us understand that investing in teachers and their learning, rather than creating more tests, is a better investment for improving student outcomes. Unlike well-intentioned policymakers who persist in their search for "silver bullet" legislation to reform schools, savvy parents already know that the focus of reform efforts should be on the classroom teacher, who can make the most difference in their children's learning.

After mixed results with accountability measures, externally designed reform programs, and reward/punishment systems meant to exact higher test scores, the focus is turning toward individual classrooms and teacher quality (*Education Week*, 2008). To improve teacher quality, teachers need to learn to teach better. So attention has shifted to professional development, formerly an occasional experience for most teachers that is now a frequent obligation for every teacher regardless of the relevance for the teacher. Vendors, district administrators, school reform leaders, and others provide menus of professional development; some reflect quality, but many violate even the rudimentary standards for effective professional development. Wechsler et al. (2007), in a study of teaching in California, reported that this state does not have a coherent approach to ensuring that teachers have the knowledge and skills to be effective, and this conclusion would most likely also be true in every state.

Perhaps the answers to concerns about education rest in the potential of a leadership structure that taps into everyone's talents within the school community, especially the teachers. There cannot be significant progress within an educational system in which hierarchical control separates managers (school principals) from workers (teachers). Leadership must be "embedded in the school community as a whole" (Lambert, 1998, p. 5). The notion of the principal as the only leader is evolving into a clearer understanding of the leadership roles that teachers must take if our schools are to be successful.

Within every school there is a *sleeping giant* of teacher leadership that can be a strong catalyst for making changes to improve student learning. By using the energy of teacher leaders as agents of school change, public education will stand a better chance of ensuring that "every child has a high quality teacher" (Wehling, 2007, p. 14). We can call upon the leadership of teachers—the largest group of school employees and those closest to the students—to ensure a high level of teacher quality by bringing their vast resources to bear on continuously improving the schools. By helping teachers recognize that they are leaders, by offering opportunities to develop their leadership skills, and by creating school cultures that honor their leadership, we can awaken this sleeping giant of teacher leadership.

In order to do this, we begin in this chapter to examine how teacher leadership emerged. Then we share our expanded definition of teacher leadership. To illustrate the definition, we provide three examples of teacher leaders who struggle with universal dilemmas teacher leaders face. We next invite teachers to assess their inclination to be teacher leaders using the Readiness for Teacher Leadership instrument. Finally, we suggest that everyone has a responsibility to support teacher leaders, because teacher leaders cannot do it alone within the existing system.

## Teacher Leadership Emerges

When we wrote the first edition of this book in the mid-1990s, the concept of "teacher leadership" was relatively unknown. We discovered the importance of teacher leadership in our work with principals and school improvement. Principals who learned with teachers about school reform were more likely to transfer their learning from professional development workshops to the work in their schools. Unfortunately, though, many of the principals were transferred to other schools, and the initiatives at their previous schools fell to whims of the next principal. The teachers who had been colearners with their former principals were disillusioned and powerless to sustain their work. We wondered how systems could be built to sustain school improvement initiatives over time in spite of who sat in the principal's office. We dreamed that in every school, there would be a critical mass of positive teacher leaders who had the knowledge, skills, and beliefs to maintain the momentum of school improvement that influenced student learning. The gap between our dream for teacher leadership and the reality of school leadership structures has been an obstacle for over 20 years.

In spite of these obstacles, today, teacher leadership is emerging, and in many schools teacher leaders are finding their voices. Previously, if we asked a principal to identify teacher leaders, most often there were long hesitations and tentative responses; finally principals responded by identifying the textbook chairperson or the team leader. Yet they did not consider these teachers as "real" leaders, and certainly the teachers in those positions did not see themselves as leaders. Currently, "teacher leadership" is a more familiar term as evidenced by the vast growth of the numbers of instructional leadership positions, the inclusion of teacher leadership in standards for teachers, collaborative work across states on licensure for teacher leaders, and the proliferation of teacher leadership literature.

A primary reason that teacher leader positions are emerging is that school systems recognize that the professional development offered to teachers does not result in changed teacher behavior in the classroom unless follow-up coaching and support are offered. Teacher leaders with titles such as literacy coach, mentor, and lead teacher provide onsite assistance for teachers. As teachers take on leadership roles, they are uniting and reaching out beyond their classrooms to influence educational policy through professional networks, such as the Teacher Leaders Network (www.teacherleaders.org) that spans the United States.

Meanwhile, the number of journals, research reports, and books focused on teacher leadership is growing (Mangin & Stoelinga, 2008). We hear from many doctoral students who are engaged in writing dissertations that study teacher leadership and its impact. Although important first steps are underway, we look forward to the unleashing of leadership talent within every school as the norm.

To tap into the potential of teacher leadership requires moving beyond changing policy, enforcing mandates, and offering professional development. These reform strategies are relatively easy compared to the challenges of guaranteeing teacher quality in every classroom, ensuring effective principal leadership, and engaging teachers in meaningful leadership responsibilities. To reach these goals, we must overcome three obstacles. First, the structure of school and school system leadership must be examined. Next, there must be a shift from the old norms of teaching in isolation and focusing on just "my students." Finally, many teachers must recognize that a broader role of teacher leadership is open and available to those who wish to assume the responsibilities. Teaching is basically a "flat" profession (Danielson, 2007, p. 14), in which a teacher's responsibilities can remain the same from the first day of teaching until retirement regardless of the level of expertise gained over the years. Although many teachers engage in collaborative work and practice shared decision making to expand their circle of influence to *all* students and *all* teachers in *their* schools, too many teachers and administrators work in parallel universes, where formal leadership still rests in the principal's office and teacher leadership is haphazard at best.

While teacher leadership is no longer an unknown idea, it is "sometimes touted, but [it is] rarely fully realized" (Berry, Norton, & Byrd, 2007, p. 48). In our work with teacher leaders, we wondered why teachers are hesitant to be called leaders even when they are active in leadership activities. Regardless of the region of the country, we found three major reasons for their reluctance. First, the quality of teacher leadership depends on the culture of the school. Teachers describe school contexts that do not encourage them to be leaders. Often teachers who are motivated to become leaders will leave these unsupportive school cultures and will seek out schools more conducive to their leadership aspirations. A second concern is that teachers feel they do not have the skills to lead other adults.

While principals and other leaders are required to learn leadership skills, teachers rarely are engaged in building these skills. Finally, the egalitarian norms of school cultures suggest that all teachers should be equal. This strong norm discourages teachers from drawing attention to themselves. Fearing the reactions of their colleagues, teachers hesitate to be singled out of the group in an environment that has valued treating all teachers the same (Johnson & Donaldson, 2007). All of these factors impede the progress of teacher leadership. As teacher leadership becomes more widely accepted in some schools, the culture of teaching has more readily embraced leadership from peers (Mackenzie, 2007).

Teacher leadership is essential for the level of complex change schools face. In order to advance these roles for teachers, it is necessary for proponents to be clear about what teacher leadership is.

## Definition of Teacher Leadership

There is common agreement that we are a long way from a widespread understanding of teacher leadership. Confusion about definitions and expectations of teacher leaders abound (York Barr & Duke, 2004). Just what does teacher leadership look like? Who are teacher leaders? In the past, when we visited groups that were interested in teacher leadership, there was a request for time to clarify the concept of teacher leadership. Now we face a different predicament. Since teacher leadership is popular in the educator's professional jargon, there is a reluctance to examine the concept, because everyone believes he or she knows what it means. Regardless of the interest or lack of interest in defining teacher leadership, we believe a dialogue about the definition provides the foundation for a common understanding in order to promote and support teacher leaders.

We arrived at our definition of teacher leadership after a review of the educational literature, careful consideration of our experiences, and much conversation with teacher leaders, principals, and others. This definition continues to evolve as we continue our exploration and learning. Our definition is teacher leaders lead within and beyond the classroom; identify with and contribute to a community of teacher learners and leaders; influence others toward improved educational practice; and accept responsibility for achieving the outcomes of their leadership.

## Lead Within and Beyond the Classroom

The professional teacher is first of all competent in the classroom through the facilitation of students' learning. Teacher leadership is allowed by other teachers when the teacher is perceived as a capable teacher of students. Little (1995) cited legitimacy for leadership as a prerequisite for teacher leaders in their influence of peers. This legitimacy can only be given by other teachers and not by a positional title. Teachers we meet clearly accept this part of the leadership role, and some even recognize that they can transfer many classroom skills to their work with peers. Teachers can be leaders of change beyond their classrooms by accepting more responsibility for helping colleagues to achieve success for all of the students and for the total school program.

The level of involvement in teacher leadership beyond the classroom depends on the context of the school and the school system as well as the teacher's willingness. Most important, teachers do not have to divorce themselves from focusing on teaching and learning to be leaders. In the past, a commonly held belief was that if you were a teacher, the only way to become a leader was to leave the classroom and possibly the school (Barth, 1988; Boyer, 1983). Few teachers are attracted to school administration, and if they prepare for this role, it is because administration appears to be their only option for affecting students more broadly. The goal of becoming an administrator as the only way of getting ahead in education is giving way to teachers finding other outlets for their leadership both inside and outside their schools.

There are differences of opinion about teachers becoming leaders by taking responsibilities outside classrooms they consider their own. When we first started working with teacher leadership, we advocated for teachers to continue to teach while contributing beyond the classroom. We feared that teacher leaders might lose their connection to the classroom. With the emerging formal roles for teacher leaders, such as those of math coach or full time mentor of new teachers, we acknowledge that teacher leaders may leave the classroom and remain quite effective in working with other teachers. Their work is still focused on the improvement of teaching and learning, but within their colleagues' classrooms. Time demands and increased workload make it difficult for some teacher leaders to remain full time in the classroom and also to take on demanding leadership roles. Formal teacher leader roles can enable teachers to be valuable contributors to school improvement as long as the teacher leaders are not pulled into quasiadministrative responsibilities that take them away from the focus on teaching and their authentic relationships with colleague teachers.

Leadership, of course, is not limited to a selected group of lead teachers or master teachers. Teachers who choose not to leave the classroom and instead to assume informal leadership roles within the school are equally valued and powerful. Drawing from their expertise and passion for teaching, these teachers influence other teachers informally through having casual conversations, sharing materials, facilitating professional development, or simply extending an invitation for other teachers to visit their classrooms.

Teacher leadership roles empower teachers to realize their professional worthwhile still maintaining the centrality of their teaching roles (Stone, Horejs, & Lomas, 1997). Although some teacher leaders may seek administrative roles, most teachers in leadership roles do not view these opportunities as steps up the ladder to the administrative ranks. These teachers want to remain close to students and are willing to assume leadership roles that will affect decisions related to their daily practice with those students.

## Contribute to a Community of Learners and Leaders

Leading beyond the classroom provides an opportunity for teachers to interact with other adults in the school. Ackerman and Mackenzie (2007) suggested that teacher leaders "live for the dream of feeling part of a collective, collaborative enterprise" (p. 237). If this dream is realized, teachers learn within the school's professional community. Barth (2001) suggested that there is a "powerful relationship between learning and leading" (p. 445). Although the concept of professional learning communities emerged as a logical way to engage the adults in the school in their own learning, the realization of this type of school culture is relatively rare. Developing a professional learning community is more difficult than most people realize. Yet when teacher leaders do join a community of learners and leaders, in contrast to an elitist group, it opens up opportunities for every teacher to be a part of the community.

Teacher leaders, though, know the value of working with their peers in "communities of practice" (Lieberman & Miller, 2004, p. 22) or their own professional learning communities. Within these settings, teachers are learning in social context rather than only learning individually (Stein, Smith,

& Silver, 1999). Teacher leadership develops naturally among professionals who learn, share, and address problems together.

When teacher leaders and principals expand professional learning communities to include the entire school, then all teachers are included in the professional learning. Hord's (2003) examination of professional learning communities reveals that teacher leaders are partners with the formal school leaders in their efforts to improve teaching and learning. Five dimensions emerge as attributes of schools that are professional learning communities. The dimensions are

1.  Supportive and shared leadership: School administrators participate democratically with teachers—sharing power, authority, and decision making.
2.  Shared values and vision: School administrators and teachers share visions for school improvement that have an undeviating focus on student learning and that are consistently referenced for the staff's work.
3.  Collective learning and application of learning: Faculty and staff collective learning and application of the learning (taking action) create high intellectual learning tasks and solutions to address student needs.
4.  Supportive conditions: School conditions and human capacities support the staff's arrangement as a professional learning organization.
5.  Shared personal practice: Peers review and give feedback on teacher instructional practice in order to increase individual and organizational capacity. (Hord, 2003, p. 7)

Teacher leaders thrive in professional learning communities that exhibit these attributes. Credible teachers are empowered to assume leadership roles with the support of their peers. A critical mass of teacher leaders engaged in a professional learning community can often maintain momentum in a school's improvement efforts even during changes in formal, administrative leadership. The lack of continuity of leadership in schools and school districts makes maintaining reforms difficult (Fullan, 2005), but a professional learning community provides the best buffer we have to prevent this level of disturbance to sustainability of improvement efforts.

Teacher leaders also reach outside their schools to a wider professional community. Participation in national educational projects, professional organizations, and other external school reform movements provide teachers with networks of other teacher leaders who reinforce improved teaching practices. Lieberman and Wood (2003) documented the value of teacher involvement in external networks. These communities of learners and leaders can be the impetus for teachers to realize that their leadership skills are valuable and can give them the courage to lead within their own school while developing both professional expertise and leadership skills.

Finally, teacher leaders know how to build alliances and networks in order to accomplish their work (Crowther, 2008). These connections help them to pull together the necessary people, funding, and other resources to support their action plans. They know the social dynamics within the school and how to connect likeminded people as well as work with the skeptics. Depending on the health of the school culture, teacher leaders can build community and collaboratively find ways to make a difference for students.

## Influence Others toward Improved Practice

Teacher leaders influence others toward improved educational practice. A key word in our notion of teacher leadership is *influence*. There is probably not another profession that provides more practice in influencing than teaching, in which students are influenced daily by their teachers. The art of transferring these skills into work with colleagues, although complex, can be learned by teacher leaders.

Leadership is influencing. Teacher leaders are approachable and influence primarily through their relationships, which become the foundation upon which teacher leaders are able to share and learn with others. Silva, Gimbert, and Nolan (2000) found in their study of teacher leaders that building relationships was critical in their work. Also, Mooney (1994) reported descriptions of teacher leaders by other teachers. Teacher leaders were described as hardworking, involved with innovation, motivating students with a variety of abilities, and available to other teachers.

Formal positions are not necessary to influence others. In fact, teachers collaborating with their colleagues are just as effective in influencing others as are individuals with formal titles who carry the power of a position (Lambert, 2003). Motivating colleagues toward improved practice relies on the personal influence of competent teachers who have positive relationships with other adults in the school. In every school there are teacher leaders who show initiative, willingly experiment with new ideas, and then share their experiences with others.

Colleagues are influenced if leaders exhibit behaviors they advocate. Teacher leaders may engage in "reaching out to others with encouragement, technical knowledge to solve classroom problems, and enthusiasm for learning new things" (Rosenholtz, 1989, p. 208). Successful teacher leaders we know are consummate learners who pay attention to their own development and model continuous learning. Sharing information and visibly improving their own practice gives teacher leaders endorsement in their work with other teachers. Teachers who are credible to their peers, who are continuous learners, and who pass relevant information about best practices to others influence their colleague teachers. While teacher leaders are working in professional communities, they are, in turn, influenced by other teachers.

This attribute of teacher leadership is the most difficult to accomplish within a teacher culture that does not easily acknowledge that a colleague may have knowledge to share. The delicate balance of relationships is a constant challenge for teacher leaders who want to influence others to work together toward the goal of improved practice. Unless this balance is achieved, teachers can remain isolated except to share "war stories" about their daily interactions with students, parents, and even administrators.

## Accept Responsibility for Achieving Outcomes

Leadership assumes accountability for results. This is a new component in our definition, and when we have shared it with different groups of leaders, there has been universal agreement that taking responsibility for one's leadership is crucial for teacher leadership to be taken seriously. One teacher shared, "If we design the leadership role, we are also obligated to accept the accountability that comes with it." As a result of these kinds of conversations with teacher leaders, the definition is expanded to include this component.

Teachers often enter leadership roles by recognizing an area for improvement and then addressing the issue. This passion for finding solutions can lead to multiple and extensive ideas that require a high level of energy and more time than is available. For these reasons and many others, teachers can become discouraged and desert the plans midstream. In contrast, teacher leaders take responsibility for follow through on commitments and for achieving outcomes.

An effective teacher leader sets the resolution of a pressing concern as a goal, gathers data to support the need for change, engages like-minded colleagues, and secures resources to make changes. Keeping the vision of a better world for students, teacher leaders persist to find ways to achieve their goals. Tichy warned us that "vision without execution equals hallucination" (Harris, 2003, ¶ 6). So teacher leaders move beyond vision, take action, and are responsible for the outcomes.

Persistence is the key to their success. With limited formal power, even in a formal role, teacher leaders know that they have to rely on their personal power to influence others, and they rarely let go of the desire to achieve desired outcomes. Ferren (2000) suggested that it takes "random acts of responsibility" committed each day to be a leader (¶ 1). Teacher leaders may achieve only partial success, but they recognize that "half a loaf" is an incremental step and may lead to an ultimate solution (Barth, 2007, p. 25).

In a study of effective professional learning communities, teachers reported that one of the most important types of support the principal provided was consistent follow-through on decisions (Moller et al., 2000). If this is true for principals, then it also applies to teacher leadership. Trust is built through experience with how much you can depend on another person. Follow-through on leadership responsibilities is important for ensuring that the principal and other teachers have trust in a teacher leader. As we have discussed teacher leadership with principals, we have found that one of the primary reasons for hesitating to share leadership is that these principals experienced disappointment when teachers became excited about a project, made a commitment to take the lead, and then did not follow through. Not only are teacher leaders accountable, but they also hold the same expectations for their colleagues.

This definition of teacher leadership helps teachers to think differently about leadership and encourages teachers to consider leadership in their schools. In contrast to an authoritarian model of leadership, this definition more closely parallels what many teachers do already. It gives them confidence to acknowledge that they are or can be leaders and still maintain their relationships with their peers.

With this definition in mind, we share descriptions of three potential teacher leaders. Each teacher faces challenges to stepping up to a leadership role.

## Three Potential Teacher Leaders

Descriptions of three potential teacher leaders illustrate the promise of rousing the giant of teacher leadership. Most educators will recognize these situations as typical.

### Latonya

An elementary teacher for five years, Latonya experienced what she believed to be an excellent preservice preparation program at a nearby university. She entered the profession with knowledge of content, instructional strategies, and communication skills that help her interact effectively with students, parents, and her peers. Latonya works with experienced teachers in a school that is governed by a school leadership team that includes teachers, parents, and administrators as well as several local community members. Latonya plans and teaches with a team of fourth grade teachers whose students meet with success. She mentors preservice teachers from the nearby university on a regular basis. Her principal recognizes her competence and often recommends her to serve on committees in the school district. She has visited other schools to observe innovations. She is encouraged by the feedback she gets from parents on her work with their children. Often she visits families in their homes when parents find it difficult to attend parent-teacher conferences.

Currently, Latonya wrestles with the role she takes in the school's change efforts. She worries about how other teachers perceive her. Do they suspect that she is hoping to move into administration, even though her real motivation is to improve daily life at school for her students and her colleagues? Latonya wonders how other teachers will react if she offers to facilitate a study group so that teachers can share ideas and materials from the professional reading they are doing. Sometimes Latonya thinks she is too assertive in meetings and wonders if she may offend her colleagues by proposing too many changes. Last week she feared she was intimidating other teachers on the school improvement team. How much leadership she should exert is a concern for Latonya.

## George

Recognizing the unlimited possibilities of teacher leadership would also be helpful for George, a music teacher who works in an urban high school. Two years ago, George left his vocation of performing with a band to become a teacher. A dedicated and competent professional teacher, George is pleased he made the switch but experiences frustration with the lack of change in the traditional high school where he teaches. George meets obstacles when he tries to persuade others that his music program should be expanded further to meet student needs. When he joined the school advisory committee, he found that little was accomplished. His experience in working outside the school in the community would, he thinks, really help facilitate the work of this committee.

After two years as a classroom teacher, he decided to pursue a master's degree. George would also like to share and to apply knowledge he is gaining in his graduate courses to the problems faced in his high school. Test scores at his school could be improved; student dropout rates are alarming. There is much improvement needed in his school. He feels that, except within the fine arts department, his colleagues will neither listen to his thinking nor value his expertise. He hesitates to step forward, though he thinks he has something to contribute. George ponders whether his principal and his colleagues will be supportive of his leadership on schoolwide issues.

## Miranda

Miranda is a special education teacher in a middle school. Over 20 years ago, she started teaching with most of the same teachers in this school. Two new middle schools opened recently in the district, and attendance boundaries changed. Her school's student population also changed drastically. Rather than the middleclass suburban population that Miranda and her colleagues have worked with for years, they are now teaching students from neighborhoods where poverty, unstable family structures, and substance abuse are prevalent. The students do not respond well to the curriculum and instructional strategies of the past. Miranda knows that the demands of a diverse student population require change in her school. She feels alone in this belief. She wants to help her colleagues cope with the new challenges they face rather than join them in doing things the way they have always done them. She recently was awarded certification from the National Board for Professional Teaching Standards and has gained confidence in her ability as a teacher leader.

Miranda would like to lead discussions with her colleagues to invite them to solve instructional problems they face. Possibly she will talk to her principal about trying to find time for professional development activities targeted to middle school strategies. She would like to initiate some coteaching inclusion strategies with a regular education colleague. She believes these approaches can help teachers cope with the changes in their student population. She feels ready to step out and exercise her leadership, but she wonders how much impact she will have on reluctant teachers who seem to value maintaining the status quo.

Dilemmas similar to those of Latonya, George, and Miranda are not unusual. These teachers can play an even broader leadership role in the improvement of teaching and learning in their schools. However, administrators, other teachers, and, most important, the structures of schools may not support the contributions such teachers could make. Not seeing teacher leadership as a legitimate activity supported by others may keep teachers like these from contributing in significant ways to change in their schools.

We view the roles available to teachers like Latonya, George, and Miranda broadly. The sheer number of possible roles for teacher leaders in schools and districts lends credence to the idea that there truly is a huge untapped resource in schools. Surprisingly, though, many of these teachers do not see themselves as leaders unless opportunities are provided for them to reflect on their potential to lead.

## Readiness for Teacher Leadership

Teachers benefit from conversations designed to raise their awareness about teacher leadership. This discussion is a prerequisite to teachers thinking about their development as teacher leaders. In school systems, district staff members often ask us to help principals identify teacher leaders. How do we know who is a teacher leader or has the potential to be a teacher leader? It is easy to identify the formal teacher leaders, because they have titles and assigned responsibilities. The informal leaders are the teachers who practice their craft in subtle ways that may not be obvious to others. We use three adjectives to help teachers and administrators identify potential teacher leaders: *competent*, *credible*, and *approachable*. Teachers usually know which teachers are competent within their classrooms, and this naturally establishes them as credible. Being approachable is a critical characteristic. There are some teachers who are competent and credible but who choose to work as individuals rather than in collaboration with others. The ability to build positive relationships is critical to becoming a teacher leader.

A valuable conversation can be initiated by raising an individual teacher's awareness about his or her potential for leadership or about recognition of fellow colleagues as potential leaders. Am I a teacher leader? Do I have the potential to be a teacher leader? What characteristics do teachers need to have to become leaders? Which of my fellow teachers might also be identified as leaders? If answering these questions helps teachers more fully understand teacher leadership, then they may be ready to explore their own development as leaders and support the development of their colleagues.

One strategy to begin exploring teacher leadership is to use the instrument in Figure 1.1. on p. 16. This is an instrument to measure readiness for teacher leadership. Once teachers are open to considering that it is their responsibility to be leaders, the checklist is a tool to generate conversation around the concept. We use this instrument as we work with groups of teachers who are relatively unfamiliar with the idea of teacher leadership. It is useful for groups of preservice teachers or experienced teachers.

## Who Is Responsible?

The responsibility for the development of teacher leaders is not limited to a single individual or group. Too often, the entire obligation is placed on the shoulders of the school principal. Others share in this responsibility. Teachers, superintendents, and district administrators, as well as leaders in colleges and universities, can be excellent advocates for teacher leadership.

### Teachers

Teachers are responsible for the support of teacher leadership. The giant cannot be awakened without teacher leaders inviting others to join together in a community of leaders. By establishing collaborative relationships among faculty members, teachers begin to take the first step toward establishing an environment in which teacher leadership can thrive. The social relationships of teachers within a school are powerful determiners of how teachers assuming leadership roles will be viewed. Members of powerful cliques within a school can encourage or inhibit teachers who are willing to take on leadership roles.

### School Administrators

Principals or assistant principals can encourage or discourage teacher initiative. These formal school-site leaders are critical to empowering teachers as leaders. They are the primary models for teacher leaders in the school and may effectively model leadership strategies and skills that teacher leaders can use. A principal's willingness to share power and to be a colearner with teacher leaders to improve classroom practice provides support for teacher leadership. Removing barriers, providing resources, and actively listening can be the most important tasks a principal does for teacher leaders.

### Superintendents and District Staff

The school rests within a larger organization, the school district. In a two-school district or a district with hundreds of schools, the decision makers at the district level influence the learning of the adults within the entire system. The influence can be tangible, such as resources allocated to professional development, or it can be intangible, such as setting the expectation that employees will learn. Just like in schools, where principals set the tone for change, superintendents and their staffs are responsible for providing the type of support that frees and encourages schools to prepare teachers as leaders. Superintendents and other staff in a school district can legitimize the efforts of developing teacher leadership by establishing appropriate policy and district culture and by being advocates for teacher leadership.

## Colleges and Universities

The role of the colleges and universities in preparing teacher leaders is significant in the continuum of teacher development. The expectation that leadership is a teacher's responsibility can be cultivated early in the undergraduate preparation of the individual (Sherrill, 1999). Collaborative arrangements, such as professional development schools or learning consortia, connect teachers with university personnel. Standards and licensure for teacher leaders are being explored in many states, so professors are beginning to examine the content of their courses to assure they are preparing their graduates for leadership roles. Development of knowledge, skills, beliefs, and attitudes about teacher leadership begins with the university or college preparation programs for future teachers. Graduate programs and courses are emerging across the country specifically designed to prepare practicing teachers for leadership. The leadership skills are as important in these programs as the curriculum and instruction content. After the teacher leaves the university, the goal should be to encourage that teacher to be a leader.

# Conclusion

The giant resource of teacher leadership must be unleashed in the support of improved student learning. When teachers recognize that they can be leaders and accept a leading role from among the array of roles available to them, positive results in schools will follow. Teacher acceptance of leadership roles, appropriate professional development, and advocacy from formal leaders in the school system can start building a critical mass of teacher leaders to improve schools. The importance of teachers in complex, ongoing, educational change efforts cannot be overstated.

# Application Challenges

## For Teachers

1. Help teacher colleagues to see the value of teacher leadership in improving student outcomes by opening the discussion in your school. Be positive, share your knowledge of the concept, and engage others in discussion. Emphasize the benefits to the improvement of teaching and learning for students, the retention of teachers, and the possibility to sustain change in the school setting. Work together to influence your principal's understanding of teacher leadership and its value.
2. Tap into the many resources available to develop yourself as a teacher leader. Professional reading, networking with other teacher leaders, and online communications can assist you in growing your understanding of teacher leadership and in building your own capacity.

## For Principals

1. Build the confidence of teachers to be leaders. Make yourself available for regular interactions with prospective teacher leaders, and authentically listen to their ideas. Support teachers in initiatives they wish to lead, and remove barriers to their success. Find ways to give

incentives (e.g., release time, resources, recognition, and problem solving assistance) to teachers who are willing to take on leadership.

2.  Grow professionally yourself in understanding teacher leadership and its possible impact on student outcomes in your building. Assure that you model professional learning and collaboration, and then work toward empowering the teachers rather than controlling them. Share professional readings and resources with teachers. Engage them in meaningful dialogue about teaching and learning.

## For Superintendents and District Level Administrators

1.  Recognize that changes in schools are enhanced by a balance of efforts from the top down and the bottom up. Attempt to put policy and practice into place that pave the way for teacher leadership. Reflect on specific ways the school district can support teacher leaders, make resources available, and provide opportunities for networking.

2.  Model leadership by working collaboratively with school administrators in ways that you would like to see principals and assistant principals work with teacher leaders. Create an understanding of teacher leadership among your building administrators, and encourage them to empower teachers in the same ways you empower your administrators.

## For College and University Professors

1.  Introduce the concept of teachers acting as leaders early in the preservice experience. Engage teacher education students in collaborative work, and build their skills to be fully functioning members of school cultures in which professional learning communities thrive. Emphasize the linkages between teacher collaboration and improved student outcomes.

2.  Examine your curriculum and preparation programs for opportunities for preservice teachers to gain a broad perspective on formal and informal leadership opportunities for teachers. Assess the extent to which your programs are encouraging leadership rather than followership among your graduates.

Figure 1.1 Teacher Leadership Readiness Instrument

## Assessing Your Readiness for Teacher Leadership

| Respond to the following statements in terms of how strongly you agree or disagree | Strongly Disagree | Disagree | No Opinion | Agree | Strongly Agree |
|---|---|---|---|---|---|
| 1. My work as a teacher is both meaningful and important. | | | | | |
| 2. Individual teachers should be able to influence how other teachers think about, plan for, and conduct their work with students. | | | | | |
| 3. Teachers should be recognized for trying new teaching strategies whether they succeed or fail. | | | | | |
| 4. Teachers should decide on the best methods of meeting educational goals set by policymaking groups (e.g., school boards, state departments of education). | | | | | |
| 5. I am willing to observe and provide feedback to fellow teachers. | | | | | |
| 6. I would like to spend time discussing my values and beliefs about teaching with my colleagues. | | | | | |
| 7. It is important to me to have the respect of the administrators and other teachers at my school. | | | | | |

Figure 1.1 (Continued)

| Respond to the following statements in terms of how strongly you agree or disagree | Strongly Disagree | Disagree | No Opinion | Agree | Strongly Agree |
|---|---|---|---|---|---|
| 8. I would be willing to help a colleague who was having difficulty with his or her teaching. | | | | | |
| 9. I can see the points of view of my colleagues, parents, and students. | | | | | |
| 10. I would give my time to help select new faculty members for my school. | | | | | |
| 11. I try to work as a facilitator of the work of students in my classroom and of colleagues in meetings at my school. | | | | | |
| 12. Teachers working collaboratively should be able to influence practice in their schools. | | | | | |
| 13. I can continue to serve as a classroom teacher and become a leader in my school. | | | | | |
| 14. Cooperating with my colleagues is more important than competing with them. | | | | | |

Figure 1.1 (Continued)

| Respond to the following statements in terms of how strongly you agree or disagree | Strongly Disagree | Disagree | No Opinion | Agree | Strongly Agree |
|---|---|---|---|---|---|
| 15. I would give my time to help plan professional development activities at my school. | | | | | |
| 16. My work contributes to the overall success of our school program. | | | | | |
| 17. Mentoring new teachers is part of my responsibility as a professional teacher. | | | | | |
| 18. School faculty and university faculty can mutually benefit from working together. | | | | | |
| 19. I would be willing to give my time to participate in making decisions about such things as instructional materials, allocation of resources, student assignments, and organization of the school day. | | | | | |
| 20. I value time spent working with my colleagues on curriculum and instructional matters. | | | | | |
| 21. I am very effective in working with almost all of my colleagues. | | | | | |

Figure 1.1 (Continued)

| Respond to the following statements in terms of how strongly you agree or disagree | Strongly Disagree | Disagree | No Opinion | Agree | Strongly Agree |
|---|---|---|---|---|---|
| 22. I have knowledge, information, and skills that can help students be successful. | | | | | |
| 23. I recognize and value points of view that are different from mine. | | | | | |
| 24. I am very effective in working with almost all of my students. | | | | | |
| 25. I want to work in an environment where I am recognized and valued as a professional. | | | | | |

## Assessing Your Readiness for Teacher Leadership
### Scoring Protocol

1) Count the number of times you chose "strongly disagree." Multiply by minus two (–2), and write the number here:
2) Count the number of times you chose "disagree." Multiply by minus one (–1), and write the number here:
3) Ignore the number of times you chose "no opinion."
4) Count the number of times you chose "agree." Write the number here:
5) Count the number of times you chose "strongly agree." Multiply by two (2), and write the number here:
6) Write the sum of these four numbers here:

~ If the number on line 6 is between 35 and 50: Virtually all of your attitudes, values, and beliefs parallel those related to teacher leadership.
~ If the number on line 6 is between 20 and 34: The majority of your attitudes, values, and beliefs parallel those related to teacher leadership.
~ If the number on line 6 is between –5 and 19: Some of your attitudes, values, and beliefs parallel those related to teacher leadership. Several do not.
~ If the number on line 6 is –6 or below: Few of your attitudes, values, and beliefs parallel those related to teacher leadership.

*Source*: © Professional Development Center, 2004.

# References

Ackerman, R. H., & Mackenzie, S. V. (Eds.) (2007). *Uncovering teacher leadership: Essays and voices from the field.* Thousand Oaks, CA: Corwin.

Barth, R. S. (1988). School: A community of leaders. In A. Lieberman (Ed.), *Building a professional culture in schools* (pp. 129–147). New York: Teachers College Press.

Barth, R. S. (2001). Teacher leader. *Phi Delta Kappan, 82(6),* 443–449.

Barth R. S. (2007). The teacher leader. In R.H. Ackerman & S. V. Mackenzie (Eds.), *Uncovering teacher leadership: Essays and voices from the field* (pp. 9–36). Thousand Oaks, CA: Corwin.

Berry, B., Norton, J., & Byrd, A. (2007). Lessons from networking. *Educational Leadership, 65(1),* 48–52.

Boyer, E. L. (1983). High *school.* New York: Harper & Row.

Crowther, F., with Ferguson, M., & Hann, L. (2008). *Developing teacher leaders: How teacher leadership enhances school success* (2nd Ed.). Thousand Oaks, CA: Corwin.

Danielson, C. (2007). The many faces of leadership. *Educational Leadership, 65(1),* 14–19.

Darling-Hammond, L., & Prince, C.D. (2007). *Strengthening teacher quality in high-need schools—policy and practice.* Washington, DC: Council of Chief State School Officers.

*Education Week* (2008). *Quality counts 2008: Tapping into teaching: Unlocking the key to student success.* Bethesda, MD: Author.

Ferren, C. (2000). Become a leader by taking responsibility every day. *The Journal for Quality and Participation, 23(1).* Retrieved December 6 2007, from http://0-web.ebscohost.com.wncln.wncln.org/ehost/pdf?vid=3&hid=115&sid=8dda2d0d-4a71–48db-bald-79cb40978d4e%40sessionmgr106

Fullan, M. G. (2005). *Leadership and sustainability: System thinkers in action.* Thousand Oaks, CA: Corwin.

Harris, B. (2003). *Noel Tichy: Leadership beyond vision.* Missoula: Montana Associated Technologies Roundtables. Retrieved December 6, 2007, from http://www.matr.net/article-9269.html

Hord, S. (2003). Introduction. In S. Hord (Ed.), *Learning together, leading together: Changing schools through professional learning communities* (pp. 1—14). New York: Teachers College Press.

Johnson, S. M., & Donaldson, M. L. (2007). Overcoming obstacles to leadership. *Educational Leadership, 65(1),* 8–13.

Lambert, L. (1998). *Building leadership capacity in schools.* Alexandria, VA: Association for Supervision and Curriculum Development.

Lambert, L. (2003). *Leadership capacity for lasting school improvement.* Alexandria, VA: Association for Supervision and Curriculum Development.

Lieberman, A., & Miller, L. (2004). *Teacher leadership.* San Francisco: Jossey-Bass.

Lieberman, A., & Wood, D. (2003). *Inside the National Writing Project: Connecting network learning and classroom teaching.* New York: Teachers College Press.

Little, J. W. (1995). Contested ground: The basis of teacher leadership in two restructuring high schools. *Elementary School Journal, 96(1),* 47–73.

Mackenzie, S.V. (2007). (How) can a new vision of teacher leadership be fulfilled? In R. H. Ackerman & S. V. Mackenzie (Eds.), *Uncovering teacher leadership: Essays and voices from the field* (pp. 373–382). Thousand Oaks, CA: Corwin.

Mangin, M. M., & Stoelinga, S. R. (2008). Teacher leadership: What it is and why it matters. In M. M. Mangin & S. R. Stoelinga (Eds.), *Effective teacher leadership: Using research to inform and reform* (pp. 1–9). New York: Teachers College Press.

Moller, G., Pankake, A., Huffman, J.B., Hipp, K. A., Cowan, D., & Oliver, D. (2000). *Teacher leadership: A product of supportive & shared leadership within professional learning communities.* Paper presented at the annual meeting of the American Educational Research Association, New Orleans, LA.

Mooney, T. (1994). *Teachers as leaders: Hope for the future.* Washington, DC: National Commission on Excellence in Education. (ERIC Document Reproduction Service, No. ED 380407).

Rosenholtz, S. J. (1989). Teachers' *workplace: The social organization of schools.* New York: Longman.

Sacks, A. (2008). *Teacher leadership at the Ford Foundation.* Retrieved November 8, 2008, from http://teacherleaders.typepad.com/shoulders_of_giants/2008/10/teacher-leaders.html

Sherrill, J. A. (1999). Preparing teachers for leadership roles in the 21$^{st}$ century. *Theory into Practice, 38*, 56–61.

Silva, D. Y., Gimbert, B., & Nolan, J. (2000). Sliding the doors: Locking and unlocking possibilities for teacher leadership. *Teachers College Record, 102(4)*, 779–803.

Stein, M. K., Smith, M. S., & Silver, E. A. (1999). The development of professional developers: Learning to assist teachers in new settings in new ways. *Harvard Educational Review, 69*, 237–270.

Stone, M., Horejs, J., & Lomas, A. (1997). Commonalities and differences in teacher leadership at the elementary, middle, and high school levels. *Action in Teacher Education, 19(3)*, 49–64.

Wechsler, M., Tiffany-Morales, J., Campbell, A., Humphrey, D., Kim, D., Shields, P., et al. (2007). *The status of the teaching profession 2007*. Santa Cruz, CA: The Center for the Future of Teaching and Learning.

Wehling, B. (Ed.). (2007). Foreword. In *Building a 21$^{st}$ century U.S. education system* (pp. 13–21). Washington, DC: National Commission on Teaching and America's Future. Retrieved February 11, 2008, from http://www.ecs.org/html/offsite.asp?document=http%3A%2F%2Fwww%2Enctaf%2Eorg%2F

York-Barr, J. & Duke, K. (2004). What do we know about teacher leadership? Findings from two decades of scholarship. *Review of Educational Research, 74(3)*, 255–316.

# CHAPTER TWO

# Teacher Leader

ROLAND S. BARTH

I WAS VISITING A MIDDLE SCHOOL KNOWN FOR ITS INNOVATION. AFTER ENGAGING A TEACHER in conversation for a while, I asked her, "Do you take on some leadership for this school?" "I'm just a teacher," she replied. "If you want to talk with the leader, he's down the hall in the principal's office."

Clearly the question struck a nerve. And her response abraded—and continues to abrade—a nerve in me. More important, this teacher's words identify and aggravate a very sore spot within our profession. It is alarming that the individuals so central to the learning process so often see themselves as incidental to the enterprise we call "school." "I'm just a teacher," indeed!

Robert Hampel spent four years studying 10 schools within the Coalition of Essential Schools and found that different factions of teachers typically emerge within each school: the "cynics," the "sleepy people," the "yes-but" people—and the teacher leaders. Even within these reform-minded schools, he found that the teacher leaders never constituted more than 25% of a faculty.

Although we might suppose that a teacher would jump at the chance to set up a computer lab for the school or to create a new block schedule, precious few opportunities for these kinds of school-wide leadership are offered to teachers—and precious few are accepted. Something deep and powerful within school cultures seems to work against teacher leadership.

Why, I wonder, has an ethos developed in schools that is so inhospitable to teacher leadership? Why is it that so few teachers and administrators view teachers as having much leadership to offer their schools?

## What Is Teacher Leadership?

What is the difference between being "just a teacher" and being a "teacher leader"? One study suggested 10 areas in which teacher leadership is essential to the health of a school:

- choosing textbooks and instructional materials;
- shaping the curriculum;
- setting standards for student behavior;
- deciding whether students are tracked into special classes;
- designing staff development and inservice programs;
- setting promotion and retention policies;
- deciding school budgets;
- evaluating teacher performance;
- selecting new teachers; and
- selecting new administrators.

These are among the conditions of schooling that affect a teacher's ability to work with students, and they are, indeed, among the domains in which teacher leadership is most needed and least seen.

Speaking about a teacher's opportunities within the classroom, Haim Ginott once said: "I've come to the frightening conclusion that I am the decisive element in the classroom. It's my personal approach that creates the climate. It's my daily mood that makes the weather. As a teacher, I possess a tremendous power to make a child's life miserable or joyous."

But can a teacher become an equally "decisive element" within the school? To be sure, some teachers enjoy a corrosive influence by subverting. Some are "sleepy" and "yes-but" people. But all teachers have the capacity to lead their schools down a more positive path, to enlist their abundant experience and craft knowledge in the service of school improvement.

In the 1970s, Ron Edmonds introduced us to the ringing phrase "All children can learn." Our profession has begun to take these words seriously, even believe them and act upon them. I would like to suggest an equally revolutionary idea: "All teachers can lead." Indeed, if schools are going to become places in which all children are learning, all teachers must lead.

Skeptics might amend this assertion to "some teachers," or "a few teachers," or even "many teachers." These low expectations are as destructive, limiting, and self-fulfilling as "some children can learn." The fact of the matter is that all teachers harbor leadership capabilities waiting to be unlocked and engaged for the good of the school.

## Who Benefits?

Since *A Nation at Risk* in 1983, most national reform reports have recommended widespread teacher leadership. The language of the burgeoning charter school movement is replete with phrases like "empowerment of teachers," "faculty participation in management," "authority of teachers," and "consensus management." Something must be in it for somebody. As it turns out, there's a great deal in teacher leadership for everybody.

### The Students

The oft-stated fundamental purpose of public education is "to equip our citizens to believe in and to participate fully in our democratic system." To accomplish this goal, we require students to take courses in civics, social studies, and citizenship. A sobering indicator of the success of our efforts is the level of voter participation in the U.S.: fewer eligible citizens register and vote in this country than in any other Western democracy. Just 51% of registered voters cast a ballot in the recent presidential election. Moreover, between 1972 and 1986, voter turnout in presidential elections among high school graduates aged 18 to 24 fell by 20%, to just 32%. Clearly, not many students who graduate from our schools really believe in, let alone practice, democracy. The hidden curriculum trumps the overt curriculum.

Few schools operate democratically. Their governance is more akin to a dictatorship (albeit usually a benevolent one) than to a New England town meeting. If students do not experience their school environment as democratic, neither do teachers. On the other hand, when teachers take on important schoolwide responsibilities, they take a huge step in transforming their school from dictatorship to democracy. This change in the leadership culture of the school is not lost on students. Ripple effects radiate throughout the building as teachers enlist student leadership to amplify their own. And the more the school comes to look, act, and feel like a democracy, the more students come to believe in, practice, and sustain our democratic form of government.

Students benefit from teacher leadership in other ways. One study of governance patterns within a thousand schools found that, "in high-performing schools (those with few discipline problems and high pupil achievement), decision making and leadership are significantly more democratic. The teachers are more involved and influential in establishing discipline, selecting text books, designing curriculum, and even choosing their colleagues than are teachers in low-performing schools."

What can we take from this study? "Students learn when teachers lead."

## The School

In order to create communities of learners, teachers must model for students the most important enterprise of the schoolhouse—learning. A powerful relationship exists between learning and leading. The most salient learning for most of us comes when we don't know how to do it, when we want to know how to do it, and when our responsibility for doing it will affect the lives of many others. This is where teacher leadership and professional development intersect.

Teachers who assume responsibility for something they care desperately about—for instance, a school's staff development day—stand at the gate of profound learning. In this way, teacher leadership provides an inevitable and fecund occasion for teacher growth. Only when teachers learn will their students learn.

Pogo advises us, "None of us is as smart as all of us." When decision making is dispersed, when many minds are brought to bear on the knotty, recurring problems of the schoolhouse, better decisions get made. The better the quality of the decisions, the better the school.

Finally, the more educators who are a part of the decision making, the higher their morale, and the greater their participation and commitment in carrying out the goals of the school. Imagine a school in which every teacher takes ownership for a portion of the entire organization! When many lead, the school wins.

## The Teachers

Most would agree that who the teacher is and what the teacher does within the classroom have a greater influence upon students' accomplishment than any other school factor. There is considerable evidence, also, that what the teacher does inside the classroom is directly related to what the teacher does outside of the classroom.

Teachers' lives are enriched and energized in many ways when they actively pursue leadership opportunities. Rather than remain passive recipients—even victims—of what their institutions deal to them, teachers who lead help to shape their own schools and, thereby, their own destinies as educators.

The teacher who leads:

- gets to sit at the table with grownups as a first-class citizen in the schoolhouse rather than remain the subordinate in a world full of superordinates;
- enjoys variety, even relief, from the often relentless tedium of the classroom; and
- has an opportunity to work with and influence the lives of adults, as well as those of youngsters.

## The Principal

If there ever was a time when the principal could ride in alone on a white horse, like John Wayne or Joan of Arc, and save a troubled school, those days are certainly over. I know of no administrator who doesn't need help in fulfilling his or her impossible job description. Parents, students, community members, universities, business partners, the central office—all have the potential to become wonderful resources for the principal. But the most reliable, useful, proximate, and professional help resides under the roof of the school house with the teaching staff itself.

When teachers pull an oar for the entire school, they offer valuable assistance to the overworked and overwhelmed principal and to the school itself. Ample evidence suggests that effective principals don't work harder than less effective principals; they work smarter. Principals who encourage and enlist teachers' leadership leverage their own.

In sum, all teachers have leadership potential and can benefit from exercising that potential. Teachers become more active learners in an environment where they are leaders. When teachers lead, principals extend their own capacity, students enjoy a democratic community of learners, and schools benefit from better decisions. This is why the promise of widespread teacher leadership in our schools is so compelling for principals, students, and teachers and for the success of schools themselves.

# Impediments

If the concept of teacher leadership is so consequential, why, then, do so few teachers contribute so little beyond their classrooms to the life of their schools? Regrettably, severe, crippling impediments stand in the way of the dream of a school as a community of leaders. Let me address four.

## Our Plate Is Full

Responsibility upon responsibility has been added to each teacher's working day: responding to parents, overseeing after-school activities, attending professional development activities, and, of course, maintaining standards. The list is staggering. As one teacher told me, "When was the last time someone said to me, 'You are no longer responsible for…?' It's always an add-on."

In this context, the "opportunity" for school leadership is an add-on, a desirable add-on perhaps, but an add-on nonetheless. When choices must be made, many teachers understandably choose to teach, not lead.

## Time

Time in schools is in finite supply and in infinite demand. For most, it is a question of living within the allotted 24 hours in a day. How many teachers have been heard to say: "I would love to chair the committee, but I don't have time"? For most it is the truth. There simply is not enough time to do it all, let alone do it all well.

Others feel they have or could make time, but they expect to be paid for it. Some unions don't look kindly on teachers who take on additional leadership functions without pay. They set limits on uncompensated time. Many teachers find they can exert more power by saying no than by saying yes. And why not? Such an "add-on" mentality eventually leads to the schoolhouse equivalent of a sweatshop.

And teachers lead demanding lives outside of school. Three quarters of teachers are women, many of whom bear major responsibility for their own children. Others are fathers, spouses, or caretakers of elderly parents. Still others hold outside jobs to make ends meet. Time is indeed precious.

## The Tests

The current wave of "accountability" and "standards" has been widely translated into standardization, tests, and scores. Increasingly, the feeling in schools is that everything must be sacrificed upon the altar of the standardized test. Accountability is ratcheted up and up by constant, comparative scrutiny of the scores by teacher, by grade level, by school, by district, by state, and by nation.

Standardized tests are having a chilling effect on the teaching profession and on the inclination and ability of teachers to assume broad leadership within their schools. Every moment of every teacher's day is being scrutinized by others to discover what changes might raise students' scores. It is virtually impossible, of course, to link a teacher's leadership of a professional development day with salutary effects on the achievement level of that teacher's students. So the teacher, mindful of what the system values and rewards, chooses not to take responsibility for shaping the professional development day. The tyranny of the tests rules, and the tests' tentacles work themselves into aspects of schooling that go far beyond the content of a student's class.

## Colleagues

Many teachers report that the greatest obstacle to their leadership comes from colleagues. If they can get by the issues of time, tests, and tight budgets, their reward is the disapprobation of fellow teachers and administrators, who wield an immense power to extinguish a teacher's involvement in school leadership.

There are many reasons why the teacher who would lead encounters resistance from fellow teachers. Opposition often comes in bizarre, enervating, and discouraging forms. Some are passive—inertia, caution, insecurity, primitive personal and interpersonal skills—while others are active.

*Inertia:* Newton's first law seems to apply to people as well as to inanimate objects. "A body at rest will remain at rest unless acted upon by an outside force." Inertia is endemic in most academic institutions. Principals lead; teachers teach. So it has been, and so it shall be.

*Caution and insecurity:* Coupled with institutional inertia is another quality familiar to many school cultures: aversion to risk. In the world of teacher leadership, danger abounds. It can be equally unsafe to lead or to follow the lead of another, especially when the leader has not been officially "designated."

Ours is a cautious profession, top to bottom. To distinguish or even to appear to distinguish—oneself from the rest places the teacher at risk. Teacher leaders regularly speak of the prevailing insecurity they experience among fellow teachers in their schools. One teacher expressed it this way: "When a teacher is truly passionate about her work, others are threatened because they don't feel it, or can't impart it to their students. Sometimes I feel impeded in my work by other teachers and administrators who are threatened by my passion and enthusiasm."

A kind of taboo among teachers in many schools, then, makes it difficult to accept or display leadership. Teachers who lead—who behave like administrators—violate the taboos of their school and may be dealt with severely by their peers.

*Personal and interpersonal skills:* A final source of passive resistance to the teacher leader is the primitive quality of the relationships among teachers. Many school faculties are congenial, but few would characterize themselves as collegial. Many teachers seem to lack the personal, interpersonal, and group skills essential to the successful exercise of leadership. The classic hallmarks of collegiality—talking about practice, sharing craft knowledge, rooting for the success of others, observing one another engaged in practice—are simply absent.

*Active resistance to teacher leadership:* Inertia, risk aversion, lack of confidence, and primitive adult relationships all thwart teacher initiatives toward school leadership. Collectively, they provide a backdrop against which more active forms of resistance from teachers play out.

Sometimes even the strong support of the principal is insufficient to cushion the teacher leader against the formidable opposition of other teachers. One teacher told the following story:

> Our building administrator, as usual, was supportive and encouraged us to take the lead in discussing this topic. We did some research, attended a conference, spoke with a couple of schools already involved in looping, and finally brought the topic to a faculty meeting for discussion. We made a presentation to the faculty following this research.
>
> The reaction of other teachers, who had been informed and updated about the upcoming discussion, was disappointing and disheartening. Most were silent. Those who did speak were unsupportive, at best. There was an unwillingness to even engage in a discussion on a topic that we thought should be, at the very least, of interest to educators.
>
> I was disappointed. I was even more disappointed (although not surprised) to learn that there had been a great deal of discussion about the topic in the teachers' room, but that discussion had not been with those of us who were initiating the discussion.

The persistent array of means teachers employ to sabotage the best intentions of others is daunting and discouraging. Many teachers are perplexed and discouraged by the unfriendliness of their school's culture and by how quickly their leadership leads to their ostracism.

## Opportunities

Happily, fellow teachers also hold the power to unlock one another's leadership potential and to foster its growth. The basic disposition of a school toward the value of teacher leadership—more than workload, time, or tests—ultimately determines whether and by what means teachers will participate in the school community as leaders.

One definition of leadership I like very much is: "Making happen what you believe in." Teachers believe strongly in many things, and those who dare to follow those beliefs and make them happen choose one of many paths available to them.

## Lead by Following

Perhaps the least risky, and therefore most common, way to influence the life of one's school beyond the classroom is to follow the lead of others. By selectively supporting the efforts of fellow teachers, one teacher can help others move mountains—and occasionally even more massive geological formations, such as schools.

Following the lead of others may seem like a modest contribution, but it often constitutes a significant, affirmative, even courageous form of leadership. For anything of consequence to get done in schools, many people are needed to contribute in a hundred subtle, periodic, and reliable ways. This can mean showing up and speaking out at an important public meeting, signing petitions, writing letters, and participating in the cheering section. The success of those at the front of the line depends on the support of those behind them.

## Join the Team

One teacher told me, "If schools are going to be run by a committee, then I want to make damn sure I'm on the committee." Teams and committees offer some safety in numbers for the cautious, companionship for the gregarious, challenge for those attempting to influence others, and greater hope of making a significant difference through combined strength. And because more perspectives are considered in a group, better decisions are often made.

When a teacher shares common ground with other members of the team, frustration with long meetings and disagreements can be tolerated, and it is often possible as a team member to "make happen what you believe in." We have all experienced the astonishing influence of a single member of a team.

And we have all seen examples of the extraordinary influence a team can have upon a school. This is why many teachers find greater satisfaction in exerting leadership by being a part of a high-performing team.

## Lead Alone

Perhaps because they are disenchanted with following the lead of others, because they experience impatience and frustration trying to work with team members, or because they have been thwarted or ignored by administrators, many teachers set out alone to influence their schools. They conceal their attempt to improve their school, such as applying for a grant to get the school wired into the Internet. They become covert, guerrilla warriors. For them it is safer, simpler, and faster—and perhaps more exciting—to go underground, disclosing what they have done only when success is certain. This way, their efforts do not depend on enlisting the support of others, and they risk no public failure should their project prove unsuccessful. If the effort succeeds, however, the impact of the guerrilla leader is often compromised by the clandestine nature of his or her work.

## Lead by Example

Different from their guerrilla cousins, solitary teachers who stay out in the open are more likely to have a positive influence upon the larger school community because they take the risk to provide a constant, visible model of persistence, hope, and enthusiasm. By their example they influence others.

Indeed, I have seen stunning examples of teachers offering leadership to their school by remaining within their classrooms. They bring others in—to observe their work, to reflect together, and to exchange their craft knowledge about teaching.

Leading by example is perhaps the purest form of leadership and the one over which each of us has the most control. The bumper sticker tells us, "You can't lead where you won't go." The flipside, known so well to these teachers, is: "You can lead where you will go."

# What It Takes

From conversations with teacher leaders, it appears that their success is related to three factors:

## Having a Goal

Teachers who can identify and clearly delimit a goal and who care passionately about and can articulate what change they want to see in the school are likely to experience some success, especially if they recognize how others might benefit from that change.

## Persisting

Teachers who succeed in influencing the school are tireless and undeterred by the obstacles that seem to leap from behind every bush. Commitment to their cause is stronger than the hurdles they encounter.

## Enjoying Half a Loaf

The real world of schools seldom allows total fulfillment of anyone's dreams. Teachers who define success as effecting an incremental change in the desirable direction, rather than as accomplishing everything they set out to accomplish, experience success and are likely to engage in subsequent initiatives.

# The Principal

Teachers may choose to exercise leadership independently, but few can successfully undertake a school improvement initiative without support from the school principal. The principal, it seems, has a disproportionate influence upon teacher leadership—for better or for worse.

## Principal as Barrier

It is disheartening that many teachers experience their school administrator, and especially their principal, as an obstacle to their leadership aspirations. They see principals holding tightly and jealously onto power, control, and the center stage.

There are good reasons why principals guard their authority. They have worked long and hard to get where they are. Now that they have secured their positions as leaders of schools, they protect those positions tenaciously.

And it is risky for a principal to share leadership with teachers. Since principals will be held accountable for what others do, it is natural that they want evidence in advance that those they empower will get the job done well. Principals are also mindful of how much care, feeding, and hand-holding must go into helping the teacher leader. Given their own time crunches, many principals believe that it is more efficient to make decisions by themselves—to hire that new teacher rather than setting up, meeting with, and managing a committee to do so.

Not surprisingly, then, many principals carefully control whether and to whom they delegate responsibility for important decisions. They offer leadership opportunities to teachers who are most likely to support the principal's agenda and who will not divert attention or energy by pursuing their own. As one teacher said, "The administrator's task is to influence a chosen few and have them advocate his position on issues indirectly."

But a pattern of repeatedly anointing the "chosen few" overloads the few while squelching the leadership potential of the unchosen many. The principal's tendency to control also gives rise to that guerrilla teacher leader, who, because he or she will never be invited by the principal to lead, must work surreptitiously.

Although they may not be aware of it, many principals transmit forbidding, unwelcoming messages about teacher leadership. A principal's disposition to share leadership with teachers (or others) seems to be related to personal security. One study found that the weaker the principal personally, the less he or she is likely to share leadership. Stronger, more secure principals are more likely to share leadership. It makes sense.

## Principal as Culture Builder

So what can the principal do to help teachers reconcile their crucial classroom work with equally crucial schoolwide responsibilities? How might more teachers be sustained rather than discouraged in their efforts to lead? If teacher leadership is crucial to the health and performance of a school, principals are crucial to the health and the performance of teacher leaders. Indeed, many do find ways of inspiring a culture of teacher leadership within their schools. Several actions seem to influence their success.

*Expect:* Principals who support teacher leadership believe in it as a central purpose of the school. The participation of teachers as leaders is much more likely to occur when their principal openly and frequently articulates this vision at meetings, in conversations, in newsletters, in memos to the faculty, and at community meetings: "Here, we expect all teachers to lead."

*Relinquish:* Principals have in their bottom drawers a few marbles of authority that came with the job and many more that they have earned over the years. Some principals play these marbles alone. Principals who support teacher leadership make sure that all the marbles are played by as many players as possible. Principals have learned that when they relinquish some of the marbles to teachers, they unlock and enlist the creative powers of the faculty in the service of the school.

*Trust:* Teachers will not become leaders within the school community if, when the going gets rough and an angry parent or a central office official makes a phone call, the principal violates the trust, disempowers the teacher, and reasserts his or her authority. It takes only a single incident of having the rug pulled from beneath a teacher leader before that teacher—and the entire faculty—secedes from the community of leaders.

*Empower*: It is common for a principal, when confronted with a sudden problem—for example, a reprimand from the fire chief and superintendent after a plodding school evacuation drill—to set up a new procedure and then recruit a trusted teacher to monitor and maintain it. Yet the fun, the learning, and the commitment arise from brainstorming and devising one's own solutions and then trying to implement them. Principals elicit more leaders and more leadership when they invite teachers to address the problem before, not after, the principal has determined a solution.

*Include*: To address a nagging school issue, the principal often selects a trusted teacher who has handled similar problems successfully. But by relying on the tried and proven teacher, the principal rewards competence with even more work. Principals who build a school culture in which teacher leadership can flourish are more likely to match an important school issue with a teacher who feels passionately about that issue. One teacher's passion may be fire safety; another's, the supply closet. Innovative solutions often come from teachers who don't know how to do something but want to learn.

*Protect*: As we have seen, teachers who reveal themselves as leaders violate a taboo and put themselves "at risk." Principals find ways to run interference and protect these members of the faculty from the assaults of their fellows. A teacher calls a meeting; the principal attends to support and show the flag. A teacher wants to share her craft knowledge about creating a multicultural curriculum; the principal "asks" that teacher to address the faculty. When it's clear to teachers that their leadership is protected, they will be more willing to exercise it.

*Recognize:* Teachers will not for long go through the heroic efforts of leading schools, in addition to teaching classes if the consequences of their work go unnoticed, unrecognized, or unvalued by others.

It's ironic that teachers, principals, and parents clearly see the value of student recognition and have assembled an array of ways to offer recognition to students, from gold stars to scholarships, while developing no comparable offerings for the outstanding work of teachers. Recognition of teachers' efforts, including their efforts as leaders, is in precious short supply in the culture of most schools. Recognition costs little, sometimes nothing in dollars, but when the alarm rings at 6 A.M., it is among the reasons a teacher keeps bounding out of bed with alacrity, ready to lead.

*Share responsibility for failure*: If, as sometimes happens, a teacher stumbles in a schoolwide effort, the principal has several options. One is to blame the teacher and remove the responsibility. This action may help the principal in the short run, but in the long run few teachers will choose to stick their necks out again. Alternatively, the principal can assume the lonely and self-punitive position of captain of the ship: "The ship has gone aground; I am responsible."

But teacher and principal can share responsibility for failure as well as for success. Usually a school community deals more kindly with mistakes made jointly by teacher and principal than by either alone. The important question, of course, is not "Whose fault is it?" but rather "What happened and what can we learn from it so we do better next time?"

*Give credit for success*: It is important that the principal share with teacher leaders responsibility for success. Principals have plenty of opportunity to be on center stage. Teachers have few and need more. Let the teacher bask in the glory of a new, distinguished fire evacuation system or take the credit for helping open a door to a summer fellowship for a colleague! Good principals are more heromakers than heroes.

Administrators who create a school culture that is hospitable to shared leadership recognize that leadership on the part of teachers does not always have to be initiated, orchestrated, or even sanctioned by the principal. These principals realize that often the most spirited, inventive teacher leadership comes when teachers themselves become disenchanted by the encrusted "way we have always done it," see a better way, and set about bringing it into their schools.

When I was a principal I worked with a teacher who could not tolerate lines. Lines of students waiting to go to the bathroom, lines of parents waiting at parent conference time, lines of teachers waiting to go to lunch. She took it upon herself to eliminate the mindless, fruitless periods of waiting in lines that so immobilize schools. We not only supported her efforts, we were all grateful for— and astonished by—how far she was able to go on her monomaniacal mission to purge the school of the dreaded lines. She was not "just a teacher"! And she taught me that school leadership that must be managed by the principal constitutes only a fraction of the leadership available to a school.

## A Different Future

The concept of shared leadership in schools goes to the heart of the principal/teacher relationship. So what shall that relationship be? Superordinate to subordinate? Adversarial? Supportive? Collegial? Cooperative? Clearly there is nothing inherent in the role of principal that causes either curtailment or support of teacher leadership: it is how the principal chooses to perform the job. By their day-to-day actions, principals build the culture of their schools. That pattern of behavior can embed teacher leadership in the school's culture, cast a wet blanket on it—or have no influence at all.

A profound ambivalence about teachers pervades our profession. On the one hand, teachers are viewed—and treated by many—as semiskilled workers who need to be more technically trained and retrained, more closely monitored, more regulated, and more frequently evaluated against ever more prescriptive requirements and standards. On the other hand, teachers are viewed by others as grownups—professionals—deserving greater opportunity for more leadership, more participation in important decisions, and greater self-governance.

In the next 10 years, 2.2 million new teachers will be needed to staff America's schools. Approximately two-thirds of the entire teaching profession will be replaced. Thus the coming decade brings with it a profound opportunity to re-create the teaching profession. What would we like it to become?

Most would agree that schools are full of an overabundance of underutilized talent. When teachers lock their cars in the parking lot each morning, too many of them also lock up astonishing skills, interests, abilities, and potential. Then they go inside and teach five classes of beginning algebra and monitor the lunchroom.

Teaching algebra is critical to the school, and so is the fulfillment of supervisory duties. Yet an opportunity resides within each new teacher, and within the veteran as well, to become a school-based leader and reformer. For only when we transform and re-create the teaching profession in this way will we be able to transform and re-create the nation's schools.

In very real ways, teachers who choose to confine their work as educators to the classroom win. They have more time and energy to devote to their teaching, to each of their students, and to their responsibilities outside of school. They are immune from interpersonal conflicts with other teachers and with the principal. They enjoy a measure of safety in the relatively risk-free sanctuary of the classroom, where they may be accountable for pupil achievement but not for their own achievement as a leader. And they may enjoy a measure of sanity each day in the often turbulent and chaotic world of the schoolhouse.

For teachers who assume leadership, the outcome is less clear. They choose to supplement their work as classroom teachers by taking on responsibility, some of the time, for some of the issues that are integral to the health and character of the entire school. By participating in the larger arena, these teachers lose what the larger group wins: time, energy, freedom from interpersonal hassle, and immunity from public criticism for efforts that might not succeed. And they probably lose, as well, a measure of sanity in their days at school and at home.

But these teachers win something more important. They experience a reduction in isolation; the personal and professional satisfaction that comes from improving their schools; a sense of instrumentality, investment, and membership in the school community; and new learning about schools, about the process of change, and about themselves. And all of these positive experiences spill over into their classroom teaching. These teachers become owners and investors in the school rather than mere tenants.

They become professionals. With our nation's schools under relentless scrutiny, with all the well-placed concern, a remarkable space exists for teachers to fill. Most concerned people know what they don't want in schools; a smaller number know where the reforming of schools ought to lead us; and very few know how to get there. We are most likely to find rich conceptions of a better school and inventive ways to attain it when teachers step into leadership roles and articulate for the public and for the profession just what school and teaching might become.

All teachers can lead! Most teachers want to lead. And schools badly need their ideas, invention, energy, and leadership.

CHAPTER THREE

# What Does Leadership Capacity Really Mean?

LINDA LAMBERT

THROUGHOUT THIS HEMISPHERE, CONFERENCES, SEMINARS, AND ACADEMIES ARE HOSTING EVENTS on leadership capacity. The Internet lists dozens of online courses about leadership capacity. Google reports more than 3 million hits under the title "leadership capacity."

What is really meant by leadership capacity? The term has been around for some time. What is my leadership capacity? What is the leadership capacity of individual teachers, our principal, our political figures? This personal usage, while central to school improvement, does not offer a framework or schema to sustain school improvement. Since the publication of *Building Leadership Capacity in Schools* (ASCD, 1998), educators use the term "leadership capacity" as an organizational concept meaning broad-based, skillful participation in the work of leadership that leads to lasting school improvement.

First, let's look closely at these terms.

• **Leadership**—and therefore the work of leadership as used within the definition of leadership capacity—means reciprocal, purposeful learning together in community.

Reciprocity is essential to solving problems and working collaboratively. Purpose suggests values, focus, and momentum. Learning is mutually creating meaning and knowledge. Community is the essential environment for experiencing reciprocal, purposeful learning. These four ideas frame a definition of leadership in which all can see themselves reflected. It is the mirroring pool of a professional culture.

• **Broad-based participation** refers to who is at the table, whose voices are heard, and what patterns of participation exist. These patterns form the structure through which the work of the school or organization is done. Also, it is within these patterns of participation (teams, cadres, learning communities, study groups) that individuals develop lasting and respectful relationships. To be effective, participation requires skillfulness.

• **Skillful participation** is the understanding, knowledge, and skills that participants either develop or bring to their engagement in purposeful learning. The work of leadership involves developing skills in dialogue, inquiry, reflection, collaboration, facilitation, and conflict resolution.

Leadership skills for adult learning parallel good teaching: A good leader is a good teacher who uses her knowledge and skills with colleagues.

By defining these terms and how they interact, we are able to understand schools' differing levels of ability to sustain improvement. Schools at varying stages of developing leadership capacity may be described as follows:

- Low leadership capacity schools tend to be principal-dependent, lack a professional culture and are significantly unsuccessful with children. Only the principal, serving as a top-down manager, is referred to as the "leader" in the school. Teacher leadership is not a topic of conversation, let alone interest. Educators in such cultures deflect responsibility while preferring blame; they avoid focusing on teaching and learning while holding fast to archaic practices. While professional relationships may be congenial, they lack the challenge of collegiality. Tests and test scores may be considered the only valid measures of student success, and promising products and performances revealed by students' work are neglected. Absent an internal accountability system, these schools are subject to the whims, demands, and pressures of parents, districts, and states.

- Moderate leadership capacity schools lack a compelling purpose and focus, are governed by norms of individualism, hold few conversations among members of the whole community, and suffer from fragmentation and polarization. Concerns regarding teachers who will "not buy in" may arise when a small group of more skilled educators form an isolated inner core of decision makers. Either scenario—dispersed and individual action or corralled and exclusive action by a few—will leave the school without a focused, professional culture. The first scenario calls for a concerted effort to create a shared sense of purpose. The second scenario requires using broad-based, inclusive strategies (e.g., norms, collaborative action research, dialogue, inquiry) to involve everyone in the work of leading the school. In a school with moderate leadership capacity, disaggregating student scores inevitably reveals a lack of success for its more vulnerable or challenged students.

- High leadership capacity schools are learning communities that amplify leadership for all, learning for all, success for all. These schools have developed a fabric of structures (e.g., teams, communities, study groups) and processes (reflection, inquiry, dialogue) that form a more lasting and buoyant web of interrelated actions. The principal is only one of the leaders in the school community and models collaboration, listening, and engagement. Each participant shares the vision, understands how the school is moving toward the vision, and understands how he or she contributes to that journey. The quality of the school is a function of the quality of the conversations within the school. Student success is revealed by multiple measures of contribution, products and performances, including the vivid presence of student voice. High leadership capacity schools hold great promise, but no guarantees, of sustainability. In other words, schools that include everyone within collaborative patterns of participation are able to develop greater levels of leadership skillfulness. This achievement can move a school closer to lasting school improvement than would otherwise be possible.

## Six Critical Factors

If high leadership capacity schools are good, why are they not always able to sustain improvement? That question usually leads to issues of values, authority, dependence, and identity within schools and districts. A study of high leadership capacity schools (Lambert, 2004) found several critical factors must be addressed to fully realize leadership capacity's promise:

1. The school community's core values must focus its priorities. Democratization and equity must be foremost among these values and are interdependent. Democratization is the means

through which staff experience and honor equity. Members of high leadership capacity schools accept responsibility for all students' learning and include all voices.

2.  As teacher leadership grows, principals must let go of some authority and responsibility. When principals lead for sustain-ability, teachers and principals become more alike than different. They share similar concerns, blend roles, and ask tough questions. They find leadership and credibility within each other through frequent conversations, shared goals, and, ultimately, collective responsibility.

3.  Educators must define themselves as learners, teachers, and leaders. How we define leadership determines who will participate. This broad perspective encompasses sharing and distributing leadership. Leadership becomes a form of learning—reciprocal, purposeful learning in community. To learn is to be able to lead. Like children, all adults can learn, all adults can lead.

4.  We must invest in each other's learning to create reciprocity. When principals engage teachers in problem solving rather than render them helpless through directives and granting or withholding permission, natural capacities for reciprocity come to life. Dependencies cause us to ask permission, to abdicate responsibilities, and to blame. Learning communities require reciprocity.

5.  The first tenet of leadership capacity is "broad-based participation." Schools must create the structures through which participation occurs. Structures for broad-based participation include teams, study groups, vertical communities, and action research teams. These are the settings in which people deepen relationships, alter their beliefs, and become more skillful in the work of leadership. Without these structures, reculturing is unlikely.

6.  Districts must negotiate the political landscape to provide professional time and development, a conceptual framework for improvement, and tailored succession practices (fitting the principal to the school).

This work requires engaging the board and the community in conversations that build an understanding of lasting school improvement. Without this groundwork, schools continually fight the same battles for time, for professional development, and for selecting principals who can take a school from where it is to where it ought to be without losing momentum or denying the worthy experiences of teacher leaders.

These factors are particularly challenging because they challenge our beliefs and traditional conceptions of leadership, how we relate to each other and ourselves and how we distribute power and authority. We consistently have called on ordinary people to do extraordinary work, and many times we succeed. We can succeed more often if we understand and implement the tenets of leadership capacity for lasting school improvement. The notion of "lasting" or sustainable improvement may well represent today's major learning edge.

# References

Lambert, L. (2004). *Lasting leadership: A study of high leadership capacity schools.* Oakland, CA: Lambert Leadership Development.

Lambert, L. (1998). *Building leadership capacity in schools.* Alexandria, VA: ASCD.

# CHAPTER FOUR

# On the Frontier of School Reform with Trailblazers, Pioneers, and Settlers

PHILLIP C. SCHLECHTY

EDUCATORS LEADING CHANGE EFFORTS NEED TO RECOGNIZE THE FIVE ROLES THAT PEOPLE PLAY in this process. People assume different roles because they vary in their experiences, their motives, and their expectations. Therefore, it's critical that staff development leaders understand who they are addressing in order to meet their vastly different needs for training, encouragement, and support.

## Trailblazers

Paradigm-breaking journeys are not for the timid, and one should not expect everyone to volunteer for such a journey. Those who take the first steps are trailblazers. They are willing to go without maps to places where no person has gone before them, without the benefit of empirically based models and with little to guide them except a belief in themselves, a desire for novelty, the freedom to try, and a vision that motivates and guides them.

The most important requirement for a trailblazer is a clear vision. Trailblazers want to know that there is some place to go that is different; they are motivated by novelty and excited by risks. Once they have a vision in which they believe, all they want and need is encouragement and support for that pursuit. Most of all, they want to be recognized and celebrated for their unique brand of courage.

Trailblazers are not egomaniacs, but they are often monomaniacs with a mission. They know where they are going even if they are not quite sure how they are going to get there or what obstacles they will confront on the way.

Staff developers and school leaders need to constantly assure trailblazers that the vision is worth the quest and that others, especially powerful others, believe that what they are about is important. But trailblazers need to be reminded that it is a community quest, not a private venture.

Trailblazers need the opportunity to read about and visit with other trailblazers. They need time to discuss and assimilate what they learn from these encounters. They need opportunities to network with others like them. Networking turns lonely ordeals into shared ordeals. Lonely ordeals debilitate; shared ordeals inspire and motivate.

## Pioneers

Closely following the trailblazers are the pioneers. Pioneers sometimes begin their journey because of intolerable conditions, but they will stay the course only if they become convinced that the new world is really better.

Like the trailblazers, pioneers are an adventurous and hardy lot and willing to take considerable risks. Like trailblazers, pioneers must learn how to link a personal quest to a larger agenda and they need assurance that the trip upon which they are embarking is worthwhile. They do not need skill development, and staff developers would be ill advised to try to provide that.

More than trailblazers, pioneers need demonstrations that the journey can be made. Pioneers, however, understand that few people can teach them "how to do it" because only the trailblazers have gone before them.

When staff development leaders are trying to recruit pioneers, their best allies are those who write about trailblazers. They need anecdotes, reports, and stories to inspire them for the journey. These stories should contain possible lessons regarding what one must know and be able to do to survive the rigors of the journey.

Pioneers are those who develop teams and build communities. This requires a different style than does the early exploration of a frontier. Trailblazers can help motivate pioneers, especially if they are colorful and good storytellers. But monomaniacs with a mission can quickly come to appear to others to be egomaniacs whose only mission is to advance themselves. Trailblazers are needed, but they are not easy to live with in the more sedate environments of committee meetings and seminar rooms. Pioneers are more suited to that work.

## Settlers

After the trailblazers and pioneers come the settlers. Settlers need to know that the world they are being asked to move to is better than the one they are leaving and that the way to get there is known. Most of all, they need to know that they are not traveling alone.

They want to know what is expected of them. They need detail and more carefully drawn maps than those who have gone before them.

Settlers are bold, but they are not adventurers. Staff development leaders must help settlers understand why the change is needed.

Settlers want assurance that the task can be accomplished and that they are not on a fool's mission. They need site visits where pioneering work is already under way, conversations with pioneers and trailblazers, testimonials from those who have tried, books and articles that provide rich descriptions of what can be expected and so on.

Settlers want skill development. They want to be sure they know how to do what will be required of them. Many potential settlers will not move until they are assured that the requisite knowledge and support are available for them.

Staff development leaders can support them with coaching, opportunities for feedback and critique, and, above all, protection from negative consequences for failed efforts.

Finally, settlers need strong, constant, and reassuring leadership that inspires them to keep going when they are tempted to turn back. Change is likely to create uncertainty, doubt, and confusion. The new practices are likely to be frightening and demanding and, at least in the short run, the results may be no better than doing things "the old way."

Staff development leaders must understand the terrain well enough to point out progress when settlers become discouraged. As they do that, they will show settlers how to identify evidence to demonstrate their progress.

## Stay-at-Homes

Stay-at-homes are not bad people. Indeed, in the long view of history, they are inconsequential people for no one remembers the stay-at-homes after the change has occurred. At the time a change is being contemplated, however, stay-at-homes receive a great deal of attention because most leaders need approval from those they want to lead. Those who do not respond enthusiastically—or at least compliantly—with the desires of change leaders are often viewed as problems.

Effective leaders seem to understand that it is probably not wise to spend too much energy trying to convince the stay-at-homes that they too need to move to the frontier. These leaders accept that some will never come along and those who do change will do so only after the pioneers and settlers have done their work very well. Of course, some will only come to the new land for a visit.

I have found that the best strategy with stay-at-homes is benign neglect, coupled with as much generosity of spirit as possible.

## Saboteurs

Saboteurs are actively committed to stopping change. Not only do they refuse to take the trip, they do not want others to go either.

Saboteurs are often lone rangers. They are not afraid of taking risks. Loneliness does not have the same meaning to them as it has for the settlers, and isolation often inspires the saboteurs to even greater effort. To be persecuted, it seems, is to be appreciated, and, in a perverse way, to be isolated or excluded is to be honored.

Saboteurs can cause trouble no matter where they are. But I have found that the best place to have them is on the inside where they can be watched rather than on the outside where they can cause trouble without it being detected until their effects are felt.

If change leaders continue to reach out to saboteurs and critics and try hard to hear what they are saying, sometimes there is much to be learned. It might be learned that some saboteurs were once trailblazers and pioneers who had the misfortune to follow leaders who did not give them the support they needed and abandoned them at the first sign of trouble.

## Conclusion

Creating commitment to change is not the same as overcoming resistance to change. To create commitment, one must understand motives. Without leaders who understand what draws men and women to the frontier and what these people need to keep going, our efforts to reform schools will fail.

# SECTION TWO

# Teacher Leaders and School Culture

# CHAPTER FIVE

# Teacher Leadership vs. School Management

## Flatten the Hierarchies

MONICA COYLE

AT AN ASCD CONFERENCE ON SCHOOL RESTRUCTURING, I MET A DISTANT COUSIN WHO AT THE time was superintendent of a large suburban school district. Through the course of the three-day conference, we met each evening for dinner, where we were joined by a principal from a small New York State district. The three of us discussed the problems inherent in school restructuring, many of which involved the issues of power and resources. What was striking about our conversations was the sense of powerlessness we each felt, even though we represented very different levels of the traditional school hierarchy. The superintendent spent most of his time talking about political constraints, warring factions within his community, limits imposed by contracts, and teacher unions. The principal talked about contracts, school personalities, paperwork, and state-imposed mandates. As a teacher, I was accustomed to the perspective of powerlessness; it was a new twist to hear about it from those I had always envisioned as having the power.

## A Hierarchical Chain of Command

Who has power in schools, and what does that say about the way school leadership is structured? Inherent in the present structure of leadership is the concept of management, a limited concept that doesn't necessarily address educational issues. Whereas management implies maintaining order, direction, and probably a fair degree of inertia, leadership in education ideally implies the setting of academic standards, goals, and modes of behavior for the entire school community and creating and nurturing structures that support those goals. While management tends to focus on the status quo, leadership must be forward-thinking.

Given the present school structure, who has the power to make a difference and exert real leadership rather than routine management? In its September 1996 report, *What Matters Most: Teaching for America's Future*, the National Commission on Teaching & America's Future noted, "Far too many people sit in offices on the sidelines of the school's core work, managing routines rather than improving learning" (25). In a large urban high school such as the one I teach in, the traditional hierarchy consists of the principal, several vice principals, and various department chairs. How involved is this typical managerial hierarchy in the school's "core work" of teaching? Few actually teach; the majority spend their days, as the commission's report suggests, addressing student disciplinary problems and daily building routines. Their major contact with the classroom teacher and student consists of processing cut slips. If class sizes increase, if students have varying learning styles and critical emotional or academic needs, if there are insufficient or outdated texts, administrators have little hands-on connection with that reality. Their work remains quite separate from the work of the classroom.

Citing a 1986 Department of Labor study, the commission noted that roughly 43.5 percent of elementary and secondary school employees were classroom teachers. "In short, for every four classroom teachers, there are nearly six other school employees in the United States" (48). Thus, more than half of the typical school staff consists of people on the sidelines, not involved in the core mission of teaching. As a result, it is easy to lose sight of that mission within a large school's bureaucracy. "In a recent eight-nation study, the United States had by far the lowest ratio of core teaching staff to other professional staff (less than 1:1), well behind the leader, Belgium, at 4:1" (48). Such a low ratio suggests that we do not place teaching at the center of the school's life. Rather than a design that is integrated and centrifugal, with all positions emanating from a central core of teaching, teaching is weighed down by a hierarchical, managerial chain of command.

Because our numbers are frequently in the minority, what kind of leadership do we who are involved in the core work of teaching exert? If school leadership consists primarily in a narrow interpretation as management, then the answer is, very little. "Historically, the only route to advancement in teaching has been to leave the classroom for administration" (National Commission 1966, 14). If that constitutes "advancement," are those in the classroom not "advancing"? Are they advancing in a way that allows them to be leaders?

The commission further says, "In contrast [to the United States], many European and Asian countries hire a greater number of better-paid teachers, provide them with more extensive preparation, give them time to work together, and structure schools so that they can focus on teaching and come to know their students well" (14). There is an implicit sense in this arrangement that teaching is the mission of the school and the teacher's role in that mission is paramount. Structuring time to work together is pivotal because it provides time for collaborative reflection and decision making, both essential components of leadership.

All of us who have spent a lifetime in teaching have encountered the skepticism about our roles from those outside the teaching community. I'm no exception. After my fifth year of teaching, my brother, a successful businessman, would periodically ask me if and when I was going to move into an administrative position. After I received my doctorate, he asked the questions more pointedly, assuming that I'd want to use my newly acquired knowledge and expertise in a broader forum than the classroom. His assumption is a natural one because our present structure doesn't encourage teachers to be leaders. As a result, those outside the teaching community (and regrettably many within) view success in teaching as something that happens outside the classroom.

# A Grant to Build an Effective School

The opportunity to teach and lead in the present system is a rare one, but I had that opportunity while chairing a three-year grant awarded to our school by the state of New Jersey. The program was called the City Schools of Excellence, and its mission was to help teachers in urban districts bring about school improvement by implementing the correlates of the Effective Schools movement. A central tenet in the grant was the New Jersey State Department of Education's belief that improvement should happen at the local school level, and teachers should be the source of the improvement efforts. A team of eight teachers worked collaboratively and tirelessly to bring about growth in school climate, curriculum, assessment, staff development, and community involvement. Duty periods were scheduled so we could meet each day, and a state liaison met with us regularly to advise and monitor our progress. Even though our efforts frequently extended well beyond the one duty period and we were still carrying a regular teaching load, the excitement of collaborating with interested colleagues and potentially making a difference in the school moved us forward.

The contrast between our activities and those of the school administration point out the differences between educational leadership and the realities of school management. Our administration's concern continued to be primarily managerial, disconnected from the actual process and needs of teaching and classroom. Our concerns were pedagogical and communal: improving school climate, exploring teaching and learning styles, establishing a curriculum council, reaching out to more parents, exciting more teachers. Because we were teachers, we were acutely aware of the problems teachers have and were eager to address them. It was a very complex and often frustrating task.

Through the process we learned how to be better leaders: how to communicate with the whole school community, how to establish and meet short- and long-term goals, how to organize our agendas and run more efficient meetings, how to structure effective staff development sessions, how to sustain energy and enthusiasm in the face of obstacles. Yet, there were many obstacles we never successfully overcame, some of which are the very obstacles impeding teacher leadership: the structure and intractability of the school schedule, the school bureaucracy, teacher complacency and isolation, overreaction to state mandates, and the tacit belief that wisdom must come from at least fifty miles away.

It took us the first year of the grant to recognize the enormity of the task of trying to be teacher leaders, creating and sustaining change. We made small inroads against the complacency and ennui of veteran faculty members who had never before experienced intensive efforts in staff development. Faculty members met more often, and talk in the faculty lounge began to circle more often around teaching, in addition to the usual personal concerns and experiences. We did not reach all of the one hundred and forty-five teachers, but many were energized by the opportunity to be more reflective about their craft.

Teacher isolation and the tyranny of the school schedule remained our chief problems. If we as teachers have no time or opportunity for collaboration about educational goals and implementation of curriculum, how can we gain a bigger picture of the entire school community and contribute to its success? Without sufficient time outside the classroom and away from students, we have difficulty reflecting on our own practice, let alone the needs and goals of an entire school. Ironically, the structure of the school day may suggest that the present system values teaching because we require teachers to spend the overwhelming majority of their time in the classroom; however, the reality of this demand weakens teachers and their leadership potential:

Despite a shorter school year, no nation requires teachers to teach a greater number of hours per day and year than the United States. American teachers teach more than 1,000 hours per year, far more than teachers in other industrialized countries, who teach between 600 and 800 hours per year, depending on the grade level....In most European and Asian countries teachers spend between 17 and 20 hours of a 40 to 45-hour work week in their classrooms with students. The remaining time is spent at school planning and working with colleagues, as well as parents and students. (National Commission 1996, 54)

Leadership requires time for leaders to reflect, confer, and then act. Perhaps, this emphasis on action is part of the American spirit, but we have seen too often in business as well as in education the ramifications of acting without sufficient reflection.

As members of our school improvement team, we were able to look at the bigger school picture together and share our separate perspectives and talents to address its needs. The rest of the faculty, however, had only rare opportunities, at isolated staff development sessions and after-school seminars, to participate in that sort of exchange. This approach made it impossible for the entire staff to develop a bigger picture of the whole school community.

## Tests That Teacher-Proof the Classroom

Another major factor influencing teacher leadership is the proliferation of state-mandated tests—externally driven assessments that affect externally driven curriculum, resulting in an increasing powerlessness among teachers. Although the ideal of a common core of graduation criteria is noble and even necessary, the implementation of this ideal frequently is not. When districts focus primarily on state competency exams rather than on the slippery process of teaching and learning, educators lose their voices and any potential for leadership they might have had, a situation that seems to be particularly characteristic of large urban districts.

In many urban schools the primary notion of education has become a skills-driven curriculum motivated by outside mandates. Large urban school districts fear state takeover if test scores do not measure up (as actually occurred in two New Jersey cities, Newark and Jersey City). To ensure that a district's scores improve, teachers are encouraged to become masters of skill and drill. It is not unusual for publishers to supply a host of workbooks, teacher manuals, computer disks, and composition guides—all targeted to the skills addressed in state-mandated tests. This approach tends to overlook the complexity of teaching and the host of skills (planned and unplanned) addressed in every class. In a recent publisher's catalogue, eight pages touted workbooks that could help students "master" state competency exams in fourteen states from New York to California. From state mandate to test designer to textbook publisher, another chain of command is formed, one that disempowers both students and teachers.

In effect, the test becomes an "instructional monitor" and assumes a tyranny never intended by the state departments of education when they established exit criteria for high school graduation (Resnick & Resnick 1985, 12). The problem exists not so much in the intention of the tests but in their design and in the response of school leaders to them. Districts remain concerned with "managing" the number of students who successfully pass the test. They are also concerned with "managing" how teachers prepare students for the tests and remediate those who have failed. Often, they look to publishers rather than to teachers for ways of helping students succeed. The not-so-subtle aim is ultimately to teacher-proof the classroom.

If districts do manage to teacher-proof instruction, then what role does the teacher have—other than deliverer of the workbook and the skills that have been targeted by the state and district? How can teachers fathom the notion of themselves as leaders if they don't have educational leadership in their own classrooms? Part of the recent interest in the charter schools movement stems from the desire to free educators from externally mandated criteria, or at least to create schools in which teachers are the leaders deciding how to respond to student needs and performance. In New Jersey alone, fifteen new charter schools have been piloted in the 1996–1997 school year.

## Internalizing the Image of Leader

Given the present structure of schools, it is difficult for teachers to view themselves as leaders or to view one another as leaders. During my three-year experience in chairing our school improvement team, colleagues frequently cautioned team members that we were trying initiatives that would never succeed, given the present structure of our school system. An anonymous note in my mailbox one day reminded me that I was not "Huck Finn on a raft." Of course, my colleague was right. It is very hard for teachers to take charge of our circumstances, to be leaders, to "light out for the territory ahead of the rest" (or even with the rest). In our efforts at leading school improvement, our team learned what Ted Sizer meant when talking about efforts in the Coalition of Essential Schools: "In a school, everything important touches everything else of importance....We are stuck with a school reform game in which any change affects all, where everyone must change if anything is to change" (34). Try to give teachers more leadership responsibility, and you affect all other structures in the school. Those who presently hold managerial power may feel threatened. In our own district, several administrators felt intimidated by our efforts and misinterpreted them as attempts to garner power. This reaction did not surprise us, but the response of some of our peers did. On days when we scheduled delayed openings for faculty breakfasts and workshops with experienced educational presenters like Heidi Hayes Jacobs or Bena Kallick, some faculty quietly remained in their classrooms, safe within the familiar isolation, protective of the only turf they felt masters of. For many teachers, leadership exists within the four walls of their classrooms, and the thought of anything beyond that is too complicated, time-consuming, and ultimately threatening.

How do we internalize the image of ourselves as leaders beyond our classrooms? The present structure does little to foster that image; in fact, it discourages teacher leadership and instead opts for managerial control of teachers and students. The irony is that the educational community is not "managing" very well with its present perspective and structure. As I indicated above, superintendents, principals, and teachers all experience a sense of powerlessness. It is for this reason that the majority of those involved in school improvement ultimately speak of school restructuring. The needs created by our present educational system go beyond tinkering with improvements. The central dilemma in school improvement is restructuring in a way that keeps people involved and invested in the core work of the school, teaching, yet free to collaborate and lead.

The National Commission on Teaching & America's Future noted that, "A career continuum that places teaching at the top and supports growing expertise should...anticipate that teachers will continue to teach while taking on other roles that allow them to share their knowledge" (24). That would require a change in how we view teachers, how we structure teacher time, and how we enable teachers to be life-long learners of their craft. It would also entail a shift from the present system of school management to one of educational leadership with teaching at the center.

Recently, *Time* magazine ran a cover story exploring the hottest jobs in our changing economy.

One of those occupations is teaching. The Bureau of Labor Statistics anticipates a projected growth of 606,000 teaching jobs between the years 1994 and 2005 (Greenwald 1997, 58). That is a formidable number, presenting an exciting opportunity to provide a fresh context for those new to the field, a context that would provide the time and structures to encourage the most capable people to enter teaching and grow into leaders of the profession while still remaining teachers.

Anyone who has been involved with teaching will recognize the humorous but sad truth in the commission's hypothetical job description of today's American high school teachers (National Commission 1996):

WANTED

College graduate with academic major (master's degree preferred). Excellent communication/leadership skills required. Challenging opportunity to serve 150 clients daily on a tight schedule, developing up to five different products each day to meet individual needs, while adhering to multiple product specifications. Adaptability helpful, since suppliers cannot always deliver goods on time, incumbent must arrange for own support services, and customers rarely know what they want. Ideal candidate will enjoy working in isolation from colleagues. This diversified position allows employee to exercise typing, clerical, law enforcement, and social work skills between assignments and after hours. Typical work week: 50 hours. Special nature of the work precludes amenities such as telephones or computers, but work has many intrinsic rewards. Starting salary $24,661, rising to $36,495 after only 15 years. (54)

Can the teaching profession attract talented, ambitious applicants, people with practical skills and idealistic intentions that can make a difference, if we adhere to the present job description? Teachers readily accept the multiple hats we wear, and we probably even feel challenged by the need for adaptability. Yet nowhere in the above description of required skills is there a mention of leadership. That skill is left for those involved in education from a distance, outside the classroom. Unless we flatten the present hierarchies that result in long distance management of teaching and create structures that empower teachers to collaborate with one another and to lead from within the heart of the school, the classroom, we will discourage the best and the brightest from entering the field and remaining in it. We will discourage true educational leadership.

# References

Greenwald, J. 1997. Where the jobs are. *Time*, 20 Jan., 55–61.

National Commission on Teaching & America's Future. 1996. *What matters most: Teaching for America's future*. New York: National Commission on Teaching & America's Future.

Resnick, P., and L.B. Resnick. 1985. Standards, curriculum and performance: A historical and comparative perspective. *Educational Researcher* 13 (April): 5–20.

Sizer, T. 1991. No pain, no gain. *Educational Leadership* 48 (May): 32–35.

Wasley, P. 1991. From quarterback to coach, from actor to director. *Educational Leadership* 48 (May): 35–38.

# CHAPTER SIX

# How Leaders Influence the Culture of Schools

KENT D. PETERSON & TERRENCE E. DEAL

PARENTS, TEACHERS, PRINCIPALS, AND STUDENTS OFTEN SENSE SOMETHING SPECIAL AND undefined about the schools they attend. For decades, the terms climate and ethos have been used to capture this pervasive, yet elusive, element we call "culture."

Although hard to define and difficult to put a finger on, culture is extremely powerful. This ephemeral, taken-for-granted aspect of schools, too often over-looked or ignored, is actually one of the most significant features of any educational enterprise. Culture influences everything that goes on in schools: how staff dress, what they talk about, their willingness to change, the practice of instruction, and the emphasis given student and faculty learning (Deal & Peterson, 1994; Firestone & Wilson, 1985; Newmann & Associates, 1996).

What is school culture, and who shapes it? Culture is the underground stream of norms, values, beliefs, traditions, and rituals that has built up over time as people work together, solve problems, and confront challenges. This set of informal expectations and values shapes how people think, feel, and act in schools. This highly enduring web of influence binds the school together and makes it special. It is up to school leaders—principals, teachers, and often parents—to help identify, shape, and maintain strong, positive, student-focused cultures. Without these supportive cultures, reforms will wither, and student learning will slip.

We have learned about the importance of school culture in a variety of ways. Over the past dozen years, we have conducted studies of school leadership, restructuring, and culture building and we have consulted with educators in hundreds of schools in the United States and abroad. Although interviewing staff highlights the importance of culture, it has often been through site visits that we have seen the power of positive cultures in action.

## The Blight of Toxic Cultures

Unfortunately, some schools have, over time, become unproductive and toxic. These are schools where staffs are extremely fragmented, where the purpose of serving students has been lost to the goal of serving the adults, where negative values and hopelessness reign.

For example, in one high school, disgruntled staff came to faculty meetings ready to attack new ideas, criticize those teachers concerned about student achievement, and make fun of any staff who volunteered to go to conferences or workshops. Teachers who support change talked about the meetings as battlegrounds, the Sarajevos of education, where snipers and attacks were the norm. Negative staff had effectively sabotaged any attempts at collegial improvement.

Even good schools often harbor toxic subcultures, oppositional groups of staff or parents who want to spread a sense of frustration, anomie, and hopelessness. Toxic schools are places where negativity dominates conversations, interactions, and planning; where the only stories recounted are of failure, the only heroes are anti-heroes.

No one wants to live and work in these kinds of schools. But it takes leadership, time, and focus to rebuild these festering institutions. Happily, most schools are not this far gone, though many have cultural patterns that do not serve staff or students.

## The Opportunities of Positive Cultures

In contrast to the poisonous places described above, many schools have strong, positive cultures. These are schools

- where staff have a shared sense of purpose, where they pour their hearts into teaching;
- where the underlying norms are of collegiality, improvement, and hard work;
- where student rituals and traditions celebrate student accomplishment, teacher innovation, and parental commitment;
- where the informal network of storytellers, heroes, and heroines provides a social web of information, support, and history;
- where success, joy, and humor abound.

Strong positive cultures are places with a shared sense of what is important, a shared ethos of caring and concern, and a shared commitment to helping students learn. Some examples might illuminate the possibilities.

Ganado Primary School in Ganado, Arizona, was once identified as one of the worst schools in the state. Now the culture is one that supports learning for its Navajo students, professional innovation for its staff, and meaningful parent involvement for its community. The principal, Sigmund Boloz, and his staff regularly meet for "Curriculum Conversations" about new instructional techniques, and they discuss new books during "Teachers as Readers" meetings. The school acclaims student accomplishment of all types during the "Celebrating Quality Learning Awards." The building, whose architecture symbolizes the four directions of Navajo beliefs, has student work and the rugs of skilled Ganado weavers displayed everywhere.

Joyce Elementary School in Detroit, Michigan, has developed a strong, student-focused culture. The school is located in an economically depressed area, but its culture is rich with hope and support. Over the past 20 years, Principal Leslie Brown Jr. has worked with his staff and parents to build a place that values its students, encourages professional improvement, and celebrates success. Regular classes for parents support their interest in learning. Staff hold high expectations for themselves and students. Joy and caring fill the hallways. A special honors ceremony with speeches, medallions for the students, and time to reflect on personal achievement attracts hundreds of community members each year.

Powerful informal professional norms characterize Central Park East Secondary School in New York City. Under the leadership of Deborah Meier, the staff and students developed a school culture with a clear vision about schooling for secondary students, linked with the coalition for Essential Schools for ideas and support (Meier, 1995). Staff exhibit a passionate professionalism and enjoy extensive opportunities for collegial dialogue, problem solving, and community building. The culture encourages student involvement in community service and teacher commitment to continual instructional development and design. The final student performance assessment remains a powerful tradition that reinforces a dedication to excellence and allegiance to learning.

At Hollibrook Elementary in Spring Branch, Texas, ceremonies and traditions reinforce student learning. Under the leadership of Suzanne Still and staff, and supported through ties to the Accelerated Schools Model, the school developed numerous traditions to create and foster increased student success (Hopfenberg, 1995). For example, faculty meetings became a hotbed of professional dialogue and discussion of practice and published research. "Fabulous Friday" was created to provide students with a wide assortment of courses and activities. A "Parent University" furnishes courses and materials while building trust between the school and the largely Hispanic community. Norms of collegiality, improvement, and connection reinforce and symbolize what the school is about.

In many other schools, local heroes and heroines, exemplars of core values, provide models of what everyone should be striving for. These deeply committed staff come in early, are always willing to meet with students, and are constantly upgrading their skills.

How do these strong cultures come about? School leaders—including principals, teachers, and often parents and community members—shape and maintain positive values and shared purpose.

## The Role of School Leaders

School leaders from every level are key to shaping school culture. Principals communicate core values in their everyday work. Teachers reinforce values in their actions and words. Parents bolster spirit when they visit school, participate in governance, and celebrate success. In the strongest schools, leadership comes from many sources.

School leaders do several important things when sculpting culture. First, they *read the culture*— its history and current condition. Leaders should know the deeper meanings embedded in the school before trying to reshape it. Second, leaders *uncover and articulate core values*, looking for those that buttress what is best for students and that support student-centered professionalism. It is important to identify which aspects of the culture are destructive and which are constructive. Finally, leaders work to *fashion a positive context*, reinforcing cultural elements that are positive and modifying those that are negative and dysfunctional. Positive school cultures are never monolithic or overly conforming, but core values and shared purpose should be pervasive and deep.

What are some of the specific ways school leaders shape culture?

- They communicate core values in what they say and do.
- They honor and recognize those who have worked to serve the students and the purpose of the school.
- They observe rituals and traditions to support the school's heart and soul.
- They recognize heroes and heroines and the work these exemplars accomplish.
- They eloquently speak of the deeper mission of the school.
- They celebrate the accomplishments of the staff, the students, and the community.
- They preserve the focus on students by recounting stories of success and achievement.

Examples abound in the schools we have already described. At Ganado Primary, Boloz and his staff constantly share stories of the many changes they have made in the school. At Joyce Elementary, Brown and his faculty celebrate the successes of their students and parents in ritual "clap outs" and larger ceremonies. At Central Park East, school leaders meet regularly with students to communicate caring and support for hard work. Hollibrook Elementary holds regular discussion groups in parents' homes to cement ties and built trust. In small and large ways, school leaders refashion the negative sides of school culture and reinforce the positive aspects.

The role of school leaders in the crafting of cultures is pervasive (Deal & Peterson, 1994). Their words, their nonverbal messages, their actions, and their accomplishments all shape culture. They are models, potters, poets, actors, and healers. They are historians and anthropologists. They are visionaries and dreamers. Without the attention of leaders, school cultures can become toxic and unproductive. By paying fervent attention to the symbolic side of their schools, leaders can help develop the foundation for change and success.

## References

Deal, T.E., & Peterson, K.D. (1994). *The leadership paradox: Balancing logic and artistry in schools*. San Francisco: Jossey-Bass.

Firestone, W.A. & Wilson, B.L. (1985). Using bureaucratic and cultural linkages to improve instruction. *Educational Administration Quarterly*, 21(2), 7–30.

Hopfenberg, W.S. (1995). *The accelerated school resource guide*. San Francisco: Jossey-Bass.

Meier, D. (1995). *The power of their ideas: Lessons for America from a small school in Harlem*. Boston: Beacon.

Newmann, F., & Associates. (1996). *Authentic achievement: Restructuring schools for intellectual quality*. San Francisco: Jossey-Bass.

# CHAPTER SEVEN

# Growing Teacher Leaders in a Culture of Excellence

LINDA SEARBY & LISA SHADDIX

HOW DO YOU CREATE A DISTRICT POOL OF FUTURE PRINCIPALS WHO UNDERSTAND AND HONOR the culture of a school community? How do you also increase the leadership capacity of teachers so that they can effectively lead from the classroom? The central administration and elected board of the Mountain Brook, Alabama school system sought to answer this question as a continuity plan for leadership that was being developed. The answer was to continue to shift the paradigm about the concept of leadership in the school system and intentionally promote a culture that would empower teachers to lead at all levels. The Teachers as Leaders program of the Mountain Brook, Alabama Schools represents that shift and is training teachers to utilize their leadership skills and contribute to the system as it fulfills its mission to offer education to its students that is effective, challenging, and engaging. This article describes their exemplary program.

## Background

Growing teacher leaders needs to be an intentional act in our nation's school systems. The principal's job in schools is becoming more complex, and it has been established that school leadership can no longer reside in one person (Ballek, O'Rourke, Provenzano, & Bellamy, 2005). Further evidence for the urgency to grow teacher leaders is the fact that public school principals are leaving the profession in increasingly high numbers. According to the Educational Research Service, nearly 40% of all principals will retire or leave the position for other reasons before 2010, causing vacancy numbers to soar (Ballek et al., 2005). Principals nearing retirement must prepare to pass the torch of leadership to those who come after them (Weller & Weller, 2002); those who will carry the torch in the future are the classroom teachers of today. It is imperative that schools invest in the leadership capacity of the teaching staff.

Schools that have high leadership capacity are those that amplify leadership for all. The guiding paradigm is that the principal is only one leader in the school community (Lambert, 2005). Schools in which teachers are becoming significant leaders have structures in place that provide opportunities for broad participation in teams, study groups, vertical communities, and action research teams. According to Danielson (2007), there are three main areas of school life in which teacher leaders can have a role: within a department, across the school, and beyond the school. In an extensive study on the work of teacher leaders, Lieberman, Saxl, and Miles (1988) focused on what teachers actually did when they took on leadership positions. While the evidence proved that the work of teachers as leaders was varied and highly dependent on the individual context of the school, Lieberman et al. did discover that it was necessary for teachers to learn an array of leadership skills while on the job. These skills include the ability to build trust and develop rapport, diagnose organizational conditions, deal with learning processes, manage the work itself, and build skills and confidence in others. Lambert, Collay, Dietz, Kent, and Richert (1996) examined the importance of "leader behaviors" that classroom teachers can exhibit, even though they are not in formal leadership roles. "Teachers emerge into new and continually expanding roles by the very nature of learning to see themselves differently and therefore behaving differently. They also do not sabotage those in other leadership roles" (p. 29). Extending this concept, Dr. Charles Mason, superintendent of Mountain Brook Schools, developed a list of how teachers could lead without being in a formal leadership position:

1. Leaders ask the right, tough questions.
2. Leaders can set the tone for meetings and discussions with their energy level, attitudes, and encouragement.
3. Leaders are mentors, one-on-one, to others.
4. Leaders anticipate needs and meet them without being asked.
5. Leaders support other leaders emotionally and professionally.
6. Leaders establish their own credibility through competence.
7. Leaders learn what they need to know and are willing to share it.
8. Leaders interpret reality for others.
9. Leaders always ask, "What is our purpose?"
10. Leaders ask the question, "Is this consistent with our values and beliefs?"
    (C. Mason, personal communication, October 16, 2006).

The Teachers as Leaders program sought to encourage teachers to see themselves in those expanding roles of leadership.

## The District's Rationale for Growing Teacher Leaders

The Mountain Brook school district, desiring to enhance the leadership capacity of its teaching staff, initiated a program that will prepare teachers for leadership roles both now and in the future. The Teachers as Leaders program was established in order to develop continuity in leadership as many administrator retirements were predicted for the near future. The program, however, was not designed primarily as a "Teachers as Future Administrators" program. Rather, it was an intentional plan to prepare teachers for continual leadership, whether that would be in their classrooms or in administration. In the Mountain Brook school system, the teacher-leader program was part of an aggressive plan developed to enhance the expectation of excellence that exists in this school system. According to Mason, the origination of the Teachers as Leaders program was conceptually tied to the culture of collaboration in the district. "All the important work we do in our district depends on teachers, and this forms our philosophy behind the Teachers as Leaders program. In our culture, there is a belief that the experts are those that are doing the job; thus, teacher leadership is extremely important. If teachers are going to collaborate effectively in groups, teacher leadership is necessary. Therefore, we needed a structure to intentionally help teachers develop their leadership skills" (C. Mason, personal communication, January 16, 2008).

The Mountain Brook Schools have been recognized with a number of state and national awards for excellence, but the culture of the district does not allow it to become complacent. Under the leadership of Mason, the district has developed a strategic plan for boosting the achievement of students who are already performing at the highest levels in the state of Alabama. The district's continuity plan acknowledges that the teachers are the most important players in that pursuit of continued excellence. The Teachers as Leaders program was designed to ensure that there would be outstanding leaders in each of the schools who would take the initiative with their peers in preserving this culture of high expectations and bring to life the three words that characterize that culture: effective, challenging, and engaging.

However, the program was also set in the context of a district with leaders who have given thought to the fact that there are principals in the school system who are getting older. The district is intentionally planning for how to retain the culture that has been developed so carefully over the last decade when those who created and fostered it start to retire. District leaders want to look for individuals who have the potential to be future administrators and have an understanding of the vision and mission of Mountain Brook Schools. According to Mason, "the district is challenged to hire the best new leaders we can, and we want to encourage teachers to consider formal leadership roles such as reading coaches and assistant principals" (C. Mason, personal communication, January 16, 2008). The three goals of the Teachers as Leaders program, therefore, were:

1. to develop a cadre of teachers who have a deep understanding and commitment to the vision of the school system—that it would be effective, challenging, and engaging.
2. to give participants the opportunity to assess and develop their own leadership skills.
3. to encourage participants to provide positive leadership wherever they find themselves serving.

## Description of the Teachers as Leaders Program

District principals were asked to nominate two or three teachers from each building who demonstrated leadership potential. Belinda Treadwell, principal of Mountain Brook Elementary, shared her criteria for selecting teachers from her building to be involved in the program:

> I listened to the comments of teachers in my building when they talked about what they want to do in the future. I looked for the pioneers and those who were engaged in continuous action research, trying new things in their classrooms. I watched for who was comfortable with collaboration. I chose teachers who were risk takers (B. Treadwell, personal communication, October 20, 2006).

Treadwell also concurred with research that cited the fact that exemplary teachers bring certain skills to the leadership role, which make it easy to for others to trust them. Such skills include relational skills, assistance in maintaining a school's sense of purpose, and the ability to improve instructional practices (Donaldson, 2007). This criterion further influenced her selection of the teachers who would become a part of the 2006–2007 Teachers as Leaders cadre.

The 2006–2007 cohort of 15 teacher leaders consisted of 13 females and 2 males, representing each of the six schools in the district. Three participants were early in their teaching careers (1 to 5 years of experience), five were mid-career teachers (6 to 15 years of experience), and six were veteran teachers (16 to 30 years of experience). There were five elementary teachers, three junior high teachers, and three high school teachers. Their ages ranged from 24 to 55, with a large cluster between the ages of 26 and 31. Eleven of the 15 participants had earned master's degrees; two had educational specialist certificates, and two were National Board Certified teachers.

Dr. David Stiles, director of Organizational Development for the Mountain Brook Schools at the time, was charged with developing the Teachers as Leaders program. He designed a protocol through which the selected teacher leaders met six times during the year for full-day experiences in understanding themselves and expanding their awareness of leadership issues. The district provided substitute teachers for the participants in the Teachers as Leaders program, allowing the participants to leave their classrooms during the school day. The first four sessions were devoted to activities that led to a great deal of self-awareness for the participants. They each completed an extensive personality inventory, and a trained consultant led the group of teachers in learning about their relationship styles, how they behaved when they were most productive, how they operated under stress, and how they would typically lead. One participant, responding anonymously in the program evaluation, shared the following:

> I am amazed at how much I learned about myself. I have always considered myself a motivated, energetic person. Going through this personality inventory, I learned that while I would make a good leader, I have so much to learn about how to "become" a good leader. This process really made me more aware of how I think of myself and how others view me as a leader.

In addition to the intense personality inventory activities, the participants had informative sessions such as an education legislation update and a presentation on how the power of personal reflection assists in developing leadership skills. Team-building activities were also an integral part of the Teachers as Leaders training. The teachers met in the summer to experience a ropes course, during which a trained facilitator led them through the challenges of working together to achieve difficult physical feats. The culminating team-building activity was a cooking challenge, held at a local restaurant that housed a corporate cook-off kitchen designed for organizations to practice working in teams. The teachers divided into two groups and were given instructions to prepare an elaborate Italian meal together in 90 minutes. They were judged on how well they cooperated, how creative they were with the recipes, and on the presentation and taste of the food. Of course, their reward was the opportunity to enjoy the gourmet lunch they had prepared! In both of these activities, the concepts of teamwork, negotiation, compromise, time management, delegation, handling crises, and dealing with multiple perspectives were explored and discussed by the teachers under the leadership of a facilitator.

## Evaluation of the Teachers as Leaders Program

An evaluation of the Teachers as Leaders program was conducted by one of us (Dr. Searby), a professor of Educational Leadership at the University of Alabama at Birmingham. A survey was given to each participant at the conclusion of the 2006–2007 cohort activities to gather qualitative data on how the participants perceived the program. The survey consisted of a series of 11 open-ended statements for participants to complete, such as "Since participating in Teachers as Leaders, I . . ."; "The most significant learning occurred for me when. . . ." Teachers who participated in the program gave it high marks; in fact, there were no negative comments made about the program at all. Participants shared comments on how much they had grown both personally and professionally through the program. Many noted that they had changed their opinions about leadership. One participant shared the following in her survey:

> Having been in the classroom for more than 15 years, I have seen teachers move from teaching in isolation to being true leaders who enact change. In the past, teachers have thought that becoming a leader in their building meant that they must come out of the classroom and become an administrator. The Teachers as Leaders program made me realize that not only can I be a leader in the classroom, but through my professional development, my sphere of influence can reach beyond the classroom and into schoolwide leadership activities.

This teacher realized that her previous opinion of leadership was based on a faulty philosophy that leaders are born, not made (Lunenburg & Ornstein, 2004). "I have always looked at leadership as something that people had or didn't have. I hadn't ever really thought that leadership is something that can grow in a person. This process really made me more aware of how I think of myself and how others view me as a leader."

As a part of the final evaluation survey, participants in the Teachers as Leaders program were asked to identify where their leadership abilities were currently being demonstrated, as well as where they would like to extend their leadership work in their school or the system. They set 1- to 5-year goals for themselves and stated what encouragement and support they would need to reach those goals. Over half of the 2006–2007 group of 17 participants stated a desire to pursue a leadership position at a different level than their current assignment.

The teachers were extremely appreciative of being selected for this program, as is depicted in the following survey comments:

> Teachers as Leaders is the best professional development I have been to in a long, long time. It has been a privilege to be a part of this group. I hope we can continue as a group—a think tank—on other projects. Put us to work for the system!

> Thank you for giving me the opportunity to learn more about myself and my leadership abilities. Affirmation of these skills is important to me and has presented the need to use them more in my school and system.

Although the Mountain Brook school system has graduated just two cohorts from the Teachers as Leaders program, it has already reaped the benefits of encouraging teachers to take more responsible leadership roles. For example, several National Board Certified teachers have emerged from the first cohort of Teachers as Leaders. Others have become new teacher mentors, chairpersons of their grade levels or departments, chairpersons of professional learning community committees, or student-teacher supervisors. In addition, one teacher became a staff development specialist; two were chosen to work on statewide curriculum committees, and one became an assistant principal. One of us (Shaddix) was a 2006–2007 Teachers as Leaders participant and has demonstrated leadership by becoming an advisor/mentor to new teachers, facilitating professional development activities, serving on school-based leadership teams, and serving on instructional support teams. Shaddix noted that, "by serving in these various leadership roles, I have noticed that my skills and knowledge about best practices in education have increased. I am much more confident, and I feel a renewed commitment to teaching and learning."

Schlechty (1990) defined teachers as leaders when they strive to influence peers to become more effective in classrooms and when they themselves become active in school governance. Shaddix advised teachers about how to take leadership roles by stating:

> I would encourage teachers who are looking to revitalize their careers to become more involved in leadership opportunities. Obtain a clear picture of the vision at your school, and take the initiative and become a vital part of that vision. Use your expertise and support and encourage other teachers. Facilitate reflection among your coworkers. Help your team make better decisions about teaching and learning. Be patient and realize that not everyone will be on the same learning curve as you, but the time you invest in people will be well worth it.

## The Future of the Teachers as Leaders Program

Viewing teachers as leaders requires a paradigm shift about the concept of leadership in a school system. As DuFour, DuFour, Eaker, and Many (2006) state, these shifts often make teachers uncomfortable. Such paradigm shifts associated with developing teachers as leaders may include moving from isolation to collaboration, from privatization of practice to open sharing of practice, and from independence to interdependence. The designers of the Teachers as Leaders program of the Mountain Brook Schools acknowledged that these paradigm shifts are important, and they will continue to refine the program components as Teachers as Leaders will be offered every other year in the district. Mason, dedicated to the continuous improvement of the program, stated, "in future years we need to make sure that the components of the Teachers as Leaders program more tightly align to the goals of our system and that we help participants grasp the big picture and overarching purpose of the program, seeing the connectedness in all that we do" (C. Mason, personal communication, January 16, 2008).

We would like to make some additional suggestions for refining the Teachers as Leaders program in subsequent years. First of all, although it is important to spend time helping future leaders enhance their self-understanding through a personality inventory, we would advise that the time spent on the accompanying interpretive activities be reduced so that a varied list of leadership topics can be covered in the course of the year's program. A possible list would include how to lead the change process, how to conduct action research in a school, and how leaders can develop resiliency. Each of these topics could be translated into creatively designed, practical experiential activities.

Secondly, teachers who are considering expansion of their leadership need opportunities to stretch their skills. We would suggest that the designers provide teachers with authentic problem-based leadership tasks that have the potential to make a significant difference in the work of the system. It was noted that one participant in this cohort said, "Put us to work for the system!" Teacher leaders want to contribute; they welcome new challenges. Perhaps each cohort of teacher leaders could be given a specific assignment that they could work on collaboratively, developing their teamwork skills and making a significant impact systemwide.

Finally, we would suggest that teacher leaders receive coaching in how to develop a professional portfolio that would highlight their leadership abilities. We would also suggest that these teachers be given the option of participating in a mock interview for an administrative position. Teachers who aspire to leadership at the principal level need encouragement to start thinking like an administrator.

The Mountain Brook school system has demonstrated its commitment to growing teacher leaders in a culture of excellence. The Teachers as Leaders program will likely continue to empower teachers to utilize their leadership skills and contribute to the Mountain Brook Schools at a higher level as it fulfills its mission to offer education that is effective, challenging, and engaging.

# Appendix

**Teachers as Leaders**
**Participant Evaluation**

**Your Demographic Information:**

M_____   F_____

Career Stage: _____     Early (1-5 years)                    Elementary_____
              _____     Mid (6-15 years)                     Middle School_____
              _____     Late (16-30 years)                   High School_____
                                                               Other_____

Your age_____
Your highest degree_____   In what area?_____
Do you plan to pursue a higher degree?  ___Yes  ___No
If yes, what degree or certification?_____

**Check all that apply:**
**Before participating in Teachers as Leaders, I…..**

_____ didn't really see myself as a leader
_____ always/usually thought of myself as a leader
_____ always planned to be a classroom teacher/ counselor, etc., my entire career
_____ thought I might someday be an administrator
_____ knew myself well, including knowing my strengths, weaknesses, giftedness, personality style, leadership style, etc.
_____ did not know myself well in the above areas
_____ thought I was a good team member and knew how to work cooperatively in a group towards a common goal
_____ had not thought much about my role as a team member on teams I was involved in
_____ thought quite often/reflected about what leaders do
_____ seldom gave much thought to what leaders do

**Write your responses to the following open-ended statements:**

Since participating in Teachers as Leaders, I…

The one thing I'll never forget about Teachers as Leaders is…

## Appendix (*continued*)

The most significant learning occurred for me when…

One thing I could have done without in Teachers as Leaders was…

Something that surprised me was…

As a result of participating in Teachers as Leaders, I have had a change of heart/mind in regard to…

My leadership abilities are currently being demonstrated in…

I have the interest and expertise and would like to be given time to engage in the following leadership work in my school or in the Mt. Brook system…

My 1-5 year goals include…

I would like to pursue a leadership position at a higher level than my current position:
_____ yes   _____no   _____ undecided   Possibilities:_____

I need the following support/encouragement to reach my goals:

My advice to future Teachers as Leaders participants would be…

I would like to nominate the following Mt. Brook staff member(s) for future Teachers as Leaders programs:

Feedback I wish to give Dr. Mason and Dr. Stiles about Teachers as Leaders is…

Additional comments:

_____you have my permission to use any of my comments in presentations or articles about Teachers as Leaders

_____ Please do not use my comments

Your Name is Optional

# References

Ballek, K., O'Rourke, A., Provenzano, J., & Bellamy, T. (2005). Keys in cultivating principals and teacher leaders. *National Staff Development Council Journal*, *26*(2), 42–49.

Danielson, C. (2007). The many faces of leadership. *Educational Leadership*, *65*(1), 14–19.

Donaldson, G. A. (2007). What do teachers bring to leadership? *Educational Leadership*, *65*(1), 26–29.

DuFour, R., DuFour, R., Eaker, R., & Many, T. (2006). *Learning by doing*. Bloomington, IN: Solution Tree.

Lambert, L., Collay, M., Dietz, M., Kent, K., & Richert, A. (1996). *Who will save our schools? Teachers as constructivist leaders*. Thousand Oaks, CA: Corwin Press.

Lambert, L. (2005). What does leadership capacity really mean? *National Staff Development Council Journal*, *26*(2), 39–40.

Lieberman, A., Saxl, E., & Miles, M. (1988). Teacher leadership: Ideology and practice. In A. Lieberman (Ed.), *Building a professional culture in schools*. New York: Teachers College Press.

Lunenburg, F. C., & Ornstein, A. C. (2004). *Educational administration: Concepts and practices*. Belmont, CA: Thomson/Wadsworth Learning.

Schlechty, P. C. (1990). *Schools for the twenty-first century: Leadership imperatives for educational reform*. San Francisco: Jossey-Bass.

Weller, L. D., & Weller, S. J. (2002). *The assistant principal: Essentials for effective school leadership*. Thousand Oaks, CA: Corwin Press.

# CHAPTER EIGHT

# Heroes, Teams, and Teachers

## A Study of Leadership for Change

MARJORIE F. HELLER & WILLIAM A. FIRESTONE

THE SECOND WAVE OF EDUCATIONAL REFORM IN THE LATE 1980S, WITH ITS POPULARIZATION OF restructuring, raised interest in new roles that give teachers more leadership responsibility (e.g., Elmore, 1990). Such changes as career ladders, teacher mentor programs, and site-based management are all supposed to give teachers increased responsibility for making decisions that affect the collective life of the school or for coaching and providing feedback to colleagues. Efforts to put such programs in place raise some of the classic problems that have concerned reformers since at least the 1950s (Firestone & Corbett, 1988). One of these is the problem of leadership for change. In fact, recent research suggests that the success of teacher leadership "innovations" depends in part on leadership provided by administrators (e.g., Little, 1988). Which administrators provide the most important leadership for change, however, seems to vary from study to study. In this regard recent studies of arrangements for teacher leadership replicate some of the ambiguities of earlier research on planned change.

The purpose of this study was to return to the earlier work on planned a change in order to reconsider the sources of leadership for change. Our intent was to address the problem in a new way. Unlike past research that suggested that certain roles were key to change (e.g., Arends, 1982; Berman & McLaughlin, 1978), our thought was that specific leadership functions had to be performed but that who performed them might not be so critical.

Our findings took us farther than we expected to go. We were impressed at the extent to which change functions were performed not by individuals or roles but by multiple roles. In fact our findings led us to question one of the most fundamental, if often unstated, assumptions about leadership—that it is the work of one person who in some sense is responsible for the change process. When we defined leadership as a set of tasks to be performed rather than the work of a role, we found many people doing those tasks, sometimes in a jointly coordinated manner and sometimes with relatively little communication. Thus, leadership for change is a redundant process where, strangely enough, it may be that no one is in charge because many people contribute. In subsequent sections, we provide a framework for thinking about leadership for change, describe the program we studied and the methods we used, provide evidence that the change functions analyzed contributed to program institutionalization, and then examine which roles contributed to various functions.

## A Framework for Leadership for Change

In the 1970s and early 1980s, the literature on planned change emphasized the need for strong leadership. Most researchers found that the principal was the *key* to change (e.g., Arends, 1982; Berman & Mclaughlin, 1978; Rosenblum & Jastrzab, 1980), but a few gave that role to the superintendent (Rosenblum & Louis, 1981), and some held out for the importance of outside change agents, although more as supports than as substitutes for internal leadership (Crandall & Loucks, 1983; Keys & Bartunek, 1979; Schmuck, Runkel, Arends, & Arends, 1977). A very few felt that teacher leadership was important (Gersten, Carnine & Green, 1982).

Some of these same apparent contradictions have appeared in recent research on new roles for teachers including those that promised moral leadership. The principal has been found important for the success of site based management (Weiss, 1993) and other innovations involving teacher leadership (Little, 1988; Smylie & Denny, 1990). However, in a study of a related program, the Coalition for Essential Schools, which empowers teachers in comparison to conventional schools, Prestine and Bowen (1993) found that the superintendent plays the decisive role. The discussion of how teachers contribute to teach our leadership tends to view them as potential impediments who must be convinced not to resist new role relationships (Little, 1988; Smylie & Denny, 1990). Still, some of the ambiguities of the old research appear in the new; researchers continue to find that some administrator or outside expert plays a critical role in making change happen, but there is no clear consensus about which role is key.

Some of these contradictory findings may result from methodological problems. For instance, studies were conducted using different levels of analysis. Rosenblum and Louis (1981) examined districtwide innovations, whereas Berman and McLaughlin (1978) looked at schools. There may also be an attribution problem. Meindl, Ehrlich, and Dukerich (1985) speak of the "romance of leadership," the tendency to ascribe observed results to leadership when other explanations may be more viable. Researchers are not immune to this romance. As an example, the research of Hall, Rutherford, Hord, and Huling-Austin (1984) set out to determine how principals contribute to program change. In part to provide alternative conceptions, Kerr and Jermier (1978) and Pitner (1986) have identified substitutes for leadership that can contribute to organizational functioning when leadership is not present and impediments keep leadership from contributing to organizational performance.

Somewhat in the Kerr-Jermier-Pitner tradition, we sought to reconceptualize leadership for change. Our thought was that successful change results not from the work of a key leader but from the effective performance of a series of change leadership functions. This line of reasoning suggests that certain tasks need to be accomplished, but it does not matter who does them. The analytic focus then is on identifying important functions, not the right roles. Similar work has been done by Louis and Miles (1990).

In previous work, Firestone (1989) and Firestone and Corbett (1988) identified six leadership functions. The first is *providing and selling a vision* of the change. A central leadership task is clarifying organizational goals and ensuring that participants focus on meeting those goals (Schlechty,

1985; Selznick, 1957). If the innovation adopted fits with broader organizational goals, the subsequent change effort is more likely to be successful because people will understand why they are doing what they are doing (Fullan, 1991). Vision must be provided in both conceptual and operational terms. Those who have examined change as a learning process have shown that teachers must know not only what procedures they are expected to follow but also what the broader purposes are (Hall & Loucks, 1977; Huberman & Miles, 1984). That way teachers understand when and in what ways it is appropriate to take the initiative. When only a broad vision is provided without details as to what is expected in practice, teachers flounder (van der Vegt & Knip, 1988). As a result, providing a vision entails specifying the major purposes of a reform, showing their links to broader goals, clarifying the procedures individuals are expected to follow, and specifying outcome targets.

The second function is *obtaining resources*. These include time, personnel, funds, materials, and facilities. Depending on the nature of the reform, time may be the most important resource for developing and learning new procedures or activities (Corbett, Dawson, & Firestone, 1984). Huberman and Miles (1984) showed that teachers often take 18 months or more to be able to use new procedures comfortably. In such cases, early evaluation may lead to premature (OK TO CHANGE?) discouraging conclusions. Materials are also important both as a reward to those participating in the project and to help people to do whatever is required (Firestone, 1980). Imagine, for instance, a teacher trying to teach a whole language curriculum without appropriate books.

Although there is a tendency to define resources concretely, knowledge and ideas also facilitate reform. Some administrators spend substantial time canvassing their colleagues and accessible experts for ideas on what constitutes acceptable compliance with regulations, what people in other schools are doing, and what more developed "innovations" are available to respond to fads and mandates (Firestone, Rossman, & Wilson, 1982). An important part of the change process is creating the learning opportunities so teachers and others can engage in the activities expected of them (Huberman & Miles, 1984). For that reason, staff development is also a crucial resource.

A third function is *providing encouragement and recognition*. The kinds of change required when using reform often entail special costs for teachers, principals, and supervisors in the form of extra effort, increased uncertainty, stress, and deviation from preferred goals. Special incentives are required to overcome these costs. Social support and encouragement are important incentives that are relatively easy to provide during the change process. A great deal can be provided through special attention from influential individuals, especially principals, superintendents, and those in visible, high-status roles (Corbett et al., 1984; Mintzberg, 1973). Providing recognition requires finesse because individuals want to stand out from the crowd while being part of a winning team (Peters & Waterman, 1982). For that reason, informal acknowledgment is sometimes more effective than more formal systems. Nevertheless, there may be room for both.

*Adapting standard operating procedures* is a fourth function. Standard operating procedures include a whole array of formal arrangements such as course sequences, textbooks, standardized tests, staff and student evaluation procedures, rules governing staff and student building assignments, lesson plans, and so forth. Sometimes these procedures can be major barriers to new policies. For instance, Gross, Giacquinta, and Bernstein (1971) found that open classrooms and other procedures that encourage teamwork and intrinsic rewards, like cooperative learning, may be incompatible with report cards emphasizing letter grades and with student tracking. Similarly, new standardized curricula and pacing schedules that ensure that all students move through the content at the same rate to be familiar with material on state-mandated test are incompatible with instructional approaches that emphasize developing individual capacities at the student's pace (Madaus, 1988). The incompatibility of new and old practices often seems predictable in retrospect, but it may not become apparent until the new approaches move out of the pilot stage and are implemented more broadly (Yin, Quick, Bateman, & Marks, 1978). For new practices to become a regular part of the system, it is necessary not only to change old standard operating procedures but also to change the rules to reflect the new, build them into the budget, and develop routines to orient newcomers appropriately (Huberman & Miles, 1984).

A fifth function is *monitoring the improvement effort.* It has become a management truism that "you get what you measure." This is one of the implications of experience with management by objectives (Hampton, Sumner, & Webber, 1978). It is also true of the effective schools research that demonstrated that student learning became more important when the principal spent more time examining and discussing student tests (Purkey & Smith, 1985). It is also important, however, to monitor processes, especially with change efforts. Mintzberg (1973) portrayed chief executives as open to a wide variety of information—wider than is available through any former monitoring or indicator system—including internal operations, external events, analyses, ideas and trends, and pressures. Such information is useful not only for ensuring that the reform is on track but also for anticipating new opportunities and problems. This wide array of information managers used to monitor their organizations also suggests that it is difficult to monitor systematically. Less formalizable approaches like "managing by wandering around" (Peters & Waterman, 1982) are important for monitoring.

The sixth function is *handling disturbances* (Mintzberg, 1973) that come from outside and in. An important part of handling disturbances is buffering the innovation from outside interference. Paradoxically, change requires much stability (Prestine & Bowen, 1993). Commitment and understanding require a great deal of time to develop as participants learn about new demands made on them (Fullan, 1985). Such participants can quickly become confused and overloaded if too many changes take place at once. This may create the unusual situation of a district or school actively embracing one innovation while just as actively opposing another for fear that simultaneous implementation will overtax the system. Sometimes, however, buffering may not enough. Occasionally, active change in external forces may be necessary, especially when state mandates prove harmful in a particular situation. Then it may be necessary to go beyond protecting people from requirements to assertively seeking a waiver from them.

Internal disturbances must also be handled. The ambiguity of the change process ensures that some surprises will always happen (Fullan, 1991). Some part of the change will be more difficult than expected; needed materials will not arrive on time; groups will start fighting over some aspect of the plan. To maintain an even flow in the implementation process it will be necessary for key individuals to drop what they are doing and deal with the unexpected situation.

These six functions should represent the bulk of tasks that must be accomplished to sustain a change process. The question that such a list raises is who performs them. The possible roles include the superintendent and other central office line officials, outside trainers or change agents associated with the program in question, principals, and even teachers. Firestone and Corbett (1988) speculated that functions like providing resources and adapting standard operating procedures that require formal authority can only be accomplished by line officials—superintendent and principals. Presumably, other functions can be fulfilled by a variety of roles. For instance, teachers are well placed to provide colleagues with encouragement and informal recognition. This is much more difficult for central administration to do by reason of distance. However, such encouragement or moral support may count for more just because it is so rare: hence, the symbolic effect of the superintendent attending a training session with teachers (Corbett et al., 1984)

# The Program and the Study

Our analytic strategy was to identify schools that differed in their success in institutionalizing the Social Problem Solving (SPS) program. Then we "backwards mapped" (Elmore, 1979–1980) by first verifying that schools had been as successful as expected with their SPS program and then exploring how well and by whom the various functions were performed. Thus, we studied schools during the institutionalization phase of change, unlike most research, which focuses on implementation. It has become conventional to divide the change process into three stages, usually referred to as adoption or initiation, implementation, and institutionalization or continuation, although there are a variety of synonyms for the first and third stages (Fullan, 1991). Although there is often some cycling back and forth between stages during any effort, institutionalization takes place after the traumatic period is passed, usually from 1 to 2 years after the formal adoption decision. In some sense it represents a second adoption decision, when the new program either becomes an accepted part of the regular system and is integrated into it or is finally cast off (Fullan, 1991). In fact, different parts of the system may make different decisions—in other words, administrators may believe a program that teachers do not really use is continuing, or teachers may keep using new approaches they learned when they were trained in a program that the administration has canceled. For our purpose, this third period is important because only at that point can one tell whether and how well a program has "stuck" in a setting. To explain how we conducted the study, we first provide background information on the program we studied—Social Problem Solving—and then describe the sample of schools chosen, data collection within the schools, and analysis procedures.

## Social Problem Solving

Social Problem Solving is much more a discrete program or curriculum than the broad restructuring reforms intended to enhance teacher leadership. It is designed to help elementary children apply critical thinking and problem-solving skills to interpersonal situations with the intent of reducing the problems of substance abuse, delinquency, the spread of AIDS, and in-school disorder (Elias & Clabby, 1989). The program is applicable to students in both regular and special education. Its more proximate objectives are to help students calm down, develop understandings of social problem situations and people in them, consider alternative actions and their consequences, and plan detailed strategies for reaching their goals. The skills are taught as more academic subjects are taught through a series of engaging lessons with multiple practice opportunities and homework assignments.

After initial discussions with program staff, a district interested in participating in SPS identifies a coordinator who selects teachers to participate—the program can begin at one grade or among special education teachers and may or may not spread from there within a school—and helps set up a system of training and consultation between those teachers and SPS staff. In later years, SPS has recommended the formation of an SPS committee in each school consisting of teachers who teach the program, the principal, and other key resource staff like guidance counselors and child study team members. After a plan for piloting the program is developed, 2–3 days of training are provided to all staff. The committee receives another day of training on program management. Part of the service the district purchases is sets of coordinated, scripted lesson materials and follow-through activities. After initial piloting, SPS staff continue to provide follow-up assistance and ongoing technical support. The team is responsible for administering selected measures to monitor program implementation, student gains, and overall program effectiveness.

## School sample

The research team worked with the SPS organization to identify nine schools that had been using the program for at least 3 years. The range was between 4 and 9 years. The intent was to identify equal numbers of schools that varied in their success in institutionalizing the program. After data collection, one school was eliminated from the study because internal sample selection criteria were not met, and it became apparent that a new principal was trying to make it appear more successful than it had been. The remaining eight schools were divided into three groups based on SPS nomination checked by fieldwork at the schools. Four schools had fully institutionalized the program—that is, all teachers who were supposed to be using the program were doing so according to the SPS consultant, and a combination of an SPS report and our interviewing indicated that the program was being used with high fidelity. Three schools had institutionalized it in a token manner; the schools continued to be affiliated with the SPS program, and there were some indications that teachers went through the motions, but use was limited and the quality was poor. The final school was classified as a mixed case in that teachers who had been in the program for a long time were at best partial users, but a new principal had started over with a subset of teachers who were much more supportive and effective in using SPS.

Table 1 presents information on the schools studied. Although the exact grade spans varied, all were elementary schools. All but one were suburban schools of at least moderate wealth with relatively low minority populations. The exception was one of the schools that had fully institutionalized the program.

## Within-School Data Collection

Because we began with a fairly explicit question about planned change, a highly structured open-ended interview guide was employed. The instrument probed three areas. First, questions verified the staff's assessment of the success of institutionalization in the school by asking about respondents' behavior, knowledge, and sentiments about SPS. Second, respondents were asked about leadership functions for change. Third, respondents were asked to evaluate the contribution that major roles in the school made to performing these functions. In this manner, informants working in various roles in the school provided perspectives on both their own contributions and those of the others, allowing for some cross-role triangulations. The guide was pretested twice with SPS teachers and principals in other schools to ensure that the language was clear and meaningful to respondents (Goetz & LeCompte, 1984).

Within each school, interviews were conducted with the principal and three teachers, usually selected by the principal. In three of the four districts, another interview was conducted with a district "gatekeeper" identified by the SPS consultant for that district. These were an assistant superintendent, a substance abuse coordinator, and a middle school principal. In the fourth district, the principal interviewed in one school was also the district gatekeeper. The SPS consultants for the districts were also interviewed about the schools they monitored. We returned to these consultants periodically when questions arose during data collection and analysis.

We conducted 42 interviews over 4 months. Teacher interviews took between 35 and 40 minutes during a teacher preparation period or specially arranged release time. Other interviews were generally longer because more time was available.

Table 1. School Sample

| School | Classification | Grades | District | Years with Social Problem Solving | Enrollment (1991–1992) | School's Socioeconomic Status[a] | Percentage of White Students | Percentage of Students on Free and Reduced Lunches |
|---|---|---|---|---|---|---|---|---|
| Full institutionalization: | | | | | | | | |
| Adams | Full | K–5 | 1 | 6 | 363 | Moderate, suburban | 81.3 | 11.8 |
| Baker | Full | K–6 | 2 | 9 | 270 | Very rich, suburban | 79.6 | 1.1 |
| Collins | Full | K–4 | 3 | 4 | 456 | Very poor, inner city | 4.8 | 90.4 |
| Davis | Full | K–6 | 2 | 9 | 298 | Very rich, suburban | 89.3 | 3.0 |
| Token institutionalization: | | | | | | | | |
| Edwards | Partial | K–5 | 1 | 6 | 379 | Moderate, suburban | 74.4 | 11.9 |
| Forbes | Partial | K–5 | 4 | 6 | 265 | Moderate, suburban | 85.3 | 7.9 |
| Grant | Partial | K–5 | 1 | 6 | 374 | Moderate, suburban | 80.7 | 9.6 |
| Mixed institutionalization: | | | | | | | | |
| Hollis | Partial | K–5 | 4 | 6 | 373 | Moderate, suburban | 90.1 | 14.2 |

[a]Socioeconomic status was measured with 10 categories developed by the state on the basis of several measures of community wealth taken from the 1980 census.

## Analysis Strategy

First, we verified the level of institutionalization of each school. Our original assessments came from these assessments of the SPS staff when we recruited the sample. Later we verified these assessments by examining teachers' responses to questions about whether they understood the conceptual framework of SPS as well as its curricular scope and sequence, incorporated lessons into their weekly schedules, and observed any changes in students' attitudes and behavior, Thus, we used teacher information to triangulate the data and verify the original assessments by SPS staff. Second, we reviewed interview information from a variety of roles to clarify the extent to which change functions had been attended to in each school and if so to what extent their contribution to whatever level of institutionalization had been noted. Through this analysis we also clarified our understanding of these functions and redefined them to some extent. Third, where functions were performed we used the interview data to identify what people in what roles contributed to the accomplishment of those function.

At each step of the way, triangulation across roles was emphasized to ensure that an accurate picture emerged. For instance, principals tended to inflate the extent to which functions were performed in their schools and their contributions to those functions. However, we checked their reports against those of teachers. As the within-school analysis proceeded, cross-school matrices were developed to show patterns of function and role performance within schools (Huberman & Miles, 1984).

# Results and Discussion

In this section we describe what the SPS program looked like in fully and partially institutionalized schools, what functions were performed and how they contributed to institutionalization, what roles contributed to function performance, and how these roles were configured.

## Social Problem Solving Institutionalized

Initial ratings of success in institutionalization were made by the SPS consultants, but these ratings were checked through on-site interviews that led to the creation of the mixed category. This category fit one school that the SPS consultants viewed as not institutionalizing the program. However, interviews revealed that a new principal had decided to focus on the few teachers who supported the program. Those teachers were using the program correctly, whereas most teachers objected to it and refused to cooperate. Schools where the program was fully institutionalized differed from those where institutionalization was only token with regard to teachers' understanding of the program, their classroom practice, and student behavior (as reported by teachers). Teachers and administrators in the fully institutionalized schools understood and supported the program's purpose. They said "Everyone [in this school] sees the value of having these coping skills starting young," whereas those where institutionalization was more token said, "Educators get on a bandwagon with a program like SPS. Then it all dies." Or "Teachers feel SPS is too personal, delving into children's lives."

The program has a specific scope and sequence for teachers to follow as well as its own language used by both instructors and students with terms like "speaker power," "listening position," "be your BEST," and "sharing circle." Teachers in fully institutionalized schools followed the scope and sequence and used this language when describing the program. As one said, "[SPS] works beautifully. Keep calm, be your BEST, speaker power. Children respond so readily." In the token schools, teachers said "I think the teachers all do it in a different way. Some don't have time." Or "I don't spend a lot of time planning, never write SPS objectives in my planbook. I don't really need anything. Actually, you just do your own thing."

Finally, since SPS is supposed to modify behavior outside the lesson itself, students should carry over what they learn in the lessons to other settings. Teachers and administrators reported that this happened in the fully institutionalized schools. One principal said, "I don't see as many students in my office; behavioral problems in the school were cut in half." A teacher observed changes "right off the bat. The very first year you would see the kids calming themselves. They accepted the techniques and enjoyed them." Such changes were not noted in the token schools.

In the mixed case school, one subset of teachers understood and supported the program, used it, and saw positive results, but the rest of the teachers did not.

## Leadership Functions

The first analytic task was to see which leadership functions were present in the fully institutionalized schools but not in the token schools (see Table 2). A function was identified as fulfilled if three of the five people interviewed said it was. Some administrators, especially in the token schools, said a function was addressed when no teachers said it was. We used SPS staff to reconcile conflicting reports from schools.

*Providing and selling a vision.* Early in SPS's history in a district, the program was usually sold in some similar way in all schools. Because the program was often implemented with a particular group of teachers at first, this initial sell was usually targeted. Still, most teachers who had been initial implementers (10 of 12 in the fully institutionalized schools; 12 of 14 in the three token schools) recalled being introduced to SPS benefits by a program advocate.

What differentiated the fully institutionalized schools from the others was that in the former the vision was maintained. One teacher at Baker told how SPS was initiated as a response to a need for behavioral control with some at-risk students and then expanded when "good changes" occurred. She said it was fully institutionalized in all grades and would be expanded to afterschool groups in the future. All three Collins teachers described both an initial and a continuing vision in both the school and the district. One said, "Five years from now, you will still see SPS in all the grades in this school with all the children, fully integrated." When asked about the future, a Davis teacher said, "It will be here, perhaps more at-risk groups, more peer coaching, and more sharing among colleagues." In the token schools, responses were more tentative. Teachers said, "Now that it's here, I would only hope that we remain committed" and "I have no knowledge of the long-range plans; the principal knows, no one else."

The pattern at Hollis, the mixed school, was quite different from the token schools. All three teachers and the principal described both the initial selling of the program and the sustained vision. Moreover, all were very positive about it. The consultant assigned to the schools later explained that these teachers carried the program as a departmentalized subject in the grades they taught because other teachers in the school had openly rebelled against it. Moreover, the current principal was much more committed to the program than his predecessor.

*Obtaining resources.* The costs to SPS turned out to be modest. Districts began with staff training, which usually required 3 consecutive days, although this was sometimes cut to 2. There was also the cost of follow-up training and trouble-shooting provided regularly by the SPS consultant.

Table 2. Summary of Interview responses about the Presence of Leadership Functions

| School | Vision | | Resources | Encouragement | Standardization | Monitoring | Handling Disturbances |
|---|---|---|---|---|---|---|---|
| | Initial | Sustained | | | | | |
| Full institutionalization: | | | | | | | |
| Adams | + | + | + | + | + | + | + |
| Baker | + | + | + | + | + | + | + |
| Collins | + | + | + | + | Ø | + | + |
| Davis | + | + | + | + | + | + | + |
| Token institutionalization: | | | | | | | |
| Edwards | + | Ø | + | Ø | Ø | Ø | Ø |
| Forbes | + | Ø | + | Ø | Ø | Ø | Ø |
| Grant | + | Ø | | Ø | Ø | Ø | |
| Mixed institutionalization: | | | | | | | |
| Hollis | p+ | p+ | p+ | p+ | p+ | p+ | p+ |

NOTE.—+ = present; Ø = absent; p+ = partial fulfillment with or among a subset of teachers.

Finally, the necessary materials and supplies were minimal. One curriculum binder contains the entire program, and there are no consumable materials. Even this cost was reduced in one school where teachers were forced to share binders. It also helps for teachers who use the program to have a common planning time.

There was not a marked difference among schools with regard to the availability of resources. Most teachers said they had the resources they needed for the program. When pressed, a few suggested that they need more joint planning time to share ideas about the present resources. However, those in the token schools worried about the future. As one said, "You will need additional workshops if you have a turnover of staff." Principals of fully institutionalized schools were more positive about getting funding. According to one, "All we need is training for new teachers. Everything is easy."

*Providing encouragement and recognition.* Few teachers in the fully institutionalized schools reported receiving formal recognition, but most got it informally. If teachers were personally asked to participate in SPS, they interpreted the invitation as recognition that they were strong, highly regarded staff members. They interpreted positive feedback after observations as encouragement. In the token schools, questions about encouragement and recognition usually drew blank looks. Although some principals in these schools said they provided encouragement, teachers disagreed. In one school the principal said, "We have to encourage teachers. Encouragement and commitment: the principal is the key. I talk a lot about [SPS]." However, one of his teachers said "I don't feel Mr.___ has a particular stake in [SPS]." In the mixed school teachers and the principal agreed that the principal verbally supported the teachers' efforts; however, this support was limited to the cadre of teachers who were actually using the program.

*Adapting standard operating procedures.* Starting a new program requires that time be found to fit it in (Corbett et al., 1984). With SPS, standard operating procedures were adjusted to make this time by building it into the formal curriculum and related evaluation procedures. According to one teacher, "The need to standardize the program and make it part of the curriculum is critical in keeping it viable. Otherwise, you're doing something no one else really expects you to do."

Teachers in three of the fully institutionalized schools described where SPS fit in the curriculum and how often they taught it. As one said, "I set aside 30 minutes once a week; we put it in our plan books." These three schools incorporated SPS into their health curriculum; two combined SPS with a substance abuse program. The exception among the fully institutionalized schools was Collins, where teachers scheduled SPS into several subjects, including social studies and current events, for different amounts of time. In the mixed school, SPS was standardized by being departmentalized. It was taught as a separate curriculum at one grade level by a designated teacher for one marking period each year.

In the token schools, standardized procedures had not been clearly defined. In two schools, the central administration had written SPS into the curriculum and specified the amount of time it should be taught. However, this decision had not been communicated effectively by the principals so none of the teachers in those schools knew how to integrate SPS into their teaching. In one of these schools, a teacher said, "If they want it to be part of the curriculum, it must be standardized and integrated. Otherwise, it's going to fall the way of all new programs introduced: by the wayside." In the third token school, one teacher said the program was in the curriculum guide for health, but another said she "forced herself into incorporating SPS into English lessons."

*Monitoring change.* In all four fully institutionalized schools, teachers reported that someone observed their teaching of SPS, checked to see that it was in plan books, and asked questions about their progress and problems. In the token schools, teachers just said that monitoring was "not done" or was only done by the SPS consultant who had no authority to follow up if the teacher was not performing adequately. In the mixed school, teachers using the program agreed with the principal that that person did monitor their SPS teaching.

*Handling disturbances.* This function overlapped with those already discussed. In all schools teachers worried about the time crunch created by competing programs. They all agreed that "it's one more to squeeze in; there's a time factor" and that "we need a longer school day." What differentiated these schools was that in the fully institutionalized ones, the disturbance created by competing curricular priorities had been resolved through a combination of a sustained vision for SPS, standard operating procedures that gave it a clear place, monitoring to ascertain that time was allocated to the program, and encouraging teachers to continue their effort with SPS. Where these functions were not well performed, primarily in token schools, disturbances erupted that threatened SPS's viability.

## Roles and Functions

The fully institutionalized schools shared the following characteristics that differentiated them from the schools with token institutionalization: a sustained vision of SPS, continuing encouragement and recognition for teachers using the program, standardized procedures that built the program into curriculum (with the exception of one fully institutionalized school), and continuing monitoring of the program. All schools had sufficient resources. Only the fully institutionalized schools handled disturbances, but this function appeared redundant with several others.

So far, however, we have not spoken to our original question of whether there is a critical role for institutionalizing change and if so whether it is the principal or some other position. To address that question we examined each role. The focus of attention is the fully institutionalized schools. This analysis suggests that the contribution of high-profile administrative roles, although important, was less than past research suggests, whereas that of teachers was larger. What was striking, however, was the redundancy with which functions were fulfilled (Table 3).

*Central administration.* By virtue of their access to external networks, superintendents and assistant superintendents often initiate changes (Carlson, 1972). They also have the formal authority to control the purse strings and the formal curriculum. Thus, one might expect the central administration to play a major role with three classic central office functions: providing a vision and resources and standardizing operating procedures. These expectations were not uniformly met.

Although one tends to think of the central office as line administrators—the superintendent and assistant superintendent—in small districts central office assignments are often delegated to others. Thus, in the district Baker and Davis were in, the middle school principal oversaw SPS in all participating schools. This principal had been the initial champion for the program when he was a principal at Baker. He negotiated the initial implementation in a few special education classes and oversaw its later spread. In Collins's district, a substance abuse coordinator had been the original program champion and continued to oversee it with some help from regular line officials.

The central office contributed substantially to the initial vision for change in seven of the eight schools; it sold the program to those schools. Someone above the school level continued to sell the vision in all fully institutionalized school, but that work was only done by line officials in Adams School's district. In Baker and Davis the vision actually came from the middle school principal.

Table 3. Roles That Fulfilled Functions in Fully Institutionalized Schools

| School | Vision | | Resources | Encouragement | Standardization | Monitoring | Handling Disturbances |
|---|---|---|---|---|---|---|---|
| | Initial | Sustained | | | | | |
| **Adams:** | | | | | | | |
| Central administration | + | ∅ | + | ∅ | + | ∅ | ∅ |
| Principal | ∅ | + | ∅ | ∅ | ∅ | ∅ | ∅ |
| Teachers | + | + | ∅ | + | + | + | + |
| External agent | + | ∅ | ∅ | + | ∅ | + | + |
| **Baker:** | | | | | | | |
| Central administration | + | + | + | + | + | ∅ | ∅ |
| Principal | + | + | + | + | + | + | ∅ |
| Teachers | + | + | ∅ | + | + | + | + |
| External agent | + | ∅ | ∅ | + | ∅ | + | + |
| **Collins:** | | | | | | | |
| Central administration | + | + | + | + | ∅ | ∅ | ∅ |
| Principal | + | + | + | + | ∅ | + | + |
| Teachers | + | + | ∅ | + | ∅ | + | + |
| External agent | + | ∅ | ∅ | + | ∅ | + | + |
| **Davis:** | | | | | | | |
| Central administration | + | + | + | + | + | ∅ | ∅ |
| Principal | ∅ | ∅ | + | + | + | + | ∅ |
| Teachers | + | + | ∅ | + | ∅ | + | + |
| External agent | + | ∅ | ∅ | + | ∅ | + | + |

NOTE.—+ = presence; ∅ = absence.

Through the force of his personal enthusiasm and commitment, he kept SPS on the "front burner" for many years. However, even in these schools, he was not the only source of this sustaining vision. In Collins, while regular district administrators showed little interest in the program, the substance abuse coordinator continued to sell the vision of the program for 5 years after it had started.

The central office provided financial resources in seven of the eight schools through contributions from the district's operating budget for ongoing training and additional materials. The only district that did not support SPS out of its regular budget was Collins, where the substance abuse coordinator was instrumental in obtaining grants for the program.

The central office also helped to standardize SPS in the curriculum in all fully institutionalized schools except Collins. Still, central office standardization is not enough. In several token schools, SPS was formally written into the curriculum, but teachers did not know this because there was no communication of formal policy. In all three fully institutionalized schools that standardized the program, either the teachers and/or the principal also contributed in this area. The absence of standardization in Collins shows the importance of having line officials involved in a program. The substance abuse coordinator who was the true program advocate in that district lacked the authority to build SPS into the curriculum.

In addition to these expected contributions, the middle school principal who advocated SPS in Baker and Davis provided continuing encouragement. Teachers at Baker reported that although he had left Baker, he continued to provide positive feedback to them. In Collins, central office encouragement came from the substance abuse coordinator who was very enthusiastic about the program and described his style as "uninhibited." His solid working relationship with the principal and external consultant as well as his informal credibility enabled him to publicly recognize teachers' and students' involvement in the program even though doing so was outside his normal authority.

For the most part, the central office was not involved in either ongoing program monitoring or handling disturbance. However, the Collins substance abuse coordinator contributed in both areas by meeting regularly with the external consultant to discuss the program and keep track of which teachers needed to be trained and to receive new materials. He also made sure that SPS continued to be a priority.

*The Principal.* The research reviewed above suggests that principals are most likely to be the "heroes" of the change process. As visionaries close to the action, they are well placed to sell a vision to teachers. When developing school budgets, they can provide resources. Because they are in the school, they can become cheerleaders for a program in a way that is difficult for the central office, and they can monitor day-to-day program use.

The principals in the fully institutionalized schools generally did not live up to the high expectations created by past research. Only two helped sustain the SPS vision. Baker's principal was viewed as generally supporting SPS, and Collins's principal was the only one seen as a strong visionary. Davis's principal was new to the school and had not yet had enough time to become familiar with all the programs there. At Adams, the principal did not support the program. In the words of the SPS consultant, this principal "doesn't harm SPS," he just "allows it to happen." In fact, he was not identified as contributing to any leadership functions.

Since funding for the program generally came from the central office, most principals did not have to get more. The Collins principal, however, had to help the substance abuse counselor secure external grants because the central office did not support the program. The Baker and Davis principals did not provide financial support, but they did provide common time for the SPS teachers to meet and got substitutes so they could be trained.

In three of the four fully institutionalized schools, the principal served as "head cheerleader," encouraging teachers after observations, during planning meetings, and through a generally positive demeanor towards the program. The Hollis principal was also extremely encouraging of teachers who were willing to try the program in that mixed school. In no case, however, was the principal the sole source of encouragement, and Adams's principal did not encourage teachers at all.

In Baker and Davis, the principals reinforced standard operating procedures, partly by communicating them, but also by contributing to periodic reviews to make sure that those procedures continued to be appropriate.

The Baker, Collins, and Davis principals also monitored SPS to varying extents by checking lesson plans, observing lessons formally or informally, discussing strengths and weakness of classroom use of the program, and providing advice. As a newcomer not yet fully versed in the program, the Davis principal probably did this the least. A teacher at Collins said that the principal "observes [SPS] very frequently; she's fully aware and our greatest supporter." By contrast, the Adams principal said he "didn't get involved" in monitoring SPS. It should be noted, however, that the principal was never the only person monitoring SPS.

For the most part, principals helped handle disturbances through their contribution to other functions. Only the Collins principal was cited by others as making sure competing programs did not push SPS out.

Finally, the principal in the mixed school contributed to most functions but only for the core group using the program. His unique contribution to standardizing procedures was to departmentalize the program and assign responsibility to interested teachers. The structural arrangement protected the program from teachers who opposed it and allowed teachers who supported it to use it with a large number of students.

*Teachers.* Teachers are generally viewed as lacking the formal authority to control resources or standardize procedures. Conceivably they could interact with peers in ways that help sustain a vision, provide encouragement, and contribute informal monitoring. However, research emphasizing the isolation of individual teachers and norms of privacy that limit discussion of curriculum and instruction discourage expectations that teachers' contributions in this area will be large (Little, 1990). In fact this isolation is just what many restructuring proposals are intended to overcome.

Thus, one of the major surprises of this research was the extent to which teachers contributed to a variety of functions. In Adams School, teachers carried the program. The program started in that district because a principal in another school and a district administrator became interested in it. The district chose to initiate a comprehensive training program for all schools in this rather large district, which enabled a team of Adams teachers to get initial orientation. The central office also formally built the program into the district health curriculum. However, it did not monitor day-to-day events, and the principal showed little interest in the program. According to the SPS consultant, what kept the program going was "a critical mass" of teachers. Convinced of the intrinsic worth of the program, they continued to promote SPS to their colleagues and provide each other with informal encouragement. In this they were helped by the SPS consultant. The teachers believed the program would work better if administrators would adjust the formal curriculum because the teachers did not think SPS fit in well. They also wanted additional workshops to update their training and opportunities to discuss what they were doing, but the teachers were able to maintain the program without a great deal of outside support.

The analysis of specific functions showed that teachers contributed to a sustained vision for SPS in all fully institutionalized schools. They understood the value of SPS, the needs it addressed, and its curricular goals. They were strongly committed to the program and convinced of its results, describing positive changes in student behavior (see above). Most important, they continued to promote this vision by reinforcing each others' efforts, encouraging each other, and initiating newcomers into the program. Teachers also provided informal encouragement to peers by sharing classroom experience with SPS. These discussions provided feedback and advice on how to deal with problems as well as ideas about teaching strategies and lesson plans. Teachers cited colleagues as among those they would most often turn to for help with SPS. These informal discussions not only provided encouragement but also served as a sort of informal monitoring to ensure that teachers used the program.

In contrast, teachers never provided programmatic resources. They simply lacked control over money, time, and personnel. Similarly, they often lacked a formal mechanism to contribute to the decisions that standardized the curriculum. Baker and Davis teachers did have such a mechanism that will be discussed below.

Teachers' contribution to successful institutionalization stemmed only in part from formal efforts to enhance their leadership. In two successful schools in one district (Baker and Davis), teacher leadership blossomed under formalized structures called SPS Resource Committees, which have responsibility for the SPS program in each school. Although principals sit on these committees, they consist mainly of experienced SPS teachers who are paid a stipend and given extra planning time to inspire, observe, monitor, and encourage their colleagues in the SPS program. Periodically, the school committees come together to meet with a district administrator to plan for district-wide training. These committees have continual access to SPS staff who can help them. The committees also address standardization issues when SPS is threatened by other programs and request district funding as needed.

Although formal structures helped teachers contribute to change management functions in two schools that fully institutionalized the program, these structures were largely absent in the other two. The culture of Collins—to some extent facilitated by the principal—was strongly collegial and promoted discussion among teachers, the principal, and the substance abuse specialist about SPS. Collins teachers communicated often with those in other roles and with each other about SPS because they believed it was very good for their students. This communication resulted in encouragement for colleagues, continual attention to getting resources, monitoring each other for problems or creative applications of SPS, and buffering the program from threatening disturbances. Thus, teacher leadership for SPS is part of a general pattern of collegial interaction and sharing facilitated by traditional authorities who are willing to share influence.

Finally, teacher leadership occurs in Adams without the assistance of a formal structure or supportive administration. The original core of SPS teachers, motivated by their belief in the intrinsic value of the program, keeps it going by fulfilling whatever leadership function they can. After starting the program, the central office has lost interest, and the principal takes little notice of it. The SPS consultant attributed continuation of the program to this critical mass of teachers, and they say they are only helped by that consultant. In fact, they believe the program would work better if administrators would build it into the formal curriculum more effectively and provide more workshops to update their training. In this case, both the program and teacher support for it continued without active administrative backing.

*External consultants.* The external consultants are employed by SPS to train school personnel. After initial training, SPS assigned one consultant to each school to become familiar with its staff and climate. The consultant then followed an annual schedule of classroom visitations and discussions with teachers and the principal to keep the program on track.

The functions of these individuals depended on a mix of SPS strategy, formal authority, and access to the schools. It was part of SPS's strategy to have the consultants help sell the initial vision to the district and schools through initial discussion, orientations, and formal training sessions. After the initial sell, however, the consultants did not try to sustain the vision. Instead, they focused on more concrete decisions about where to introduce the program and how to expand it and improve instruction. This change of focus from vision to tactical issues appears to have been an oversight rather than a conscious decision (personal communication with Maurice Elias, one of the founders of SPS, July 15, 1992). Like teachers and, to some extent principals, external consultants lacked the authority to allocate resources or standardize SPS procedures by making formal curricular decisions.

The function where the role of the consultant differed most between the fully institutionalized schools and the token was monitoring. The consultant was the strongest monitor in the fully institutionalized schools because teachers could count on this person to visit, observe, and provide feedback on their use of SPS in the classroom. She or he was recognized as a person with experience and knowledge who was used to solve problems, brainstorm new strategies, and model lessons. The consultant also gave feedback to principals and others on the status of the program as well as advice on how to improve it.

Although consultants engaged in similar activities in the token schools, the results were not the same because of lack of principal support. Teachers believed they could ignore the consultant because the principal did not support that person. Phrases like "We can invite her in" and "Some teachers don't use her at all" signaled this lack of support.

Consultants also provided support and handled disturbances in the fully institutionalized schools. This was done as part of the consultant's regular contact with teachers that provided the opportunity to encourage them. Again, the consultant engaged in the same activity in other schools, but the effects of this encouragement were undermined by lack of principal support.

## Metaphors for Change Leadership

As expected, the role-by-role analysis challenged the centrality of both the principal and district leadership to change leadership. However, it is also suggested that there was more complexity in the relationships among roles than had originally been expected. To organize this complexity, we considered past literature and our own data to identify four metaphors that might be used to describe change leadership more holistically: the hero, the gatekeeper, the division of labor, and the team. Although this analysis helped clarify the issue, no metaphor fit our data well. Moreover, consideration of these metaphors reinforced a more important conclusion: that leadership for change can be accomplished in several ways.

The hero metaphor has been discussed most frequently in past research. It is implicit in all the analyses suggesting that one role is key or central or crucial to the change process. This metaphor has been criticized by Corbett and D'Amico (1986), who suggest that if one waits for a hero, change will never happen in some places. At a minimum, the hero is an internal idea champion (Daft & Becker,

1978) who finds out about a program and sells it internally. There was certainly evidence of internal advocacy, especially by the middle school principal in the Baker-Davis district and the substance abuse counselor at Collins. However, when applied to change leadership functions, the hero metaphor suggests that one role fulfills all or most of them alone. The closest administrator to that metaphor may have been the current Baker principal who fulfilled all the functions except handling disturbances, but this person was supported substantially by the central administration, teachers, and the external agent. An even closer approximation was the teachers at Adams who maintained SPS in their school in spite of the principal's lack of interest and only formal support—financing and standardization in the curriculum—from the central office. Even in Collins the most striking observation was not the heroic struggles of the substance abuse counselor so much as the way that person had support from other places.

The term "gatekeeper" is often used in informal analyses of planned change to identify those who determine whether a program is allowed to enter or not. The gatekeeper may not fulfill any functions personally but can keep others from doing so or otherwise stop program implementation. Although we did not see any of this negative gatekeeper behavior—principals were apathetic but not actively opposed to the program—Rollow and Bryk (1995) describe it poignantly. In the school they studied, the principal provided modest encouragement for a university effort to help teachers improve their language arts teaching until she read an evaluation that she construed as critical to her. At that point, she signaled her displeasure with the program in such ways that all teachers who were loyal to her—virtually all teachers in the school—refused to participate in the program.

There are two alternatives to these one-person metaphors. The first is the division of labor where each function is centralized in one role but different roles perform different functions. Strict division of labor was never observed. In 22 out of 24 instances where a function was performed in a fully institutionalized school, it was performed by two or more roles. The exceptions were both in Adams school where teachers were on their own.

A better fit was the team metaphor where functions were performed redundantly. The utility of the team idea is that it suggests that the work of performing functions need not be done by one person or even one role. However, that image implies that the joint performance of change management tasks was coordinated. We never saw that tightly choreographed performances that one associates with a football team where plays are tightly scripted in advance and one person—again in the heroic mold—calls those plays. The closest approximation to this came in the standardization area where district decisions about where SPS would fit in the curriculum were only effective when communicated by the principal and monitored by both the principal and the consultant.

Some schools were more like a basketball team where there is often more joint improvisation than in football. That seemed to occur with encouragement where individuals made decisions to reinforce others based on observed performance rather than any tight definition or role responsibility. Even here, however, the idea of interdependence implied by good team basketball exceeds what we observed in several schools. What was striking was that people in very different roles fulfilled the same function, sometimes with collaborative teamwork, but often redundantly with little coordination.

One formal arrangement contributed to team performance. This was the creation of SPS resource committees in Baker and Davis Schools. These committees enhanced communication between the district and the schools as well the principal and teachers within each school. The committees helped reinforce the SPS vision in those schools and through more regular contact to encourage and recognize efforts related to the program. At the same time, because these committees were charged with evaluating the programs in their schools, principals in particular had input into the district curriculum decisions that standardized the program. Moreover, these committees created the expectation that their planning work would allow the principal and teachers input into future resource allocation decisions. Thus, SPS resource committees appeared to offer the promise of more collective management for the program and to increase coordination among the various roles.

## Conclusion

There are a number of limitations to this study. First, unlike most change research, which focuses on implementation, this study examined institutionalization. This decision helps identify the success of the change process. Trying to predict ultimate success of a change at adoption or during implementation is notoriously difficult. We have lost the dynamics of the implementation process itself, which is especially strenuous and perplexing for those going through it. The contributions of various roles and functions may be different during that stage and later on.

The second limitation is that this is a study of a single innovation. Although SPS deals with interpersonal behavior and is useful for preventing drug use and misbehavior, it is more like a conventional curriculum than restructuring innovations like Coalition for Essential Schools or programs to bring about teacher leadership or site-based management. It is hard to know how these findings will generalize to different curricular areas or, more to point, to structural changes.

Still, the study illustrates the utility of shifting focus when studying change leadership from a search for key roles to an analysis of the functions that support the process of implementation and institutionalization. When comparing schools that had institutionalized a program with those that had not, we found a subset of functions performed in the first group, but not in the second. These include providing a sustained vision of the change, offering encouragement, and monitoring its progress. These were especially useful to institutionalizing at least this program. Providing essential resources also appears helpful, although sufficient resources were also found in the schools that only established the program in a token form. Adjusting standard operating procedures is another important function, although one school managed to sustain the program without such procedures. Finally, handling disturbances does not appear to be an activity that is distinct from the others.

What is striking in light of most past research is that we did not find a critical leader in charge of the change process. In contrast to earlier work, in our study the principal did not stand as the key to the process. One of our fully institutionalized schools, Collins, had a strong principal, and although quite supportive, she was not the prime mover in institutionalizing SPS there. The Baker principal contributed to most of the change functions in that school, but additional work was done by others. What was most intriguing was the redundancy in leadership for change. This redundancy took two forms. First, functions were performed by many people, often in different roles. Typically, a function like maintaining a sustained vision for a program was performed by several roles, teachers and the central office, for instance, or the principal, the external change agent, and the teachers together. Sometimes, when a function was performed by only one role, it was still done collectively as when the Adams teachers worked together to provide each other with encouragement. Sometimes this redundancy was orchestrated in a teamlike manner, but often it seemed to just happen.

Second, there is a certain redundancy in the change management functions themselves. Handling disturbances, for instance, depends on monitoring and to some extent overlaps with that function as well as providing encouragement and resources. Although a redundant set of functions does not meet the scientific criterion of orthodoxy, it proves useful for practitioners. The functions themselves are mutually reinforcing. The more of each that is done, the better, and doing one helps accomplish others. Moreover, a list with some redundancy assures that critical issues are attended to.

Another important observation concerns the contribution of teachers to change leadership. In this study, teachers were not passive subordinates who either took orders from above or resisted change as they are sometimes portrayed in the literature. Where SPS was institutionalized, they actively helped to sustain the program vision, monitor progress, and provide encouragement. Indeed, in one school teachers carried the program in spite of a lack in interest among those with greater formal authority. The teacher leadership was not the heroic redefinition of a school's mission nor the wielding of power and influence. Although more prosaic, it exemplified the mutual teaching and mutual support described by Johnson (1990), Little (1982), Rosenholtz (1989), and others that provide the argument for structural changes to promote teacher leadership.

Perhaps the most significant practical implication of our findings is the challenge to the "commonsense" view that someone has to be in charge to make change happen. We did not find "key leaders" of change efforts. When one defines leadership as certain kinds of work, what turns out to be crucial in that the work gets done. When that work is done redundantly, and sometimes jointly, it is hard to find any one person who is responsible for the accomplishment of change. This view of leadership is quite similar to that of Louis and Miles (1990). They discuss what administrators can do to facilitate change. However, their cases, like ours, illustrate how change results from joint and redundant coping by a number of people.

Perhaps more important, this work reminds us that, however unlikely, teacher leadership is possible in schools as they are currently structured and that it can complement leadership coming from other sources. In some instances, teacher leadership can maintain constructive pedagogical changes in spite of administrators' apathy. When planning a variety of changes, from new instructional strategies to more elaborate forms of restructuring, teachers should be considered as more than passive recipients or sources of resistance to change. To the extent that change leadership is provided redundantly and jointly, teachers have an important and original contribution to make on their own.

# References

Arends, R. I. (1982). The meaning of administrative support. *Educational Administration Quarterly*, 18(4), 79–82

Berman, P., & McLaughlin, M. W. (1978). *Federal programs supporting educational change: Vol. 8. Implementing and sustaining innovations.* Santa Monica, CA: Rand.

Carlson, R. O. (1972). *School superintendents: Careers and performance.* Columbus, OH: Merrill.

Corbett, H. D., & D'Amico, J. J. (1986). No more heroes: Creating systems to support change. *Educational Leadership*, 44, 70–72

Corbett, H., Dawson, J., & Firestone, W.A. (1984). *School context and school change: Implications for effective planning.* New York: Teachers College Press.

Crandall, D.P., & Loucks, S.F. (1983). *A road map to school improvement. Vol. 10. People, policies, and practices: Examining the chain of school improvement.* Andover, MA: The Network

Daft, R.L., & Becker, S.W. (1978). *The innovative organization.* New York: Elsevier.

Elias, M.J., & Clabby, J.F. (1989). *Building social problem solving skills: Guidelines from a school-based program.* San Francisco: Jossey-Bass

Elmore, R.E. (1979–1980). Backward mapping: Implementation, research and policy decisions. *Political Science Quarterly*, 94, 601–616

Elmore, R.E. (1990). *Restructuring schools: The next generation of educational reform.* San Francisco: Jossey-Bass

Firestone, W.A. (1980). *Great expectations for small schools: The limitations of federal projects.* New York: Praeger.

Firestone, W.A. (1989). Using reform: Conceptualizing district initiative. *Educational Evaluation and Policy Analysis*, 11(2), 151–165.

Firestone, W.A. & Corbett, H.D. (1988). Organizational change. In N. Boyan (Ed.), *Handbook of research on educational administration* (pp. 321–341). White Plains, NY: Longman.

Firestone, W.A., Rossman, G.B., and Wilson, B. L. (1982). *Only a phone call away: Local educators' views of regional education service education agencies*. Philadelphia: Research for Better Schools.

Fullan, M.G. (1985). Change processes and strategies at the local level. *Elementary School Journal*, 85(3), 391–421

Fullan, M.G. (1991). *The new meaning of educational change*. New York: Teachers College Press.

Gersten, R., Carnine, D., & Green, S. (1982). The principal as instructional leader: A second look. *Educational Leadership*, 40(3), 47–50.

Goetz, J.P., & LeCompte, M.D. (1984). *Ethnography and qualitative design in educational research*. Orlando, FL: Academic Press.

Gross, N., Giacquinta, J.B., & Bernstein, M. (1971). *Implementing organizational innovations: A sociological analysis of planned educational change*. New York: Basic

Hall, G.E., & Loucks, S. (1977). A developmental model for determining whether the treatment is actually implemented. *American Educational Research Journal*, 14, 263–276.

Hall, G.E, Rutherford, W.L., Hord, S.M., & Huling-Austin, L.L. (1984). Effects of three principal styles on school improvement. *Educational Leadership*, 41(5), 22–29.

Hampton, D.R., Summer, C.E., Webber, R.A. (1978). *Organizational behavior and the practice of management*. Glenview, IL: Scott, Foresman.

Huberman, M.J., & Miles, M.B. (1984). *Innovation up close*. New York: Plenum

Johnson, S.M. (1990). *Teachers at work: Achieving success in our schools*. New York: Basic

Kerr, S., & Jermier, J. (1978). Substitutes for leadership: Their meaning and measurement. *Organizational Behavior and Human Performance*, 22(3), 375–403.

Keys, C., & Bartunek, J. (1979). Organization development in schools: Goal agreement process skills and diffusion of change. *Journal of Applied Behavioral Science*, 15, 61–78

Little, J.W. (1982). Norms of collegiality and experimentation: Workplace conditions of school success. *American Educational Research Journal*, 82(3), 325–340

Little, J.W. (1988). Assessing the prospects for teacher leadership. In A. Lieberman (Ed.), *Building a professional culture in schools* (pp. 78–108). New York: Teachers College Press.

Little, J.W. (1990). The persistence of privacy: Autonomy and initiative in teachers' professional relations. *Teachers College Record*, 91(4), 509–536.

Louis, K.S., & Miles, M.B. (1990). *Improving the urban high school*. New York: Teachers College Press.

Madaus, G.F. (1988). The influence of testing on the curriculum. In A.N. Tanner (Ed.), *Critical issues in curriculum: Eighty-seventh yearbook of the National Society for the Study of Education* (pp. 83–121). Chicago: University of Chicago Press.

Meindl, J.R., Ehrlich, S.B., & Dukerich, J.M. (1985). The romance of leadership. *Administrative Science Quarterly*, 30, 78–102

Mintzberg, H. (1973). *The nature of managerial work*. New York: Harper and Row

Peters, T.J., & Waterman, R.H., Jr. (1982). *In search of excellence: Lessons from America's best run companies*. New York: Harper & Row.

Pitner, N.J. (1986). Substitutes for principal leadership behavior: An exploratory study. *Educational Administration Quarterly*, 21, 23–42.

Prestine, N.A., & Bowen, C. (1993). Benchmarks of change: Assessing essential school restructuring efforts. *Educational Evaluation and Policy Analysis*, 15, 298–319.

Purkey, S.C., & Smith, M.S. (1985). School reform: The district policy implications of the effective schools literature. *Elementary School Journal*, 85, 353–389.

Rollow S., & Bryk, A.S. (1995). Catalyzing professional community in a school reform left behind. In K.S. Louis et al. (Eds.), *Professionalism and community: Perspectives on reforming urban schools* (pp. 105–133). Thousand Oaks, CA: Corwin.

Rosenblum, S., & Jastrzab, J, (1980). *The role of principal in change: The Teacher Corps example*. Cambridge, MA: ABT

Associates.

Rosenblum, S., & Louis, K.S. (1981). *Stability and change*. New York: Plenum.

Rosenholtz, S.J. (1989). *Teachers' workplace: The social organization of schools*. New York: Longman.

Schlechty, P.C. (1985). District level policies and practices. In R.M.J. Kyle (Ed.), *Reaching for excellence: An effective schools sourcebook* (pp. 117–130). Washington, DC: U.S. Government Printing Office.

Schmuck, R., Runkel, P., Arends, J.M., & Arends, R.I. (1977). *The handbook of organizational development in schools*. 2nd ed. Palo Alto, CA: Mayfield.

Selznick, P. (1957). *Leadership in administration*. New York: Harper & Row.

Smylie, M.A., & Denny, J.W. (1990). Teacher leadership: Tensions and ambiguities in organizational perspectives. *Educational Administration Quarterly*, 26, 235–259.

van der Vegt, R., & Knip, H. (1988). The role of the principal in school improvement: Steering functions for implementation at the school level. *Journal of Research and Development in Education*, 22, 60–68.

Weiss, C.H. (1993, April). *Decision making and teachers' roles in school reform*. Paper presented at the annual meeting of the American Educational Research Association, Atlanta.

Yin, R.K, Quick, S., Bateman, P., & Marks, G. (1978). *Changing urban bureaucracies: How new practices become routinized, executive summary*. Santa Monica, CA: Rand.

# SECTION THREE

# Teacher Leaders and Student Learning

# CHAPTER NINE

# Leadership for Student Learning

Redefining the Teacher as Leader

INSTITUTE FOR EDUCATIONAL LEADERSHIP, INC.

## The Initiative

OF THE MYRIAD PROBLEMS THAT HAVE PLAGUED AMERICAN PUBLIC EDUCATION IN RECENT YEARS, few have resisted resolution more stubbornly than the complex of issues surrounding school leadership. While we sense that it is not working as well as it must, there has been no concerted national call to find out why—and to suggest how to improve it. Yet without richly qualified, dedicated, and enlightened state-of-the-art professional and political leadership, efforts to bring about genuine reform to enhance student learning are destined to suffer, possibly even to fail. Sadly, the American public and the nation's political leaders have yet to acknowledge the intrinsic seriousness of this matter.

This is the backdrop to the *School Leadership for the 21st Century Initiative*, a national effort led by the Institute for Educational Leadership (IEL) to clarify the issues of school leadership, shepherd them into the spotlight of public policy, and debate where they belong. To prod the process, the Institute created four task forces of experts, practitioners, business leaders, elected and appointed government officials, and others who met for a day and a half each in 2000 to probe one of four levels of school leadership—state, district, principal, and teacher—and examine ways to improve it as part of a massive, long-needed upgrading.

Not surprisingly, the task forces yielded differences in ideology and in how to approach the considerable dilemmas of leading public education. Had such differences not risen to the surface, the national debate about school leadership that the Initiative hopes to spark would be less spirited and robust than we expect it to be.

## Introduction

No single principle of school reform is more valid or durable than the maxim that "student learning depends first, last, and always on the quality of the teachers." Experts may disagree about how highly to value the size of a class or school, how the system functions, or whether it is adequately funded—but nobody's list of education's priorities fails to place teacher quality at or very near the top.

As a front-running national concern, the issue of improving teacher quality has taken on a controversial life of its own that extends beyond the world of public education and into our political culture, where it was a spotlighted feature of the presidential campaign of 2000. On a seemingly nonstop basis, this core element of schooling in America has become an editorial staple, the rationale for countless legislative debates, and the subject of numerous books, reports, and commentaries by commissions, task forces, councils, working groups, scholars, and journalists.

Typifying this concern most recently is *Investing in Teachers*, an analytical dissection of public school teaching in early 2001 complete with a package of recommendations by the National Alliance of Business in conjunction with the U.S. Chamber of Commerce, the National Association of Manufacturers, and the Business Roundtable.

Any issue of public policy that can arouse the concern of the nation's media, politicians, scholars, and business interests—and have most of them on or near the same page—clearly demands more than just the rhetoric it usually receives.

How much good such attention is doing teachers and student learning is debatable. Indeed, a strong case can be made that its yield has been relatively modest, that, in fact, it has resulted in fewer tangible gains for teachers than those produced by the National Education Association (NEA) and the American Federation of Teachers (AFT) in helping to raise teachers' salaries and benefits, while working to stimulate the recognition and political backing that an undervalued line of work deserves.

In the early years of the new century, public school teaching still lags behind its nominal professional peers, both within and outside of public service, in public esteem. It is a dignity-challenged profession that often is more reviled than praised or even appreciated, and its members have few legitimate opportunities to defend it. It is no secret (but, rather, a national shame) that average salaries for teachers remain at or near the bottom of professional wage scales, while prospects for advancement in the conventional, career-oriented sense are all but shut off. Except through the teacher organizations, most of the profession's members normally have little or no effective representation in the key organizational, political, and pedagogical decisions that affect their jobs, their profession, and, by extension, their personal lives. These indispensable professionals to whom the nation entrusts its children daily rarely even have their own offices, computers, or telephones.

Mischaracterized though they often are as incompetent know-nothings, teachers are, paradoxically, also widely viewed as education's "franchise players," its indispensable but unappreciated leaders in the truest meaning of the word. It is unarguable that they instill, mold, and ultimately control much of the learning and intellectual development of the young people in their charge. It would be difficult to find a more authentic but unacknowledged example of leadership in modern life.

Yet we are loath as a nation to consider whether our roughly 2.78 million public school teachers should have any consequential role in schooling beyond that of closely controlled human mechanisms for funneling information into schoolchildren—and then getting out of the way. The infinite potential the nation's teachers possess for sharing their hard-earned knowledge and wisdom with players in education's decision-making circles—or even for becoming part of these circles—remains largely unexploited. There are a growing number of glittering exceptions, but they do not add up to much in American public education's universe of 46-plus million students, 15,000-odd school districts, and 100,000-plus schools. If they constitute a trend toward recognizing the teacher as leader, it is surely a slowly developing one.

Even as some of education's smartest people try to explain how the term "teacher leader" can have real meaning, their message is too often lost in the Byzantine maze of educational governance that runs our schools. The notion that classroom teachers should be part of education's policy-shaping, decision-making system—and that they may actually be able to help redefine it and their own role—is hardly new, but the record nearly a generation after the current incarnation of school reform began refutes any serious claims that this is happening on a significant or measurable basis.

Throughout their discussions, Task Force members consistently underscored two linked themes: 1) the vital role of the teacher in providing instructional leadership, especially at a time when the demands of up-to-date management, political pressure promoting tests and standards, and the near-universal obsession with across-the-board accountability are making principals more conscious of what happens in classrooms; and 2) the constantly reiterated proposition that well-prepared professional teachers are central to the decades-long push for school reform. In these pages, we will attempt to sift the evidence that emerged from the discussions of the IEL Task Force on Teacher Leadership, highlight the dilemmas that seem to surround the issue, and make the case that it is not too late for education's policymakers to exploit a potentially splendid resource for leadership and reform that is now being squandered: the experience, ideas, and capacity to lead of the nation's schoolteachers.

## Teacher Leadership at Ground Level

Within the Task Force on Teacher Leadership there was strong sentiment that "the system has not been organized to treat teachers as leaders." The main paths to leadership for teachers who were interested have been 1) becoming an administrator—an obstacle-strewn route entailing added academic work, closely watched training, and tough competition for the few available slots; 2) organizing or hooking up with activist-type teacher movements (mainly in urban settings); and/or 3) becoming involved in local union affairs, thereby helping to improve conditions of work in the profession. As a group, however, the Task Force was more inclined to believe that, despite many impediments, the existing system is ripe for teacher-driven change from within—that is, for "teacher leadership" intrinsic to the role of teachers in the classroom, school, and larger policy environment.

Given a reinforcing school culture and a self-confident principal willing to experiment and to share some power, the raw potential for teachers to become a serious force in local school policy would appear to be enormous. Writing in the *Phi Delta Kappan* of February 2001, Roland Barth, a strong supporter of teachers as movers and shakers in schools, notes that, although "something deep and powerful within school cultures…seems to work against teacher leadership," there are at least ten areas, all of them having an impact on teacher-student relationships, where teacher involvement is actually essential to the health of a school:

- choosing textbooks and instructional materials;
- shaping the curriculum;
- setting standards for student behavior;
- deciding whether students are tracked into special classes;

- designing staff development and in-service programs;
- setting promotion and retention policies;
- deciding school budgets;
- evaluating teacher performance;
- selecting new teachers; and
- selecting new administrators.

To professionals in other fields, exercising responsibilities comparable to these would usually be "no-brainers," mere starting points leading to the serious participation in the affairs of their organization that they had come to expect. It has long been part of the accepted wisdom in most sectors of the economy and the human services, certainly since the information age became a reality, that vertical hierarchy in organizations is giving way to horizontal information-sharing networks and collective decision-making. Rigid structures are becoming an anachronism, while organizational fluidity is taken for granted. In the human services model of 2000 (except, in most cases, education), leadership is conceived as being more transformational than transactional. And hearing all sides of an issue before setting policy and making final judgments is a fact of life, not a distant goal, as is still the case in most of public education's executive corridors.

Although the literature on the teacher as leader is thin, and some critics would argue that the products of today's teacher training institutions are not really qualified to take on more than the day-to-day responsibilities of managing a classroom full of children, contrary anecdotal evidence abounds. Across the country, teacher leaders have been making their presence felt beyond the classroom walls. These are teachers who seek and find challenge and growth. Writing almost ten years ago, Meena Wilson of the North Carolina-based Center for Collaborative Leadership, who interviewed high school teachers their peers had judged to be leaders, reported that such individuals support their colleagues, are "risk-oriented and collaborative," are often role models for students (although less so for their teacher colleagues), and are especially effective in mentoring or "peer-coaching." In the absence of valid statistical data, that is probably about where things stand in 2001.

In his *Phi Delta Kappan* article, Roland Barth states, "Few schools operate democratically." But when teachers take on leadership roles beyond the classroom their schools can become more democratic than dictatorial, and everyone benefits. The more democratic a school culture, "the more students come to believe in, practice, and sustain our democratic form of governance." In similar ways, teachers, principals, and the school itself will be strengthened in their roles. A more participatory ambiance is unlikely to materialize in settings where teachers' daily lives are overloaded with a staggering list of obligations, time is a precious commodity, and a climate of circumspection rather than creativity prevails in the school.

Teacher leadership is not about "teacher power." Rather, it is about mobilizing the still largely untapped attributes of teachers to strengthen student performance at ground level and working toward real collaboration, a locally tailored kind of shared leadership, in the daily life of the school. Teachers must be an essential part of that leadership, never more so than when issues of instructional leadership are at stake. Teacher leadership can be a big part of the answer to questions like the following:

- How can we create the "professional community" that research shows is essential to peak school and student performance?
- How can we create school environments where each student is known and treated as an individual?

- What can be done to increase the quality of teachers and enhance the professionalism of teaching and teachers?
- How can the necessary bridge be made between challenging academic standards and accountability and what goes on in the classroom?
- What can be done to ensure that state and national policies to reform education are informed by the realities of the school and classroom and to enhance the probability of successful policy/reform implementation?

Teacher leadership is no fantasy. The case is too strong that it is becoming an increasingly visible presence in our schools and that it can contribute much to improving their health and performance. But implying that the teacher as leader is poised to become a controlling force in the near future is delusional.

If there is one urgent requirement that cannot be emphasized too often as teacher leadership inevitably becomes more influential, it is that teaching must become a genuine profession rather than one still seeking public legitimacy. Without greater recognition of them as partners in making schools work better rather than as semiskilled functionaries, too many teachers are fated to remain second-class citizens in their workplace. School districts are becoming aware of these needs through reports such as Public Agenda's "Just Waiting to Be Asked?" and other sources, even if many schools, colleges, and departments of education may pay them too little attention.

There is no single path to enlightened teacher leadership, but there probably has never been a better time to examine ways to make it a positive fact of life. With 2.2 million teachers slated to leave the field in the next ten years, the American school can become a different—and better—place in the second decade of the 21st century. There is no shortage of models of teacher leadership; the job now is to choose what might suit a particular school or district and set about making it happen. Education's decision-makers must now make up their minds to do exactly this.

## Clashing Images

In *Choosing Excellence*, the prize-winning veteran education journalist John Merrow describes teaching as "the noblest profession" and "the heart and soul of a school." In the same pages, though, he quotes a teacher's description of his world as "rushed, crunched, and isolated." And to this characterization, Merrow suggests, could be added "distrusted" and "undervalued."

Underscoring and expanding Merrow's observations, Stanford University's Linda Darling-Hammond, a member of the Task Force, adds, in "Educating Teachers: The Academy's Greatest Failure or Its Most Important Future?", that the ability of teachers is one of the most powerful determinants of student achievement—more influential, in fact, than poverty, race, or the educational attainment of parents. But if they are to do the job right, she points out in *The Right to Learn: A Blueprint for Creating Schools That Work*, teachers must have help in the form of "more intensive teacher training, more meaningful licensing systems, and more thoughtful professional development." In other words, the systems that support teacher development need to be much better than they are.

These comments by two thoroughly credentialed, nationally respected observers who want public education to succeed encapsulate a lot of the prevailing wisdom about teachers and their profession. Perhaps unintentionally, they also cast a shadow of doubt on the proposition that teaching is yet, in fact, a *bona fide* profession comparable in most ways to such stalwarts as, for example, medicine, law, and architecture. Even though most parents of schoolchildren (one-fifth of the population) like their children's teachers, it would be hard to find another supposedly professional field that triggers such consistent overall criticism and so many reminders of its alleged shortcomings.

Clearly, teaching lacks many of the qualities that stamp a real profession. Income, one of the more reliable determinants of professional status, still presents a discouraging picture. Data from the federal Bureau of Labor Statistics and other sources put elementary and secondary school teachers in roughly the same wage bracket as telephone installers, nurses, and mail carriers, below that of police officers, detectives, and firefighters, and, when employee benefits are factored in, at a level of income comparable to that of senior noncommissioned or lower-level commissioned officers in the military services (who, however, have the option of retiring in their upper thirties or low forties with 20 years of service and of going on to second careers).

The debate over whether teaching is a legitimate, full-fledged profession whose members can or should be part of public education's leadership ranks evokes mixed responses. Vocal support for their inclusion, especially by the NEA and AFT, is generally strong though too often as a generality rather than as a reality. But those who doubt that teachers belong in the councils of leadership have a bulging arsenal of arguments such as the menial indignities of much of the work, the lack of independence, the still-inadequate reward system, and the possibility that teacher leadership might actually mean union control. Indeed, many of the hard realities of public school teaching tend to undercut the satisfying features of a career in the classroom. Some of the demeaning facts of the teacher's work life are so routinely accepted as natural features of the job that they are usually not even discussed when teacher issues appear on the agendas of school boards, editorial meetings, or campaign platforms. But they remain sizable burrs under the saddle of a line of work that strives for professionalism while tolerating practices that few, if any, professions would countenance.

Examples of how seriously the American teacher is being "rushed, crunched, and isolated"—and generally disrespected—pervade the field. With some exceptions, the very nature of today's schools militates against innovation, much less relatively free expression or professional "leadership" by anyone other than statutory supervisors. Teaching is a "flat" career lived out in jobs and schools that Vivian Troen and Katherine C. Boles described in *Teacher Magazine* as "legacies of their 19th-century industrial-style origins, with principals viewed as bosses and teachers as replaceable workers on an assembly line. This history has bred a school culture of isolation and egalitarianism that effectively stymies all attempts at reform." This is not the stuff of leadership-in-waiting.

The teacher who may lack the healthy self-respect that sustained encounters with energetic young people demand is destined to be additionally frustrated by the strictures that too often epitomize daily life at work. Disillusioned by daily, even hourly, indignities such as ceaseless interruptions by public address announcements, being ordered to "teach to the test," and a legion of others, 30 percent of all new teachers now last less than five years, while half of those in urban schools are gone within three. They see little hope of gaining the respect and relative autonomy that a true professional usually expects. And some, routinely assigned as new teachers often are to a district's worst schools, leave during or at the end of their first year—frustrated, disillusioned, and often self-doubting. Teaching is no longer a lifetime career. And that weakens it—immeasurably.

At the day-to-day level, the career itself has always had deflating qualities. To succeed within it, teachers in many systems have traditionally needed only to do enough to get by and, if ambitious, take off-duty courses in almost any field, even irrelevant ones, in order to ensure relatively regular pay hikes and occasional bonuses within a carefully calibrated salary schedule. As in most taxpayer-supported endeavors, it is not easy to fire anyone for inadequate performance. In most settings, little or no credibility is given to the experience-based judgments or opinions of teachers. To do their jobs right, responsible teachers in many systems lay out as much as $1,000 annually for essential equipment and learning materials that budget-conscious school officials decline to provide.

As for the "shared decision-making" that, in one form or another, typifies the workplace in many professions, one teacher summarized his and his peers' reaction to how it works in education with the pithy observation that "as soon as they make a decision, they share it with us."

But for every, or nearly every, shortcoming in the vastness of teaching there is usually a mitigating plus or at least a plausible cause or explanation. If they don't step forward to challenge existing leadership or harbor ambitions of their own beyond the classroom, many teachers contend, it is because they prepared and signed on to work directly with schoolchildren, not bureaucrats. Whatever the ambiance in the school may be, this is what they are most satisfied doing. Although most appointed school officials began as teachers, numerous studies indicate that teachers generally have little interest in succeeding them; they have found the niche in the classroom where, depsite agonizing and demanding days that can sometimes seem like weeks, the satisfactions can be genuine and personal.

This is not to imply that teachers do not value recognition. They do. Rewards such as cash bonuses, awards, and various kinds of incentive grants are always welcome. But they are not always enough. Teachers are the core professional resource in every school in the nation, and they must be involved wherever possible in policies and decisions affecting how that resource is deployed. Such participation is a practical application of what Richard Elmore of Harvard calls "distributive leadership."

Some researchers have made the case that, as a matter of personal choice rooted in their own personalities and value systems, teachers crave neither the limelight of public attention nor the responsibilities and headaches of leadership of any kind outside their classroom fiefs. Most have not attended prestigious, high-pressure colleges and universities where competition and careerism may be campus-wide preoccupations. But any stereotype of today's teacher as what the education writer Harriet Tyson, in *Who Will Teach the Children?*, calls "the noble, literature-loving spinster of earlier eras" also has no validity today. John Goodlad, one of the most esteemed oracles of public education, contends that, contrary to popular impressions, education is actually attracting idealistic, bright, and able people who are "alert to the stupidity of much of the simplistic reforms that are being proposed, which they know won't work. Their bosses don't want bright people around who are going to resist when they impose things on them. So the schools lose the best, and who can blame them for leaving?" (Merrow 2001)

These clashing images of our nearly three million teachers do not seem at first glance to leave much room or hope for them to take on a conspicuous role in school leadership, especially in an ambiance of high-stakes testing and the ever-increasing politicization of education. To buy into this perspective is to underrate a huge and diverse population of caring Americans. Some of the very characteristics that shape informed leadership are exactly what our teachers possess—in abundance.

## Rationales and Roadblocks

### Beleaguered Bosses

As it is presently constituted, educational leadership needs all the help it can get. Whether at the level of the school building, district, or state, today's education leaders have few admirers, many skeptics, and a lot of tough critics. Media commentators, both print and electronic, as well as reformers of various ideological leanings, dismiss them all too glibly as comprising an obstructive "establishment," while others simply label public education's front offices and its inhabitants "the blob." Whatever it is called, and whether or not it is performing well, this guiding force in America's schools, its leadership, no longer enjoys the necessary trust of much of the larger population.

Since the principals, district leaders, and school board members who are the subjects of this criticism are reluctant to fight back in public, even though most of the negative judgments of them are unwarranted, the idea that existing forms of school leadership are failing us has gained traction. And it goes beyond that. With some signal exceptions, incumbents are often savagely labeled by the media, in particular, as (pick one or a combination) unimaginative, dictatorial, risk-averse, imperious, regulation-addicted, initiative-squashing, power-hungry, anti-intellectual, time-serving bureaucrats wedded to a past that modern leadership doctrine outgrew decades ago. These charges are bandied about with little regard for the real-world problems that plague education's top brass. They are mostly wrong, and they hurt. They also complicate efforts to bring teachers into leadership roles.

## Democracy Sidelined

As the discussions of the Task Force on Teacher Leadership proceeded, it was clear to this representative group of educators and concerned lay leaders that they were confronting a concept—the teacher as a vital part of the policy-framing and governing processes—that may have been around for a long time but which has somehow never loomed large in the nation's school systems. Given the problems that teachers are experiencing at the turn of the century and the popular impression that they need badly to take care of their own house, it is perhaps understandable that becoming part of the structure of leadership at this time is a back-burner issue. It deserves better.

As long as school leadership remains mostly top-down and hierarchical, there is little chance that teachers will ever be more than fringe players—available as a resource when called upon, but seldom directly and continuously involved in decisions of substance. School district leaders often trot out the buzzword of teacher leadership as an established reality in their domains, but, Troen and Boles contend, touting participation by teachers in routine matters in the school rather than just in their classrooms is "somewhat like calling a banana republic a democracy if a few of its citizens are allowed to vote." Authoritarian governance styles may have fallen out of favor in most sectors of society since these words were written in 1993, but what appears to have replaced them is sometimes neither better nor appreciably more democratic, notably in the schools.

As leadership in business, technology, various professions, and public institutions has become more participatory and representative over the past 30 years, education has also taken to boasting of the inclusion of teachers, its lowest-ranking professionals, in its policy-creation and management processes. But the level of inclusion ordinarily does not deserve to be bragged about. True, classroom teachers in many schools are at least tangentially involved in their principals' and district leaders' concerns about curriculum, supplies, discipline, testing and standards, student and family problems in the school, and a few other classroom-specific concerns. In addition, some schools promote at least a veneer of participation though principal-led "leadership councils" or their equivalents. And most principals, especially those in middle and high schools, ask classroom teachers to take on the posts of department chairs, team and grade leaders, heads of curriculum committees, and others—often with extra pay and/or slightly reduced teaching schedules.

The greater likelihood, though, is that the teacher's role in school leadership is still limited to what goes on in or directly affects the classroom: how to teach creatively within narrow curricular specifications, how to organize class time, how to assess progress, how to deal with troubled children and their families. The expertise and good judgment of classroom teachers in all of these matters patently strengthen a school's capabilities, but they do not constitute leadership as it should be defined—or, in the case of teachers, redefined.

## What Teachers Can Contribute

Teachers offer something beyond expertise. But at a time when nearly all of public education is in the grip of the rush to politically mandated tests, standards, and accountability, they may be under heavier pressure than they have ever known. The special qualities that the excellent ones possess—knowledge of children and subject matter, empathy, dedication, technique, sensitivity to communities and families, readiness to help, team spirit, ability to communicate, and many more—should be in even greater demand than ever.

These attributes also are an essential side of school leadership. But in the realm of school wide policy as distinguished from what happens in the classroom, the unique voice of teachers is too seldom heard or their views even solicited. Addressing this point, *The Metropolitan Life Survey of the American Teacher, 2000: Are We Preparing Students for the 21st Century?* found that many secondary school faculty members felt alienated, that substantial numbers felt "left out of things going on around them at their school" or that "what they think doesn't count very much at their school." It is readily apparent that, except in unusual cases, the basic decisions that affect the work lives of teachers, as well as the performance of their students, come from on high, from top-down leadership in its most pristine form. In most settings, teachers have little or no say in scheduling, class placement, how specialists are assigned, decisions on hiring new teachers, and, perhaps most telling at ground level, the preparation of budgets and materials. This is not the stuff of professionalism.

## How They Are Prepared

Today's teachers are coming into the job market as the unevenly prepared products of some 1,300 schools and colleges of education that have historically constituted a largely change-resistant system. Reports about the escalating number of teacher preparation institutions that are breaking with tradition are refreshing, but they are still exceptions in a carefully preserved corner of academe that abhors revolutionaries, discourages mavericks, and is not too comfortable with mild dissenters. Organizations such as the revitalized National Council for Accreditation of Teacher Education (NCATE) have their hands full trying to help transform these institutions into the modern, first-class learning centers they must become if our teachers are to resist a beckoning slide into mediocrity.

The professionalism (and the beginnings of a consciousness about the teacher as leader) that should be a core feature of teacher training is not easily acquired in these settings. Though most teacher-training institutions claim to be making their curricula more responsive (and several hundred appear to be succeeding), many parent universities have few qualms about treating them as what John Merrow describes as "cash cows," that is, revenue-suppliers for other parts of the university where expenses are higher, such as programs in law, medicine, engineering, and nursing. Linda Darling-Hammond adds, "If you are preparing to be a teacher, you can expect about half of the tuition money that you put into the till to come back to support your preparation." This is training on the cheap, and it carries no guarantees of success.

While a heavy concentration on classroom teaching methods (to the detriment of substantive academic subjects) often appears to be the *raison d'être* of teacher training faculties, more institutions need to think about exposing future teachers to discussions of the larger policy issues of education. Although a growing number of institutions have made progress in this area, too many new teachers still report for duty largely uninformed in the essentials of the professional, cultural, and political worlds they are to inhabit—and what they do know they have often acquired on their own. There is a growing and encouraging realization that teachers need practical knowledge about contemporary family life, immigrant and minority group children, and the political and social currents that swirl about public education. However, too few teacher training institutions offer courses that treat these subjects in sufficient depth, and practically none below the graduate level scratch the surface of training in management and leadership.

## On-the-Job Frustrations

Teacher training is not the only obstacle. Once hired and in the pipeline, young teachers often find that what they have learned in their four or more years of preparation has not equipped them for what they may encounter in their new classrooms. In a few districts, although hardly the norm, there are horror stories: freshly minted teachers assigned to instruct high schoolers in out-of-subject content areas, decaying and unsafe buildings, students with daunting family problems, neighborhoods with scarcely controllable violence, facilities comparable in some grotesque cases to those in their cities' jails. Newcomers come to realize all too soon that their education professors were either poorly informed about the downsides of teaching or that they simply didn't bother to share their knowledge and perspectives. More than they ever would have anticipated, new teachers too often enter a world in which administrative orthodoxies repeatedly combine with indifference in confronting often overwhelming problems. Rocking these boats is all but impossible when personal survival becomes the newcomer's mantra.

As policy analyst Denis Doyle observed in the March 2001 issue of *The School Administrator*, modern workers are "self-guiding problem solvers and troubleshooters. No longer…is passivity valued. To the contrary, independence and initiative are." Except, he might have added, in a huge swath of the country's classrooms where "go along to get along," a favorite slogan of Sam Rayburn, a long-time Speaker of the U.S. House of Representatives, normally sets the mood and tempo. This may have been the path to political success in a bygone era, but it is no prescription for school leadership or reform—or even a miniscule role in them—in the 21st century.

## Unions and Teacher Leadership

A frequently cited barrier to grass roots teacher leadership is the supposedly pervasive, even controlling, role of the National Education Association and the American Federation of Teachers in the work lives of the nation's teachers. This description may apply in some districts and political settings where union functionaries may appear to rule the roost, but it distorts reality. Although the literature on the teacher as leader usually downplays the teacher organizations and the mass media are seldom kind to them, the inescapable fact is that most of the tangible gains teachers achieved in the second half of the 20th century would not have materialized without union activism and leadership. Many critics and analysts conveniently forget that the relatively decent salaries teachers now receive (decent, that is, compared to what they might be earning without successful union-led negotiations), their employee benefits packages, and their success in lobbying in Washington, state capitals, and local districts for increased funding for education owe much to union leadership. All have had a positive impact on how teachers are treated and perceived. They also strengthen the potential of teachers as leaders.

The commonly heard accusation that the unions have been so focused on bread-and-butter concerns that they have shown little interest in educational content is also mostly spurious. Admittedly, there are periods when strikes and other political-type concerns are dominant and professional matters must take a back seat—way back, sometimes. And members do have legitimate complaints about the overly bureaucratic style and operational methods of some union headquarters. But the long-run effect of the unions' presence has been to elevate the professional stature and self-regard of teachers, and this can only be positive. If further proof were needed, it came in a study revealing that states with a higher percentage of teachers represented by unions tended to report higher SAT and ACT schools than those with less representation. Based on their research as summarized in the Winter 2000 issue of the *Harvard Educational Review*, the three coauthors of the study (Steelman, Powell and Carini) said, "That we found such a strongly consistent positive relationship across so many permutations of analysis should give pause to those who characterize teacher unions as adversaries to educational success and accountability."

## The Push for Professionalism

Happily, the quest for professionalism and the stature that goes with it—without which the idea of the teacher as leader would be a far-off dream instead of an achievable reality—finally appears to be gaining serious momentum. There are now countless examples scattered around the country, many of them in the form of intensified but greatly broadened teacher training programs, of institutions where visionary educators simply refuse to kowtow to established ways of doing things. Many are altering the balance between method and substance in preparing teachers. They are strengthening their content preparation as well as preparation for content pedagogy, curriculum development, and assessment. Several hundred of these programs blend undergraduate and graduate programs into five-year regimens from which the student gains two degrees while experiencing protracted involvement in school life far beyond the minimal opportunities that conventional practice teaching affords. Others offer teaching internships, often in a growing number of professional development schools, that provide sustained exposure while enabling the candidates as individuals and in teams to decide whether teaching really is their best career option. Promising though these examples of progress may be, they are still a minority in the 1,300-institution domain of teacher preparation. Less dramatic but likely to be equally effective in the long run, notably in helping to pave the way to teacher leadership, are broader kinds of influences such as these:

### The National Commission on Teaching & America's Future

The 1996 report of the prestigious National Commission on Teaching & America's Future (NCTAF) called for no less than a thorough revamping and restructuring of the teaching profession, which, it declared, had suffered from decades of neglect. Likening itself to the Flexner Report of 1910, which led to the transformation of the medical profession, the Commission's report, *What Matters Most: Teaching for America's Future*, provided a detailed blueprint for recruiting, preparing, supporting, and rewarding excellent educators. Such terms as "overhaul," "reinvent," and "call to action" dot this historic report, which lays out a detailed agenda for restructuring the world of the American teacher. Unlike so many "blue ribbon" commissions, the NCTAF has also been able to monitor progress and to assist 20 states and nine school district partners in reaching its goals.

## The NCATE Effect

In a quietly effective fashion, and with the backing of numerous education organizations, the reform-minded National Council for Accreditation of Teacher Education (NCATE) has helped get all but a few states to raise the standards bar for classroom teachers. Working with state agencies and teacher training institutions, NCATE is leading the way in insuring that colleges have a content-oriented system in place to facilitate assessment and that state licensing requirements are aligned with accreditation standards—a tough, thankless task destined to generate few headlines. Participation in the State/NCATE Partnership Program vaulted from 19 states in 1990 to 46 in 2001—proof that at the least, as the National Conference of State Legislatures asserted, NCATE "is a cost-effective means to upgrade teacher preparation in the states." In practice, it is much more. Though probably not yet fully quantifiable, the effects of these NCATE-guided steps toward accountability and measures to upgrade the profession are almost certainly being felt across the country in the early years of the new century. They exemplify education reform in action in a manner that should benefit both the quality of the teaching enterprise and the institutional and governmental infrastructure that supports it.

## National Board Certification

The respected National Board for Professional Teaching Standards (NBPTS) epitomizes the ideal of the high-quality American teacher. Established at the recommendation of *A Nation Prepared: Teachers for the 21st Century* of 1986, a product of the Carnegie Foundation's Task Force on Teaching as a Profession, the NBPTS has established nationally applicable qualifications and procedures for certifying teachers that may be the most rigorous yet sensible of recent times. Those who survive a lengthy, costly, and demanding process are widely recognized as embodying all the attributes of top-flight professional teachers. The roughly 10,000 who have successfully completed the NBPTS regimen (4,727 of them in 2000—the admittedly slow pace has been quickening) achieve almost instant recognition, usually receive tangible rewards such increased pay and advisory roles, and inevitably become role models for their colleagues.

## Alternative Certification

Alternative certification, that is, credentials awarded teacher candidates who have not spent four or five years training to become teachers, has beckoned for over three decades to diverse groups and individuals. It has taken different forms and exposed public education to different breeds of aspiring teachers. Frowned upon by many mainstream educators and institutions, alternative certification nevertheless does represent something new and possibly invigorating in the field. The National Commission on Teaching & America's Future recognized that the aggressive policies needed to put a qualified teacher in every classroom include developing different approaches to preparation including alternative pathways to teaching for mid-career professionals, college graduates with no teaching certification, and paraprofessionals.

Although they are numerically miniscule in terms of the numbers of teachers prepared, alternative certification programs have been around, in one version or another, since at least the mid-1960s. The possibility exists that some of them may over time embody a different, more venturesome style of leadership than that which the products of conventional teacher training generally provide.

As a rule, the backgrounds of these nontraditional teachers reveal more diversity than is found in the teaching force in most typical schools. When Teacher Corps, the Johnson Administration's then-revolutionary program to prepare young people to serve in urban districts, began in 1965, it drew recent Peace Corps volunteers, liberal arts majors already working in non-teaching jobs, professionals from other fields, and a broad mix of public service-oriented young people. These roughly 3,500 feisty recruits survived an obstacle course that combined low-paying two-year internships in inner-city classrooms, "volunteer" work in low-income communities, and course work in schools of education—all of which usually led to a legitimate graduate degree and certification. The national Teacher Corps effort cost the federal government roughly $500 million from 1965 to 1981. It produced a lot of committed leaders for education, especially teachers (and future leaders) from minority groups.

Subsequent "alternative" programs have dotted education's landscape in 40 states. By 2000, according to the American Association of Colleges for Teacher Education, as many as half of the group's member institutions offered at least one alternate route, and *Education Week* and the Pew Charitable Trust's *Quality Counts 2000* estimated that 80,000 people had been licensed in nontraditional ways, 8,000 of them in New Jersey alone. Teach For America, a heavily publicized 12-year-old program to place liberal arts graduates of elite colleges and universities in inner city classrooms for two years before they start their "permanent" careers in other fields, now has 4,000 alumni. Although critics cite the lack of adequate preparation for the program's graduates, it has been claimed that more than half of TFA teachers have stayed in public education, where many of them are well regarded. Some who have left the classroom have gone into administrative posts, several have become charter school founders, and one, Sara Mosle, has been an outstanding writer for the *The New York Times Magazine* and *The New Yorker*, mostly on education, as well as a mentor of inner city children after leaving teaching.

Though statistically insignificant in the nearly three million-person behemoth that is America's teaching force, these and other unconventional programs now include former military officers, business people, police officers, government employees, and professionals from other sectors. Many were successful but "unfulfilled" in their previous careers and bring "leadership personalities" to the school. Others, such as those in paraprofessional career ladder programs that eventually lead upward to teaching posts in urban areas, come at teaching from a different job perspective, that of classroom aide. Often sponsored by the American Federation of Teachers, these "para-educators" usually live near the schools in which they work, know how their students live and what they endure daily, and, quite often, are also seasoned advocates and activists. This brand of leadership is not always welcome in the schools, but it surely helps keep policy-framers' feet to the fire.

## Business Speaks Up

In *Investing in Teaching*, the 2001 report calling for "a renaissance in teaching," the National Alliance of Business and three of the most potent national organizations representing both large corporations and small business focused heavily on "an agenda that will elevate teaching to a profession" through improved preparation and professional development, NBPTS certification, higher pay, and, among others, access to job-related opportunities for growth such as mentorships, peer assessors, and possibilities of becoming adjunct university faculty members. With the understandable exception of its emphasis on readying students for success in the workplace (and then for higher education and life, in that order), *Investing in Teaching* could have been issued by a coalition of distinguished educators and policy-makers rather than business leaders.

The simple fact that a coalition of powerful business groups produced a thoughtful and constructive document in 2001 on teaching in America underscores the critical importance of the subject. The form and direction of the sponsors' follow-up will merit close watching. Exercised properly, the clout of such giants as the U.S. Chamber of Commerce, the Business Roundtable, and National Association of Manufacturers behind this NAB product could be enormously helpful in promoting and nurturing teacher leadership.

### Material Rewards

The salary structure for teachers has historically been a disincentive for young people to enter the field. In the booming economy of the 1990s and early 2000s, in particular, the urge to teach has been squelched to an unknown degree by the explosive growth of salaries for young college graduates almost everywhere else in society. While teacher salaries are rising, they still do not suffice, as Public Agenda pointed out in 2000 in *A Sense of Calling*, which found that three-fourths of a cross-section of teachers it polled agreed "strongly" or "somewhat" that they are underpaid. But change is in the air. In early 2001, *Education Week* reported that at least 39 governors and legislators in 28 states from Alabama to Washington were making pay raises for teachers a high priority. Reflecting the mood of the times, their proposals were usually made in one or a combination of three forms: across-the-board raises, performance-pay plans, and cash bonuses.

Tying wage increases directly to teacher leadership, NEA President Bob Chase said, "we need to look at how we induct people into the profession and let them be part of the decision-making process in schools." Decision-makers or not, many teachers still double as late shift and weekend waiters and waitresses, bartenders, supermarket and department store cashiers, and sales clerks. There is a long way to go, even in places such as affluent Montgomery County, Maryland, where starting salaries for teachers are rising to $38,683 annually, but where most of the system's teachers still cannot afford to own houses. This jurisdiction had ten applicants for every vacancy in 2000, while the less prosperous neighboring Prince George's County was still scrambling to fill vacancies even after the 2000–2001 school year began. Selfless though many teachers may be, money and agreeable working conditions still matter very much.

## Taking Ownership

As the nation comes to recognize the need to involve teachers more directly in shaping policy and contributing their knowledge and perceptions to decision-making processes, it is clear that concerned groups must do their part (and more) to make this happen. Situated as they are on the lowest rungs of education's professional hierarchy, teachers need a lot of help if their voices are to be heard and heeded. Therefore, to a large degree it is up to players and groups such as these to pitch in:

**Teachers:** Across the country, teachers are fully aware of the larger demands of school reform, and most are looking for ways to do their job better. Part of the quest for improvement must come from within. As one Task Force member indelicately put it, "Get in the game." Leadership is not handed out like blue books for a college examination. It is largely up to teachers themselves to locate and exploit opportunities for the professional growth and personal development that will increase their qualifications and credibility for leadership. Teaching is admittedly an exhausting, demanding job and a huge time-devourer, but people in many other professional fields are under similarly ferocious pressure. Yet they somehow manage to get published, to take on advocacy roles, to volunteer time and expertise, and otherwise improve themselves, their profession, and, most important, the products they may be developing, serving, or processing.

**School Districts:** Of the multitude of services school districts can provide or support to better the performance of teachers (and therefore of their students), none quite matches that of resources—pertinent, up-to-date materials for schools, for classrooms, for students, and, too often lost in the shuffle, for teachers themselves. Resources include increased pay (where clearly and fairly merited) as a district-wide priority, adequate allowances for otherwise unprovided classroom materials, and, of special significance, advanced training that bears on the teacher's job. Too many districts are content to support (at least partially) offerings for "advanced" training that have no realistic connection to the needs and responsibilities of the teacher but that represent a bureaucratic step toward salary hikes and improved status. With occasional exceptions, school systems assign a low priority to in-service training, which too often consists of a couple of days off during the school year and a few days of "planning" in late August or early September. No career field pays less attention to enhancing the qualifications of its professionals or their development than does public education.

**Teacher Unions:** Solidarity is important, but achieving it within unions should not mean discouraging members from launching independent initiatives to help improve school performance (or that of teachers). Too, unions have been asserting a more active presence in matters affecting instruction and school-wide matters rather than limiting themselves to the bread-and-butter issues that have traditionally been their bailiwick. Local union leaders, in particular, should explore specific ways to capitalize on the still largely untapped strengths of their members, especially those whose specialized knowledge could contribute to developing more competent and enlightened school leadership in the instructional realm.

**Higher Education:** As described earlier, NCATE, the National Board for Professional Teaching Standards, and the National Commission on Teaching & America's Future, among others, are doing much to professionalize teaching. But most of higher education, specifically the huge majority of mostly prosperous colleges and departments that do not consider themselves to be trainers of future public school teachers, is notably absent from any aspect of school reform. This may be a tired issue, but that does not mean that it should not be addressed. It may take political pressure on state legislatures or trustees, but at least some of the seemingly limitless intellectual and physical resources of the nation's great universities should be used to help fulfill the academy's implicit civic obligation to play a strong role in such obvious areas as development, leadership training, and instructional content.

**Business Organizations:** Thousands of corporations and business leaders, as well as the national and local organizations that represent their interests, have long been directly involved in trying to make schools more productive and efficient. Their support is becoming, on the whole, a welcome ingredient in contemporary school reform, especially in promoting achievable academic standards, different kinds of evaluation, and maximum feasible accountability—and, equally important, in aligning all three. Although corporate experience in these areas does not always transfer easily to public institutions, the business community should promote its basic premises and be prepared to offer a helping hand. At the same time, businesses that have developed (and applied) systems of shared responsibility in management should come forward to share their experience with school systems.

**Mass Media:** Both the print and electronic media have been ambivalent in their treatment of teachers. Locally-based media often run positive stories about the achievements of innovative teachers, while the national media tend to be critical of the performance of the profession as a whole. With rare exceptions, however, neither has paid much attention to the enhanced role that teachers can and logically should play as part of a school or district's policy apparatus. Yet large and middle-size school systems have media relations specialists whose job is to provide timely and accurate information on such topics. (Smaller systems do not customarily have the resources to employ public relations specialists, but the need there is ordinarily not as great. Teachers in small districts tend to get more respect, and they are often more involved in deliberations of policy issues.) There are countless ways to draw attention to the leadership potential of teachers, and public relations professionals should be able to help build a public climate sympathetic to the idea.

## Leadership in Your Own Backyard

Leadership in public education is a matter of guiding a community to realize its potential to do the best job it can for its children. There are many priorities but only limited resources with which to succeed. And no action can really succeed without consensus for a focused, shared vision of what must be done. IEL encourages you to:

- *Gain consensus* on and backing for your community's vision and goals for its schools. If held strongly enough, they will help guide the community in a constructive fashion, especially when the issues become complicated and controversial, and the going gets rough.
- *Involve* representatives from as many different sectors as possible—education, government, business from both the "old" and "new" economies, the communications media, and others.
- *Do your homework* by collecting as much data and information as possible about teacher leadership issues in your community—challenges, opportunities, previous performance, the goals you have set, and the situation in communities with characteristics generally similar to yours.
- *Examine teacher leadership issues* within the broader framework of the community's shared education goals. Analyze your teacher leadership structures with a view to improving them if they appear to fall short.
- *Discuss and debate* the particular teacher leadership challenges, opportunities and options for action described in this report, using your community's shared education goals as the framework.
- *Plan* specific teacher leadership actions that will work for your community, so that your friends and neighbors are aware of the significance of school leadership issues.

Many of these actions are basically political, and leaders must engage the general public in this work. Taxpayers want good schools and generally agree that this will require investment. But most people have little or no understanding of the importance of teacher leadership. This means you will need to start building public awareness for the concept and support for options and approaches such as those described in this report.

## Suggested Questions

To provide a starting point for discussion in your community, this report provides a number of questions that you might want to examine. Expect that differences of opinion and temporary impasses will surface in your discussions, just as they did in the task force meeting. Maintaining focus on group goals and respecting all participant perspectives will keep your discussions on track.

### Recruiting Quality Teachers for Our Schools

- Are we facing a shortage of qualified, motivated teachers in our community?
- What kind of teacher turnover rate does our community have? What reasons do teachers give for leaving the profession?
- Do teachers in our community feel isolated and alienated or do they feel their input is valued in school decisions?
- Are the teacher salaries in our community competitive? Are the schools clean, safe, and well-maintained?
- What recruitment efforts are in place to ensure an adequate supply of qualified and effective teacher-leaders?
- Do teacher demographics in our community mirror the demographics of the student body? If not, how can we support more representative recruitment practices?
- From what sources do we recruit our teachers? Are we satisfied with the results?
- Does our community recruit teachers from alternative preparation programs?

### Supporting Quality Teachers

- Are new teachers in our schools provided instructional support, technical resources, and mentoring? What about a community orientation and assistance finding affordable housing?
- Do teachers in our community have frequent and meaningful opportunities for peer networking and collaboration? Do our schools encourage action research and the sharing of effective instructional approaches?
- Do the preparation and professional development our teachers receive expose them to policy issues, management and leadership skills, and the pedagogic implications of demographics, politics, and cultures?
- Are there adequate numbers of substitute teachers and other incentives for teachers to participate in professional development activities outside the school building?
- Are the roles of teachers differentiated?
- Is teaching in our community a "flat" career or is there a ladder for professional advancement?

### Ensuring Leadership Opportunities for Teachers

- What opportunities for teacher leadership do our schools and our district support?
- Which unions or groups, if any, represent our teachers in salary discussions? Are they open to examining a greater leadership role for teachers?
- Are skilled teachers positioned to provide instructional leadership?
- Are teachers in our community actively involved in designing curricula and selecting textbooks and instructional materials?
- Are teachers actively involved in professional development activities such as developing and

presenting in-service training, mentoring, peer coaching and the like?

- Do teachers have meaningful input into the school budget process? Do teachers in our community supplement the school budget from their own pockets?
- Do teachers have active roles in selecting and evaluating administrators and teachers in our community?
- Are teachers actively involved in setting school and district policy for student behavior, promotion, retention, and discipline?

### Evaluating and Recognizing Quality Teachers

- Does our community or school district have professional standards for teachers? How do they relate to student performance standards?
- Are our community's teachers evaluated on a regular basis? How do these evaluations provide teachers with the information they need to grow professionally?
- How are accountability measures applied to teachers? Are principals, teachers, and students provided with the resources and supports needed to meet rigorous accountability measures?
- What incentives are built into our teacher evaluation and accountability systems to encourage lifelong learning and to recognize teacher leaders for their contributions and accomplishments?

### Ensuring Community Support for Quality Teachers and Teacher-Leaders

- How can we promote better public understanding of teacher leadership roles?
- What community members, resources, and organizations are potential partners in supporting quality teachers and teacher-leaders?
- How do we communicate with the community and our stakeholders? How can we improve our communications strategies?
- Do we have a strong, positive relationship with the media serving our community?

## References

Abrams, D. (2001, February 21). Hiring teachers gets trickier for other counties. *Montgomery County Gazette*. Available at http://www.gazette.net/search/

Barth, R.S. (2001, February). Teacher leader. *Phi Delta Kappan 82*, (4).

Blair, J. (2001, February 2). Lawmakers plunge into teacher pay. *Education Week*. Available at http://www.edweek.org/edsearch.cfm

Bradley, A. (2000, April). Presto, change-o. *Teacher Magazine*. Available at http://www.edweek.org/edsearch.cfm

Darling-Hammond, L. (1999, January-February). Educating teachers: The Academy's greatest failure or its most important future? *Academe 85*, (1).

Darling-Hammond, L. (1997). *The right to learn: A blueprint for creating schools that work.* San Francisco, CA: Jossey-Bass.

Darling-Hammond, L. & Loewenberg Ball, D. (1998). *Teaching for high standards: What policy-makers need to know and be able to do.* Philadelphia, PA: National Commission on Teaching & America's Future and Consortium for Policy Research in Education.

Doyle, D. (2001, March). A liberal education. *The School Administrator.* Arlington, VA: American Association of School Administrators. Available at http://www.aasa.org/publications/sa/2001_03/doyle.htm

*Education Week* & Pew Charitable Trust. (2000). *Quality counts 2000: Who should teach?* Bethesda, MD: Education Week. Available at http://www.edweek.org/sreports/qc00/

Elmore, R.F. (2000). *Building a new structure for school leadership.* Washington, DC: Albert Shanker Institute.

Farkas, S., Foley, P. & Duffett, A. with Foleno, T. & Johnson, J. (2001). *Just waiting to be asked? A fresh look at attitudes on public engagement.* New York, NY: Public Agenda. Available at http://www.publicagenda.org /specials/pubengage/pubengage.htm

Farkas, S., Johnson, J. & Foleno, T. with Duffett, A. & Foley, P. (2000). *A sense of calling: Who teaches and why.* New York, NY: Public Agenda. Available at http://www.publicagenda.org/aboutpa/aboutpa7.htm

Koppich, J.E. (2001). *Investing in teaching.* Washington, DC: National Alliance of Business.

Merrow, J. (2001). *Choosing excellence.* Lanham, MD: Scarecrow.

Metropolitan Life Foundation. (2000). *The Metropolitan Life survey of the American teacher, 2000: Are we preparing students for the 21st century?* New York, NY: Metropolitan Life Insurance Co. Available at http://www.metlife.com/ Companyinfo/Community/Found/Docs/2000pdf.html

Milken, L. (2000). *Teaching as the opportunity: The Teacher Advancement Program.* Santa Monica, CA: Milken Family Foundation. Available at http://www.mff.org/publications/publications.taf

National Commission on Teaching & America's Future. (1996). *What matters most: Teaching for America's future.* New York, NY: Author. Available at http://www.nctaf.org/publications/whatmattersmost.html

Perez-Rivas, M. (2001, March 26). Teachers moving beyond paychecks. *The Washington Post.* Available at http://www.washingtonpost.com

Steelman, L.C., Powell, B. & Carini, R.M. (2000, Winter). Do teacher unions hinder educational performance? Lessons learned from state SAT and ACT scores. *Harvard Educational Review, 70* (4).

Task Force on Teaching as a Profession. (1986). *A nation prepared: Teachers for the 21st century.* New York, NY: The Carnegie Foundation.

Terry, P.M. (1999–2000). Empowering teachers as leaders. *National Forum of Teacher Education Journal 10E,* 3. Lake Charles, LA: National Forum Journals. Available at http://www.nationalforum.com/TERRYte8e3.html

Troen, V. & Boles, K.C. (1993, November 3). Teacher leadership: How to make it more than a catch phrase. *Teacher Magazine.* Available at http://www.edweek.org/edsearch.cfm

Tyson, H. (1993). *Who will teach the children?* San Francisco, CA: Jossey-Bass.

Urbanski, A. & Erskine, R. (2000, January). School reform, TURN, and teacher compensation. *Phi Delta Kappan 81,* 5. Available at http://www.pdkintl.org/kappan/kurb0001.htm

Wilson, M. (1993, March). The search for teacher leaders. *Educational Leadership, 50,* 6.

# CHAPTER TEN

# Teachers, Learners, Leaders

ANN LIEBERMAN

WHAT IF TEACHERS RAN THEIR OWN PROFESSIONAL DEVELOPMENT THROUGH PROJECTS? And what if teachers themselves received funding for these projects? What if the purpose of such projects was not only to spur individual professional learning, but also to develop leadership skills and initiate an exchange of knowledge among one's peers?

In Ontario, Canada, teachers pursue this kind of self-designed professional learning through the publicly funded Teacher Learning and Leadership Program (TLLP). Since the 2007–08 school year, 1,500 people—mostly teachers—have initiated 225 teacher learning projects through TLLP, 83 percent of which have been collaborations among several educators.

Part of the beauty of this professional learning structure is that it represents a successful joining of the education policy arm and teachers' unions. The program meshes education research, education policy, and teaching practice and is a prime example of how researchers, policymakers, and practicing teachers can work together instead of pursuing conflicting agendas.

## The Context: Building a Collaboration

The province of Ontario serves 2 million students, and approximately 120,000 teachers work in Ontario's K–12 public schools. English, French, Catholic, and nonreligious K–12 schools all receive public funding through the provincial government. The Teacher Learning and Leadership Program was developed in 2003 in the context of a new Ontario provincial government. From the start, the new education minister deliberately avoided the kind of "top-down" approach to education policy that many Canadian teachers felt had characterized past approaches. The new administration was determined to create a professional development program for teachers that was supportive, collaborative, and sustainable.

In 2005, recognizing that all stakeholders needed to come together if they hoped to enhance education in Ontario, Ontario's education ministry called together a Working Table on Teacher Development. All groups who represented Ontario's schools—including the Ontario Teachers' Federation (OTF) and its affiliates—were included. This Working Table was charged with making recommendations for how the government and other bodies should support teachers' professional learning, keeping in mind that teacher quality is the single most important factor in student learning. To inform this work, the ministry assigned two university professors, Kathy Broad and Mark Evans, to write an extensive literature review on the best content and delivery modes of professional development for experienced teachers (Broad & Evans, 2006).

## Defining Professional Learning and Opting for Choice

The Working Table first made distinctions among *training* (skills all teachers must learn to do their job, such as lesson planning); *staff development* (a systemwide set of learning activities driven by the system's needs, such as enhancing early literacy instruction); and *professional development* (self-chosen activities that teachers can do individually or as a group, such as action research). The Working Table participants decided that the ministry should focus on supporting the latter kind of learning. Teachers have different learning styles and professional needs, and they should have the chance to pursue those needs independently. At the same time, any ministry-supported program should give teachers choice and connect teachers' needs to the goals of the ministry of education and other official bodies. Effective professional development needs to positively affect students as well as teachers. Toward that end, the group concluded that a high-quality teacher learning program should be:

- *Built on the three Rs of respect, responsibility, and results.* The program must respect the complexity of teachers' learning and, ultimately, be responsible for boosting students' success.
- *Attentive to adult learning styles.* Teachers should have choices of meaningful, relevant, and substantive content and ways to learn.
- *Goal-oriented.* The program should be clearly connected to improved student learning as well as to changes in daily practice, remaining respectful of varied contexts.
- *Sustainable.* It should provide appropriate resources (including a clear support system from colleagues) and time for practice and self-assessment.
- *Supported by research and data.* This base in research would ensure that professional development reflects up-to-date theories and practice (Working Party on Teacher Development, 2007).

The Working Table affirmed that this program should tap into the tremendous resource of experienced teachers who can provide peer leadership and that grantees should be strongly urged to team up with fellow classroom teachers, resource teachers, or other players in the education field.

## Creating a Teacher-Led Program

These ideas formed the basis for Ontario's teacher learning and leadership program. The program was designed and developed—and continues to be sustained—collaboratively by the ministry of education and the Ontario Teachers' Federation (OTF), who decide together which teacher projects of the many submitted will be funded.

At the beginning of the school year, teachers submit a description of their proposed project and a request for funds (most range from $1,000 to $10,000). All funding is used to cover costs for materials and teacher release time; lead teachers don't receive a stipend for spearheading their projects. Teachers must show how their project will address participants' professional learning and contribute to student learning; they must also delineate the experience that different teachers will bring to this effort. They outline a budget and show how they will measure both students' learning and their own, and they describe how they will share the learning with colleagues. Teachers are encouraged to expand their project to other schools, networks, and regions; 91 percent of projects have included other schools in the teacher leaders' boards (the Canadian equivalent of a district), and 43 percent have reached beyond their board—for example, by developing a conference or websites.

After a panel chooses the cohort of Ontario teachers whose projects will be funded that year, the ministry and OTF sponsor a conference to introduce essential leadership knowledge to these educators and show support for them. Presenters clarify any questions about finances and offer training sessions to draw out skills among project leaders (typical sessions include "Developing and Delivering a Dynamic Workshop" and "Persuasion, Not Pontification: Promoting Your Project").

As teachers from past cohorts describe their successful projects to those just starting out, teacher leadership multiplies. Meeting with other participants in the beginning not only motivates project participants, but also helps them realize they are part of something larger than themselves: Their learning can improve students' lives as they stretch themselves and become members of a developing professional community.

## A Look Inside the Projects

A glance at TLLP-funded projects gives an idea of the breadth and depth of teacher learning that's possible when teachers organize professional development connected to their own contexts, strengths, interests, and needs. Projects range from "Working Together to Improve Boys' Literacy" (in both French and English) to "Engaging Young Readers with E-Books" to "A Plan for Work-World Readiness." There are projects focused on every subject in K–12 schools and projects that integrate music into language arts, science, and social studies. Teachers have devised support strategies for students falling through the cracks. In one project called "The Success Room," teachers work with any 7th or 8th grader who is struggling with academics or work habits; they sometimes bring the students' peers into the process. For example, if a student hasn't been handing in homework, a teacher in the Success Room talks with both the student and his or her classroom teacher and arranges a support system to help that student succeed.

To get inside the power of the program, let's look at two projects up close.

### Fostering Math Talk

Math teacher Nicole Walter Rowan realized that she and other teachers at Agnew H. Johnston Public School, a K–8 bilingual school in Thunder Bay, Ontario, needed a deeper understanding of how to help students think and talk about math. Walter Rowan and a group of 12 colleagues—several of whom had earlier participated in an action research project on "math talk"—wanted to address students' weaknesses and uncertainties in math. The teachers decided to work on improving both their practice as teachers and their students' math awareness.

Four educators, forming the leadership team of the project, worked collaboratively with interested classroom teachers to deepen their collective understanding. They aimed to build a community of like-minded professionals. Supported by a university professor and a staff developer from a New York-based group called Math in the City, this leadership team helped their fellow teachers explore and practice math talk strategies.

In several workshops the team led during the school day, the teachers studied teacher talk and actions as portrayed on a video (part of Pearson's Young Mathematicians at Work series) that modeled actual teachers fostering student discourse during math class. The leadership team, along with outside consultants, identified exemplary teaching strategies appearing at key points in the video—for example "teacher asks students to apply one student's strategy that was different from their own to solve a problem"—and discussed these strategies with the learning community.

As teachers watched the video together, they practiced spotting instances in the lessons in which teachers modeled each of these effective strategies and students displayed heightened mathematical awareness. Teachers in the video prompted students to "turn and talk" about math understandings at pivotal moments in exploring math concepts, and the Agnew teachers saw how the experienced teachers sensed when to stop kids at a pivotal moment. Through these workshops, the group developed a shared vocabulary and began to envision what a classroom involved in collaborative mathematical problem solving could look like.

Two teachers from the leadership team then planned and cotaught lessons with other team members. Each coteaching session included planning, delivering instruction together, and debriefing. The focus of how lessons were planned and cotaught differed, depending on the needs of each teacher and his or her learners, but the focus generally centered on teacher and student talk and the effect of the chosen strategies on students' thinking.

The impact of this learning project was powerful. Teachers developed more confidence in how to question students and elicit responses that showed math understandings. Many went public with their teaching for the first time. Shared pedagogical knowledge and vocabulary made it easier to view one another's instructional practices with a critical lens and give feedback. The team members began to realize that their own practice was authenticating and expanding the research they were learning about. Eventually, a nearby school board took notice of the Agnew team's work, and this board is now supporting its own similar initiative.

## Spreading the Graphic Novel Gospel

Matt Armstrong, Heather Murphy, and Anne Doorly, teachers at Adult High School focused on spreading a practice they had honed—using graphic novels to boost older struggling readers' literacy—throughout a wider circle. In Canada, an adult school is one in which students older than 18 can retake courses they must pass to pursue a diploma or take additional courses, such as English as a second language. Armstrong, Murphy, and Doorly had found graphic texts to be a promising resource with adult learners who need motivation to continue reading or who are still learning reading skills. They had developed extensive strategies for how to use graphic texts fruitfully, organized all their notes on how to use these texts into an easy-to-share binder, and were primed to provide workshops on this instructional practice to others.

The team started by introducing these materials to five English teachers in the team's own school. As a result of these workshops, all five began using graphic novels in their classes as well, and they saw struggling students become heavily engaged in reading.

At the school board's English professional development day, Heather Murphy and Anne Doorly shared strategies on using graphic texts with about 150 teachers from other schools. They provided participants with an electronic version of several graphic texts, including *Persepolis* by Marjane Satrapi and a version of John Steinbeck's *Of Mice and Men*.

The team expanded its presentations to additional groups of teachers that year and the following year. As they presented to each new audience, the team learned more about how to facilitate their peers' learning; for example, they learned their peers mostly wanted hands-on, practical ideas. A video produced by the Ontario Teachers' Federation shows this teacher learning in action.

### Joining Learning and Leadership

Teachers teaching teachers is a powerful strategy for finding, developing, and using all talents. Teacher Leadership and Learning recently funded its fourth cohort of projects, and the ministry plans to keep the program going. TLLP shows what can happen when teachers propose professional development efforts centered on what they know, what they want to learn, and what they hope to share with peers. The program recasts the traditional paradigm that stresses compliance rather than collaboration, disparages teacher unions rather than builds shared solutions, and imposes research on teachers without rooting new knowledge in everyday teaching and learning. This program is also a robust example of how practice, research, and policy can join to change learning for both teachers and students.

## References

Broad, K., & Evans, M. (2006). *A review of literature on professional development content and delivery modes for experienced teachers.* Toronto: Canadian Ministry of Education.

Working Party on Teacher Development. (2007). *Report to the Partnership Table on Professional Learning.* Ontario: Ontario Ministry of Education.

# CHAPTER ELEVEN

# Teacher Leadership

## Alive and Thriving at the Elementary Level

S HERRY  W ILLIS

D URING THE SUMMER OF 2007, THIRTY-FOUR SELECTED KINDERGARTEN TEACHERS FROM ACROSS the state of North Carolina came together to begin a journey purposefully crafted to enhance their instructional practice and to build their leadership capacity. This group of teachers, identified as North Carolina Kindergarten Teacher Leaders, was a key component of the state's early childhood initiative known as The Power of Kindergarten (Power of K). The impetus for this initiative arose from concerns voiced by a number of kindergarten teachers, administrators, and members of the North Carolina Birth Through Kindergarten Higher Education Consortium. These educators were highly concerned that developmentally appropriate practices in North Carolina kindergarten classrooms were being diminished if not lost entirely.

Members of the Early Childhood Division of the North Carolina Department of Public Instruction (NCDPI) listened to the concerns and quickly responded. An eight-member Kindergarten Think Tank composed of kindergarten teachers, administrators, and other early childhood professionals was organized. The Think Tank first created a position paper that defined the purpose and requirements for North Carolina kindergartens in the 21st century. Next, plans were made for selecting a cadre of teachers to become leaders in implementing and sustaining the kindergarten program described in the position statement. Interest in the initiative was high—over two hundred kindergarten teachers from all regions of the state applied to become a Kindergarten Teacher Leader. Thirty-four teachers were selected to begin an intensive three-year process of professional development designed to expand their knowledge of child development, learning environments, instructional intentionality, developmentally appropriate practice, and leadership skills. These teachers were expected to assume leadership roles within their schools, in their local school districts/regions, and at the state level. Possible leadership roles included serving on school improvement teams and system-level committees; conducting local, district, and regional professional development; and developing demonstration classrooms.

Ten of the Kindergarten Teacher Leaders recently participated in a study (Willis, 2010) designed to understand the experiences of North Carolina kindergarten teachers as they worked to establish, sustain, or improve developmentally appropriate practices in their classrooms. Developmentally appropriate practices are those research-based teaching and decision-making practices that take into account how each child learns, each individual child's growth and development, as well as the child's cultural values (Copple & Bredekamp, 2006). The study served to identify sources of support for these teachers as well as any barriers they encountered in their jobs. The study also served to discover how teachers coped with or resolved any challenges they experienced. The results of this study were intended to inform administrators and central office personnel of the needs and concerns of teachers committed to a developmentally appropriate approach to teaching kindergarten. These needs could inform system-wide and local school allocation of resources, professional development plans, teacher recruitment and retention strategies, and school improvement plans.

The participants in the study proved to be quite passionate in their beliefs favoring a developmentally appropriate approach to teaching; they desired to be as developmentally appropriate as possible in their teaching practices. Acutely aware of the academic standards for which they are held accountable, the kindergarten teachers wanted to be able to teach those standards in ways that were relevant to children. More specifically, they wanted children to be engaged in rigorous, challenging, active learning experiences that honor the ways children learn best. Developmentally appropriate classrooms, which the teachers in the study highly regarded, are thoughtfully designed to include learning centers, movement, exploration, meaningful hands-on learning experiences, and projects that support children's curiosity, interests, and natural eagerness to learn. The teachers serve as both *guides to* and *directors of* learning (Copple & Bredekamp, 2006; Katz, 2000; Rushton, 2001). The teachers did not believe that a more academic approach, often favored by other kindergarten teachers in their schools, was the best practice. That approach placed children in learning environments that resembled traditional first-grade classrooms. Those settings placed a heavy emphasis on teacher-directed learning, isolated skills, whole-group instruction, and worksheets, with children spending extended time sitting at tables or desks. Children had little opportunity to engage in problem solving, decision-making, or self-initiated projects within authentic contexts.

Most of the teachers in the study reported being required to follow some kind of system mandate that ran counter to their philosophical beliefs about developmentally appropriate practice as a significant barrier. These mandates involved the use of scripted commercial reading and math programs with whole groups of children. The teachers, strong in their knowledge of developmentally appropriate practices, worked creatively to adapt the programs in order to provide more effective and meaningful learning experiences for children. Other barriers reported by the teachers included the lack of meaningful and differentiated professional development aligned with the needs of early childhood teachers; the lack of meaningful feedback from administrators; and the feeling of being ignored and undervalued as professionals. These barriers were most challenging as the teachers felt they had little control in trying to overcome them.

## Implications for Administrators

Several implications for administrators in North Carolina can be drawn from the study. These implications relate to understanding and supporting the needs of teachers as well as nurturing their leadership capacity, recruiting and maintaining high quality teachers, and providing them with meaningful professional development.

The ten North Carolina Kindergarten Teacher Leaders in this study were quite adamant in their belief that using a developmentally appropriate teaching approach was the best practice for educating young children. These Kindergarten Teacher Leaders truly wanted the help and support of administrators in order to be most effective in their practice. Teachers in the study found this source of help to be lacking or reported passive support from their administrator at best. Passive support occurred when administrators basically left the teachers alone, trusting them to do what they thought was best. Though the teachers appreciated any kind or means of support, they preferred active support from informed administrators. Active support included having the administrator in their classrooms frequently and for extended lengths of time; receiving meaningful feedback related to their practice, with knowledgeable suggestions for improvement; and recognition or praise for worthy endeavors.

It would not be a stretch to say that the number of North Carolina principals who are highly knowledgeable in the areas of early childhood education and child development is relatively low. If administrators are to be true instructional leaders in their schools, they must know and understand what is going on at every grade level and in every classroom and why. Being well informed is the only way they can meaningfully coach teachers to improve their practice. This level of knowledge also informs the administrator when celebrations of success are warranted. I have illustrated this point with principals during a professional development session with them. Using the analogy of a golf game, I described a scenario that included unheard of practices in the game of golf, but "golf-like" enough to someone not familiar with the game. These practices included driving the golf cart up on the green and placing a tee on the putting green. At the end of the scenario I asked the audience of principals if they saw any problems with the scenario I described. Only two principals, the golf-pros of the group, raised their hands wildly. "Don't ever drive your cart on the green!" one exclaimed. The other one said, "You don't use tees on the putting green!" The analogy was then applied to observing a kindergarten classroom. An administrator, who is not knowledgeable about what is observed, cannot tell the difference between appropriate practice and inappropriate practice; can make no meaningful suggestions for improvement; and has no idea what to consider praiseworthy.

Principals must have available to them some means for gaining knowledge about child development and early childhood education. They must learn how the practices used in a developmentally appropriate kindergarten classroom impact a child's success beyond kindergarten. They should know what to look for in developmentally appropriate kindergarten classrooms—what teachers should be doing and what children should be doing—so that the integrity of this teaching approach is upheld. Few, if any, educational leadership programs provide such coursework related to early childhood education. Until that happens, it will be up to administrators to seek out this important information. Online courses could be specifically designed for this purpose with special emphasis on how the administrator can support instruction and teachers at the primary level.

Many administrators practice classroom "walk-throughs" designed to collect and document information about what teachers and students are doing. The administrator looks for evidence of specific researched-based strategies proven to have a high impact on student achievement. It would be helpful to administrators to have the checklist of practices "translated" to show how the practices might be represented in a developmentally appropriate kindergarten classroom. It is highly interesting to note that many of the research-based practices administrators are to look for in all classrooms at elementary, middle, and high school levels are the very practices they would find in a developmentally appropriate kindergarten classroom—differentiated instruction instead of whole-group instruction, student learning projects, small-group instruction, cooperative learning, and active, meaningful learning experiences.

A new state teacher evaluation instrument in North Carolina was fully implemented during the 2010–2011 school year. A small group of educators is actually working on a principal-support document for this instrument—a document specifically designed to inform principals of how the new evaluation instrument aligns to practices in Pre-K and kindergarten classrooms. Principals who are new to the instrument and not strong in early childhood knowledge will be grateful for this information. They need to make all efforts to secure and use the document once it becomes available.

## Teacher Recruitment and Retention

Recruiting and retaining quality teachers is a high priority for all school systems. Once excellent teachers are recruited for specific positions, it then becomes important to retain those teachers for as long as possible. It is helpful to know what factors keep teachers in the classroom.

In the study, four teachers at one time or another considered leaving the classroom because of high levels of dissatisfaction. The teachers experienced low levels of esteem and lacked a sense of belonging. Curriculum decisions made at the system level often did not take into account input provided by the kindergarten teachers. Some of the teachers shared experiences indicating that no attempts were ever made to seek out their teacher voice. When mandates were issued requiring that teachers follow scripted teachers' manuals, the kindergarten teachers felt they were being given the message that the school system did not consider them competent to plan and teach based on the known needs of children.

If states are serious about keeping good teachers who have the knowledge and disposition to dedicate their lifework to young children, then school systems and local schools must act to honor the work of these teachers and to meet their needs. Administrators must demonstrate by word and action that they believe kindergarten has a valuable place and purpose within the school program. Kindergarten and kindergarten teachers cannot be relegated to a lower level of importance when it comes to providing resources, making schedules, and offering teachers support in terms of professional development. They cannot be ignored to accommodate the needs of teachers and students in tested grades. Kindergarten teachers are often the most knowledgeable teachers in the school in the area of child development. Their expertise is needed when critical instructional decisions affecting children have to be made.

Primary teachers do want to have a voice in making decisions at school and system levels that will affect them and their students. Teachers want their input to be seriously considered rather than just being a moot exercise. When their ideas are taken seriously, teachers' esteem is raised; their sense of autonomy is increased; they feel their opinions are valued and appreciated. School systems and schools would be very smart indeed to make it a standard practice to solicit opinions from and involve teachers in decision making as much as possible. Decisions are more likely to be supported if a feeling of ownership and involvement has been established.

## Professional Development

The teachers in the study experienced a high level of support, esteem, and sense of belonging through their involvement with the Power of Kindergarten. All school systems should use this model to organize and support their kindergarten teachers as a professional learning community. Regularly scheduled meetings would afford teachers opportunities to network and learn from each other, to gain knowledge through professional development designed to meet the differentiated needs of kindergarten teachers, and to provide teachers the opportunities to share and discuss concerns with school and system-level administrators. Teacher leadership would be supported when the teachers are encouraged to lead the professional development or discussion sessions.

The North Carolina Kindergarten Teacher Leaders could not be more glowing in their descriptions of the positive impact the Power of Kindergarten initiative has had on their professional lives. The word "empowered" was used again and again to explain the effects of their increased knowledge and leadership skills. The teachers reported that they were better able to implement developmentally appropriate practices without fear of reproach from colleagues or administrators; they were also much stronger in effectively articulating their philosophy and their classroom practices to administrators, colleagues, parents, and other stakeholders.

The current participants are at the end of the three-year initiative. Plans are underway to sustain the powerful network that has been established. Demonstration classrooms are being discussed and developed. The Kindergarten Teacher Leaders are now available to provide support and professional development for teachers in their regions. Administrators have been encouraged to seek out these leaders and use their expertise to support their own kindergarten teachers.

## Nurturing Leadership

No one should think that primary teachers are unable or uninterested in assuming leadership roles at the local, district, or state levels. Teacher leadership at the primary level is alive and thriving. This dynamic was certainly evident in the case of the teachers involved in the North Carolina Kindergarten Teacher Leader initiative. These teachers have been, in their own words, "empowered" to serve as models for teaching kindergarten in a way that honors how children learn best and makes learning meaningful; they stand ready to share their knowledge with others through professional development. The teachers are also assuming leadership roles in their schools, their school districts, regions, and even at the state level to make sure that the kindergarten teacher-voice is heard.

It is important to remember that over two hundred kindergarten teachers from all corners of the state initially applied to be selected as a Kindergarten Teacher Leader. They eagerly pursued the opportunity to assume the role of being a leader. For some, it was the first leadership opportunity ever extended to them. Changes must be made in the way some people view teacher leadership—it is not a role reserved only for upper elementary, middle, and high school teachers. Administrators are key players in this process.

Administrators must be fully knowledgeable about how to develop and nurture the leadership capacity in all teachers—*at all levels*. In other words, administrators must know, understand, and value, the contribution each teacher makes to the total school program; they must identify and enhance teachers' strengths; they must identify and meet teachers' needs. Having this information, administrators can help teachers craft the leadership skills needed in their classrooms, in the school, and in other places.

As a former kindergarten teacher, and now as an elementary school principal, I have experienced both sides of teacher leadership. While teaching kindergarten, I was encouraged and supported to assume leadership roles in the school system. Resources were provided so that I could develop a demonstration classroom for area kindergarten teachers to observe. I do understand what primary and elementary teachers need in order to feel professionally valued and supported. As principal, I am charged with the responsibility to provide all teachers—primary and elementary teachers—with opportunities for professional growth designed to build their leadership capacity. It is a responsibility I take seriously. I must also provide opportunities and encourage teachers to apply their leadership skills within the school setting and beyond. These opportunities often translate into teachers engaging in shared decision-making, leading parent meetings and professional development sessions, and actively serving on school and system-wide committees. School then becomes a true learning community where everyone works in tandem to support student achievement in the 21st century, as well as teachers' professional growth.

# References

Copple, C., & Bredekamp, S. (2006). *Basics of developmentally appropriate practice*. Washington, DC: National Association for the Education of Young Children.

Katz, L. G. (2000). Another look at what young children should be learning. *ERIC Digest*, Retrieved April 28, 2007, from http://www.ericdigests.org/2000–1/look.html

Rushton, S. P. (2001). Applying brain research to create developmentally appropriate learning environments. *Young Children*, 56(5), 76–82.

Willis, S. R. (2010). *North Carolina kindergarten teachers and developmentally appropriate instructional practices: A phenomenological study* (Unpublished doctoral dissertation, Western Carolina University, 2010).

# CHAPTER TWELVE

# Teacher Leadership in High Schools

## How Principals Encourage It, How Teachers Practice It

### Institute for Educational Leadership, Inc.

TEACHER LEADERSHIP IS EMERGING AS A CRITICAL COMPONENT OF HIGH SCHOOL REFORM. This is the major conclusion of the most recent analysis of school leadership by the Institute for Educational Leadership (IEL), which has been investigating and reporting for almost a decade on ways to improve leadership for student learning.

IEL launched the School Leadership for the 21st Century initiative in 2000. Its studies, surveys, and analyses document dramatic challenges facing schools and identify why school leadership needs to be transformed. Through four reports on Leadership for Learning, IEL has called for these substantial changes:

- Reinvent the principalship
- Redefine teachers as leaders
- Recognize the role of states
- Restructure school districts.

IEL's initial call to redefine the teacher as leader was based on the work of the Teacher Leadership Task Force. That Task Force's report, *Redefining the Teacher as Leader* (IEL, 2001), emphasized that teacher leadership is not about "teacher power." Rather, "it is about mobilizing the still largely untapped attributes of teachers to strengthen student performance at the ground level." This can happen through "real collaboration—a locally tailored kind of shared leadership—in the daily life of the school." The Task Force also found a noticeable lack of respect for teachers. Their profession is viewed as anything but "a vital part of the policy-framing and -governing processes." Most teachers, the report pointed out, "have little or no effective representation in the key organizational, political, and pedagogical decisions that affect their jobs, their profession, and, by extension, their personal lives." More importantly, the report lamented that the resources for leadership and reform among teachers—their experience, ideas, and skills—were being "squandered."

These findings echoed many of the same sentiments reported earlier in the MetLife 2000 Survey of the American Teacher. It reported that many secondary school faculty members felt alienated. Substantial numbers believed they were "left out of things going on around them at their school," or that "what they think doesn't count very much at their school."

This document, IEL's second study on teacher leadership, focuses on how principals foster teacher leadership in high schools. In 2006, the MetLife Foundation provided funding for IEL to support a new initiative, the MetLife Task Force on Teacher Leadership in High Schools. Although its study is limited in scope, the MetLife Task Force has identified a group of high schools where principals support teacher leadership, and where teachers are taking on new leadership roles and responsibilities. These schools provide a better understanding of two issues: 1) the conditions that foster teacher leadership and 2) the different roles that teachers can assume. The study focuses on the perspective of principals, because they sit atop the traditional power structure and control access to decision-making in a school.

Engaged educators are central to the reform of high schools. The National High School Alliance, an IEL-based partnership of 50 organizations working to transform high schools for all youth, cites the empowerment of educators as one of the six principles needed to transform traditional, comprehensive high schools into schools that foster high academic achievement, close the achievement gap, and promote civic and personal growth in all high school age youth. Without strong teacher buy-in, according to the Alliance, "successful high school reform in support of better student outcomes is simply not possible" (IEL, 2005).

## What Is Teacher Leadership?

Teacher leadership has historical roots that run deep and confirm that the norms of collegiality and collaboration are significant to quality teaching, the instructional climate, and student achievement. Though the concept is not new, Smylie & Denny (1990) assert that "what is new are the increased recognition of teacher leadership, visions of expanded teacher leadership roles, and new hope for the contributions these expanded roles might make in improving school."

Redefining leadership in schools is central to understanding its impact on student outcomes. Current research calls for moving away from the traditional administrative hierarchy towards a more distributed model of leadership. The research describes a type of teacher behavior that reaches beyond classrooms to create the climate and the organization necessary for learning. The behavior is not so much an act of instruction as an act of leadership essential to the whole school, which Spillane, Halverson, and Diamond call "distributed leadership" (Spillane et al., 2001). Their evolving description of distributed leadership is: "that [leadership] which is stretched over people (leaders and followers) and place." It also has been defined as "an emergent property of a group or network of interacting individuals, contrasting it to conceptions of leadership that focus on the actions of singular individuals" (Bennett et al., 2003).

This study used a definition of teacher leadership drawn from a meta-analysis of teacher leadership research since the early 1990s by York-Barr and Duke (2004):

> Teacher leadership is the process by which teachers, individually or collectively, influence their colleagues, principals, and other members of the school communities to improve teaching and learning practices with the aim of increased student learning and achievement. Such team leadership work involves three intentional development foci: individual development, collaboration or team development, and organizational development.

They contend there are recognizable conditions that must exist for teacher leadership to develop. These conditions mirror the theory behind distributed leadership, and provide a framework that covers School Culture and Context, Roles and Responsibilities of Teachers, and the Structural System of the School. Within each of these categories there are individual conditions that, when occurring simultaneously, allow teachers to act in leadership roles. (See Table 1.)

York-Barr and Duke's definition of teacher leadership is consistent with IEL's guiding principles about developing leadership that knows learning and development, that can cross boundaries, and that influences organizations and systems. The York-Barr and Duke definition of teacher leadership and their framework of conditions necessary for the development of teacher leadership was used to build the conceptual framework for this study.

## Seeking out Teacher Leadership

IEL identified 76 schools in which teachers are playing vital leadership roles. Using a large, national survey and interviews with a smaller subset of teachers and principals, IEL found schools where teacher leadership is practiced, identified what teachers are doing as leaders, and documented the many ways in which principals foster that leadership.

Almost 300 principals responded to the MetLife Task Force on Teacher Leadership Survey (MTL Survey), a voluntary survey about teacher leadership in high schools. Three criteria, drawn from research about the optimal conditions for the growth of teacher leadership and from recent federal legislation, helped to winnow the data and identify a subset of high schools where teacher leadership was in practice. The criteria were:

1. the principal responded that he or she led the school with others
2. the presence of a leadership team in the school
3. the high schools met adequate yearly progress (AYP), as defined by their states, for two or three years prior to the survey.

The ability to meet AYP was the only quantitative measure of student success and, thus, a critical part of the sample selection. In order to obtain and understand the stories about the practice teacher leadership, IEL staff conducted telephone interviews with principals and teachers in six high schools that qualified for the final sample, chosen on the basis of diverse demographic characteristics. A final subset of 76 schools met the criteria and was used for the data analysis.

As a benchmark for its own work, IEL used the initial cohort of Breakthrough High Schools (BTHS) for comparisons. These are high schools identified by the National Association of Secondary School Principals (NASSP) as being successful with high-poverty, high-minority student enrollments. In these schools, the student population is at least 50 percent minority, at least 50 percent qualify for free and reduced-price lunch, and at least 90 percent graduate and enroll in postsecondary education. According to NASSP, principals in these schools facilitate professional development for their teachers, encourage staff collaboration, and personalize the learning experience for all students. IEL found that practices in the high schools included in its study are very similar to those found in the highly successful BTHS. Throughout this report, IEL compares the findings from the national survey to those from the survey of BTHS principals.

## TABLE 1. Conditions for Teacher Leadership

| | |
|---|---|
| **School culture & context** | • Schoolwide focus on learning, inquiry and reflective process<br>• Encouragement for taking initiative<br>• An expectation of teamwork and shared responsibility, decision making, and leadership<br>• Teaching professionals valued as role models<br>• A strong sense of community among teachers that fosters professionalism |
| **Roles & responsibilities** | • Colleagues recognize and respect teacher leaders who have subject-area and instructional expertise<br>• High trust and positive working relationships exist both among teacher peers and with administrators<br>• Teacher leadership work central to the teaching and learning processes (as opposed to administrative or managerial tasks) is routinely assigned<br>• Interpersonal relationships between teacher leaders and the principal flourish |
| **Structures** | • Provision of adequate access to materials, time, and space for activities that facilitate teacher leadership (ex., professional development) |

# Creating a Picture of Teacher Leadership in High Schools

This report documents what IEL learned about how principals support teacher leadership and what it looks like in high schools in which it is practiced. It presents an analysis of the findings and concludes with questions designed to stimulate conversations about how to encourage and maintain teacher leadership in high schools. The data include responses from the principals of the final sample of 76 high schools, and the interviews with principals and teachers from the six high schools.

The data produced five general conclusions:

- Teacher leadership is being fostered and practiced in large and small high schools in different parts of the country.
- Principals are supportive partners.
- Teachers are doing more than teaching.
- Teachers become leaders because they recognize a need.
- Principals, teachers, and students benefit from teacher leadership.

## 1. Teacher leadership is being fostered and practiced in large and small high schools in different parts of the country.

The MTL Survey found that many of the principals in the study believed in collaboration. When asked, "Who leads your school?," they overwhelmingly replied that they lead their schools in collaboration with others in the school community. This mirrors the NASSP Breakthrough High Schools, where principal leadership sets high levels of expectations for teachers and understands that an effective school depends on leadership from all members of the school community.

Another indicator that teacher leadership is being practiced in these schools is the presence of leadership teams. All 76 principals reported formally involving other staff members in a team designed to oversee, manage, and coordinate instruction. Ninety-seven percent of the principals viewed meeting with the leadership team as important to the work of leading the school. Principals valued this interaction higher than any of the other activities they were asked about, such as attending department or curricular meetings.

Forty-two percent of the principals interact with members of these leadership teams in formally scheduled meetings at least once a week; 40 percent report meeting formally a few times per month. Principals meet with their leadership team far more frequently on an informal basis, however, than they do in formally scheduled appointments. About 75 percent report having informal team contacts more than two times per week, while only 5 percent have formal meetings more than two times per week.

The principals in these schools vary in their levels of experience and certification. Two-thirds of the 76 principals in the survey sample hold regular or standard certification; 20 percent have advanced certification. Principal experience ranges from those in their first year of leadership (11 percent) to principals with 33 years in the position, and even one with 22 years at the current school. More than one-third (38 percent) have five or fewer years of experience as a principal. Only three percent had no experience as teachers; more than 50 percent had been teachers for at least 10 years.

According to the data, this collaborative leadership approach occurs across the country, but is more frequent in Virginia, Texas, Michigan, California, and Ohio. It is found in various community settings, from large urban districts with many high schools to small rural districts with one high school. The principals in the data set work in districts that enroll a range of more than 200,000 students to only 350 students, although most districts enroll fewer than 5,000 students. High schools in the survey had as few as 55 students and as many as 3,500; most were in the 1,000 to 1,500 enrollment range. The schools generally included grades 9–12, although a few were grades 8–12 and a few spanned grades 6–12.

## 2. Principals are supportive partners.

Principals in both the survey and interviews reported they are working to engage teachers as effective stakeholders, not merely job holders. Teachers in interviews confirm their principals' efforts to foster collaboration and leadership. They appreciate the principals' collaborative attitude about instruction and curriculum and feel comfortable asking for instructional help. They view their principals as visionary instructional leaders who are their partners, rather than their administrative supervisors.

One teacher commented that "teachers need to feel supported," and once they do, they are better able to address needs they see either within the system or with particular students. According to another teacher, "whoever wants access to leadership, can have it." When asked about professional development activities, one teacher explained that "the principal takes care of us with anything we need to enrich the experience for students." For one principal, the mantra is: "Tell me what you need." Most teachers also reported having autonomy in their classrooms and freedom to use an array of additional instructional resource materials to support student learning.

These principals also make great efforts to develop a sense of connectedness with both teachers and students. In the interviews, principals indicated that they adhere to an open door policy and welcome daily visits from all teachers. Principals also reported that they get out of their offces and into classrooms, not to check up on teachers, but rather to support them. One principal stated, "I like to cultivate trust with my teachers."

In interviews, principals explained they also use teamwork to create a shared focus on various aspects of the school organization to promote gains in student achievement. These included:

**Study of school leadership**. One principal asked all teachers involved in leadership to read *Results Now: How We Can Achieve Unprecedented Improvements in Teaching and Learning* (Schmoker, 2006). The book focuses on better teacher leadership. The teachers now participate in regular discussions about implementing Schmoker's ideas in the school. These teachers also serve as resources to other teachers who are reading and using the book.

**Lesson planning**. Teachers at another school are using *Understanding by Design* (Wiggins and McTighe, 2005). This is a framework developed by the Association for Supervision and Curriculum Development for designing and aligning curriculum, assessments, and instruction. The framework explains that it is more effective and efficient to plan lessons based on "big ideas" rather than on content standards alone. Once an academic goal has been set, teachers plan backwards to set benchmarks. Teachers also are encouraged to use a planning day at the end of a goal for feedback and reflection, assessing the outcomes for the goal. The school provides a substitute for the entire day, and all teachers in the school receive training on the design work.

**Transforming old models**. One school partnered with the Institute for Student Achievement to create small learning communities, with the goal of transforming the school into smaller, more personalized learning environments. Through professional development and ongoing training activities, teachers were active partners in supporting the implementation of the model.

Principals also reported they want students to have a sense of belonging to the school community and enthusiasm for learning, rather than passive attitudes. Their belief is that students will be more motivated and engaged when they feel a sense of place.

## 3. Teachers are doing more than teaching.

In interviews, teachers reported that they increasingly hold roles and are responsible for functions that are not traditionally considered part of their job. They are gaining access to school-level decision making. They serve as resources for other teachers and are also expected to be "go-to people" for the principal. Principals confirmed and elaborated on teacher involvement in leadership functions. The comparison group, the BTHS principals, also confirm this importance. More than 80 percent of the principals in the MetLife Survey reported that teachers in their schools are involved in creating a collaborative work environment; 93 percent of the BTHS principals reported this. Similarly, 72 percent of the MetLife Survey respondents indicated that teachers are involved in building and communicating a vision for their schools; 71 percent of BTHS principals said the same thing. Other indicators of teacher leadership cited by principals included teacher involvement in: setting performance standards for students (66 percent), establishing curriculum (67 percent), determining the content of professional development for teachers (67 percent), and setting discipline policy (57 percent).

While teachers have taken on many new responsibilities, they are still not involved in several key areas of school decision-making. Principals reported much lower involvement of teachers in hiring new full-time teachers (34 percent), deciding how the school's budget will be spent (37 percent), and evaluating other teachers (5 percent).

Teachers who were interviewed described changes made by their principals to the traditional high school structures, in order for teachers to gain access to leadership roles and responsibilities. The principals were creative with the daily schedule to allow for more concurrent planning time for all teachers within each grade. Teachers also may meet vertically across grades to discuss individual student learning. Teachers in one school develop cross-content, ad-hoc "learning advocacy teams" to address immediate needs of struggling students. Teacher leaders also are more involved in curriculum planning, often working during the summer months at the request of principals.

Teacher accountability in these schools no longer is just about academic achievement. Teachers in one school, for example, informally "adopt" 3–4 students and are responsible for their academic and personal development. They do this, according to one teacher, because they believe in "sacrifice and humility to keep the vision alive." Similarly, in another school, teachers are informally responsible for helping 10–12 students with any personal issues that arise.

Teachers also report they use data to inform their planning. In addition to test scores, they might look at the results of answers to specific items on tests to focus learning on weak areas. Though tremendously helpful, use of this practice is limited because of time constraints. Teachers in small learning communities make frequent use of data to inform their instruction, identify students in need of support, and design appropriate interventions. These might include on-going reports to parents, extra-curricular learning opportunities, mentoring, guest speakers, and motivational strategies. Teachers in one school participated in a data retreat to learn how to better use data to inform decisions that support student learning.

## 4. Teachers become leaders because they recognize a need.

Teacher leaders reported they are not satisfied to let the system work without their help. If a student is not challenged or a mathematics department needs retuning, teacher leaders recognize the needs and devise solutions. Teacher leaders believe it is their role to engage students in learning rather than just teach their lessons. It is clear they have common attributes and philosophies that inspire them to be "catalysts for change." Generally, they believe in modeling and leading by example. Though they do not tend to think of themselves as leaders, they know they must be willing to be "out front" in order to be effective and create change. Some teachers use special training on engaging students; others develop their own strategies, usually working with colleagues. Teacher leaders feel responsible for their students' success—academically, socially, and emotionally.

Teachers who were interviewed had varying levels of experience, from 7–28 years in the classroom. What did not vary was the level of preparation. All of the teachers had subject-level certification and expertise. Many were certified in several areas, and some had multiple graduate degrees.

It is generally agreed that high schools focus on subjects and content areas, while elementary schools focus on students. As a result, the practice of teacher leadership is different in high schools. Teachers reported that traditional education systems in high schools act as barriers to teacher leadership. An unspoken code of conduct discourages professional initiative among teachers; and those who go against this code can be seen as a threat by some colleagues. This issue is particularly acute for high schools, institutions generally characterized by deeply entrenched, hierarchical systems.

## 5. Principals, teachers, and students benefit from teacher leadership.

As documented by the research on distributed leadership, teacher involvement outside of the classroom benefits the whole school. Principals benefit from teacher leadership because they have a committed group of stakeholders working for improved student success in their schools. As all of the principals reported in the interviews, they view their teacher leaders as vital members of their administrative teams. Without the involvement of teacher leaders, the principals and their schools would not be as successful. Teachers also benefit. Their teamwork and their efforts beyond the classroom create a sense of ownership and community, which leads to better working environments.

Most importantly, students benefit from teacher leadership. Although AYP is an imperfect measure of student success, all of the schools in the survey sample met AYP for either two or three years prior to the survey. Thirty-four percent met AYP for the two years before the survey; 66 percent met AYP for three years. The MetLife Survey group actually scored higher than the BTHS group; 50 percent of those schools met AYP for three years.

Looking only at AYP does not provide a comprehensive measure of student progress. As the research illustrates and current national conversation reflects, it is important to consider other indicators such as graduation rates, college-going rates, and student disciplinary infractions. One teacher recommended looking at any relationship between teacher attendance and teacher leadership. Noting that teachers in her school rarely take days off, she suggested that there may be a definable relationship between teacher attendance and student outcomes.

## How Much Teacher Leadership Is Enough?

The York-Barr and Duke (2004) definition of teacher leadership that anchors this study suggests that there are three different levels of influence within an education system—fellow teachers, principals, and people at other schools across a district. A framework developed by Terry Dozier, a MetLife Task Force member and Director of the Center for Teacher Leadership at the Virginia Commonwealth University School of Education, refines this idea, asserting that teacher leadership can be measured on three levels, thus showing where leadership is strongest and identifying training needs. The definition also suggests that leadership is not static. It requires dynamic movement and development at all levels. Dozier's framework illustrates this through a pyramid.

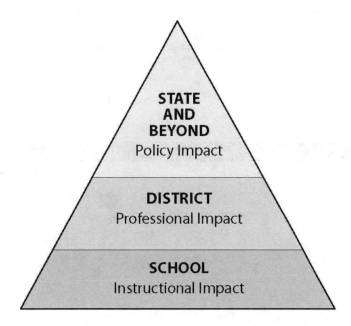

The Dozier framework shows the scope of the impact of teacher leadership at each level. At the school level, at the lowest level of influence, teachers directly affect students in their classrooms. At the district level, teacher leaders work with their colleagues to produce better outcomes for all students in the school. At the state level and beyond, teachers advocate for positive policy changes.

By looking at the roles and responsibilities assumed by teachers and matching them to the levels of impact, IEL can identify the levels where teacher leadership is more prevalent and, conversely, can identify levels where teacher leadership is lacking.

Table 2 outlines the essential roles and responsibilities of teacher leaders from 1986–2008. It identifies 20 years of research on teacher leadership and documents that teacher leadership has been focused primarily at the school level. The table shows the evolution of thought regarding areas where teacher leadership is necessary, becoming more specific and more role-oriented than task-oriented—but remaining school focused. Two decades ago, the Carnegie Task Force stated that teachers should be involved in developing operational policies and procedures. In 2007, ASCD specifically articulated the need for teachers to take on those tasks by being school leaders and catalysts for change.

This is a new role that does not appear in the other lists and crosses over into a district-level influence.

As mentioned before, the analysis of principals' responses highlighted four areas where teachers were less involved: evaluating teachers, hiring new full-time teachers, setting discipline policy, and deciding how the school's budget will be spent. Yet, these are specific tasks that affect the entire school.

Policymakers continue to pay little, if any, attention to teachers' knowledge in the development of education policy. "Our culture underestimates teachers—not only the complexity of their work, but also their potential to contribute substantively to the dialogue about school reform" (Berry et al., 2007).

The results of this study show that opportunities for teachers to be involved on the district level are still very limited. The processes of district and state level education policies vary, and sometimes principals do not have access to decision-making structures. In some districts, for example, certain tasks such as curriculum development or discipline policymaking take place at the district, not the school level. Therefore, the placement of the roles and responsibilities arrayed in Table 2 is based on a generalized understanding of the ways in which schools and districts operate.

| TABLE 2. Roles & Responsibilities of Teachers | | | |
|---|---|---|---|
| **Source** | **School** | **District** | **State & Beyond** |
| Carnegie Task Force on Teaching as a Profession (1986) | • Set performance standards<br>• Frame a curriculum<br>• Establish a school mission | • Develop operational policies and procedures | |
| Roland Barth, Harvard Principal's Center (2001) | • Choose textbooks and instructional materials<br>• Shape the curriculum<br>• Design staff development and in-service programs<br>• Set standards for student behavior<br>• Decide whether students are tracked into special classes<br>• Decide school budgets<br>• Evaluate teacher performance<br>• Select new teachers<br>• Select new administrators | • Set promotion and retention policies | |
| Cindy Harrison & Joellen Killion, Ten Roles for Teacher Leaders, Educational Leadership (2007) | • Resource provider<br>• Instructional specialist<br>• Curriculum specialist<br>• Classroom supporter<br>• Learning facilitator<br>• Learner<br>• School leader<br>• Mentor<br>• Data coach | • Catalyst for change | • Catalyst for change |
| MetLife Task Force on Teacher Leadership in High Schools Survey (2008) | • Establish curriculum<br>• Set performance standards<br>• Serve on leadership team<br>• Create a collaborative work environment<br>• Build and communicate a vision for the school<br>• Determine content of professional development<br>• Evaluate teachers<br>• Hire new full-time teachers<br>• Decide how the school's budget will be spent | • Set discipline policy | |

## The Ultimate Goal of Teacher Leadership

There is general research agreement that leadership has a significant impact on student learning. And, "although the empirical evidence is limited, research suggests that teacher leaders can help other teachers to embrace goals, to understand the changes that are needed to strengthen teaching and learning, and to work together towards improvement" (Leithwood and Riehl, 2003). Ideally, effective teacher leadership results in better student outcomes.

A recent publication from the National Commission on Teaching and America's Future states, "We must expand our understanding of the educational leader beyond the traditional authority figure of the principal....Instead we must consider new types of instructional leadership within various educational contexts, such as teacher leaders" (Schneider and Zigler, 2007). BTHS provide solid examples of how principal support and teacher leadership can lead to measurable results, such as post-secondary attainment as high as 90 percent. BTHS high school principals have confirmed that promoting staff collaboration and growth were some of their key strategies in improving results for students (Hale and Rollins, 2006).

Being effective necessarily means that everyone in a school participates in the decision-making process and is accountable for student achievement. As the National High School Alliance concludes in *A Call To Action* (IEL, 2005), empowered educators and accountable leaders are two of the core principles necessary for creating enduring change in high schools. Not only is teacher leadership basic to school success, it can also be used at the district level to develop policies and practices that create the right conditions for learning across a district.

This study was not intended to be comprehensive. Rather, it was to take the next step in helping school leaders and policymakers think about teacher leadership by illustrating that leadership in tangible ways. It gives us a sharper picture of teacher leadership in high schools, and indicates the need and identifies the areas for further research.

## Continuing the Conversation

There is evidence of an emerging use of teacher leadership in high schools, but it is a nascent practice that requires support from the principal. "Teachers know firsthand what is needed to improve student learning. But...need specific knowledge, skills, and dispositions to be successful change agents" (Dozier, 2007).

This study reveals concrete, positive examples of teacher leadership, but also identifies specific areas where that leadership is underdeveloped or nonexistent. In addition, it raises several important questions about teacher leadership from four perspectives: policies, principals, teachers, and students.

### *Do school or district policies support institutionalizing teacher leadership?*

Systemic practices that support teachers as leaders, such as common planning time, should be built into school and/or district policies. As IEL learned in this study, teachers' voices are rarely present in policy discussions at the district or state and beyond levels. As a result, teachers do not have an impact on the very policies that affect them the most.

## What policies and programs can increase the capacity of principals to support teacher leadership?

Supportive principals are critical to teacher leadership. Currently, several innovative principal training programs include a focus on developing the skills necessary to foster collaborative work environments. All programs to prepare principals should include this focus. In addition, all teacher preparation programs should include a focus on understanding teacher leadership and increasing the teacher's capacity to lead.

## What policies and programs can increase the capacity of teachers to be part of the decision-making processes at the school level? At the district level? At the state and beyond level?

This study documents that teacher leadership and involvement at the school level are weakest in the area of school-wide decision making on such matters as school budgets and teacher selection. There may be lessons to be learned from the research on collaborative/professional learning communities that would help prepare principals who could support teachers as integral part of policy decisions. The study also documents that teacher leadership is weak at the district level and almost nonexistent at the state and beyond level. This makes it impossible for teachers to advocate for policy change in support of improved student outcomes. Teacher leaders want to be engaged in policymaking, but know that they need training—as well as encouragement—to help them achieve this goal (Center for Teacher Leadership, 2003).

## What policies would make it possible to assess the impact of teacher leadership on student outcomes?

In order to draw the connection between teacher leadership and positive student outcomes, it is necessary to have indicators of teacher leadership that are tied to indicators of student outcomes, aside from simply AYP. Further research might produce indicators for teacher leadership, as well as broader, more inclusive and informative measures of student achievement, and identify strategies for identifying how teacher leadership has an impact on student achievement.

IEL's earlier report on teacher leadership lamented the squandering of this resource and affirmed its importance. This report provides a slightly clearer picture of the condition and the status of teacher leadership as described and as practiced in high schools across the country, documenting the level and scope of the impact of teacher leadership. Educating all of our children and young people requires all hands on deck. In fact, the National High School Alliance reminds us, "without these [teachers] practitioners, successful high school reform in support of better student outcomes is simply not possible" (*Call to Action*, IEL, 2005). We invite decision makers at all levels to join in an important conversation—asking and seeking answers to questions about teacher leadership—a required strategy if our nation is to educate all our children and young people.

# References

Barth, R.S. (February 2001). "Teacher Leader." *Phi Delta Kappan 82*, 443–447.

Bennett, N., Wise, C., Woods, P., & Harvey, J. (2003). *Distributed Leadership* (Full report). National College for School Leadership, Oxford, UK.

Berry, B., Norton, J., and Byrd, A. (2007). "Lessons from Networking." *Educational Leadership, 65* (1), 48–52. Association for Supervision and Curriculum Development, Alexandria, VA.

Center for Teacher Leadership. (2003) "Teacher Leaders: Self-Perceptions and Training Needs." [Survey]. Virginia Commonwealth University, Richmond, VA. *http://www.ctl.vcu.edu/ tl_surveyresults.htm*

Dozier, Terry K. (2007). "Turning Good Teachers into Great Leaders." *Educational Leadership, 65* (1), 54–59. Association for Supervision and Curriculum Development, Alexandria, VA.

Hale, Elizabeth and Rollins, Kwesi. (June 2006). "Breakthrough Principals…Leading the Way to Increased Student Learning." *Principal Leadership*, National Association of Secondary School Principals, Reston, VA.

Harrison, C. and Killion, J. (2007). "Ten Roles for Teacher Leaders." *Educational Leadership, 65* (1), 74–77. Association for Supervision and Curriculum Development, Alexandria, VA.

Institute for Educational Leadership. (2005). *A Call to Action: Transforming High School for All Youth*. National High School Alliance, Institute for Educational Leadership, Washington, DC.

Katenmeyer, M. and Moller, G. (2001). *Awakening the Sleeping Giant: Helping Teachers Develop as Leaders*. Corwin Press, Thousand Oaks, CA.

Leadership for Student Learning: Redefining the Teacher as Leader. (April, 2001). School Leadership for the 21st Century Initiative: A Report of the Task Force on Teacher Leadership. Institute for Educational Leadership, Inc.

Leithwood, K. et al. (2007). *How Leadership Influences Student Learning*. The Wallace Foundation, New York, NY.

Leithwood, K.A. and Riehl, C. (2003). *What We Know About Successful School Leadership*. Laboratory for Student Success, Temple University, Philadephia, PA.

Litke, Erica. Member, MetLife Task Force on Teacher Leadership in High Schools, in conversation August 8, 2007, with Sarah Manes.

Lortie, D. (1975). *Schoolteacher: A Sociological Study*. University of Chicago Press, Chicago, IL.

National Center for Education Statistics. Common Core of Data. *http://nces.ed.gov/ccd*

Olson, Lynn. (April 16, 2008). "Lack of School Leadership Seen as a Global Problem." *Education Week*. Editorial Projects in Education, Inc., Bethesda, MD.

Organization for Economic Cooperation and Development. (June/July 2008). *Improving School Leadership, Volume 1: Policy and Practice*. Organization for Economic Cooperation and Development, Paris, France.

Schmoker, M.J. (2006). *Results Now: How We Can Achieve Unprecedented Improvements in Teaching and Learning*. Association for Supervision and Curriculum Development, Alexandria, VA.

Schneider, Carri and Zigler, Ted. (2007). "Views from the Trenches: Two Practitioners Reflect on the Need for a National System of Educational Leadership Preparation." *Building a 21st Century Education System*. National Commission on Teaching and America's Future, Washington, DC.

Smylie, M.A., and Denny, J.W. (1990). "Teacher Leadership: Tensions And Ambiguities in Organizational Perspective." *Educational Administration Quarterly, 26*, 235–259. University Council for Educational Administration and Corwin Press, Thousand Oaks, CA.

Spillane, J.P., Halverson, R., & Diamond, J.B. (2001). "Investigating School Leadership Practice: A Distributed Perspective." *Educational Researcher, 30*(3), 23–28. American Educational Research Association, Washington, DC.

Task Force on Teaching as a Profession. (1986). *A Nation Prepared: Teachers for the 21st Century.* The Carnegie Foundation, New York, NY.

Teachers Network Leadership Institute. (2007). *Making the Case: Real-Life School and Classroom Scenarios.* Teachers Network, New York, NY.

Wiggins, G. and McTighe, J. (2005). *Understanding by Design.* Association for Supervision and Curriculum Development, Alexandria, VA.

York-Barr, J. and Duke, K. (2004). "What Do We Know About Teacher Leadership? Findings from Two Decades of Scholarship." *Review of Educational Research, 74*(3), 255–316. American Educational Research Association, Washington, DC.

# CHAPTER THIRTEEN

# Teachers Talk About Teaming and Leadership in Their Work

SHARON CONLEY & DONNA E. MUNCEY

TEACHERS JUGGLE MANY ROLES IN THEIR WORK LIVES. THROUGHOUT THE PAST 15 YEARS OF school reform, many teachers have been asked to juggle more and faster as reformers seek to expand the roles teachers play. One issue in the preparation of teachers of high quality might well be how teachers come to juggle these roles successfully. In this article, we focus on the strategies four teachers have used to incorporate two roles, teaming and leadership, into their work lives.

## School Reform and Teachers' Work

The initial phase of this nation's recent educational reform movement began in the 1980s and was predicated on the bureaucratic belief that teachers lacked sufficient motivation to invest in improving their teaching.[1] The second phase of reform, which has come to be called the teacher professionalism movement, gained currency as reformers came to realize that even the most highly motivated teachers would fall short of their goals in school organizations that did not respect their professional judgment (Lieberman, Saxl, & Miles, 1988). Indeed, the past decade of reform has been marked by a growing emphasis on the desirability of moving to more professional models of school organization and management.

An assumption of many reform proponents has seemed to be that the professional would both supplant the preceding bureaucratic model and promote reform throughout the schools. Both models assumed that the reform would lead to improved teaching and learning for students as well as to enhance the attractiveness of teaching so as to recruit and retain teachers of the highest possible quality.

Within the broad parameters of the teacher professionalism movements, two analytical strands have emerged. The first strand is oriented towards creating change through enhancing teachers' roles as leaders (Berry & Ginsberg, 1990; Devaney, 1987; Lieberman et al., 1988). This form seeks to provide teachers "a chance to move beyond the role of student instructor and to work at the school or district level assisting other teachers, developing programs and policies, or performing administrative responsibilities" (Smylie, 1994, p. 132).

The second strand is oriented towards enhancing teacher teaming as a mechanism for school change and as a way to break down the isolation of the individual classroom teacher (Kruse & Louis, 1997; Maeroff, 1993). As Maeroff (1993) notes, "team building can be the beginning of [teacher] collegiality where none existed before" (p. 9). While the first strand focuses on changing roles for individual teachers, the second focuses on changing teachers' role through new organizational configurations, clusters of teachers designated as "teams."

Some school reform initiatives tend to emphasize one strand over the other. For example, analysts suggest that career ladder, mentor teacher, and lead teacher programs place a primary emphasis on teacher leadership (Devaney, 1987; Smylie, 1994). School grade-level teams and interdisciplinary teams, by contrast, tend to emphasize teacher teaming (Kruse & Louis, 1997; Maeroff, 1993). Other reform initiatives, however, such as the Coalition of Essential Schools, encourage teachers to engage in reform that promotes both teacher leadership and teacher teaming as strategy for change. Within such an environment, teachers are asked to embrace and enact skill, beliefs, and activities aimed toward increasing collaboration as well as being assertive about their rights to participate as leaders in the school. Teachers whose work lives are already full may find much that is problematic in embracing these values and using these new skills, which are conceptually distinct and possibly contradictory.

## Why Leadership and Teaming?

To appreciate why simultaneous emphases on leadership and teaming may be contradictory, we must return to the above distinction between bureaucratic and professional models of organization and school reform. Conceptions of these models are closely related to Burns and Stalker's (1961) distinction between "mechanistic" and "organic" organizational systems. The mechanistic system emphasizes a "hierarchic structure of control, authority, and communication, vertical interaction between superiors and subordinates, and rules formulated by superiors to govern subordinates (Burns & Stalker, 1961, p. 120). The "organic" system, in contrast, emphasizes a "network structure of control, authority, and communication," a "lateral rather than vertical direction of communication," and "a content of communication which consists of information and advice rather than instructions and decisions" (Burns & Stalker, 1961, p. 421).

These models suggest possible contrasts between teacher teaming and leadership. Teaming is most often envisioned as an egalitarian enterprise, whereby members of the teacher team are accorded a more or less equal voice in decision making. Teacher leadership, in comparison, more explicitly recognizes that even within a professional model, a hierarchy still exists within the school. Furthermore, while teaming emphasizes lateral interactions among teacher peers, teacher leadership stresses more vertical interaction, both between teacher leaders and other teachers and between teacher leaders and administrators.[2]

Thus, to some extent. When viewed as distinct strategies or practices, teacher teaming might appear more closely aligned with the organic professional model than teacher leadership; it seems to envision a less hierarchical mode of school organization. However, Burns and Stalker (1961) noted that "while organic systems are not hierarchic in the same sense as mechanistic, they remain stratified" (p. 421). This suggests that it would be premature to judge teaming as more closely aligned with the professional model than teacher leadership.

Moving from organization to the work level of analysis, some additional distinctions between teacher teaming and teacher leadership can be noted. Smylie (1994), describing work redesign initiatives in general, says that they aim to provide "(a) additional renumeration and status for accomplishment and new responsibilities; (b) greater task variety; (c) increased authority, control, and autonomy in work; and (d) more opportunities for collegial interaction and individual professional learning and development" (p. 133). Indeed, both teacher leadership and teacher teaming seem to emphasize task variety and professional learning (Kruse & Louis, 1997; Pounder, 1995; Smylie, 1994). However, teacher leadership may place greater emphasis in authority, control, autonomy, remuneration, and status (Smylie, 1994), while teaming may accentuate collegial interaction (Kruse & Louis, 1997; Maeroff, 1993; Pounder, 1995).[3]

Despite these distinctions, there seems to be potential benefit from examining both approaches concurrently within current school restructuring initiatives in order to understand better (a) what activities are associated with teaming and teacher leadership in restructured schools, (b) what distinctions, if any, teachers make between teaming and leadership in restructured settings, (c) whether individual teachers in restructured schools embrace and enact both approaches (or prefer one over the other) in doing their work, and (d) what effect these approaches have on the nature of teachers; work and classroom practices. Until now, examination of these two concepts as simultaneous emphases in teachers' work has gone unexplored. At the same time, teachers in restructuring schools have been participating in both (Muncey & McQuillan, 1996).

Therefore, we are interested in teachers' sense-making about their participation in teacher leadership and teaming. We asked ourselves: Do teachers identify contradictions between their roles as teacher leaders and as members of a team, and, if so, how do they resolve them? In two restructuring schools, we explored four teachers' perceptions of their own roles as leaders and members of teams. We examined whether they saw continuity or compatibility in their roles as well as whether they found one or both satisfying and for what reasons.

The results of our preliminary research suggest that teachers found one of the roles to be most comfortable for them. Although the teachers participated in work organized both ways, two teachers preferred leadership and two teachers preferred teaming. In addition, to the degree that teachers perceived tensions between teacher teaming and teacher leadership, they appeared to rely on their own individual sense-making to help guide the development of context-sensitive solutions to resolving perceived inconsistencies in their own work stemming from these simultaneous emphases.

## Learning from Teachers

Two elementary and two secondary teachers shared their views about teacher teaming and teacher leadership with us during the 1994–1995 school year.[4] Each teacher had held multiple leadership roles and team memberships, as summarized in Table 1.

Our conversation touched on many aspects of teaming and leadership, school structure, and restructuring. The following mini-portraits provide a sense of the teachers, as well as their experiences and views about teaming and leadership and the skills needed to be leaders and members of teams, The names of teacher and schools in the mini-portraits are pseudonyms.

Table 1. Reported Leadership Roles and Team Memberships for Four Teachers

| School | Leadership | Teaming |
|---|---|---|
| **Elementary** | | |
| Ms. Jackson (24)* | Chapter One team leader; Head teacher; Mentor teacher; Former instructional coordinator, career ladder | Chapter One team; Cross-grade level meetings; Norms group; School faculty |
| Ms. Rossi (10) | Instructional coordinator, career ladder; Former chair, first-grade team | First-grade team; Cross-grade level meetings |
| **Secondary** | | |
| Ms. Grant (21) | 10th-grade team leader; Former team leader in middle school | 10th-grade team; Site-based management team |
| Ms. Patrick (20) | Head, writing resource center | 11th-grade team; Site-based management team; Department chair group; State committee |

\* Number of years of teaching experience are in parenthesis

## Ms. Jackson

A Chapter One coordinator at Benjamin Roberts Elementary School (located in a small urban schools district in the Southwest) for over 20 years, Emily Jackson works with elementary school students who need extra assistance in order to succeed in school. In addition to her role as Chapter One coordinator, Ms. Jackson has held several other leadership positions at Benjamin Roberts.

> When I was on career ladder, I was instructional coordinator for about 4 years.[5] In the past, I was active in leadership in our association. [Now] I'm in it but not in leadership positions…Also, I am head teacher, and one of my assignments is to work with all new teachers.

As head teacher, Ms. Jackson also mentors teachers identified by the principal or the district as needing support and fills in for the principal in his absence.

When the topic shifted to Ms. Jackson's participation in teaming efforts, she again offered multiple examples of this part of her work including her role as head teacher.

Inside my own area of teaching, I have three instructional assistants that work with me. We are also a team. I also supervise the ESL [English as a Second Language] program. So I see that as a team of two. This year I'm now the liaison between this school and our [district] Head Start program. My role there has been to help the Head Start teachers help their children make a transition between Head Start and our school. We also have a…teacher assistance team [to screen referrals for students to have testing assessments] made up of three classroom teachers, me, and the school counselor, who chairs it.

As head teacher Ms. Jackson is also included in a cross-grade level team. She noted, "I feel like that is a team." She also characterized the faculty as a whole as a team. She continued, "I [also] served on a committee this year where we [were] trying to decide what the implicit and explicit norms are that we see in our school. We'd never done [that] before." She noted that this team's decision making was accomplished by consensus.

There was no real leader of the team. The principal acted as one of the team. It was all equalized. But…because I've worked here so long, I have a lot more history. And because I work with different grade levels and different situations, I sometimes can see things differently, I gave a lot of input…But there wasn't really any leader…We were all equal.

But when asked how she describes her role on other teams, Ms. Jackson said she was "a leader facilitator," offering the following examples of her work.

I do a lot of communicating with…classroom [teachers]. I also see myself developing a lot of material…This year, we modified process writing for the second grade. I brainstormed the modification with [an aide]…I know what I want it to look like and I take the time to make the thing a model [for the others]. So that's where I see myself as a facilitator.

We asked Ms. Jackson what skills teachers need to be productive members of a team.

They need good listening skills. They need to be analytical…they need to have confidence to express opinions and not be afraid to disagree with everybody else. You know, to see things from different points of view. Other than that, they need one more skill, and to see it as a valuable thing that they're doing by being on a team. They need to value it so that they will put the time into it.

Asked what skills teachers should have to hold leadership positions, she replied:

They need good interpersonal skills. This is not a skill, but they need to be a person of integrity so that people will feel free to talk to them and know that it's going to be held in confidence. They have to be willing to invest time into people. Skill-wise, they need to be very organized. They also need to be analytical…You usually don't view an analytical person as a person who has interpersonal skills. But they need both, I think leaders have to be able to view themselves as facilitators. It's their job to help everybody else get their job done.

After a short pause, she added

I don't even know how to say this, but they need to lead without creating fear. Other people should not fear their authority.

Throughout her interview, Ms. Jackson stressed the leadership aspect of her work consistently. Even when addressing teaming, she used leadership as the frame and talked about her role as leader on the teams. This was most noticeable when she discussed her team of aides, but was also somewhat present in her discussion of the norms group, particularly when she emphasized the knowledge she was able to bring to the team by virtue of being at the school a long time.

## Ms. Rossi

Dana Rossi has been teaching for 10 years and is currently a first grade teacher at Benjamin Roberts School. As a member of the first-grade team, Ms. Rossi noted that a lot of their meetings are ad hoc in nature, but that they cover a lot of conversational ground.

> We do a lot of planning together in first grade. We eat lunch together every day out in the center, and talk about school as well as other things. We sit out there in the afternoons and talk about different things we can do for the next day. We usually sit down once a week formally and go through things that we want to do in reading, and ideas for math…We talk constantly . . .
>
> We talk about lesson-planning activities we're going to do, about how activities went, and things that we had planned to do…We talk about testing. We talk about students and different problems they might have, trying to come up with solutions for them. Different curriculum questions might come up. We talk about different school situations, such as a district or a school policy or a program that's come in and how we're going to do it in our school or our classroom.

She offered some examples of the kinds of decisions made by the team.

> Well, we make decisions on when to present our curriculum…and when to do our testing. We come up with how we would like to report the testing, you know, even though [that] has to be cleared through the administration. I'm not sure that we make administrative decisions, but I think…we can come together to make suggestions to the administration…[The] four of us can also show different ways to do [things]. So we can listen to each other and say, "Yes, you do it that way; I don't," not saying one's right or wrong.

Turning to her leadership roles, Ms. Rossi explained that she served as the first-grade team leader (grade-level) chair 3 years ago. She described some of the expectations of and activities associated with that role.

> The grade-level chair has meetings with Doug [the principal]. They meet every couple weeks or once a month depending on what he has on the agenda. They take care of the ordering of materials; although [the team] as a group [does] the ordering, they actually have to write it out and turn it in. They do the separating of materials at the beginning of the year as they come in. They take care of any district capital items that need to be ordered; it has to go in through them. They do a lot of the paper work…They take care of field trips…although, you know, we have found with the four of us that we work so well together, we don't leave it all on the one person.

Interestingly, Ms. Rossi talked extensively about her participation in the career ladder, noting that she recently became an instructional coordinator. However, she did not describe this position as a leadership role.

When asked whether she considered herself a team leader, teacher, a teacher mentor, a teacher leader, an administrator, or something else, she replied: "I don't think it becomes any of those…I think you're a teacher with other responsibilities and [that] you are compensated for doing it."

Ms. Rossi described the skills needed to be a productive member of a team.

> I think [teachers] need to be open. I think they need to be able to listen. I think they need to be able to hear both sides without judgment. I think they need to be able to state their opinions and back it up or follow it without being intimidated. I think they need to be able to get along with people.

She also described the skills needed to be an effective leader of a team.

> I think…because they represent our grade level with other people, they need to be able to be open. They need to be able to listen. Plus, I think they need to be aggressive to make sure that our side is heard.

She added:

> I don't think our grade-level chair makes big decisions. I think if there's a big decision made, you know, normally it's done as the team.

Throughout her description of her work, Ms. Rossi's membership on teams and commitment to the idea of teaming was dominant. Although she had held leadership positions within the school, she prefers to think of herself as a "teacher with other responsibilities," stressing the collaborative aspect of teaming over the supervisory or positional roles of leadership.

## Ms. Grant

Patricia Grant, now in her 21st year of teaching, has spent most of those years teaching life science to middle school students and earth science, chemistry, and biology to evening high school students. She works at Stafford High School, a newly created school in a rapidly growing suburb of a large Eastern city.

In addition to her classroom responsibilities, Ms. Grant is the 10th-grade team leader. She described her role.

> I'm the communication and the liaison between my teachers and Mr. Smith [the principal]. If they have questions, I can go directly to Mr. Smith and get answers. And he in turn can share things with me that I can share with my teachers directly. [Also], when Mr. Smith wants feedback, the team members make a decision about how they feel about something and then we [the team leader] take it [back to him].
>
> We [team leaders] also are supposed to help new teachers as they come to the school…Sometimes I'm the lead teachers, a helping teacher. When somebody's having problems,…either [they] come to me directly or I'll say, "Look, can we bring it up at a team meeting" and maybe somebody else has some ideas that we can share. I'm not the only good teacher on the team . . .
>
> Our school philosophy is to try and teach through integration as much as possible…I'm responsible for overseeing the integration. If somebody brainstorms, "Oh, let's do this project," then it falls to me to kind of supervise, monitor how it happens, and make sure that it happens.

As team leader, Ms. Grant is also responsible for monitoring student progress—"I keep a running list of students we've discussed and how they are doing and we review it at the team meetings"—and for making decisions about acceleration, that is, "moving the kids" to a "higher-level class." She explained that as the team leader she "can organize the team and say, 'Okay, what do you think; should we do this?' And help them come to a decision on that."

Ms. Grant also feels it is part of the team leader's role to keep communication channels open and public. Her interest is in helping the team do what needs to be done in the best interests of students. In her view, keeping communication open means that she might also go to the team for information and advice.

> Sometimes I have trouble with a student. But I go to another team member and say, "All right, what are you doing that gives this person success? Maybe it's something I can use to help the student." Sometimes I need help. My teachers are all equal to me. They're all teachers. They have their own strengths…It's a give and take on the team.

She noted that she does not have evaluative responsibilities for team members. When asked whether she considered herself mostly a teacher, a teacher mentor, a teacher leader, an administrator, or something else, Ms. Grant responded:

> I've never thought about it. I guess more often I'm a teacher leader. Actually, I consider myself part of my team. I just happen to be given the position of team leader, but I really consider myself part of the working team. And when they need me to, then I'm the one that steps in to make sure the group stays on task…But otherwise, I'm part of that working team because I have students also.

Asked to describe the qualities of a good team member, Ms. Grant responded, "They have to be people oriented and student oriented. [There have to be] some flexible people on the team." Similarly, she notes that the skills needed to be a good leader were "flexibility, and again, being child oriented, people oriented." She reiterated that time management was a big issue.

In sum, Ms. Grant muted her leadership role somewhat, repeatedly describing herself as part of the grade-level team. She seemed to view her position as team leader in terms of both its potential to facilitate and support the team's work as well as the service the role provides as a mechanism to ensure smoother and more open communication throughout the school. Her emphases on the classroom level and on being student centered were evident in most of the examples she offered throughout the interview.

## Ms. Patrick

Barbara Patrick, our second teacher from Stafford, is a 20-year veteran of teaching, a field she came to as a second career following a position in journalism. Currently, Ms. Patrick teaches two classes and coordinates the school's writing center. In addition, she belongs to several teams at Stafford.

> I'm the writing resource teacher…I kind of cross the teams. There are times when I work with all the grade levels—depending on what projects they're on. Because I also teach one 11th-grade class, the AP language class, I'm technically a member of the 11th-grade team. But this year I have assisted the 9th- and 10th-grade teams in their projects. [I've worked with all the teams] because writing is kind of the connector. I don't go to all of the [grade-level team meetings] on a regular basis, but if they're doing a project that involves a writing aspect or writing across the curriculum, [a team will] invite me to come…I do go to all the 11th-grade [meetings]. I'm solidly an 11th-grade team member.

When asked if she was a member of any other teams, Ms. Patrick added: "I am part of the site-based management team too and even though there is not a writing department, I also am part of…the department chair group." Ms. Patrick described the work of the 11th-grade team:

There's a purpose for every meeting…At almost…every meeting we talk about upcoming school-wide events…We talk about issues that the team leaders together [have agreed that they] would like to share via the teams. These might be workshops…and student opportunities—those kinds of thing. And because the accelerated programs [for students] are worked through the team leaders, we talk about…a lot of the material that comes through accelerated programs, and about student problems. And then we've been trying to focus on integration of instruction, so that sometimes becomes the focus of the meeting.

She then described her role on the 11th-grade team as that of a "writing teacher role more than a classroom teacher [because] the [team members] will sit there and talk about students that I only know because of [my] writing role, not because they're my students."

When asked whether she considered herself a teacher, a teacher mentor, a teacher leader, administrator, or quasi-administrator, Ms. Patrick continued describing her role before answering.

Part of the writing resource role is team teaching, mentoring beginning teachers, and helping teachers who want to start new projects they have never done…you know, a math teacher who thinks he wants to do math journals and is scared…[And] I'm also the staff development rep for the school…I think the [roles] go together. And so there are some training issues that come up. Staff development kinds of things…So I guess that I would say quasi-administrative.

Ms. Patrick also sits on a state committee charged with rethinking high school assessment:

I meet with the folks in [a nearby city] who are going to present the proposal to the state board of education in July. I'm the only educator on that committee; it's mostly politicians or representatives of associations…Monday at the faculty meeting, [the principal] has asked me to share where they are now and what I think politically is going to happen.

Ms. Patrick described the skills needed to be productive members of a team.

Teachers have to know how to be a team member and I don't think we're trained for that. In fact, another teacher—who is a department chair—and I were going to suggest to the principal that next year…we start [training teachers] the skills for success, the enabling skills that transcend all content. Let's use those as the integration connectors before content, because sometimes the content projectors are kind of contrived…We're going to ask him for some training on team building and team membership…and I think we have to be better listeners.

When asked what kind of skills people would have to have as a team leader, Ms. Patrick suggested "conflict resolution" skills. She suggested that a less-than-effective team leader might well be "bright and energetic," but also want or need to be in charge. Such a team leader might "want to own it all," and make decisions for the team. So it might end up seeming like "a one-way street," rather than a collaborative effort to decide what needs to be done and how. A team leader who operated that way would soon become a source of frustration and resentment. These reactions would most certainly lead to less cooperation among team members. Even if such team leaders had good ideas, they might easily become a blocking force, rather than a facilitator of change or of teamwork.

In sum, Ms. Patrick enjoys her dual role as writing resource person and classroom teacher and finds her membership on the grade-level team provides her with opportunities to share her expertise with others and learn more about the 11th-grade curriculum and students. She tended to frame her responses to our questions in terms of her role as writing resource teacher, describing herself as a quasi-administrator and emphasizing the work she does with other teachers throughout the interviews.

# Comparing Teachers' Sense-Making

The four teachers have had unique experiences as members of teacher teams and in leadership positions. What sense can we make from looking across their descriptions and their statements about teaming and leadership? Through our analysis, we found that by comparing the views of the two classroom-based teachers, then those of the two non-classroom-based teachers, we could best distinguish the ways by which these teachers used their participation in the forms of work (teaming and leadership) to contribute to their sense-making about their teaching.[6]

Perhaps not surprisingly, the teachers who were not classroom based (Ms. Jackson and Ms. Patrick) shared many views about their roles as leaders. Both highlighted mentoring, modeling, and translating external programs (e.g., "essential elements of instruction" for Ms. Jackson and "writing across the curriculum" for Ms. Patrick) into the school. They additionally emphasized (or mentioned) their work as liaisons—to Head Start or (district) staff development. Finally, both emphasized the "special roles" they play in the school. As head teacher, Ms. Jackson plans with the principal and "subs" for him in his absence. Ms. Patrick crosses teams and attends department chair meetings owing to her position as writing resource teacher.

The two teachers differed in their views of teaming: Ms. Jackson described team participants' roles as either leaders or team members, emphasizing the difference between the two. In fact, some of the groups she referred to as teams seem to be supervisory relationships. For example, she noted that the ESL program that she supervises is "a team of two." Furthermore, even when discussing the consensus-based team, Ms. Jackson still asserted her role was special.

In contrast, Ms. Patrick saw team leaders and members in more egalitarian terms, as was evident when she described the potential pitfalls of a team leader who "wants it all." Even though she used more egalitarian terms, Ms. Patrick still emphasized her leadership role (writing resource teacher) more than her teaching role (her AP class) when she talked about teaming. Both teachers framed their work in terms of their leadership roles rather than their team membership.

The non-classroom based teachers shared one further similarity. Both ascribed somewhat different skill requirements to team members than to team leaders. Ms. Jackson, for example, said that leaders need to be able to "lead without creating fear" and need to have "integrity so that people will feel free to talk to them." Ms. Patrick said that leaders needed to have effective "conflict resolution skills." Neither of these skills were ascribed to team members who instead were said to need "good listening skills," "confidence to express their opinions, " and to be "analytical" by one teacher (Ms. Jackson) and "know how to be a team member" by the other (Ms. Patrick).

The classroom-based teachers, Ms. Rossi and Ms. Grant, were most similar in their views of teams. Both highlighted than teams exchange opinions, translate district and school policies into action, and suggest policies to staff. Ms. Rossi also said that the team makes teachers' workloads more manageable while Ms. Grant noted that the teams facilitate student placement.

Further, when both teachers talked about leadership, they emphasized that the leadership role was downplayed on their teams. Ms. Rossi described the leader's role as handling "paperwork" and routine administrative matters as opposed to supervising the team. Ms. Grant remarked several times that "My teachers are all equal to me" and that "It's a give and take on the team."

However, Ms. Grant was more acknowledging of her leadership role on the team ("I'm the one that steps in to make sure the group stays on task") than Ms. Rossi, who also downplayed the supervisory and evaluative aspects of her leadership role as instructional coordinator in the career ladder program. Somewhat congruously, she observed that people "higher" up in the district have some control of the career ladder program, thus highlighting the decision-making roles of *others* in leadership roles. Nevertheless, both teachers' participation in work organized by teams was the dominant framework these teachers used, even when they described the leadership roles they have.

Finally, the classroom-based teachers shared the view that the skills needed to be team members and leaders were fairly similar. Ms. Rossi said that both leaders and team members needed to be "open" and "able to listen." Ms. Grant said that they needed to be "people oriented," "student oriented," and "flexible."

In sum, the classroom-based teachers emphasized teaming and viewed skills needed to be teacher leaders and team members as fairly similar. By contrast, the non-classroom-based teachers highlighted the leadership, organization, and decision-making aspects of their work and distinguished between the skills needed to be good leaders and members of teams.

## Preferred Roles

At that start of this chapter, we asked whether teachers identify contradictions between teacher leadership and teaming and, if so, how they resolve them. Our cases generally suggest that teachers do not identify contradictions between leadership and teaming in the work they do. However, the teachers we spoke with do express preferences for, or appear to favor, one or the other role. Moreover, this preferred role appeared to provide the frame teachers use to make sense of the work they are doing.

Although all the teachers in our study played both roles, as leaders and members of teams, they seemed to use the preferred role to make sense of both roles. Ms. Jackson, for example, viewed herself as a leader and framed her responses to many questions about teaming from that perspective. She noted, for instance, that she was included on teams because she is a leader. Ms. Rossi downplayed leadership on the team and, when discussing her leadership role, emphasized the administrative tasks she did as opposed to the influence she exercised because of that role.

Furthermore, in their responses to many questions, the two teachers who emphasized teacher teaming also stressed teacher collegiality and reciprocity as when, for instance, Ms. Rossi said, "[The] four of us can also show different ways to do [things]. So we can listen to each other and say, 'Yes, you do it that way; I don't,' not saying one's right or wrong."

In contrast, the two teachers who emphasized teacher leadership tended to emphasize that their work and decision making take place within a school hierarchy. These teachers fit (and described themselves) most closely within a category of "quasi-administrator" that emphasizes a rung in the authority hierarchy below the administration but above teachers. They stressed the work they do to support and mentor other teachers as opposed to the work they do in their own rooms and on their teams. Recall Ms. Patrick describing her cross-team work as the resource writing teacher. This finding tentatively supports our earlier suggestion that a key difference between leadership and teaming may lie in the differential emphases placed within the professional model on hierarchy and egalitarianism.

Given the amount of variability we saw in these four teachers concerning their perspectives of what teaming is, and their reactions to and impressions of both teaming and leadership, our study reinforces Hargreaves's (1996) argument that it is misleading to speak of "the" teacher's voice as a "singular voice that…embodies qualities that are generic to all teachers and teaching" (p. 13). Consistent with this perspective, we would argue that what is needed is a fuller understanding of the perspectives that exist and a deeper understanding of why this diversity of perspectives can become a basis for solid restructuring in some cases, while in other cases it can become the basis of arguments, opposition, or resistance that keep schools from restructuring in the first place (Kruse & Louis, 1997; Muncey & McQuillan, 1996).

## Conclusion

Our work has implications for those who are studying efforts to bring about school change in a professional model of reform. Those attempting to understand change by focusing on one strand of the professional model, leadership or teaming, are likely to obtain a misleadingly simplistic view of teachers' work lives. An examination of both strands appears to be a more powerful way of understanding the complexity of teachers' work and being respectful of that complexity.

In addition, such examination might help educational researchers gain insights into the complexity of teachers' work on its own terms rather than, for example, by comparative analysis with other occupations and less-related work spheres. Further, seeking teachers' perspectives on multiple strands of teachers' work may give researchers and practitioners useful insights concerning the effects of current reforms on enhancing teachers' quality and their overall impact on teachers' work lives.

In studying how teachers incorporate teaming and leadership into their work lives, we learned that teachers can and do balance many seemingly contradictory roles and skills. One question is, are the skills and roles teachers are expected to embrace being emphasized in teacher preparation and teacher professional development programs? We found that the teachers with whom we spoke excelled in their classrooms and in their interactions with peers in part by successfully incorporating new roles and skills in their work lives. We have much to learn from them as we attempt to determine how to prepare and support teachers of the highest quality for the schools and classrooms of the next century.

## Notes

1. One reform approach involved teacher merit pay. This initial reform impulse was consistent with the bureaucratic tradition because non-teaching reformers, in tying teacher pay to externally created performance measures, attempted to increase the system's control over teachers and their work (see Bacharach & Conley, 1986).
2. One consequence of the team may be that they exert influence on school site decision making (Erb, 1987).
3. However, Kruse and Louis (1997) suggest that teams may increase teacher authority and control. They state that "teacher authority is increased as influence over [varied] decision areas extends beyond the individual classroom and becomes a matter for public discussion and critical examination" (p. 263).
4. Teacher interviews were conducted in two schools that national project directors nominated as exemplary school restructuring sites. The elementary school was participating in a state-sponsored, district teacher "career ladder" program. The high school had recently opened with an organization and management structure that emphasized teaming. Each school seemed to have an emphasis; the elementary school on teacher leadership and the high school on teaming. Two face-to-face interviews and one telephone follow-up were conducted with two teachers in each school. From our visits to the sites and subsequent individual interviews, it became clear that both teacher teaming and leadership were aspects of the structure of these schools and mechanisms for supporting reform. More extensive case studies of each teacher were prepared (see Muncey & Conley, n.d.) from which these necessarily brief mini-portraits were excerpted.
5. In the district's career ladder, teachers advance through successive career steps that are associated with increased pay. The instructional coordinator has some supervisory responsibilities for teachers.

6. We also explored three additional lenses: views all teachers shared, points about which teachers from the same level of schooling (elementary or secondary) mostly agreed, and views about which there was seemingly little agreement among any of the teachers. We included the classroom and non-classroom-based comparison here because it helps us to best see how people differ in their views. The elementary and secondary teacher comparison mostly fleshed out what specific teams and leadership responsibilities were like. One area in which little agreement emerged among the teachers were sources of dissatisfaction with work. Areas of most agreement had to do with students' success and other sources of job satisfaction.

# References

Bacharach, S.B., & Conley, S.C. (1986). Education reform: A managerial agenda. *Phi Delta Kappan, 67*, 641–645.

Berry, B., & Ginsberg, R. (1990). Creating lead teachers: From policy to implementation. *Phi Delta Kappan, 71*, 616–621.

Burns, T., & Stalker, G.M. (1961). *The management of innovation*. London: Tavistock Publications.

Devaney, K. (1987). *The lead teacher: Ways to begin*. Paper prepared for the Task Force on Teaching as a Profession, Carnegie Forum on Education and the Economy. New York: The Carnegie Forum.

Erb, T.O. (1987). What team organization can do for teachers. *Middle School Journal, 18*, 3–6

Hargreaves, A. (1996). Revisiting voice. *Educational Researcher, 25*, 12–19.

Kruse, S., & Louis, K. (1997). Teacher teaming in middle schools: Dilemmas for a school wide community. *Educational Administration Quarterly, 33*, 261–288.

Lieberman, S., Saxl, E.R., & Miles, M.B. (1988). Teacher leadership: Ideology and practice. In A. Lieberman (Ed.), *Building a professional culture in schools* (pp. 148–166), New York: Teachers College Press.

Maeroff, G.I. (1993). *Team building for school change: Equipping teachers for new roles*. New York: Teachers College Press

Muncey, D.E., & Conley, S. (n.d.). *Teacher leadership and teaming in teachers' work*. Working paper.

Muncey, D.E., & McQuillan, P.J. (1996). *Reform and resistance in schools and classrooms: An ethnographic view of the Coalition of Essential Schools*. New Haven: Yale University Press.

Pounder, D. (1995 October*). Faculty work teams: Paradoxical influences on teachers' work, work experiences and attitudes*. Paper prepared for presentation at the 1995 University Council of Educational Administration Conference, Salt Lake City, UT.

Smylie, M.A. (1994). Redesigning teachers; work: Connections to the classroom. In L. Darling-Hammond (Ed.), *Review of research in education, 20* (pp. 129–177). Washington DC: American Educational Research Association.

# Teacher Leadership and Professional Learning Communities

CHAPTER FOURTEEN

# A Pedagogy of Collective Action and Reflection

## Preparing Teachers for Collective School Leadership

Joseph Kahne & Joel Westheimer

"Actions speak louder than words," goes the popular aphorism. Although university-based teacher educators frequently find themselves immersed in words, most are deeply concerned with actions. In fact, teacher educators work to influence the actions of scores of prospective teachers who pass through their classrooms each year primarily through the words of educational research and theory. Even more important, a growing number of teacher educators struggle to demonstrate to their students the connection between action—in this case teaching—and the academic literature associated with pedagogy and learning. These educators hope to prepare teachers who are thoughtful consumers of education theory and research, and as a result, think carefully and critically about their own practice.

At the same time that teacher educators are seeking to close the gap between research and practice, schools are demanding another set of skills and practices from teachers (and hence from teacher education). School reformers now hope that teachers will become leaders who work together across corridors, departments, and disciplines to foster educational reform (Barth, 1990; Lieberman, 1995; Louis & Kruse, 1995; Maeroff, 1993; McLaughlin, 1993). The ability to work with colleagues in a strong school community is seen as essential in the school restructuring efforts that have characterized education reform over the past decade (Hargreaves, 1994; Murphy, 1990). Because forms of teacher collaboration and community have thus far been underconceptualized, however, they make up a weak foundation for school change. As Andy Hargreaves (1994) suggests about teacher collaboration and community, "much of the burden of educational reform has been placed upon their fragile shoulders" (p. 187).

The emphasis on school-based decision making, team teaching, interdisciplinary curriculum, and teacher professionalism has led teacher educators to consider new approaches to teacher preparation (Goodlad, 1990; Grossman & Richert, 1996; Merz & Fuhrman, 1997; Shulman, 1989). Important reports such as the Holmes Group's (1986) *Tomorrow's Teachers* and the Carnegie Task Force's

(1986) *A Nation Prepared: Teachers for the 21st Century* were issued with an eye toward meeting the challenges posed by these new school structures and priorities. Although these ambitious reports aspired to broad goals not likely to be attained any time soon, they helped create dialogue about possibilities for change in the way we prepare teachers to work in schools. They spurred a shift in focus from technical proficiency to teacher leadership. Methods for preparing teachers to build meaningful school communities, however, remain vague (Westheimer & Kahne, 1993). Although reformers argue that teachers must be "organized, mobilized [and] led" (Lieberman, 1988) to overcome the norms of autonomy that pervade teaching, the means of such organization, mobilization, and leadership are rarely specified (Westheimer, 1998). As a result, many newly restructured schools encounter serious obstacles because teachers come to them ill equipped to work together in designing interdisciplinary curriculum, making scheduling decisions, or planning schoolwide activities (Beane, 1997; Lieberman, 1995; Murphy, 1990).

Those interested in narrowing the gap between research and practice generally do not focus on how to teach teachers to collaborate or design and manage a school as a professional community. Conversely, those promoting collaboration and community among teachers in schools do not often point to narrowing the gap between research and practice as a means of furthering their goals. In this article, we bring together these two teacher education reform agendas—preparing teachers for collective school leadership and bridging theory and practice. Specifically, we suggest a pedagogy of collective action. By this we mean a process through which teachers collectively design, implement, and reflect on curricula. Bridging theory and practice is at the heart of this process. Student teachers learn to collaborate and build a professional community at the same time as they bridge private teaching practices with public educational research and theory.[1] We ground this discussion in a detailed analysis of an actual program to highlight the complexity of this challenge and some of the dilemmas faced by those with this agenda.

## Toward a Pedagogy of Collective Action, Collective Reflection, and Teacher Leadership

In what follows, we describe the Experiential Curricula Project (ECP), a two-term, experimental course sequence for prospective teachers designed to provide participants with a rich experience as a community of teachers by engaging them in reflective practice.[2] Each year, the ECP worked with 16 to 25 prospective teachers. The teachers examined the role of experience in education, studied a variety of curriculum theorists, and explored their personal and professional experiences in classrooms. In addition, they designed, implemented, and reflected on three experience-based curriculum units for classes of 9th and 10th graders from two local high schools.

Before describing the project in more detail, it is worth mentioning the role experience plays in preparing teachers for collective practice and leadership. Why is this endeavor called the Experiential Curricula Project? Why not the Collective School Leadership Project or the Teacher Community Project? In other words, why place experience at the heart of a program designed to promote collective leadership among new teachers? The simple response is that experience drives the curriculum of the ECP. Analysis of students' prior experiences and engagement of students in new collective experiences provides a powerful vehicle for integrating discussion of theory and practice. In addition, as the description below details, the emphasis on experience also supports the development of a professional community.

To highlight the ways students and instructors use prior and current experience to structure collective efforts, we focus on three phases of the curriculum. Collectively, the prospective teachers (a) generate theory from their own experiences, (b) develop and implement curricula in local schools, and (c) follow each curriculum implementation with a structured process of reflection, which informs the development of subsequent curricula (see Table 1).

Table 1. The Experiential Curricula Project's Two-Term Course Sequence

**First term**

| | |
|---|---|
| Weeks 1 through 3 | Identify characteristics of powerful curriculum both from students' "private" experience and from "public" theory |
| Weeks 4 through 6 | Develop first curriculum |
| Week 7 | Implement first curriculum in local school |
| Weeks 8 through 10 | Assess curriculum, engaging in collective and individual analysis |

**Second term**

| | |
|---|---|
| Weeks 11 through 13 | Examine normative dilemmas in curriculum development |
| Weeks 14 through 15 | Develop second curriculum |
| Week 16 | Implement second curriculum in local school |
| Weeks 17 through 18 | Assess first and second curricula; integrate accumulated theory in developing third curriculum |
| Week 19 | Implement third curriculum in local school |
| Week 20 | Reassess validity of original private and public theories; adjust theories accordingly; explore impact on individual and collective teacher practices |

## Collectively Generate Theory from Individual Experience

Those seeking to bridge theory and practice (but not necessarily seeking to promote collective teacher practice and leadership) might approach a course in curriculum design in the following manner. First, students read the work of various education theorists to gain a conceptual understanding of the matters at hand. Next, the professor presents the class with examples of various approaches to teaching for students to consider. Finally, perhaps as the term project, students design their own lesson plans or perhaps a unit to share with the professor and the class. When possible, students may even test out these lessons in conjunction with their individual student teaching assignments. This approach is consistent with many recent conceptual models for teacher education (Fullan, Galluzzo, Morris, & Watson, 1998; Goodlad, Soder, & Sirotnik, 1990).

The ECP shares a number of these features: students explore educational theories, consider practical applications, and devise curricula that they implement in local schools. But there are also important differences that promote the blending of theory and practice and lead to a collective orientation to work in schools. Perhaps the primary difference is in the use of a collectively generated theory of curriculum and pedagogy. Students share their individual experiences, categorize these experiences, and integrate them with what they are reading to create a working theory of teaching and learning generated collectively by the class. We explain this process in some detail below.

Rather than beginning by reading and discussing the conceptual foundations of curriculum design, students share stories of their best and worst educational interactions with each other in small groups. They are discouraged from selecting general experiences (a seventh-grade algebra class they enjoyed, for example) and asked to focus on particular positive and negative interactions (e.g., a time when local politicians provided feedback on a community-based project they had completed). Over the following week, each student develops a written description of a significant educational interaction he or she had. The descriptions include the type of activity, assessment of success or failure of the activity, and speculation on the reasons for success or failure. In the seminar, students and the instructor work to identify common features of these interactions. Negative interactions, for example, are sometimes traced to miscommunication, a betrayal of trust or abuse of authority, a violation of boundaries, or a dehumanizing feeling. Features that the class often associates with positive interactions include experiences in which students and teachers engage in meaningful relationships, break down their traditional roles, overcome real or perceived limits, or produce a tangible product. Examples of these categories drawn from students' writing are compiled, typed, and distributed to the class. These documents chronicle the seminar members' individual experiences and privately held theories.

Over the following 3 weeks, each of these categories or features is reinterpreted as students reflect further on their experiences and examine the writings of curriculum theorists. As they assess the implications and desirability of Noddings's (1992) ethic of care, for instance, they are asked to reflect on the relationship of this ethic to their own conceptions of good educational interactions. Positive features are then extracted and refined. Students consider and debate curriculum theorists' work or "public" theories (Cole, 1990) with explicit reference to their own varied experiences. Through these discussions, the prospective teachers work to develop a coherent and agreed-on set of characteristics of powerful teaching and learning experiences. In one seminar, for example, the class focused on the importance and influence in curriculum design and implementation of teacher charisma, leadership opportunities for students, challenges that build on students' talents and abilities, and extended multidisciplinary projects.

Using students' collectively compiled experiences in schools to examine critically more public theories of teaching and learning brings the two closer together, enriching students' understandings both of their own experiences and of scholarly texts. Teachers start with individual theories based on personal experience about what works in classroom practice. Of course, these privately held theories are not always productive. To "become educated as a teacher," note Bullough and Gitlin (1995), these "commonly held assumptions about teaching must be challenged and tested. . . . Masquerading as common sense, [teachers'] private theories need to be made explicit so they can be criticized and, when found wanting, reconstructed" (p. 15). By collectively examining these theories through narrating and analyzing individual experiences, private theories are put to public scrutiny. At the same time, public theories are put to the test of experience by analysis based on teachers' own principles of practice derived from their experience. As Schwab (1959/1978) notes, "Any theory of practice finds its full meaning only as it is put into practice and gains its 'verification' only as it is tested there" (p. 169). As students described the process, engaging in conversations about professional practice "gave me a sense that my experiences and what I had to say mattered," "helped us learn from our experiences," and enabled the class to "use the more theoretical readings as a sounding board for our intuitions."

In addition, engaging students in deep conversations about practice informed by their experiences, analysis of their particular context, and a knowledge base with regard to teaching and learning supports the development of an emerging professional community (Little & McLaughlin, 1993; Louis & Kruse, 1995; Rust, 1999; Shulman, 1989). For many of the teachers, these discussions lend legitimacy to their own experiences while creating a common base of experiential knowledge and a familiarity with each other's values and orientations—essential ingredients for an emerging professional community of teachers (Little & McLaughlin, 1993; Newmann, 1994). These settings also enable students to experience dynamics associated with the sense of trust, respect, and common purpose that advocates of professional communities prize. As one student noted,

> In this class, I always felt totally comfortable talking. . . . When you know people more, you really want to know what they have to say. . . . It was more than my own participation, it's this overall professional respect for each other's thoughts and ideas, and that makes a huge difference.

## Collectively Develop and Implement Curriculum Projects

Following their collaborative analysis of powerful learning experiences, the prospective teachers in the ECP then begin to design their own educational activities. Rather than develop and implement these activities individually, however, they do so collectively.

Communities, as John Dewey (1900/1956) made clear, are built from the collective experiences of their members. The process by which experiences are shared through collective action and reflection both builds community and defines it. Collective action can create a commonly understood set of experiences from which to generate theory and incorporate the research and theory of other educators. Collective reflection, in turn, requires community and also strengthens it (Bullough & Gitlin, 1995).

Schools led by communities of teachers who are responsible for making curricular, organizational, and sometimes financial decisions require that newcomers are well versed about the benefits, commitments, tensions, and trouble spots that emerge when people work together in demanding environments. Research to date has indicated that without adequate preparation, expectations for teacher collaboration in teacher-led schools are easily thwarted (Leithwood & Menzies, 1998; Little, 1990). To prepare teachers for work in these types of schools, teacher education programs should make it a priority to model what communities of professionals might look like and to give new teachers a positive experience designing curricula within such a community. The impact of such an experience can be enormous (see Westheimer & Kahne, 1993). As one student explained when interviewed by another for her action research project,

> The idea of creating a community of learners . . . you can talk about that . . . but to see it happen is another thing entirely. . . . The way we not only planned and implemented the [curriculum], but the way it worked . . . Something happens over time, people make connections. Those connections have carried us through the two terms, through the three trips, but at the same time, they're a basis from which we can make connections to the kids.

By providing the opportunity for preservice teachers to experience professional communities, teacher educators also make it possible for them to develop the insight, knowledge, and orientation needed to pursue collective practice in newly restructured schools.

The students in the ECP work together designing a curriculum for classes of 25 to 30 students from a local urban high school. The curriculum is then implemented over a 2-week period, which features a 2-day overnight curriculum, outdoors and away from the norms and constraints of traditional school settings. Preliminary and follow-up educational activities take place at the school site. As they begin to plan their curriculum, the class forms working committees, each with specific responsibilities. One committee coordinates transportation and develops curricular activities for the bus ride and walk into the campsite where everyone will be spending the night. Another designs a curriculum for small groups of the high school students. Other committees handle logistics, whole-group projects, outing themes, and pretrip and posttrip activities to be implemented at the high school. The prospective teachers sit on as many as three committees. The class also chooses a curriculum coordinator. This person works across the committees to ensure coherence and communicate ongoing developments.

For the next 3 weeks, the students meet together as a class and in the smaller committees. They discuss their options, goals, and teaching strategies in light of their own categories of curriculum design and each week's readings. They deliberate, report back to the class, and seek to improve on one another's ideas.

One year, for example, the transportation committee proposed that three class members, posing as park rangers, greet the high school students during their walk into the campsite. The rangers would ask the students to participate in a poll and then facilitate a discussion on policies related to park use and access.[3] As the class of prospective teachers explored this possibility, they decided to adopt park policy as a curricular theme for the weekend. The small group activities committee later suggested that the high school students cycle between five workshops, each addressing ethical, political, and environmental concerns of park use. The whole group projects committee designed a forum in which groups of students would deliberate, write position papers, and make presentations that support their positions. Each committee contributed similarly as the class went back and forth between committee and whole class meetings until a coherent design for the entire curriculum was created. "In that first week of planning," another prospective teacher wrote,

> all of the committees met and came up with plans. . . . Each group laughed and joked as they presented their part, even when the rest of the class was seeming skeptical. . . . The following week, the committees met again and were able to take the best aspects of the ideas which had been tossed around earlier, and add new

twists. By the following Tuesday, we were no longer asking "Do you really think it's going to happen?" Now we were wondering how we were going to fit everything in!

Once implementation of the curriculum begins, the prospective teachers are in charge. Decisions, from disciplinary measures and logistics to on-the-fly curricular revisions are left to the discretion of the class. The course instructor provides some feedback, consultation, and oversight but does not run the event. Assessments of the curriculum and of the students' performance as teachers are the focus of the classes that follow each weekend curriculum implementation.

## Collective and Individual Reflection

Having had the opportunity to test their curriculum ideas, the prospective teachers enter the second term of the course during which they design two additional curricula for new groups of students. As a starting point, the class systematically considers their previous experience, revises their priorities and assumptions, and researches the new conditions they will face. For the next 10 weeks, the students prepare detailed plans for this curriculum and the next. During this time, the class also reads further about innovative curriculum design (e.g., Elliot Wigginton's [1986] *Foxfire*) and explores a number of normative issues related to pedagogy. This phase of the program—when students reflect on one curriculum, read educational literature, and design the next curriculum—offers the best opportunity to collectively integrate theory with practice. The ways the class members integrate their experiences and home-grown theories with the research and theoretical models developed by others are best illustrated by a discussion that arose concerning creativity and pedagogy, a topic familiar to teacher educators.

Prospective teachers had just returned from a 2-day curriculum in which they had facilitated discussions and activities about the then-current presidential campaigns. They observed that when groups of students were asked to make creative presentations about presidential platform issues, the results were less than inspired. Most groups had one or two students read a lengthy written statement in monotone while the other group members stood behind. One group split the reading among all of the group members. The effects were predictable. Few in the audience listened carefully to their classmates' presentations, the presenters took little pride in their performances, and minor disciplinary problems required sporadic attention from the prospective teachers. Why, the prospective teachers wondered, were the presentations so lackluster? They had given the students the freedom to present in any way they wished and had even encouraged them to be creative.

As the class explored possible answers to this question, much debate ensued. A number of student teachers were hesitant to give up their long-held theory that if schools would simply diminish the constraints imposed on student behavior, they would free students' natural capacity for innovation and creativity. Others pointed out that the outcome of their planned activity demonstrated the opposite. The students were afforded plenty of freedom to be creative but chose traditional means to present their work. The students' private theories came head to head with their experience and with some of the research they had read and summarily dismissed as not child-centered enough. As one student explained,

> We talked about all the drawbacks of teacher-centered classrooms. . . . But when we went and did our curriculum, even though we didn't intend for it to be this way, the activities depended on us, and upon our setting up the situation. And that was one of the things that we talked about as being a negative in the traditional classroom, that the teacher shouldn't have to be the center of attention that way.

As the class further discussed freedom and pedagogy, they began to consider the antecedents of creativity. Were freedom and encouragement enough? Do children in educational settings tend toward creative expression, or do they tend to replicate patterns of behavior they commonly see? Would the modeling of alternative presentation styles expand the range of creative options that children consider or would it simply substitute a new dominant presentation style for the old one? As they examined these questions, multiple interpretations of the experience and its causes emerged. The class revised its theory to accommodate new understandings of the relationship between pedagogy and creativity.

It is common in teacher education to rely on theories to shape students' understanding of educational interactions and outcomes. Zeichner and Tabachnick (1981) have shown that such reliance is unwise because new and veteran teachers alike are likely to make decisions based on their own experience even if research contradicts their judgment. New teachers see the connection between theory and practice as tenuous, and teacher educators find approaches for meaningful integration of the two to be elusive. Teacher education students routinely report that their university coursework does not inform their teaching and that their experience with children is accorded little value in university classrooms. As Mike Atkin (1989) writes, "a great many teachers and administrators believe—and say, with conviction—that educational research is irrelevant, wrong-headed, or both" (p. 200). This is particularly troubling in light of the series of educational reforms intended to give teachers greater responsibility and control over the schools in which they work. If we are to take seriously the notion that meaningful change is going to come only when directed by those who will implement it, then the ways practitioners understand and respond to theory-based and research-driven reforms are very important indeed.

In the example described above, students' assumptions with regard to the best way to encourage creativity were called into question by their collective experience working with high school students. They found that freedom to be creative did not necessarily result in creative expression, and they returned to their original assumptions about the public theories they had read to reconsider them. "In that second visit to the readings, we were struck by what some of the education authors had to say," one student noted, "that maybe the ones we had dismissed had a point, that maybe this was more complicated than we had expected." Privately held theories of class members were challenged and adjusted accordingly.

The activities described above provide a strategy for integrating theory and practice and for incorporating systematic reflection in teacher education. Teacher educators have drawn attention to the importance of forging these links in teacher preparation and staff development programs (Atkin, 1992; Bullough & Gitlin, 1995; Cochran-Smith & Lytle, 1992; Gore & Zeichner, 1991; Kroll & LaBoskey, 1996). More important for our argument here, however, is that the process of collectively generating and revising theory became a lesson for student teachers in what meaningful collective work is like. These reflective experiences derive much of their power from their expressly collective nature. In contrast to student teachers' sharing their individual experiences and asking their peers for advice, students implemented this curriculum together. Several students echoed one student's observation that "there was such a sense of common purpose that made [these conversations] meaningful. . . .We had an opportunity to be an expert and to learn the expertise of others." The shared experience enabled discussions among the prospective teachers about their teaching and its effects, which in turn facilitated a kind of professional collaboration that would have been much harder to create had the students worked individually.

## Not All Work Is Collective

It is important to note that not all the work in the ECP is collective. Through action research projects, each student teacher conducts a study related to the three curricula designed and implemented by the entire class. One student, for example, assessed the consistency of the curriculum the class developed with a set of principles John Dewey (1938/1963) provides in *Experience and Education*. Another wrote a qualitative study of the impact of the 2-day curriculum project on the high school students' attitudes toward traditional educational experiences.

Individual projects are essential for teacher preparation. Indeed, teachers in schools will do the great majority of their work individually. Our point is not that all of teaching must be a collective enterprise. Rather, we are suggesting that individual efforts should be related to a collective, if broadly defined, endeavor. In this case, the action research projects were combined into a volume of written work from which students could draw in the more general discussions of curriculum design and classroom practice that take place toward the end of the seminar. The findings of some of these projects, however, lead us to several points of concern.

## Balancing the Way Schools Are with the Way We Would Like Them To Be

Teachers must be prepared for the institutions they are likely to enter as well as those they hope to create. Although we found that the ECP inspired teachers to think creatively, work collectively, and utilize educational theory and literature as partners in curriculum design, the nontraditional aspects of the project that made this possible also raise important questions.

The ECP helped prepare students for leadership in restructured schools by redefining the norms of teaching so that these prospective teachers were free to develop an interdisciplinary curriculum and authentic learning experiences that built on the high school students' interests and needs. The teachers engaged in theory building; learned from their own experiences in a structured, analytic manner; incorporated the work of education scholars; shared knowledge with each other; and worked in concert. The experience ignited many students' passion for entering the field. "This seminar," wrote one student, "has fueled my interest and excitement about education. More than ever I am sure that I want to go into the field." Another student wrote that the time spent planning the curriculum together was "more inspiring than any other professional experience I have had. . . . I have never been so exhausted and so willing to do more than the night before our final curriculum." For the 3 years the course sequence was taught, students consistently emphasized the inspirational power of the experience.

On the other hand, these inspirational field experiences, which allow prospective teachers to explore freely the practices expected of them in the finest restructured schools, differ dramatically from the schools in which most are likely to work. They planned curricula for settings in which many of the norms and barriers that constrain experience-based approaches, team teaching, and collaborative planning were not operative. The curricula student teachers created could not be easily implemented in most schools.

This is an especially important consideration given the current climate in a vast majority of schools. Highly restrictive, state-level curriculum frameworks and increasing use of standards-based evaluations and high-stakes testing for teachers and students can severely curtail new teachers' capacities to teach as a community of colleagues who locate their teaching and curriculum development in the primacy of their own and their students' experiences. Standards, high-stakes testing, and competency testing for both students and teachers are currently the noisiest and most prevalent educational conversations, and few calls for experience-based learning or innovative collective teaching can be heard above the din. Forty-nine states have now adopted higher academic standards as one of the major strategies for educational improvement (Clark & Wasley, 1999). Test scores are frequently used for decisions with regard to tracking, promotion, and graduation (National Research Council, 1999). Especially in districts where low test scores and high-stakes policies threaten students, teachers, and principals, a test-centered pedagogy and curriculum will frequently dominate (Brabeck, 1999; Goodlad, 1999; Shepard, 1991; Wiggins, 1993). In many cases, opportunities for collective school leadership are constrained or are focused solely on raising students' test scores.

Many teacher educators emphasize the importance of giving student teachers real experiences in real schools. We are prepared to argue for the importance of providing positive, even utopian, experiences for new teachers (in a profession that has resisted change for decades). However, there is often a conflict between teacher education that seeks to prepare teachers for collective action (which includes collective decision making with regard to both the goals of schooling and ways to pursue these goals) and schools that are under increasing pressure to focus on test scores. This raises difficult questions with regard to the balance of adequate preparation for existing schools, on one hand, and effecting change, on the other (see also Barton, 1999; Cochran-Smith, 1991). Until a new educational narrative arises about what good schooling looks like (Goodlad, 1999), such dissonance will remain a challenge to teacher educators seeking to implement a new vision for collective action and collective reflection in teacher-led schools. This is not to say that the concern over the basics and subject matter knowledge is without basis. The degree to which the curriculum designed by teacher education students ties into mandated curriculum frameworks and subject matter expectations also merits careful consideration. A focus on community and collegiality among teachers does not guarantee rigor in curriculum development. One preservice teacher found in her action research project, for example, that the high school students failed to make meaningful connections between the weekend curriculum planned by the student teachers and the academic subject matter they regularly studied in school. One high school student who said she really valued the weekend experience also said that the projects did not "tie into anything academic" that she was learning in school.

Over the 2-day curriculum, the high school students engaged in numerous academically oriented activities—they wrote position papers on political issues as well as short stories. They debated ethical and philosophical issues and studied maps and environmental science. It may well be that the high school students simply did not recognize this curriculum as educational even though it actually was. But, we should not ignore either their critique or the limited connections they made between the curriculum and their education in school. Those involved in the ECP design fell prey to the most common critique of this approach. By basing their curriculum in meaningful experiences and by not tying these experiences to a systematic and sequential examination of subject matter, the high school students, though engaged in each experience, did not connect these experiences and what they were learning from them to what they were studying in school. In some important respects, the freedom from curriculum guidelines and educational norms that the preservice teachers found inspiring led to fewer connections to academic subject matter.

The need to free prospective teachers to develop powerful educational visions and to imagine new possibilities, although important, may come into conflict with the need to prepare them for schools as they currently exist. The tension between accommodation and change—not a new one to practitioners working in restructuring schools—is one with which teacher educators will need to grapple. The types of exciting opportunities that engender passion, commitment, and the ability to innovate will have to be balanced by direct work in more traditional school settings.

## Teaching Collective Work by Bridging the Theory/Practice Divide

In explaining the importance of making teachers partners in the pursuit of theory, Atkin (1989) echoes Edgar Schein's dictum that there are times when understanding a human system can come only from trying to change it. It is not so much that actions speak louder than words, then, but rather that actions inform words, or for our purposes here, that experience (practice) informs theory. Without action, without meddling in the practical minutia of curriculum design and implementation, teacher education courses are limited by the constraints imposed when operating in a closed system without context. Conversely, educational research and theory are critical to developing and improving practice. We already know that when theory and practice are kept distinct, new teachers, when confronted with the challenge of action (teaching), will follow the lead of their own prior and current experiences to the exclusion of informed consideration of theory (Bracey, 1989; Goodson, 1991; Johnston, 1994; Zeichner & Tabachnick, 1981). For both new and veteran teachers engaged in classroom practice, theory is, after all, only words, and actions speak louder.

By collectively exploring the relationship between theory and experience, however, student teachers can learn not only to challenge privately held theories but to carefully consider public ones. They also learn to work together in establishing deep and meaningful principles of collective practice. If teacher educators are going to be successful in addressing the dual goals of uniting theory and practice and preparing teachers for collective leadership in the demanding environment of newly restructured schools, then schools of education must consider substantial changes in the curriculum and design of their programs. As one student in the program wrote, "Teachers of teachers must model their models." To foster schools in which teachers examine their own experiences in light of education theory while working within a professional community to improve the school culture and curriculum, teacher educators must provide these experiences for their students.

The ECP is not a formula to be replicated. It is one example of a program that worked toward these changes. Students shared important individual experiences, collectively identified characteristics of powerful curricula that reflect these experiences, and collectively developed, implemented, and systematically reflected on their own curriculum for high school students. These activities, in turn, develop the kind of familiarity, trust, and sense of common purpose characteristic of vibrant professional communities. By engaging students in collective actions designed to stimulate collective reflection, teacher educators sow the seeds of these communities. In addition, this process provides students with the opportunity to experiment with numerous practices promoted by advocates of school restructuring. Rather than taking part in abstract consideration of site-based management, team teaching, and interdisciplinary curriculum, for example, the students assess the merits and drawbacks of these practices through firsthand experience. Similar opportunities are worthy of further exploration in the contexts of other programs.

## Notes

1. Private theories, as described by Cole (1990), are those orientations and assumptions that are born out of personal experience, whereas public theories are those encountered in scholarly research and writing. For further discussion of the distinctions between private and public theories and practices, see Cole (1990) and Griffiths and Tann (1992).

2. Joel Westheimer conceived of, created, and directed the Experiential Curricula Project at Stanford University. He also taught the program's two-term course sequence. Joseph Kahne spent 1½ years studying the program. He observed all but two classes, attended special weekend trips, interviewed the students, and, with Westheimer, examined student work. The authors contributed equally to this chapter.

3. This idea was met with enthusiasm by some who believed it would excite the students and was criticized by others who felt it was manipulative. Students discussed ways possible problems could be avoided, and although not all students were convinced that this approach made the most sense, they were sufficiently assured to support their more enthusiastic colleagues with the activity.

## Acknowledgment

We would like to thank the participants in the Experiential Curricula Project, Mike Atkin, Marilyn Cochran-Smith, Gary Lichtenstien, David Scanlon, Lee Shulman, and two anonymous reviewers for invaluable comments on earlier drafts, and Mark Alter for supporting the completion. We are especially grateful to Marshall Smith and all the students who participated in the Experiential Curricula Project.

## References

Atkin, M. (1989). Can educational research keep pace with educational reform? *Phi Delta Kappan, 71*(3), 200–205.

Atkin, M. (1992). Teaching as research. *Teaching and Teacher Education, 8*(4), 381–390.

Barth, R. (1990). *Improving schools from within: Teachers, parents, and principals can make a difference.* San Francisco: Jossey-Bass.

Barton, P. (1999). *Too much testing of the wrong kind: Too little of the right kind in K-12 education.* Princeton, NJ: Educational Testing Service.

Beane, J. (1997). *Curriculum integration: Designing the core of democratic education.* New York: Teachers College Press.

Brabeck, M. (1999). Between Scylla and Charybdis: Teacher education's odyssey. *Journal of Teacher Education, 50*(5), 346–351.

Bracey, G. (1989). Why so much education research is irrelevant, imitative, and ignored. *American School Board Journal, 176*(7), 20–22.

Bullough, R., & Gitlin, A. (1995). *Becoming a student of teaching.* New York: Garland.

Carnegie Task Force on Teaching as a Profession. (1986). *A nation prepared: Teachers for the 21st century.* New York: Carnegie Corporation.

Clark, R., & Wasley, P. (1999). Renewing schools and smarter kids: Promises for democracy. *Phi Delta Kappan, 80*(8), 590–596.

Cochran-Smith, M. (1991). Learning to teach against the grain. *Harvard Educational Review, 61*(3), 279–310.

Cochran-Smith, M., & Lytle, S. (1992). Communities for teacher research: Fringe or forefront? *American Journal of Education, 100*(3), 298–324.

Cole, A. L. (1990). Personal theories of teaching: Development in the formative years. *Alberta Journal of Education Research, 36*(3), 203–222.

Dewey, J. (1900/1956). *The school and society.* In *The child and the curriculum and the school and society* (pp. 3–159). Chicago: University of Chicago Press.

Dewey, J. (1938/1963). *Experience and education.* New York: Collier Macmillan.

Fullan, M., Galluzzo, G., Morris, P., & Watson, N. (1998). *The rise and stall of teacher education reform.* Washington, DC: American Association of Colleges for Teacher Education.

Goodlad, J. (1990). *Teachers for our nation's schools.* San Francisco: Jossey-Bass.

Goodlad, J. (1999). Whither schools of education? *Journal of Teacher Education, 50,* 325–338.

Goodlad, J., Soder, R., & Sirotnik, K. (Eds.). (1990). *Places where teachers are taught.* San Francisco: Jossey-Bass.

Goodson, I. (1991). Teachers' lives and educational research. In I. Goodson & R. Walker (Eds.), *Biography, identity, and schooling: Episodes in educational research* (pp. 137–149). London: Falmer Press.

Gore, J., & Zeichner, K. (1991). Action research and reflective teaching in preservice teacher education: A case study from the United States. *Teaching and Teacher Education, 7*(2), 119–136.

Griffiths, M., & Tann, S. (1992). Using reflective practice to link personal and public theories. *Journal of Education for Teaching, 18*(1), 69–84.

Grossman, P. L., & Richert, A. E. (1996). Building capacity and commitment for leadership in preservice education. *Journal of School Leadership, 6*(2), 202–210.

Hargreaves, A. (1994). *Changing teachers, changing times: Teachers' work and culture in the postmodern age.* New York: Teachers College Press.

Holmes Group. (1986). *Tomorrow's teachers: A report of the Holmes Group.* East Lansing, MI: Author.

Johnston, S. (1994). Experience is the best teacher; or is it? An analysis of the role of experience in learning to teach. *Journal of Teacher Education, 45*(3), 199–208.

Kroll, L. R., & LaBoskey, V. K. (1996). Practicing what we preach: Constructivism in a teacher education program. *Action in Teacher Education, 18*(2), 63–72.

Leithwood, K., & Menzies, T. (1998). A review of research concerning the implementation of site-based management. *School Effectiveness and School Improvement, 9*(3), 233–285.

Lieberman, A. (1988). Expanding the leadership team. *Educational Leadership, 45*(5), 4–8.

Lieberman, A. (1995). Restructuring schools: The dynamics of changing practice, structure, and culture. In A. Lieberman (Ed.), *The work of restructuring schools* (pp. 1–17). New York: Teachers College Press.

Little, J. (1990). The persistence of privacy: Autonomy and initiative in teachers' professional relations. *Teachers College Record, 91*(4), 509–536.

Little, J., & McLaughlin, M. (1993). Introduction: Perspectives on cultures and contexts of teaching. In J. Little & M. McLaughlin (Eds.), *Teachers' work: Individuals, colleagues and contexts* (pp. 1–8). New York: Teachers College Press.

Louis, K. S., & Kruse, S. D. (1995). *Professionalism and community: Perspectives on reforming urban schools.* Thousand Oaks, CA: Corwin Press.

Maeroff, G. (1993). Building teams to rebuild schools. *Phi Delta Kappan, 74*(7), 512–519.

McLaughlin, M. (1993). What matters most in teachers' workplace context. In J. Little & M. McLaughlin (Eds.), *Teachers' work: Individuals, colleagues, and contexts* (pp. 79–103). New York: Teachers College Press.

Merz, C., & Fuhrman, G. (1997). *Community and schools: Promises and paradox.* New York: Teachers College Press.

Murphy, J. (1990). Helping teachers prepare to work in restructured schools. *Journal of Teacher Education, 41*(4), 50–56.

National Research Council. (1999). *High stakes: Testing for tracking, promotion, and graduation.* Washington, DC: National Academy Press.

Newmann, F. M. (1994). School-wide professional community. *Issues in restructuring schools* (Issue Report No. 6). Madison: Center on Organization and Restructuring of Schools, University of Wisconsin–Madison.

Noddings, N. (1992). *The challenge to care in schools: An alternative approach to education.* New York: Teachers College Press.

Rust, F. (1999). Professional conversations: New teachers explore teaching through conversation, story, and narrative. *Teaching and Teacher Education, 15*(4), 367–380.

Schwab, J. (1959/1978). The impossible role of the teacher in progressive education. In I. Westbury & N. Wilkof (Eds.), *Science, curriculum, and liberal education: Selected essays*. Chicago: University of Chicago Press.

Shepard, L. (1991). Will national tests improve student learning? *Phi Delta Kappan, 73*(3), 232–238.

Shulman, L. (1989). Teaching alone, learning together: Needed agendas for the new reforms. In T. Sergiovanni & J. Moore (Eds.), *Schooling for tomorrow: Directing reforms to issues that count*. Boston: Allyn & Bacon.

Westheimer, J. (1998). *Among schoolteachers: Community, autonomy, and ideology in teachers' work*. New York: Teachers College Press.

Westheimer, J., & Kahne, J. (1993). Building school communities: An experience-based model. *Phi Delta Kappan, 75*(4), 324–328.

Wiggins, G. (1993). Assessment: Authenticity, context, and validity. *Phi Delta Kappan, 75*(3), 200–208, 210–214.

Wigginton, E. (1986). *Sometimes a shining moment: The Foxfire experience*. New York: Anchor/Doubleday.

Zeichner, K., & Tabachnick, B. (1981). Are the effects of university teacher education "washed out" by school experience? *Journal of Teacher Education, 32*(3), 7–11.

# CHAPTER FIFTEEN

# Professional Learning Communities

## A Bandwagon, an Idea Worth Considering or Our Best Hope for High Levels of Learning?

R<small>ICHARD</small> D<small>U</small>F<small>OUR</small>

I<small>T SHOULD SURPRISE NO ONE THAT THERE ARE FACULTIES THROUGHOUT</small> N<small>ORTH</small> A<small>MERICA THAT</small> refer to themselves as professional learning communities (PLCs) yet do none of the things that PLCs do. Conversely, there are faculties that could serve as model PLCs that may never reference the term. A school does not become a PLC by enrolling in a program, renaming existing practices, taking the PLC pledge, or learning the secret PLC handshake. A school becomes a professional learning community only when the educators within it align their practices with PLC concepts. Therefore, any valid assessment of the impact of PLC concepts on a school or the compatibility of those concepts with the middle school model would first need to determine if PLC practices were actually in place in the school. Only then would it be possible to determine the impact of those practices on the learning of both students and adults.

The May 2006 issue of the *Middle School Journal* included the article "Learning Communities in 6–8 Middle Schools: Natural Complements or Another Bandwagon in the Parade" (Patterson & co-contributors, 2006). The authors based the article on interviews and surveys of the staff members of two middle schools that considered themselves to be in the very early stages of implementing professional learning community concepts. In brief, the authors discovered there was widespread confusion regarding the term and that teachers saw little potential benefit in the PLC concept. They concluded the article by offering the caution that, while PLC ideas "are worth considering," educators should be wary about "jumping on the bandwagon" and following a "recipe-driven process."

If the educators in these schools are confused about the term, "professional learning community," they are not alone. As I observed in an earlier article, the term has been used "to describe every imaginable combination of individuals with an interest in education—a grade-level teaching team, a school committee, a high school department, an entire school district, a state department of education, a national professional organization, and so on. In fact, the term has been used so ubiquitously that it is in danger of losing all meaning" (DuFour, 2004, p. 6). As Fullan (2005) has cautioned, "terms travel easily . . . but the meaning of the underlying concepts does not" (p. 67). Thus, it is not surprising that some educators would express uncertainty regarding terminology.

## The Wrong Focus

The authors of the "Bandwagon" article did not focus much on practices; instead they focused on terminology, structures, and perceptions. They described one school's structural change from "eight teams to four learning communities." Teachers were perplexed by the change, saying their learning communities "still act like teams" and merely represented the merging of two teams into one. The second school continued to assign teachers to one of seven "teams" but added two "learning communities" on the basis of the location of teacher classrooms. Teachers in this school focused on "the structural aspects of learning community" and saw it as "a way of organizing or containing students." In both instances teachers expressed confusion regarding vocabulary and a preference for the "team" format over "learning communities." The authors presented little evidence that the educators in these schools actually engage in PLC practices. Had they studied a school that was a PLC in fact rather than in name only, they would have found that teachers were organized into collaborative teams that focused their collective efforts on certain critical questions such as:

1.  Are we clear on the knowledge, skills, and dispositions each student is to acquire as a result of this course, grade level, and unit we are about to teach?
2.  Have we agreed on the criteria we will use in assessing the quality of student work, and can we apply the criteria consistently?
3.  Have we developed common formative assessments to monitor each student's learning on a timely basis?
4.  Do we use the formative assessments to identify students who are having difficulty in their learning so that we can provide those students with timely, systematic interventions that guarantee them additional time and support for learning until they have become proficient?
5.  Do we use data to assess our individual and collective effectiveness? Do assessment results help us learn from one another in ways that positively affect our classroom practice?
6.  Does our team work interdependently to achieve SMART goals that are Strategic (linked to school goals), Measurable, Attainable, Results-oriented (focused on evidence of student learning rather than teacher strategies), and Time-bound?
7.  Are continuous improvement processes built into our routine work practice?
8.  Do we make decisions by building shared knowledge regarding best practices rather than simply pooling opinions?
9.  Do we demonstrate, through our collective efforts, our determination to help all students learn at high levels?
10. Do we use our collaborative team time to focus on these critical issues?

Researchers who have studied schools where educators actually engage in PLC practices have consistently cited those practices as our best hope for sustained, substantive school improvement (Darling-Hammond, 2001; Fullan, 2005; Louis & Marks, 1998; McLaughlin & Talbert, 2001; Newmann, 1996; Reeves, 2006; Saphier, 2005; Schmoker, 2005; Sparks, 2005). Those practices have been endorsed by the National Staff Development Council, the National Association of Secondary School Principals, the National Association of Elementary School Principals, the National Commission on Teaching and America's Future, the National Board of Professional Teaching Standards, and the National Forum to Accelerate Middle-Grades Reform. They certainly "complement" the recent recommendations presented in *Success in the Middle* by the National Middle School Association (2006) and *Breaking Ranks in the Middle* by the National Association of Secondary School Principals (2006).

It would be inaccurate to portray PLC concepts as a fad, bandwagon, or recipe. We have known for decades that students benefit when the teachers in their schools work in collaborative teams (Little, 1990), establish a guaranteed and viable curriculum to ensure all students have access to the same knowledge and skills (Marzano, 2003), monitor student learning on a frequent and timely basis (Lezotte, 1997), use formative assessments to identify students who need additional support for learning (Reeves, 2006), and demonstrate high expectations for student achievement through a collective commitment to help all students learn (Brophy & Good, 2002). These concepts represent more than "ideas worth considering": they continue to represent best practices for meeting the needs of all students.

## The Wrong Timing

Had the authors of "Bandwagon" set out to describe potential problems in the early stages of the implementation of the PLC concept, a case could be made for studying schools immersed in their first and second year of the initiative—if the schools were actually implementing PLC concepts. However, the authors proclaimed their purpose was to assess the potential of the concept by studying schools that did not have sufficient time to make valid assessments. As Fullan (2001) wrote: "One of our most consistent findings and understandings about the change process in education is that all successful schools experience 'implementation dips' . . . a dip in performance and confidence as one encounters an innovation that requires new skills and understanding" (p. 40). As a result, Fullan concluded, people are likely to feel anxious, confused, and overwhelmed in the early stages of innovation.

Another researcher put it this way: "Everything looks like a failure in the middle. Predictable problems arise in the middle of nearly every attempt to do something new. . . . Stop an innovation because of these problems, and, by definition, that initiative will be a failure. . . . Change-adept organizations support initiatives through the difficult middle period" (Kanter, 1997, p. 11).[1]

The schools studied in the Patterson and associates article (2006) had neither implemented PLC concepts nor had enough experience to assess the effectiveness of those concepts. Had schools been described that had pushed through the implementation dip to drive PLC concepts deep into the culture of their schools—the nationally recognized Freeport Intermediate School in Brazosport, Texas;

the award-winning Adams Middle School in Westland, Michigan; Levey Middle School in Southfield, Michigan, which has not only closed but shattered the achievement gap between students of different races; Woodlawn Middle and Twin Groves Middle in suburban Chicago, where more than 90% of students meet state proficiency standards; or any of hundreds of other middle schools that actually do what learning communities do—they would have observed very different results and heard very different opinions regarding the potential for PLC concepts to make schools better places for learning for students and teachers.

## Conclusion

School reform efforts in the United States have followed a predictable pattern. An improvement initiative is launched with great enthusiasm, only to be buffeted by confusion, criticism, and complaints. Many educators then abandon the initiative and continue their quest for the quick fix that will result in deep cultural changes that are unaccompanied by anxiety and concerns. Hosts of researchers, however, have concluded that substantive change inevitably creates discomfort and dissonance as people are asked to act in new ways (Marzano, Waters, & McNulty, 2005; Fullan, 2005; Sarason, 1996). We cannot avoid the discomfort, but we can determine how we will respond when the going gets tough. As Schlechty (2005), a veteran observer of school reform has concluded, "One of the most fundamental problems confronting those who would transform schools . . . is the problem of persistence of effort" (p. 23).

In his study of organizations that made the leap from "good to great," Collins (2001) found that the transformation was never the result of "a single defining action, no ground breaking program, no one killer innovation, no miracle moment" (p. 14). The improvement was always the result of "a cumulative process, step by step, action by action, decision by decision" (p. 165) and "pushing in a constant direction over an extended period of time" (p. 169). Greatness required persistence, fierce resolve, and consistent, coherent effort over the long haul. There were no shortcuts.

The professional learning community concept does not offer a short cut to school improvement. It presents neither a program nor a recipe. It does provide a powerful, proven conceptual framework for transforming schools at all levels, but alas, even the grandest design eventually degenerates into hard work. A school staff must focus on learning rather than teaching, work collaboratively on matters related to learning, and hold itself accountable for the kind of results that fuel continual improvement. When educators do the hard work necessary to implement these principles, their collective ability to help all students learn inevitably will rise. If they fail to demonstrate the discipline to initiate and sustain this work, their school is unlikely to become more effective, even if those within the school claim to be a professional learning community. The rise or fall of the professional learning community concept in any school will depend not on the merits of the concept itself, but on the most important element in the improvement of any school—the collective capacity, commitment, and persistence of the educators within it.

## Note

1. The phenomenon where measurable success does not immediately follow the implementation of a new initiative is called the "J-curve" effect. For a more complete discussion of how the J-curve phenomenon applies to educational innovations, see Erb, T. O., & Stevenson, C. (1999). Middle school reforms throw a "J-curve": Don't strike out. *Middle School Journal*, 30(5), 45–47.

## References

Brophy, J., & Good, T. (2002). *Looking in classrooms* (9th ed.). Boston: Allyn & Bacon.

Collins, J. (2001). *Good to great: Why some companies make the leap . . . and others don't*. New York: Harper Business.

Darling-Hammond, L. (2001). *The right to learn*. San Francisco: Jossey-Bass.

DuFour, R. (2004). What is a professional learning community? *Educational Leadership*, 61(8), 6–11.

Fullan, M. (2001). *Leading in a culture of change*. San Francisco: Jossey-Bass.

Fullan, M. (2005). *Leadership and sustainability: System thinkers in action*. Thousand Oaks, CA: Corwin Press.

Kanter, R. M. (1997). *On the frontiers of management*. Boston: Harvard Business School Press.

Lezotte, L. (1997). *Learning for all*. Okemos, MI: Effective Schools Products.

Little, J. W. (1990). The persistence of privacy: Autonomy and initiative in teachers' professional relations. *Teachers College Record*, 91, 509–536.

Louis, K. S., & Marks, H. (1998). Does professional community affect the classroom: Teachers' work and student experiences in restructuring schools. *American Journal of Education*, 106, 532–575.

Marzano, R. (2003). *What works in schools: Translating research into action*. Alexandria, VA: Association for Supervision and Curriculum Development.

Marzano, R., Waters, T., & McNulty, B. (2005). *School leadership that works: From research to results*. Alexandria, VA: Association for Supervision and Curriculum Development.

McLaughlin, M., & Talbert, J. (2001). *Professional communities and the work of high school teaching*. Chicago: University of Chicago Press.

National Association of Secondary School Principals. (2006). *Breaking ranks in the middle: Strategies for leading middle level reform*. Reston, VA: Author.

National Middle School Association. (2006). *Success in the middle: A policymaker's guide to achieving quality middle level education* [Electronic Version]. Retrieved November 26, 2006, from National Middle School Association http://www.nmsa.org/portals/0/pdf/advocacy/policy_guide/NMSA_Policy_Guide.pdf

Newmann, F. (Ed.). (1996). *Authentic achievement: Restructuring schools for intellectual quality*. San Francisco: Jossey Bass.

Patterson, J. A., & 16 co-contributors. (2006). Learning communities in middle schools: Natural complements or another bandwagon in the parade? *Middle School Journal*, 37(5), 21–30.

Reeves, D. (2006). *The learning leader: How to focus school improvement for better results*. Alexandria, VA. Association for Supervision and Curriculum Development.

Saphier, J. (2005). *John Adams' promise: How to have good schools for all our children, not just for some*. Acton, MA: Research for Better Teaching.

Sarason, S. (1996). *Revisiting the culture of the school and the problem of change*. New York: Teachers College Press.

Schlechty, P. (2005). *Creating the capacity to support innovations*. Louisville, KY: Schlechty Center of Leadership in School Reform.

Schmoker, M. (2005). No turning back: The ironclad case for professional learning communities. In R. DuFour, R. Eaker, & R. DuFour (Eds.), *On common ground: The power of professional learning communities* (pp. 135–154). Bloomington, IN: Solution Tree.

Sparks, D. (2005). *Leading for results: Teaching, learning, and relationships in schools.* Thousand Oaks, CA: Corwin Press.

# CHAPTER SIXTEEN

# Teacher Leadership Continuum

## How Principals Develop and Support Teacher Leaders

ANN S. ALLEN & KATHLEEN TOPOLKA-JORISSEN

Imagine the excitement as you begin your new teaching assignment. You arrive in a small rural town; the mayor, the preacher, and the president of the bank greet you at the train station. You are the town's new teacher. You have been selected from a pool of enthusiastic, educated, and morally sound graduates from the state's Normal School. Young and idealistic, you venture far from home to fulfill a lifelong dream.

The town's one-room schoolhouse is your stage. The town's school age children become your pupils to teach, love, and lead. Your place in the town's social order depends on your ability to organize and assess appropriate lessons and curricula, prepare students for the academic demands of their chosen vocations, manage discipline of students ranging from age 5 to 16, keep the schoolhouse and outhouse clean, oversee playground and lunchtime activities, insure that there is enough wood cut to keep the building warm, and inform parents of students' progress or struggles. If your pay is determined by the number of students attending, then you are also charged with recruitment and retention of students.

THE RESPONSIBILITIES SET FORTH BY THE TOWNSFOLK FOR A YOUNG ADULT WITH DREAMS AND ideals of a smooth-running school near the turn of the 19th century challenged teachers not only to provide instruction but also to provide leadership. Teacher leadership began when tutors were hired to educate young men from powerful families. The tutors were charged not only to teach curricula but also to teach thinking, moral decision making, and social skills. Responsibility for all aspects of the school rested with the teacher of the one-room schoolhouse. The industrialization of the nation led to larger schools with many teachers and one principal teacher, who was responsible for assisting with the managerial tasks associated with a larger facility, staff, and student body. The current age of accountability requires teachers, principals, students, and parents to respond to a myriad of dilemmas ranging from discipline to curriculum to health concerns. Teachers can no longer meet the needs of all students single-handedly. All teachers must provide leadership.

## What Is Leadership?

Leadership has been defined in many ways. Many definitions and theories focus on leadership traits (McClelland, 1985; Stogdill, 1981; Yukl, 2002). Others focus on skills (Northouse, 2004; Mumford, Zaccaro, Harding, Jacobs, & Fleishman, 2000; Yukl, 2002). What trait and skill theories have in common is a focus on individuals in formal leadership roles. However, in the context of a model in which leadership is shared across an organization or school, the definition of leadership takes on a more diffuse nature. Spillane (2006) defines leadership this way:

> *Leadership* refers to activities tied to the core work of the organization that are designed by organizational members to influence the motivation, knowledge, affect, or practices of other organizational members or that are understood by organizational members as intended to influence their motivation, knowledge, affect, or practices. (2006, pp. 11–12, emphasis in original)

The primary purpose of this kind of influence, according to Elmore (2004) must be the "improvement of instruction and practice" (p. 66). Furthermore, because leadership aims to improve practice, it requires continuous learning and modeling. (Elmore, 2004, p. 67). Actions that are directed toward the improvement of instructional practice, then, may be categorized as leadership practices, regardless of the role of the person engaging in those practices. What is the role of the principal in schools where adults in a range of roles engage in influencing "the motivation, knowledge, affect, or practices" of other members of the school community, with the intention of improving instructional practice?

According to Lambert (1998), the role of the principal becomes more critical than ever in a shared leadership school community. A primary goal of a principal committed to collective work as the key to student growth across the school will be to develop the leadership capacity of everyone in the school. Lambert says:

> Viewing leadership as a collective learning process leads to the recognition that the dispositions, knowledge, and skills of capacity building are the same as those of leadership. Leadership capacity building, then, can be defined as broad-based, skillful participation in the *work of leadership*. (Lambert, 1998, p. 12)

A principal committed to building leadership capacity will engage teachers and others in the school community in the work of leadership in several ways.

## Hiring Teachers Capable of Leadership Work

In schools developing leadership capacity, principals seek teachers who value collaborative learning and work and who see their responsibilities as extending to all the students in the school, not just to their own classes. Principals look for teachers who are a good "fit" for the school culture. In preparing to interview for entry-level teaching positions, teachers need to be prepared to respond to questions such as:

1. Describe a time when you worked on a team to solve a problem. What was the problem? How did your team approach the problem? What role did you play on the team?
2. Assume that you collect data from your first unit test, using the common assessment that your team has developed. You see that your students have scored lower on one section than

those of the other teachers on your team. What will you do?

3. Think of a time when you were working with another person or team, and the group was unable to agree upon a course of action. Describe that situation. What did you do?

Just as teachers need to be prepared to answer questions, they also need to be prepared to ask good questions and to share work samples. In preparing a file of materials to share with prospective employers, teachers should select at least one project that reflects the work of a collaborative effort and be prepared to describe their roles in developing the project. Questions teachers might ask to determine whether a school is committed to shared leadership include:

- How often does the (third-grade team or math department) meet to work on instructional issues?
- What are the current priorities for the (third-grade team or math department)?
- In reviewing your Web site, I noticed that math scores have been steadily rising for the past three years. What has caused this significant improvement?

## Participation Through Leadership Structures

Teachers in leadership capacity building schools can expect many opportunities to participate in leadership and to engage in the shaping of structures and processes that facilitate participation. For example, schools in which leadership capacity is developing are likely to use a School Improvement Team or School Leadership Team as a key structure that involves representatives from each grade level or subject, as well as parents and support staff, in reviewing data, establishing short and long term goals, implementing action research, monitoring progress, and communicating across the school. Flowing from the School Improvement Team will be grade level, subject area, or interdisciplinary work teams, focused on discrete aspects of more global school goals. For example, a third grade team may target fluency as a means of improving student achievement in reading, using a variety of agreed-upon methods for ensuring the success of all third graders.

## Engaging in Collaborative Inquiry

Traditionally, teachers have practiced in isolation from each other. In schools where developing leadership capacity is a goal, teachers expect to collaboratively investigate their practice. This dynamic involves going beyond simply sharing materials and ideas to exploring together to find solutions to shared problems of practice. Nelson (2009), points out:

> Dialogically, teachers' interactions shift from sharing teaching activities to critically questioning relationships between common activities, learning goals, and student learning. The essential characteristic in this shift is teacher learning through the analysis of student work, teaching artifacts, and relevant professional resources. Teachers generate knowledge that can inform larger school and district initiatives. (pp. 551–552)

Because such inquiry requires time for reflection, dialogue, data review, and discussion among team members, principals building leadership capacity will develop schedules that provide sufficient time for teachers to work together. For example, Glenn Marlow Elementary School in Hendersonville, NC, allocates common planning time each week for each grade level team. Over a two-year period, teachers have identified needs for more active engaged student learning strategies, studied learning styles, and developed differentiated lessons geared to a range of student learning styles.

In schools where leadership is the lever for school improvement, the role of the principal becomes vastly different from traditional views of the formal school leader. Principals assume the role of steward, entrusting all members of the educational community who are committed to achieving the collective goals and vision with respect and with support and assistance.

What are some of the specific strategies principals promote and support in order to build school and leadership capacity? In our work with schools, we have observed that savvy principals use their understanding of the school culture and developmental readiness of their teachers to design collaborative learning processes that best match teachers' orientation to professional inquiry and learning. Similar observations have been noted by Copland (2003). Moving along a continuum from novice to advanced, principals create opportunities for teachers to begin by analyzing data and helping each other learn and develop strategies to address learning problems. As teachers become increasingly comfortable with their participation in the work of leadership, they move into deeper inquiry, studying teaching and learning through direct observation. Schools and teachers at advanced levels become concerned with internal accountability and methods of integrating change initiatives across the entire school. Table 1 illustrates the continuum with examples of teacher leadership at each stage. To illustrate the continuum of participation in the work of leadership, we will present examples of strategies that represent each stage.

Table 1. Continuum of Teacher Leadership in Collaborative Learning

| Novice | Intermediate | Advanced |
|---|---|---|
| Book study | Train the trainer | Shared examination of student work |
| Individual classroom level action research | Group action research | Development of common assessments |
| Teacher-led professional development activities | Mentoring (with protégé' observations) | Direct observation |
| | | Teacher learning walks |

## Book Study as a Strategy for Novice Professional Learning Communities

In schools where teachers are accustomed to working in isolation, strategies such as book studies are effective in bringing teachers together to focus on a topic of common interest. Glenn Marlow Elementary School in Hendersonville, North Carolina, is a good example of a school that used a common concern about student learning as a catalyst for collaboration through book study. In examining their student achievement data, the teachers noticed a dip in learning for students transitioning from second to third grade and from fifth grade to middle school. They decided to learn more about their students as learners and more about themselves as teachers. As Principal Jan King explained,

"The teachers wondered why their students weren't more engaged. After all, the teachers were planning these great lessons!" The teachers explored two questions:

- How do our learning styles affect our instructional decisions?
- How do styles-based lessons affect student engagement and performance?

To answer the first question, teachers assessed their own learning and teaching styles and the learning styles of their students, using a small grant to purchase teaching and learning style inventories. They also purchased copies of a book to study together, in order to learn about teaching and learning styles. This initiative enabled the teachers to transform their grade-level teams into professional learning communities (PLCs), in which the teachers identified a student learning problem and worked together to identify strategies for addressing the problem. This approach illustrates the power of teacher leadership, even in its novice stages. As Lieberman and Miller (2008) say, "Much of current professional development activity rests on the assumption that there are best practices *out there*. In professional learning communities, this belief is replaced by the conviction that the best practices are *in here*; they can be uncovered by mining inside knowledge" (Lieberman & Miller, 2008, p. 22). Through sharing their self-assessment data and their perspectives on the ideas presented in the book, the teachers began to lead each other in learning.

## Moving to the Intermediate Stage with Action Research

As they used their common planning time to examine the data from the inventories, the Glenn Marlow teachers discovered that they had been designing lessons that matched the way *they* learned best—instead of considering the way *the children* preferred to learn. That provided sufficient motivation for the teachers to move into action research. Their grade-level meetings became action research meetings, in which they worked together to design lessons and to commit to trying strategies that would better engage their students. Together the teachers used the ideas they had learned in their book study to develop lessons that gave students many options for active, engaged learning. To assess the impact of the new strategies they were implementing, teachers began to bring samples of student work to their grade-level/PLC meetings, thus breaking down the barriers of isolation further and developing norms of trust. As Lieberman and Miller (2008) point out, "Professional learning communities . . . offer an alternative to the norms of privacy and secrecy and build the capacity of teachers to make their work public" (p. 24). In order to perform the work of leadership, teacher leaders need to progress to this level of trust.

## Advanced Stage Teacher Leaders Learning Through Direct Observation

The idea for teacher learning walks emerged from a supervisory practice commonly referred to as classroom walk-throughs. Principals began to see the benefit of teachers visiting other classrooms to seek ideas, strategies, and find common ground to begin discussions surrounding pedagogy and best practices. Learning walks can be simple informal visits shared between two or three colleagues seeking particular information such as student engagement techniques, use of a specific teaching tool such a learning map, or they can be more organized and engage the entire faculty and staff in formal professional development. In this model, the entire school becomes the context for teachers as leaders and learners. The focus is always on learning, not evaluating, and reflection is a key learning process at every stage of the process.

The more formal version of teacher learning walks includes the staff in a planning meeting which is led by any willing facilitator. The staff identifies shared goals or needs frequently taken from school report cards or school improvement plans. They then generate a list of indicators or "look fors" to guide the three- to five-minute snapshot visits. A schedule that involves all teachers being observed by at least one group and all teachers visiting at least three classrooms with at least one other teacher provides the necessary structure for using this process as school-wide professional development.

Teams of two to five teachers visit a classroom together, observe the action using the agreed-upon indicators for three to five minutes, and then step into the hall to discuss what they saw. The hallway conversation centers on what was observed, what was seen that is included on the indicator list, and any other positive ideas that one of the observers would like to borrow. The team decides on a question or two to ask later when the whole faculty meets for reflective dialogue and then moves on to the next class. After school the visitors have an opportunity to provide only positive feedback to those they observed and ask questions to help deepen their understanding of the techniques or approaches they saw.

The after-school conversations are where professional dialogue begins in earnest. Teachers are recognized for the hard work that occurs in each classroom. We have heard comments such as, "I knew we had a good school, but after visiting several classrooms today, I am really proud to say that we have some fantastic teachers here!" A physical education teacher commented, "No one ever came to see me teach before. It was nice to connect on an instructional level with other teachers." He went on to say that after visiting a third-grade classroom during a spelling lesson he planned to get the weekly spelling lists from teachers to use as students did calisthenics at the beginning of his class each day. He planned to have them do push-ups and jumping jacks while spelling!

Less formal teacher learning walks include visiting teachers in one grade level or content area and just picking up skills and ideas by watching for a short period of time. Visiting in a team of two or more helps teachers work together to develop ways to immediately apply in their own classrooms the good strategies they observe in their colleagues' classrooms. As learning walks become a professional norm in a school, teachers invite each other to come to see a "special" lesson or a new strategy to address a student learning goal.

## Integrating a Continuum of Strategies to Build School Capacity

As teachers become increasingly comfortable with shared inquiry and collaboration, they will naturally integrate novice, intermediate, and advanced strategies. One way to integrate levels of teacher leadership is to combine a "train the trainer" model of professional learning with site-based PLC work and learning walks.

Frequently teachers attend professional development events that teach how to present materials, support adoption of a specific program or curriculum, or even provide new tools to deliver instruction. These events are usually costly to the district and not practical for the entire staff to attend. If only one or two teachers attend, they may have difficulty implementing what they have learned, because they have no site-based support for their efforts. Sending one or two teachers to promising professional development sessions may be practical and contribute to school improvement, provided that those teachers assume leadership in sharing new information with colleagues.

One of the schools we have worked with has used a specific workshop—"Worksheets Don't Grow Dendrites"—to create a year-long focus, integrating teacher leaders presenting new material to all the other teachers (novice stage), all teachers adapting strategies for engagement into their lessons (intermediate), and using the teacher learning walk process for all teachers to see the strategies in practice and then engage in dialogue to analyze their practices and impact on student learning (advanced stage). Three teachers from the school attended a regional workshop and followed up by sharing two or three strategies a month during regular faculty meetings. Each month the teachers used the examples presented at the workshop as their indicators during teacher learning walk days. Their after school discussions focused on successful uses of the strategies, extensions they had discovered, and future plans to implement the skills and techniques they were developing.

An example of this integrated approach at the high school level is a school where the School Improvement Team had established the goal of integrating technology across the curriculum. The school had received a grant for ELMO tools Smart Boards, and Promethean boards. Many teachers had the technology in place in their classroom but were unsure of how to use it effectively. One Smart Board sat in a hallway, unused for three months. During teacher learning walks, all teachers saw some of their colleagues using technology in ways that inspired their own lesson designs. Within a matter of weeks, most of the Promethean boards were being used every period of the day. The once-lonely Smart Board became a vital tool in the Spanish teacher's classroom, helping her move vocabulary practice at a faster pace than a chalkboard ever could. Some of the older tools continued to be used because teachers saw that the tools supported student learning and made their teaching practice more efficient.

## Summary

Although there is no prescription or recipe for engaging teachers in the work of school leadership, the momentum for teacher engagement in the work of leadership is increasingly evident in schools. When teachers begin to meet to focus on student learning and their deep-seated commitment to improve their own professional practice, in order to ensure success for all students, teacher leadership has the potential to build school capacity. Lambert's (2003) assertion, "It is what people learn and do together, rather than what any particular leader does alone, that creates the fabric of the school" (p. 20) captures the essence of distributed leadership. When educators learn and work together to improve instruction and practice, schools develop the capacity to fulfill their mission for students.

## Discussion Topics

### Assessing Readiness and Planning for Teacher Leadership

Imagine how teachers in your school might begin to share their wealth of knowledge. Building communities of practice involves engaging the members of your school in authentic activities which connect their knowledge, skills, and practice to each other.

- How would you assess your school's current level of readiness for teacher leadership—novice, intermediate, advanced?
- What strategies would you recommend to engage teachers in the work of leadership?
- What ideas do you have that could build communities of practice?

## Case study

Your school buzzes with the excitement and bustle of a new school year. The annual "welcome back" teacher meetings this year offered a new twist. Your principal has organized several new committees that need teacher leaders to serve as committee chairpersons. There are also leadership opportunities in other positions. Select one of the following committees or leadership opportunities and describe your qualifications for the position, how you envision this committee addressing student learning needs, and what you would do to facilitate the group to define and achieve its goals.

| | |
|---|---|
| School Improvement | Student intervention process |
| Grade level leader | Department chair (content specific) |
| Literacy initiative | Professional learning community |
| Textbook adoption | Mentor for entry year teacher |
| Community outreach | Testing coordination |
| District Science Fair | School to Work representative |

# References

Copland, M. A. (2003). Leadership of inquiry: Building and sustaining capacity for school improvement. *Educational Evaluation and Policy Analysis, 25*(4), 375–395.

Elmore, R. F. (2004). Building a new structure for school leadership. In R. F. Elmore, *School reform from the inside out: Policy, practice, and performance.* Cambridge, MA: Harvard University Press.

Lambert, L. (1998). *Building leadership capacity in schools.* Alexandria, VA: Association for Supervision and Curriculum Development.

Lambert, L. (2003). *Leadership capacity for lasting school improvement.* Alexandria: ASCD.

Lieberman, A., & Miller, L. (2008). Developing capacities. In A. Lieberman & L. Miller (Eds.), *Teachers in professional communities: Improving teaching and learning* (pp. 18–28). New York, NY: Teachers College Press.

McClelland, D. C. (1985). *Human motivation.* Glenview, IL: Scott, Foresman.

Mumford, M. D., Zaccaro, S. J., Harding, F. D., Jacobs, T. O., & Fleishman, E. A. (2000). Leadership skills for a changing world: Solving complex social problems. *Leadership Quarterly, 11*(1), 11–35.

Nelson, T. H. (2009). Teachers' collaborative inquiry and professional growth: Should we be optimistic? *Science Education, 93,* 548–580. DOI:10.1002/sce.20302.

Northouse, P. G. (2004). *Leadership: Theory and practice* (3rd ed.). Thousand Oaks, CA: Sage.

Sergiovanni, T. J. (2007). Administering as a moral craft. In T. J. Sergiovanni, *Rethinking leadership: A collection of articles* (2nd ed.). Thousand Oaks, CA: Corwin.

Spillane, J. P. (2006). *Distributed leadership.* San Francisco, CA: Jossey-Bass.

Stogdill, R. M. (1981). Traits of leadership: A follow-up to 1970. In B. M. Bass (Ed.), *Stogdill's handbook of leadership* (pp. 73–97). New York: Free Press.

Yukl, G. A. (2002). *Leadership in organizations* (5th ed.). Upper Saddle River, NJ: Prentice Hall.

# Teacher Leadership:
# The New Foundations of Education

# CHAPTER SEVENTEEN

# Turning Good Teachers into Great Leaders

TERRY K. DOZIER

TEACHERS OF THE YEAR, NATIONAL BOARD–CERTIFIED TEACHERS, PRESIDENTIAL MATH AND Science awardees, and Milken educators—the public generally considers these exemplary classroom teachers to be teacher leaders. In their schools, they mentor new teachers, lead school improvement efforts, develop curriculum, and provide professional development for their colleagues. Administrators tap them to serve on school, district, and state committees.

But how do accomplished teachers view themselves? To what kinds of leadership roles do they aspire? And what skills do they need to be effective leaders?

In February 2003, the Center for Teacher Leadership at the Virginia Commonwealth University School of Education set out to answer these questions by conducting an online survey of 300 of the most accomplished teachers in the United States.[1] Sixty percent of those surveyed—179 teachers—responded, representing 37 different states. Of the respondents, 102 were National Board–certified teachers, and 92 were Teachers of the Year. Ninety-eight percent of respondents had received other awards for excellence in the classroom.

## What Teachers Think About Leadership

The survey results have several important implications for those who want to promote and support teacher leadership.

*Recognized teachers are confident about themselves as teacher leaders.* Ninety-seven percent of respondents considered themselves teacher leaders, and 96 percent believed that others saw them as leaders.

*Recognized teachers engage in many leadership roles.* Ninety-three percent have conducted professional development sessions for colleagues; 83 percent have engaged in curriculum development; 84 percent have served as department chairs, team leaders, or grade-level chairs; and 84 percent have mentored new teachers. Clearly, schools are already using accomplished teachers as leaders.

*Recognized teachers lack training in the new leadership roles they are asked to assume.* Eighty-two percent reported that they have not received training for all the leadership roles they have been asked to take on. Most administrators apparently assume that an outstanding teacher of students will be a good teacher of teachers. However, working with colleagues requires a different skill set.

*Recognized teachers desire new leadership roles.* When asked to identify the top three areas in which they have *not* served as leaders, but would like to serve, 95 percent of respondents chose (1) advisor to policymaking group, (2) teacher recruitment, and (3) education policy and issues. This mirrors national studies that report that teachers believe they have no input in decision making, even within their own schools (Marvel, Lyter, Strizek, & Morton, 2006). Moreover, this lack of input in decision making is a major reason teachers cite for leaving the profession (Ingersoll, 2003).

*Recognized teachers want training to help them become effective in the policy arena.* Although accomplished teachers want to be engaged in policymaking, they recognize that they do not have the necessary knowledge and skills to be effective in this area. When asked to identify the top three aspects of teacher leadership for which they need additional training, respondents selected (1) understanding education policy and issues (65 percent); (2) working collaboratively with education policymakers (64 percent); and (3) interpreting education research (40 percent). *Every* respondent chose either understanding education policy and issues or working collaboratively with education policymakers as an area in which they needed training.

## Policy Lessons from Teacher Leaders

There have long been calls for teacher leadership in education reform, among them the Institute for Educational Leadership's 2001 report *Leadership for Student Learning: Redefining the Teacher as Leader*. Nevertheless, teachers still have few opportunities to develop the skills they need to become effective leaders. The literature on teacher leadership documents a consistent absence of training for those asked to assume new leadership roles. Teachers are expected to have the necessary skills on entry into leadership positions or to develop those skills on the job (Katzenmeyer & Moller, 2001; O'Hair & O'Dell, 1995). The success or failure of teacher leaders has most often depended on context and on the experience and personal characteristics of the teacher.

Accomplished teachers realize that to be effective leaders in the policy arena, they must deepen their knowledge of education policy and sharpen their skills in influencing change. To provide the kind of policy training that teachers want and need, the Center for Teacher Leadership developed an online leadership course, *Teacher as Change Agent*, with funding from the AT&T Foundation. The following teacher profiles—drawn from the course and from the Center's Virginia Teacher Leaders Network—not only illustrate the knowledge, skills, and dispositions that teacher leaders need to be effective, but also highlight the importance of promoting and supporting teacher leadership.

### Join with Others

Pearl Quick, a middle school art teacher, believed that Virginia's art standards needed to be revised for clarity and for better alignment with the National Visual Art Standards. Using her position as president of the Virginia Art Education Association (VAEA), Pearl proposed that the board convene committees around the state to collect input from art teachers. A revision committee made up of representatives from the state's five VAEA regions considered the art teachers' feedback. At the end of a two-year process, the state Board of Education endorsed the suggested changes.

Pearl noted that one important way to effect change, especially in specific content areas, is through active involvement in a professional organization. When it comes to teacher leadership, there is strength in numbers.

## Use Data to Fuel Reform

Concerned about the effects of mandated testing on students in the Richmond Public Schools—especially kindergartners and 1st graders—1st grade teacher Sarah Ford helped create the Richmond Education Association's Testing Committee. The group spent a year looking at research; developing and conducting a survey to capture the perspective of all teachers in the district; analyzing survey results; and meeting with district leaders, outside experts, and interested parents. The report lists main concerns, such as the effect of mandated testing on instruction and teacher morale, and includes recommendations, such as reducing the number and frequency of mandated assessments to allow teachers time for creative and enrichment activities.

The final proposal was presented to the school board with the full support of Concerned Parents for Assessment Reform, a new advocacy group that parents formed as a result of Sarah's efforts. The school board has now created a task force that includes members of the testing committee, parents, and district administrators. The group has already agreed to eliminate the developmentally inappropriate test for kindergarten and 1st grade students and is working to implement additional changes. Sarah increased her chances of success by doing her homework, working with a team and other important stakeholders, and making sure that she had data to back up her recommendations.

## Communicate and Build Relationships

Sharon Nelson, a high school chemistry teacher, believed that school districts in Wisconsin needed high-quality induction programs to support new teachers. Working with the New Teacher Center at the University of California–Santa Cruz and initial funding from the Goldman Sachs Foundation, she established the Wisconsin New Teacher Project, whose mission is to provide guidance, training, and support to school districts as they develop and implement new teacher induction programs. Sharon and Tom Howe, a high school social studies teacher, also launched the Dane County New Teacher Project, a pilot consortium site of 14 school districts.

Surprisingly, their initial efforts met with some resistance until Sharon and Tom focused on two essential skills: communication and building relationships. As Tom explained,

> Rather than dismissing those who couldn't see the long-term benefit of induction and mentoring, we talked about how we might communicate our project's goals, purposes, and importance in ways that resonated with our audience and touched them in ways important to *their* purpose and mission. We also connected with people inside the state teachers' union and the state Department of Education who shared our beliefs around education. Finding allies within institutions, building relationships with individuals, and communicating clearly were important to our success.

Today the Wisconsin New Teacher Project is working in more than 40 districts.

## Use Your Spheres of Influence

Gail Ritchie, a National Board–certified teacher (NBCT) in Fairfax, Virginia, was inspired to use her new learning from the online teacher leadership course to revise the time-consuming and unwieldy process for soliciting, reviewing, and disseminating the results of leadership projects undertaken by NBCTs. In her role as the National Board program manager for her district, Gail met with the new assistant superintendent for professional learning and training to explain her plans for streamlining the process by eliminating redundant steps, such as having both curriculum specialists and a committee of NBCTs review projects.

Gail invited a committee of National Board-certified teachers representing different grade levels, areas of expertise, and viewpoints to help refine the plan and create a fair process. On the basis of feedback from assistant superintendents and directors in her school system, Gail revised the proposal and presented it to the district superintendent and his leadership team, who approved the new process. Gail's understanding of the district's chain of command and her successful use of her spheres of influence resulted in a smoother, more efficient submission process that enabled students and teachers to quickly benefit from innovative projects.

## Seize the Moment

Lori Nazareno, a National Board–certified teacher in Miami-Dade County Public Schools in Florida, helped create a professional organization of the district's more than 600 NBCTs, whose primary purpose was to improve teaching and learning. Despite state funding for NBCTs to mentor new teachers and the group's repeated efforts to share its expertise, Lori knew that district leaders were not using these accomplished teachers effectively.

When Miami-Dade hired Rudy Crew as the new superintendent, Lori wrote him a letter offering to explore ways in which NBCTs could participate in the many reforms that he planned for the district. Crew accepted Lori's offer. Lori and a colleague shared with him a list of recommendations on how the district could better position these accomplished teachers as leaders. These recommendations resulted in a school board policy that involved assigning NBCTs to provide professional development at schools identified as being at risk for low performance. School and district administrators are now seeking out these teachers to provide professional development and help reconfigure district professional development programs.

Lori's experience points out the importance of timing. She noted,

> I'm receiving phone calls and e-mails six and seven times a week from district personnel asking for our input, advice, and assistance on a growing number of initiatives. It's amazing what has happened because we seized an opportunity when it presented itself.

## Learn the Language

Susan Graham, a middle school family and consumer science teacher, attended teacher forums sponsored by the Center for Teacher Leadership and the Virginia Department of Education. The experience of sharing her own views and listening to the perspectives of other stakeholders opened her eyes to the complexity of working in the policy arena. As Susan explained,

Here, I began to learn the etiquette of policy discussion—that the language of policy debate and political debate differed, that consensus was not concession, and that changing policy for public education was complex and required great patience. I have discovered that to become a teacher leader requires great tenacity and a willingness to accept small successes.

### Follow Your Passion

Dodie Magill Rodgers, a kindergarten teacher, used her celebrity as the South Carolina Teacher of the Year to plan a statewide celebration of the 25th anniversary of kindergarten education in her state. Seeing the need for full-day kindergarten, especially for disadvantaged students, Dodie decided to use the celebration as a way to push for change. Dodie organized all the kindergarten teachers in South Carolina to host birthday celebrations and invite their local legislators. At these celebrations, politicians (and the media who follow them) received buttons and bumper stickers displaying the slogan "Half Day, Half the Way."

Although it was a tough fight that took the careful nurturing of relationships between state legislators and teachers over several years, South Carolina now has full-day kindergarten, thanks to Dodie and her colleagues. Her advice to teacher leaders?

> Go for it *if* it is a cause in which you believe passionately. I could never have mustered the strength, determination, or courage to see this project to completion unless it had been a cause I believed in with all my heart.

## Supporting Teacher Leadership

Because teachers know firsthand what is needed to improve student learning, promoting and supporting teacher leadership are crucial to the success of any education reform effort. But teacher leaders need specific knowledge, skills, and dispositions to be successful change agents. To strengthen teachers' leadership capacity, the Center for Teacher Leadership provides teachers with key resources: information on current issues that influence education and the teaching profession, National Board–certification preparation courses, training in how to work with student teachers, and mentor and leadership training.

But training alone is not enough. Teachers need opportunities to break out of their isolation and build professional networks of teachers who share a vision of education excellence. To this end, the Center for Teacher Leadership hosts statewide teacher forums, the Virginia Teacher Leaders Network, and an online discussion group dedicated to connecting teacher leaders throughout the state.

Teachers have a perspective that we can't get from anyone else. By helping good teachers become great leaders, we plant seeds that will enhance our profession and enable students to reap the reward they deserve—a high-quality education.

## Note

1. The teachers surveyed were members of the National Board for Professional Teaching Standards Network Advisory Committee, the Southeastern Virginia NBCT Network, and the electronic mailing lists of the National Teacher Forum and the Virginia Teacher Forum.

# References

Ingersoll, R. (2003). *Is there really a teacher shortage?* Philadelphia: University of Pennsylvania, Consortium for Policy Research in Education.

Institute for Educational Leadership. (2001). *Leadership for student learning: Redefining the teacher as leader.* Washington, DC: Author.

Katzenmeyer, M., & Moller, G. (2001). *Awakening the sleeping giant: Leadership development for teachers.* Thousand Oaks, CA: Corwin Press.

Marvel, J., Lyter, D. M., Strizek, G. A., & Morton, B. A. (2006). *Teacher attrition and mobility: 2004–2005 teacher follow-up survey* (NCES 2007–307). Washington, DC: U.S. Government Printing Office.

O'Hair, M., & O'Dell, S. (1995). *Educating teachers for leadership and change.* Thousand Oaks, CA: Corwin Press.

# CHAPTER EIGHTEEN

# The Search for Teacher Leaders

MEENA WILSON

MORE THAN 2.5 MILLION TEACHERS IN 15,500 SCHOOL DISTRICTS ACROSS THE COUNTRY STRIVE to develop the skills, attitudes, and knowledge of young people.[1] The quality of their work determines the future well-being and economic welfare of a generation of Americans. Education can make a difference.

The general assessment, though, seems to be that education is not making enough of a difference. *Why do students not achieve as they should?* This tough issue has resisted glib policy solutions and thereby has created a window of opportunity for teacher leaders.

## Sketching the Picture

Do teacher leaders exist? Who are they? How do they think, feel, and behave? How do they show leadership? Do they have any impact on the system? I began my search for teacher leaders by asking more than 400 teachers at all six high schools in one school district to nominate teachers that they regarded as leaders. Despite their difficulty with my request, the reasons listed (by more than 100 teachers) for nominating a colleague, were remarkably consistent.

Followers sketch this picture of their leaders:

- They are hard-working and highly involved with curricular and instructional innovation.
- Their creativity is demonstrated by their power to motivate students from a wide range of backgrounds and abilities.
- They are gregarious and make themselves available to other teachers as a resource or an advocate.
- They energetically sponsor extra-curricular activities for young people.

These responses were cursory answers to a simple question: Who is a teacher leader? To give the portrait more detail, I used a reputational nomination procedure to elect 13 of 355 teachers for intensive interviews. With demographic data from these interviewees, a fuller picture of teacher leaders emerges. A typical leader is 42 and has taught for 18 years, at the same school for almost 13 years. More than half of them have served as formal leaders, either as department chair for an average of 11 years and/or as a committed representative of the teachers' union for at least 3 years. They usually hold a master's degree.

How do these men and women compare with leaders from other fields—for example, business? Choosing a template to understand and assess the leadership ability of these teachers was not easy. Theories about leadership are numerous, and transcribed interviews yielded 560 pages of description. I eventually selected the widely disseminated Kouzes and Posner (1990) model as the best tool for understanding teacher leadership.

In *The Leadership Challenge: How to Get Extraordinary Things Done in Organizations*, Kouzes and Posner describe the leadership behaviors of 1,300 middle and senior managers in private and public sector organizations across the country.[2] Briefly, leaders *challenge the process* because they are risk-takers who capitalize on opportunities. As idealists who communicate expressively, they *inspire a shared vision*. Since they like teamwork and instinctively nurture the talent and energy of colleagues, leaders *enable others to act*. Leaders are role-models and planners who *model the way*. By serving as coaches and cheerleaders, they *encourage the heart*.

Interviewees candidly shared thoughts and feelings, making it possible to understand their strengths and limitations as leaders. Let me share the evidence and the exploratory understanding I gained about teacher leadership.

## Seekers of Challenges and Growth

First, in common with other leaders, teacher leaders seek challenge, change, and growth. Here are some of their comments:

> Today was something different. We worked on a grant-writing project and are submitting a building grant proposal. We are so excited about it that we can hardly see straight.

> I think one ought to like what one is doing, so I expend a lot of energy creating situations that I will like. I don't want to get stagnant.

> I had so much fun learning about 9th graders. I see so many neat and exciting things that I can do, things that if I were a 9th grader would really interest me.

The teacher leaders I spoke with go out of their way to find innovative, exciting programs, both for the benefit of their students as well as themselves.

## Supporters of Colleagues

At the same time, teacher leaders feel like family: informal, reassuringly dependable, and supportive of colleagues.

My sense is that anytime you get teachers who work together talking about kids, problems, and curriculum in a supportive way, they feel better about themselves, and there is more energy. All of that has positive consequences for kids in their classrooms.

A number of us feel that one of the most significant things we ever did was arrange to have lunch together outside the faculty lounge.… It was an environment where everybody had given you permission to be elated about things that worked and cry about the things that didn't. The end result is that it created relationships that made possible a lot of sharing and encouragement to try things when you were nervous.

I created materials that we then passed out to everybody who was teaching that subject in my department. I have a personal interest in digging out information that I think may be helpful to somebody else even if I can't use it at that particular moment.

Thus, these teachers busily pursue novel opportunities but continue to be nurturing and cooperative people. Using leadership jargonese, they are risk-oriented and collaborative. Clearly, these leaders both "challenge the process" and "enable others to act."

## Role Models for Students, but Not Teachers

Third, leadership is the process of bringing forth the best from oneself and others. Unfortunately, these teachers do not as yet seem to lead colleagues. However, the Kouzes and Posner model shows they are potent leaders of students.

Around here I have a reputation of working hard and pushing the kids hard.…Some people just hold kids' hands.

I like to be able to love my students. When I get letters from them after they have graduated or when they come back to see me and tell me that what we did in class was right and that it worked for them, that's the kind of positive stroke that I think teaching is all about.

They'll come in early and sit down, and they won't look at you, but they just want strokes. Their parents don't ever talk to them. Ever. Their parents ask you questions like, "Who is my son? Who does he go around with? What's he like? What does he do?"

I would caution student teachers always to be flexible with the kids, but not to leave them with no structure, because many times we are the only structure, the only model, these kids have.

In the eyes of their colleagues, leadership skill with students is what uniquely qualifies some teachers as leaders in their schools. Ironically, teacher leaders do not see that simply by "walking their talk," they inspire and influence others. They fail to understand that role modeling is a powerful form of leading.

I don't know that we are leaders, because we are not out championing any cause. We don't do what we do for recognition. We are here because we enjoy teaching, and we like to improve the quality of our teaching and help kids. I think because we do these things, people notice us.

I think of him as a master teacher, and that is how he gets his influence…[by] modeling what an excellent teacher should be as far as relationships with students and content. His leadership hasn't been with anything he has done outside the classroom.

This lack of understanding of how they can play a leadership role, just by "modeling the way," has some unfortunate consequences. As committed and competent professionals, teacher leaders could invigorate their schools. But if they do not recognize that role models are critical to school improvement, their leadership potential is aborted.

## Coaches and Cheerleaders

Fourth, coaching and cheerleading "encourage the heart" of workers in any organization.

Historically, teachers have not coached other teachers, but the following comments are telling in their portrayal of the need for, and the potential efficacy of, peer-coaching.

> When I am God of Education, for at least two years, nobody will be in a classroom by themselves.

> I am excited about mentoring because it is a support system for new people who sometimes feel they have just been thrown to the wolves. That is such a terrible thing to have happen to somebody who is full of new ideas, and there is nobody out there to bounce ideas off or vent frustrations on.

> When we first started peer-coaching, the people who came forward weren't the new teachers. It was the person with 18 or 20 years in who came to the first meeting and said, "What can I do?" "If I could do this, I could do a better job." They were the ones who…were looking for something to re-energize their life and their teaching.

> Peer-coaching gave teachers the power to try things, to seek out innovation, to find out about what was going on in other places.

Yes, committed and competent professionals can invigorate their schools when they choose, and are formally chosen, to be role models, coaches, and cheerleaders. The question remains: Is their ability to "model the way" and "encourage the heart" likely to be put to systematic use in any school district?

## What About a Shared Vision?

One leadership behavior that they did not demonstrate was "envisioning a unique and ideal future." These teachers seemed to register dreams too hazy to shape an ideal school. Though committed to idealistic personal goals, they were tentative about schoolwide goals. While recognizing that a leader is "a strong personality who has some sense of where she is going and what she wants to do," only two asserted that teachers are entitled to express "an idea of what they want the school to be like, and a willingness to work toward that, rather than just being in the environment and existing and coping with it."

Some themes emerged: Teacher leaders want schools to be communities with more resources for instruction and greater influence and control for teachers. However, these ideas were not expressed persuasively enough to "inspire a shared vision."

A useful picture of teacher leaders had taken form. This picture had light and dark aspects and areas of gray as well. Yet other goals of the study were unmet. Leaders or not, did these teachers have an impact on their high schools? Did their initiative win them recognition and influence? How was their influence demonstrated in interactions with colleagues? Was the teacher's exercise of leadership supported by the organizational culture of their school? What part could teacher leaders play in the drama of school reform?

## The Costs of Playing by the Rules

The findings of the next phase of this study are disconcerting. The very capabilities that distinguish teacher leaders from others in the high school environment—risk-taking, collaboration, and role modeling—produce tensions between them and colleagues.

Administrators, for example, often prefer to avoid risks. Interviewees typically observed that:

> It's not what the kids learn that matters to them; it is whether the boat is rocking or not.

> Sometimes we have different missions in schools. As an administrator, one of your missions is order and discipline. That is important within the building, and that is a primary mission for them. If they are not doing that job, nothing else works. If you have multiple missions, at times they are going to conflict with one another.

These comments cut to the heart of the conflict between the administrative need to maintain order and risk-taking attitudes that naturally generate some disorder.

Nevertheless, most of these teacher leaders choose a non-adversarial stance toward principals, and their credibility as innovators usually enables them to push their own priorities. Teacher leaders accept that administrators have different agendas, and they adjust by adopting a live-and-let-live attitude.

Also, collaboration between administrators and teachers is a new rule of the game. Traditionally, administrators have not expected to be influenced by teachers. Teacher leaders, in general, find this restrictive attitude toward teacher initiative to be distasteful. For example:

> I'm not saying that all administrators come with a chip on their shoulder ready to do their thing. It's just that they have been trained to say, "This is what we are going to do," trained to not ask teachers, to not accept any kind of direction from teachers.

Teacher leaders prefer to cooperate with others in order to create learning options for their students, themselves, and others. However, administrators, by habit, seem averse to teamwork that disregards rank-based authority. Teacher leaders do not like this traditional attitude but pragmatically choose to ignore the impasse.

Finally, teacher leaders often are dismayed by the behavior of colleagues who don't seem to want the best for students. Leaders are committed to student welfare. They like young people and willingly devote tremendous time and energy to students as individuals; they focus on students first and subject matter second. As they put it:

> We have teachers who don't like kids. They don't get from behind their desks…they have to have authority; they have an "us vs. them" mentality. They talk about "bad kids" and how they are going to take them on.

Too many high school teachers are content-oriented instead of kid- and process-oriented.

Yet, they choose not to censure less-committed colleagues, partly because they believe that "professionalism" requires the freedom to choose the ends and the means you wish to adopt for your classroom.

So, just as school-culture norms prevent teacher leaders from demanding public air-time for their risky teaching ideas and recognition for their collaborative style, professional norms restrain them from openly criticizing teachers whose commitment to students is low. Given these cultural and professional norms, "teacher leadership" sounds hollow. When a teacher leader does not audaciously insist on the best for all young people, is he or she really a leader?

## Teacher Leadership: A Feminine Paradigm?

Thus, this research indicates that the school culture, as perceived by these teachers, does not reward (and perhaps obstructs) risk-taking, collaboration, and role-modeling. In fact, leadership traits such as initiative, an instinct for teamwork, and commitment actually can create stress for teacher leaders in their relationships with colleagues.

Despite frustration, teacher leaders manage conflict, but not by becoming confrontational. On the contrary, they prefer persuasion. Their choice of strategies seems to demonstrate nontraditional ideas about whether leaders are important and how change occurs. Many of these teachers voiced the following thoughts:

- The label of "leader" sets a person apart from peers and diminishes his or her ability to bring about change.
- Leadership is a role played by one person in a group. The role seduces the leader into believing that he or she is the mouthpiece of the group. Given a strong group of competent people, a leader may not be necessary.
- Secondary teachers value their autonomy and do not wish to lead or be led.
- As a group, teachers should exercise more control over the initiation and implementation of change.
- Participatory decision making is critical. Any teacher who wishes to participate in a particular decision should be encouraged to do so.

What do such statements suggest? Maybe these teachers misunderstand the nature of leadership. Or conceivably, as individuals, they are reluctant to give up their enjoyment of good teaching for the uncertain satisfaction of good leading. Certainly, not one interviewee aspired to become an administrator.

A third supposition is that if the behaviors and attitudes commonly regarded as demonstrating leadership are not acceptable to these teachers, perhaps they prefer a style of leading that is not as yet prevalent. Notably, a majority did not consider themselves leaders, despite their influence on colleagues and appointment to leadership positions. Could it be that lacking an alternate set of rules for playing the leadership game, they choose to bow out of the leadership arena?

Their preferences are theoretically and practically significant. Rosener differentiates between so-called masculine and feminine styles of leading.[3] The masculine style uses structural power, which is based on authority associated with position, title, and the ability to reward and punish. The feminine style relies on personal power, which is based on charisma, work record, and contacts. Masculine versus feminine styles of leading also are labeled transactional versus transformational.

Additionally, these teachers prefer shared leadership, with roles and tasks distributed among members of a group. Individuals move in and out of membership. Perchance, these teachers' hazy notions of leadership hint at a dynamic organizational form for which an organizational chart does not as yet exist. Can this organizational form be described (for want of better terminology) as feminine rather than masculine? Unfortunately, not enough information is available to warrant such generalizations.

## Dilemmas and Dreams

Paradoxically, though the teachers described here are highly proficient leaders of their students and themselves, in their work with colleagues they appear to be reluctant leaders who exercise incomplete leadership. Their remarks illustrate how their influence in the high school is curtailed by school-culture and professional norms as well as self-imposed limits. For example, they neither accept nor fulfill their leadership role in the school due to prevalent misconceptions about professionalism and leadership. To be fair, though, they seem to reject the leader's job because they like neither the structure that props up leaders, nor the style the role requires.

For me, my research led to some answers but raised an even bigger question: Can "teacher leadership" be more than a semi-fulfilled potential? I hope so. I hope the school of the future will be a formal but nonhierarchical system that nourishes informal arteries of influence, a place where the pulse and rhythm of good teaching and learning are driven by the capabilities of teacher leaders. It seems to me that only then will the potential contribution of these teachers to their schools be realized. Only then will we genuinely begin the work of fashioning school environments within which it is possible for every student to achieve.

## Notes

1. *Newsweek* (Fall/Winter 1990), special issue entitled "The Future Is Now."
2. J.M. Kouzes and B.Z. Posner (1990), *The Leadership Challenge: How to Get Extraordinary Things Done in Organizations*, (San Francisco: Jossey-Bass).
3. J.B. Rosener (June 1990), *Leadership Study: International Women's Forum* (available from the Graduate School of Management, University of California, Irvine).

# CHAPTER NINETEEN

# Inch by Inch, Row by Row

## Growing Capacity for Teacher Leadership

MARY JEAN RONAN HERZOG & EMILY BRUMLEY ABERNATHY

TEACHER LEADERSHIP HAS FLOURISHED IN THE PAST 15 YEARS. THERE HAVE ALWAYS BEEN teachers who are leaders, but the abundance and growth in the attention to the specific term *teacher leadership* indicate that it has moved from concept to praxis. A library search for books on "teacher leadership" resulted in a long list (554) of related titles, but the first one with "teacher leader" in the title was Bolman's 1994, *Becoming a Teacher Leader: From Isolation to Collaboration*. The number of related links that occur from broad internet searches of "teacher leader" is rather astounding. For example, Google Scholar = 7000+; Google = 7,300,000; Google Advanced Search = 108,000; Amazon.com = 1200+; Education Week, 2009–2010 = 200. Yes, teacher leadership is out there, and it is huge and growing, with more publications in the recent past than in its early days in the mid-1990s.

## Precursors to Teacher Leadership

Before teacher leadership became a part of the education lexicon, there were precursors. John Dewey (1903) linked democracy itself with the role of the teacher. He criticized the schools for the "autocratic principle" of placing the decisions in the hands, first in "…a body of men who are outside the school system itself, who have not necessarily any expert knowledge of education . . ." to "…the transfer of authority to the school superintendent . . .," thus leaving the teacher out of the process, even so far as to make curriculum decisions and select textbooks. More than one hundred years ago, Dewey argued for deeper and more authentic involvement of teachers in making school policies and practices. He said, "…until the public-school system is organized in such a way that every teacher has some regular and representative way in which he or she can register judgment upon matters of educational importance, with the assurance that this judgment will somehow affect the school system, the assertion that the present system is not, from the internal standpoint, democratic seems to be justified" (1903, p. 195).

Through the twentieth century, the role of the teacher has been a continual source of discussion, but in practice, it has generally been relegated to a traditional role in an authoritarian institution, or as Apple (1986) described it, teacher-as-technician. From the 1980s to the present, two parallel forces have been in operation. The accountability and standards movements have pressured teachers to focus on test scores, keeping teachers firmly stationed in the technician camp. At the same time, there have been considerable efforts to change the traditional paradigm and transform teacher work to active participation in the governance of democratically structured schools. Both of these opposing forces continue to vie for the top. Teacher empowerment was around for a while, but it had a slightly militant connotation and located teachers on the opposite side of the fence from their administrators. Master teacher, on the other hand, put teachers in the same camp as administrators, but it had a hierarchal connotation raising them above regular teachers. Among the efforts to remake teachers in a more participatory, radical light were several "teacher as" models, for example, "teacher-as...-transformative leader, -researcher, -reflective decision-maker, -transformative intellectual, -curriculum planner..." (See theories on teacher roles in Connelly & Clandinin, 1988; Cochran-Smith & Lytle, 1990; Cochran-Smith & Lytle, 1999; Giroux, 1988; Kincheloe, 1991.) The teacher as researcher theory has more recently evolved into practitioner research in the work of Cochran-Smith and Lytle (2009) where they develop the theory of "inquiry as stance."

The concept of the teacher leader, on the other hand, emerged in the 1990s, at a time when the notion of servant leader, credited to Robert Greenleaf's (1977) essay, was popular in universities. Teacher leader, within the servant context was a more accommodating and collaborative, less threatening idea than the earlier and continuing iterations from teacher empowerment to teacher as intellectual researcher. This observation is not meant to suggest that teacher leadership promotes teachers as servants, but the halo surrounding servant leader has made teacher leader a more acceptable moniker. In spite of the incredible numbers of books written, studies conducted, and sheer depth of work completed in the last three decades, both in the academy and in the schools, for the most part, teachers' roles have changed very little.

## Teacher Leader Staying Power

Why does teacher leadership have traction while so many other teacher roles have never gained a foothold? Will it have staying power and make a lasting impact resulting in structural change in the teaching profession? Or will the establishment endorsement turn it into one more mandate, co-opted by the departments in charge?

Teacher leadership may have reached a tipping point commonly used in schools and teacher preparation. Teacher leadership seems to be a phenomenon that started small, with articles and books and groups of teachers and other educators chatting about it, and it has spread through grassroots efforts, networks, tons of articles and, the Internet. It was not originally mandated by the authorities. Like so many educational bandwagons, it did not explode like wildfire, catch on quickly, rise, fall, and fizzle out. Gayle Moller, co-author of a widely used book on teacher leadership, said in a recent interview with the Teacher Leader Network (TLN, 2009) that it was virtually an unknown concept in 1996 when the first edition of *Awakening the Sleeping Giant* (Katzenmeyer & Moller, 1996) was published. Despite its growing maturity and popularity, teacher leaders are not in every school, nor has a differentiated professional scale been universally embraced. "Distributed leadership" is commonly discussed today, but it cannot yet be said that the structure of school staffing has truly changed. However, perhaps, we are entering a new stage in the teaching profession in which teacher leadership will become a norm and the schools will be laboratories for democratic practices. Perhaps teacher leadership will have staying power.

# Preparing Teacher Leaders

The literature in this reader reflects a high level of agreement on the need, meanings, definitions, roles, and preparation of teacher leaders. If teacher leadership is to have that staying power, it will have to become part of the established curriculum in teacher preparation programs and state education departments. Several states have passed legislation adding a teacher leader endorsement to the standard teaching license (National Association of State Boards of Education (NASBE, n.d.). Georgia, Illinois, and Louisiana have been offering teacher leader endorsements for several years. The "Five State Teacher Leadership Consortium" is a partnership for sharing related curriculum and policy among Alabama, Delaware, Kansas, Kentucky, and Ohio. Maryland and Massachusetts have created new roles for teacher leaders. Generally, eligibility for preparation programs leading to a teacher leader endorsement is for experienced teachers, and in some states, it comes as an addition to a master's degree. In North Carolina, teacher leadership has become a required standard for all beginning and advanced teacher preparation programs (North Carolina Professional Teaching Standards Commission [NCPTSC], 2007). In fact, teacher evaluation in North Carolina has changed from the decades-old, standard, behaviorist TPAI-based (Teacher Performance Appraisal Instrument) criteria to one heavily laden with teacher leadership factors. The first category of the rubric is teacher leadership, and *all* teachers are expected to be leaders in their classrooms, schools, and profession. (See the NC teacher evaluation rubric at http://www.ncptsc.org/Teacher%20Evaluation%20Booklet%20%20Fill%20In%20Forms.pdf.) How can every teacher possibly be a leader? That is a tall order, and it runs the risk of getting watered down so much that it becomes just another meaningless phrase. It may end up like the idea "diversity" which is everywhere in education standards and has become just another word. Teacher leaders in the schools and educators preparing new teachers have to work to keep it alive and avoid its becoming nothing more than a semantic change.

Charlotte Danielson's (2007) essay, "The Many Faces of Leadership," in which she categorized teachers into two broad camps, the formal and the informal teacher leaders, provides a lens for preparing teacher leaders for new roles. The formal leaders are in official positions such as department head and instructional coach, while the informal leaders "emerge spontaneously and organically from the teacher ranks....They take the initiative" (p. 16). Teacher leadership, she said may take place within a department or team, across the school, or beyond the school. Both the formal and informal leaders have often risen to their positions without any training in leadership skills. They learned on the job, through trial and error. Intuitive leaders can be effective, but they could be more successful with leadership training in facilitating group problem solving, team building, effecting school change, and curriculum development. With the growing number of states and universities developing programs for teacher leader endorsements, the need for high quality preparation is urgent.

Our own institution, Western Carolina University, was an early adopter of teacher leadership. When Gayle Moller joined the faculty in 1998, we established a course entitled "Teacher Leader" and made it a requirement for the Master's programs in teaching. For several years, Master's students have been learning teacher leadership practices, including developing a plan for solving a school-wide problem. It has become such an established part of the curriculum that, when all the teaching programs were revised, teacher leadership became part of the undergraduate coursework and the Master's programs developed two courses, an introductory and an advanced teacher leadership course. The graduate students in the Master of Arts in Teaching (MAT) program, an alternative path to teaching for college graduates, work alongside experienced teachers in the Master of Arts in Education (MAEd) program to develop their action plan. The growing network of teachers working in teacher leadership positions in the schools has a positive influence on the MAT internships, creating a mentoring, nurturing climate for emerging teacher leaders.

In the next section of this chapter, we introduce Emily and her reflections on teacher leadership through her practicum and internship experiences. She is a beginning teacher who has the capacity to learn to become a teacher leader. In her internship, she worked with teachers, two of whom were models of teacher leadership, and she reflects on her observations and interactions with them.

## Emily: A Potential Teacher Leader

*Emily is a graduate student working on her Master of Arts in Teaching. She graduated from a liberal arts college with a bachelor's degree in English, and she decided that she wanted to become a teacher. She studied Teacher Leadership in the Master's program, and at the end of the program now, she reflects on her experience as an intern in a public high school in the region.*

I began my internship during my fourth semester of graduate school in the MAT with a concentration in English. One thing courses cannot prepare you for, no matter how well designed, is the lives of your students and the reality of their community. The school is the lowest performing school with the highest percentage of free and reduced lunch in a large, rural county. The school, with a student population of approximately 1,300, had a significant gang presence, and gang-related violence was not uncommon. The home environment most often accompanying this economic situation is one of low literacy and little parent involvement in their children's educations. Many parents were so busy trying to provide food and shelter that education took a necessary backseat. In the worst cases parents had significant economic, social, and psychological problems of their own. The high dropout rate for the high school was a major concern and the focus of much attention within the school and the community.

The picture I have painted of this rural high school, while certainly not ideal, is not at all uncommon. What was unique about this school, which I will now refer to as Rural Mountain High, was its diversity. Despite its rural location, RMHS had a large diverse student body in a predominantly white county. Latinos, Eastern Europeans, and African Americans made up a large portion of the school. Regardless of a widespread lack of interest in formal education, the students had uncanny survival skills. While middle-class students are generally oriented toward some form of higher education, most students at RMHS did not have college on their radar.

What fascinated me most about the students I got to know was not how much they hated school, but how much they liked it. A safe place, with responsible adults, food, friends, games, sports, and structure made school a refuge. However, class work and learning were not necessarily a high priority. The teachers I met during my internship spent significant time and effort trying to motivate the students to become invested in their own education. Teachers used both rewards and carefully structured assignments guaranteed to result in success on some level with any effort on behalf of the learner.

Clearly, the student body of RMHS requires smart, dedicated teachers with a special set of skills for responding to their students' needs. During my internship, there were two teachers who stood out as particularly successful teacher leaders in this challenging environment: Linda Black and Daniel Taylor (names have been changed) were both teacher leaders, but they went about their teaching and leadership activities very differently. Mr. Taylor was my host teacher, providing me with plenty of opportunity to observe his teaching style. Both Linda and Daniel had huge success with their students, across all diversity. Linda was a "formal leader" according to Danielson's (2007) model. She was department chair, a member of several school committees, and a teacher organization, and she was pursuing a master's degree in teaching with technology. Daniel, who emerged from the ranks as an "informal leader" was, I believe, on every school committee and chair of several, including the Graduation Initiative Committee. In addition, he was pursuing his National Board Certification and was also a member of a teacher organization.

As teacher leaders, Linda and Daniel actively sought opportunities to develop school programs that addressed student needs and provided useful support. The right way to educate cannot be mandated by federal, state, or local government. Teacher leaders seek to identify community, school, and individual students' needs and then implement programs, strategies, and support structures to meet those needs. One example of this is the graduation initiative committee. A local publication wrote an "exposé" on Rural Mountain High School, naming it a "dropout factory" and to be sure, the dropout rate at RMHS was the highest in the county. In the aftermath of the article, which hurt morale and resulted in a massive lack of faith in the school from the students and community, the Graduation Initiative Committee was formed. It sought to identify students at risk for dropping out as early as possible and develop and cultivate a support network for those students. The faculty members and the school counselors involved in the support network took time to seek the students out and inquire about their well-being. The committee even went so far as to find out which teachers had been influential in the individual student's life as far back as elementary school and to get those educators involved in supporting the student's academic success. Daniel helped form this committee while Linda was a member. The committee's success was obvious and came about quickly; the graduation rate improved dramatically.

Teacher leaders, like Linda and Daniel, are visible throughout the school, on action committees and organizations, but their greatest achievements in leadership are witnessed by their students behind the doors of their classrooms. Soft spoken and earnest, Linda had her classroom arranged in collaborative groups of four desks facing each other. She followed the state-recommended division of instruction where instructional time is divided between self-selected reading, guided practice, teacher-led reading, and independent student work. Ms. Black had books on shelves surrounding her classroom and had an in-class library system. Essential questions for daily lessons, vocabulary, and literary terms, along with assignments, were clearly visible on her dry erase board. Linda kept manipulative items and a cascading water timer (a plastic rectangle with colored oil inside—when turned upside down the beads are forced through a sort of maze and turn a water wheel as they collect at the bottom) for students with attention deficit disorders and more kinetic learning styles. She did not have discipline problems. Every lesson included technology. She signed up for the computer lab for every class virtually every day. Most lessons included video clips, projected images, or audio files. As a teacher pursuing a Master's in Teaching with Technology, she certainly incorporated and applied her graduate learning into her high school classroom. Linda did not raise her voice; she very rarely had discipline referrals; her students were awake and on task, and two or three could always be found in her room during her planning period or after school. While Linda was not outspoken, she followed the school, county, district, and state rules explicitly, and did not seek leadership positions within the school; she was, nevertheless, a prime example of a teacher leader.

Linda was the chair of the English Department simply because she was asked, and though she was a member of the Graduation Initiative Committee and attended every meeting, she was not outspoken. However, I found it encouraging and inspiring that a teacher could follow the rules with such precision and still have meaningful, fulfilling lessons and classes while utilizing and applying the innovative knowledge and techniques acquired in graduate school. Even though Linda was not my host teacher, her door and file cabinets were always open to me. The previous year, she and a history teacher co-developed an AP course based on writing across the curriculum with English and history. They co-taught lectures, had common assessments and assignments, and from all accounts, they and their students greatly benefited and enjoyed the experience of what must have been a very challenging course. Linda is a perfect example of a teacher leader: a developing professional seeking higher education and content pedagogy, a mentor for new teachers, a curriculum innovator, and a holder of school office. However, her leadership style was totally unassuming. Other teachers in the school may not even know how much and how deeply she contributes to student success and a positive school climate.

The two traits Daniel and Linda had in common were a dedication to their students and the fact that they were both teacher leaders; the similarities stop there. While Linda was quiet and unassuming, Daniel was an extrovert. He had a larger than life personality, was outspoken at meetings, the lunch table, and school pep rallies. For pep rallies he would don a costume and wig and perform antics around the gym, stirring up the crowd. In spite of his self-described outlandish behavior at pep rallies and his constant joking, he was on virtually every committee or council, usually by invitation of the administration. He was involved in the politics of the school with the community, was pursuing his National Board Certification, and took on interns every other semester. Unlike Linda, Daniel was a very visible leader in the school; he was continuously asked to make up councils, initiatives, and committees because he continuously said "yes." Daniel was a formal teacher leader, like some described by Danielson (2007): he held offices throughout the school and did not hesitate to offer his insight or opinion on any matter that came into his sphere. Sometimes teachers resent those who become leaders because of the attention they get, but for the most part, the teachers I observed seemed happy the department was being represented by teachers like Daniel and Linda, and they were not the ones sacrificing their afternoons.

Behind the closed doors of the classroom, Daniel began each lesson with a joke, riddle, or amusing story. He liked to begin by putting students at ease and gaining their cooperation through humor. It was rumored that students with greater academic challenges were placed in his classrooms because they tended to be more successful in a more relaxed environment. I don't know that I can speak to the level of challenge these students experienced, but I can speak to the fact that he maintained discipline by allowing significant freedom and that what he asked his students to do, they did. I did not see him struggle to wring work out of a reluctant class; his students seemed to understand the implicit reciprocal agreement: I give you freedom, you give me cooperation. Daniel's students loved him; they loved his class, and they did work. Daniel noticed details about his students that needed outside involvement. While I was teaching, he would observe the class and, once class ended, would set up counseling appointments, eye exam appointments, and make phone calls to parents. To an untrained eye, Daniel appeared casual and relaxed, but he was extremely vigilant in the attention he paid to the well-being of his students.

Rural Mountain High School is a perfect environment for teacher leaders to blossom and flourish. The administration, particularly the principal, openly encouraged teachers to become involved in school leadership and made it known that he had an ear for new ideas. In faculty meetings he would propose issues and ask for potential solutions from his faculty. I witnessed many teacher-led initiatives across the school from food drives to a teacher committee charged with researching and implementing a new discipline model for the entire school. It was not at all uncommon for teachers to stay after school for make-up work and extra help. As an intern, I found doors, ears, and file cabinets open to me in every direction, even across departments. Observing such real, and such different, teacher leaders as Daniel and Linda, provided teacher leadership models for me. Although I will focus on my students and classroom when I get my first teaching job, I will gradually look for opportunities to be involved in school-wide initiatives. I see teacher leadership in my future.

As the teacher leader movement continues to grow, change may finally come to the teaching profession. It is long past time for teachers to have professional opportunities with differentiated staffing and for schools to have a more equitable distribution of leadership. How many times and for how many decades must it be said that teachers have few opportunities for advancement other than to quit teaching and become administrators? Informal teacher leaders will continue to emerge, but all teachers should have explicit opportunities for promotion within the teaching profession. In particular, teacher leaders should be prepared, like Linda and Daniel, to work with their colleagues, to help solve classroom and school problems, and to nurture and mentor interns and new teachers. In addition, they should be able to do this professional work within their school day, teaching part of the time, and leading during the rest of the day. New teachers, like Emily, will, hopefully, be the beneficiaries of the transformation of the teaching profession so that teachers have, as Dewey argued more than 100 years ago, "deeper and more authentic involvement in making school policies and practices" (1903, p. 195) and can truly advance without having to give up what they are at heart: teachers.

## References

Apple, M. (1986). *Teachers and texts: A political economy of class and gender relations in education.* New York, NY: Routledge and Kegan Paul.

Bolman, L. G. (1994). *Becoming a teacher leader: From isolation to collaboration.* Thousand Oaks, CA: Corwin Press.

Cochran-Smith, M., & Lytle, S. L. (1990). Research on teaching and teacher research: The issues that divide. *Educational Researcher, 19*(2), 2–11.

Cochran-Smith, M., & Lytle, S. L. (1999). The teacher research movement: A decade later. *Educational Researcher, 28* (7), 15–25.

Cochran-Smith, M., & Lytle, S. (2009). *Inquiry as stance: Practitioner research in the next generation.* New York, NY: Teachers College Press.

Connelly, F. M. & Clandinin, D. J. (1988). *Teachers as curriculum planners: Narratives of experience.* New York, NY: Teachers College Press.

Danielson, C. (September, 2007). The many faces of leadership. *Educational Leadership, 65*(1) 14–19.

Dewey, J. (1903). Democracy in education. *The Elementary School Journal, 4*, 193–204.

Giroux, H. A. (1988). *Teachers as intellectuals: Toward a critical pedagogy of learning.* Granby, MA: Bergin & Garvey.

Greenleaf, R. K. (1977). *Servant leadership: A journey into the nature of legitimate power and greatness.* New York, NY: Paulist Press.

Kincheloe, J. L. (1991). *Teachers as researchers: Qualitative inquiry as a path to empowerment.* New York, NY: Falmer Press.

National Association of State Boards of Education. (n.d.). Teacher leadership: State actions. Retrieved from http://www.nasbe.org/leadership/leadership-continuum/teacher-leadership/state-actions

North Carolina Professional Teaching Standards Commission. (2007). North Carolina Professional Teaching Standards. Retrieved from http://www.ncptsc.org/Final%20Standards%20Document.pdf

Teacher Leader Network. (2009). Teacher leadership 3.0—An interview with Gayle Moller. Retrieved from http://teacherleaders.typepad.com/tln_teacher_voices/2009/07/teacher-leadership-30-an-interview-with-gayle-moller.html

# CHAPTER TWENTY

# Educating School Leaders for Social Justice

NELDA CAMBRON-MCCABE & MARTHA M. MCCARTHY

GRAVE CONCERNS EXIST ABOUT LEADERSHIP PREPARATION PROGRAMS' LACK OF RELEVANCE IN preparing school leaders to address the crisis conditions facing many children and schools in this country. As the efficacy of existing preparation programs is questioned, specific concerns also are raised about the extent to which social justice issues are being considered in the development of new approaches and standards for preparing leaders. Although policy makers express a concern for creating more just, equitable schools, new standards and licensure requirements do not explicitly encompass social justice concerns (Marshall, 2001; Oliva, 2001).

The prevalence of social justice language in educational settings and scholarship portends a new movement with as many meanings as actors on the scene. This visibility is cause for celebration as well as unease. With popular use, both liberals and conservatives have embraced the term social justice to rationalize similar as well as polar opposite strategies. In the policy arena, educational accountability policies tend to construct the meaning of social justice in narrow market-based terms that attempt to remedy the so-called deficits students from diverse backgrounds bring to school (Marshall & Parker, 2009). When policy makers are asked to identify social justice elements in their states, they point to high academic standards and stringent assessment strategies (Cambron-McCabe, 2009; Marshall & McCarthy, 2002). Consequently, elimination of the achievement gap between Caucasian students and students of color has become the signifier for the political commitment to fairness and equal educational opportunity. The by-product of this policy discourse of accountability, standards, and quality is safe language that eschews more controversial confrontations about race, class, gender, sexual orientation, and systemic inequities (Cambron-McCabe, 2009). In this climate, school administrators desiring to create inclusive, just schools find themselves constrained by rules, regulations, and state controls (Foster, 2004).

Within a social justice context, school leaders are being called on to take up the role of transformative intellectuals, public intellectuals, or critical intellectuals—that is, individuals who engage in critical analysis of conditions that have perpetuated historical inequities in schools and who work to change institutional structures and culture (Burrello, Lashley, & Beatty, 2001; Dantley & Tillman, 2009; Foster, 2004; Giroux, 1997). But traditional leadership preparation programs and licensure requirements give only token consideration to social justice concerns (Marshall, 2004). In this chapter we examine the emerging social justice discourse in the educational administration field and discuss its implications for reconceptualizing preparation programs for more just schooling. We begin by delineating the multiple dimensions of social justice leadership, particularly noting its broad construction not only as the identification of institutional and societal inequities affecting race, gender, sexual orientation, and disability but also as the assumption of an activist role for school and social change. Next, we explore several issues that are significant in preparing school leaders for social justice critique and activism. We conclude with a discussion of the implications for educational administration faculties and programs.

## An Emergent Social Justice Discourse

Social justice scholarship and conversations have become prominent in leadership journals and conferences. Momentum intensified in the educational administration field in 1999 when 140 scholars convened by Catherine Marshall organized as Leadership for Social Justice. These scholars targeted their research and practice on creating an understanding and capacity to do social justice work. An impressive body of work has amassed during 4 years that gives educational administration programs grounding to articulate more clearly what social justice means and how the field might move these ideas into the practice of leadership.[1]

Social justice is informed by multidisciplinary inquiry that struggles to accommodate distinct ontological and epistemological foundations. Tensions arise as some perspectives are validated and others are excluded. In creating a new social justice discourse for leadership, we argue that educational administration scholars must engage in an ongoing critical dialogue drawing on diverse theoretical perspectives. Although structural-functional and positivist research paradigms continue to influence inquiry in educational administration, alternative social justice perspectives have emerged under the banners of multicultural leadership, feminist leadership, critical African American and Latino leadership traditions, and so on (Dantley, 2003; Larson & Murtadha, 2002; Lopez, 2003). These critiques move us from merely an examination and naming of inequities to intentional action to make radical, fundamental changes in societal structures, including schools.

Social justice scholarship in educational leadership exhibits some broad, common themes. Scholars emphasize moral values, justice, respect, care, and equity; always in the forefront is a consciousness about the impact of race, class, gender, sexual orientation, and disability on schools and students' learning (Dantley & Tillman, 2009).[2] Foster's (1986) early work in critical theory echoes through this emerging social justice discourse. The crucial questions for Foster involved what ends are being pursued, whom do they benefit, and whom do they harm. The unmasking of the distortions around us, however, was only the beginning of his critique. He maintained that leadership must be critically educative: "It can not only look at the conditions in which we live, but it also must decide how to change them" (Foster, 1986, p. 185). This call for activism to challenge entrenched institutional structures reproduced by the dominant culture unites a number of other scholars (Bogotch, 2002; Goldfarb & Grinberg, 2002; Grogan, 2004; Gruenewald, 2003; Marshall, 2004).

In deepening and expanding the social justice discourse, some educational leadership scholars argue that race and racism in society must become a central and integral aspect of the leadership knowledge base (Donmoyer, Imber, & Scheurich, 1995; Lopez, 2003; Parker, Deyhle, & Villanas, 1999). When race is included in preparation programs, typically the emphasis focuses on a surface level of inequitable treatment as opposed to probing the pervasive and systemic nature of racism in society (Donmoyer et al., 1995; Lopez, 2003). Critiques of racism too often lead to "decontextual- ized and deracialized political theory of conflict, yielding a sanitized view of racial politics in the United States" (Lopez, 2003, p. 77) that produces racially neutral understandings of policies and schools. New legal scholarship in critical race theory (CRT) directs attention to the invisibility of racism and through counternarratives portrays racial realities rather than the dominant privileged sto- ries (Delgado & Stefancic, 2001; Lopez, 2003; Parker et al., 1999). This scholarship adds an impor- tant dimension to the social justice discourse; CRT stresses that laws alone will not alter racism and that the values and knowledge underpinning a racially neutral construction of democracy work to maintain racism.

Other contested terrain with implications for a social justice discourse includes gender and sex- ual orientation. Today's battles in statehouses over gay marriages point to the deeply contentious issues in this arena. News reports highlight how devastating the violence and harassment can be for queer students in public schools. Courts grapple with defining rights in the absence of specific constitu- tional language. Lugg (2003) reminded the educational administration field that protecting students and educators from harassment because of gender or sexual orientation, although important, is not social justice. Drawing on queer legal theory, she attempted to illuminate legal and regulatory sys- tems that privilege and enforce heterosexuality and other forms of oppression. Again, school lead- ers and scholars are urged to take an activist stance in making deep structural issues around gender and sexual orientation explicit as they work to change them.

The emerging social justice discourse calls on school leaders to question the assumptions that drive school policies and practices to create more equitable schooling. To meet this challenge, school leadership programs must prepare new leaders to critically inquire into the taken-for-granted struc- tures and norms that often pose insurmountable barriers to many students' academic success.

## Issues Affecting Leadership for Social Justice

From our perspective, four broad issues must be carefully considered in any serious attempt to recon- ceptualize what it means to lead with a concern for social justice in today's schools. School condi- tions reveal that expectations for leaders have shifted substantially, but we continue to prepare administrators for traditional roles in traditional school settings (see Hess & Kelly, 2005). At this junc- ture, educational administration scholars can help shape radically new roles and expectations for school leaders; inequitable practices and conditions demand fundamental changes in the ways we think about school reform and leadership. Reform issues around the standards movement, selection of leaders, student achievement gap, and privatization of education may simply reinforce and tighten the pre- sent system that marginalizes many students and educators.

### The Standards Movement

Standards-based reforms create new challenges regarding both the assessment of leadership prepa- ration programs and the alignment of these programs with social justice commitments. The standards movement, accompanied by high-stakes testing, affects virtually every level of education from K-12 schooling to teacher and administrator preparation. The standards drive the curriculum, and standards-based tests are used as prerequisites to grade promotion, high school graduation, and teacher and administrator licensure. This movement has evoked substantial controversy. Some view these reforms as the best strategy to ensure that no child is left behind (see Paige, 2003). They contend that equal educational opportunities will be realized if schools are held accountable for all students achieving the standards, but others argue that these developments are hindering the creation of vibrant and intellectually challenging education programs at all levels (see Gronn, 2002). These critics assert that standards-based school reforms have replaced efforts to achieve diverse student populations.

Standards-based reforms for school leaders focus on the standards developed by the Interstate School Leaders Licensure Consortium (ISLLC). The ISLLC standards address the school leader's role in connection with developing a shared vision of learning; sustaining a school culture conducive to learning; ensuring appropriate management of school operations and resources; facilitating collaboration with families to respond to diverse needs; acting with integrity and fairness; and responding to the schools' political, social, economic, legal, and cultural context. As of 2004, about four-fifths of the states had adopted the ISLLC standards for administrative licensure or had developed their own standards based on ISLLC.

Standards for school leaders have been proposed by various professional organizations and government agencies over time, but the current standards movement, based on the ISLLC model, differs in several respects. First, these standards focus attention on the centrality of student learning as each begins with the notation that school administrators are school leaders who promote success for all students (Council of Chief State School Officers, 1996).

Second, there has been surprising agreement among educators and policy makers on the validity of the ISLLC standards. Many state policy makers view ISLLC and other standards-based reforms as the solution to problems associated with school leadership and university preparation programs (Marshall & McCarthy, 2002). National and state criteria for the accreditation of educational leadership preparation programs, including the *Standards for Advanced Programs in Educational Leadership* of the National Council for Accreditation of Teacher Education (NCATE), reflect the ISLLC standards. In fact, the Educational Leadership Constituent Council (ELCC), which includes representatives from all national practitioner organizations focusing on school leadership, has merged its standards with ISLLC and NCATE for use in accrediting leadership preparation programs. The major thrust of this consolidation is for leadership preparation program accreditation and administrative licensure to be based on performance measures in line with the ISLLC standards (Cibulka, 2004; National Policy Board for Educational Administration, 2000). By 2004, ELCC had reviewed 178 educational leadership programs, of which 137 (77%) achieved "national recognition" status (Cibulka, 2004, p. 3).

Despite the consensus among policy makers regarding the merits of standards-based education reforms, this movement also has critics (Bracey, 2000; Merrow, 2001). The very act of creating standards, noted Gronn (2002), is an inherently biased process in which preference is given to a particular perspective and other points of view are silenced. The ISLLC standards have not been universally embraced in the field of educational administration (English, 2000; Furman, 2000; Maxcy, 2000). Specifically, questions have been raised about whether the standards give sufficient attention to social justice issues such as diversity and whether they represent a negative reduction toward a single correct method (English, 2004).

Standards, of course, lack significant meaning without valid mechanisms to determine that the standards have been met. The assessments used to determine that standards are satisfied, however, do not necessarily produce fair results whether for K-12 students or for teacher and administrator licensure. For example, studies indicate that African Americans score an average of one standard deviation below Caucasians on teacher licensure tests (Hedges & Nowell, 1998; Mitchell, Robinson, Plake, & Knowles, 2001). Similarly, slightly more than 40% of the Caucasian applicants receive certification from the National Board for Professional Teaching Standards, whereas only about 11% of African American applicants are successful (Bond, 1998). These data have dramatic implications for the racial composition of public school personnel in our nation. At a time when student bodies are becoming increasingly diverse, the opposite trend may occur among public educators, partially as a result of assessment tests used as a prerequisite to licensure.

A standards-driven paper-and-pencil test is the most popular strategy used to assess that school leaders meet the ISLLC standards. Thirteen states condition administrative licensure on the passage of the School Leaders Licensure Assessment (SLLA), a performance-based assessment developed by the Education Testing Service (ETS). A number of other states are considering the adoption of the SLLA. This instrument consists of a set of vignettes to which individuals respond. The test is then evaluated by a national group of trained assessors based on predetermined criteria. In some states professional standards boards link accreditation of leadership preparation programs to how well their students perform on the SLLA. Thus, the stakes are extremely high for everyone involved.

In the near future, across most states, the successful passage of SLLA may very well become a prerequisite to administrative licensure, an exit examination in university preparation programs, and/or a criterion for program accreditation. If so, the ETS instrument will greatly influence the content and components of school leadership preparation programs. Universities will be forced to align their admissions process and curriculum with the high-stakes test. This does not necessarily mean that preparation programs will be narrowed or negatively affected if we are certain that SLLA measures what is considered essential for moral leaders who can guide schools toward becoming humane, challenging, learning-centered communities (McCarthy, 2002b).

Yet, many critics are concerned that current assessment instruments, like SLLA, do not give individuals the opportunity to demonstrate some important leadership behaviors such as tolerance, creativity, vision, and commitment to social justice (Bracey, 2000). Merrow (2001) declared that "bad tests, used to make high-stakes decisions, are the enemy of good (i.e., high) standards" (p. 653). In short, assuming the standards are appropriate (which continues to be debated), if the tests that assess whether they are met are poorly written, biased, or not aligned with the intent of the standards, the process will not be effective. Fears are voiced that reliance on SLLA and similar tests to judge both individuals and leadership preparation programs could take educational leadership preparation in detrimental directions and impede efforts to increase diversity among our public school educators (English, 2000, 2004).

Nonetheless, the standards movement, and its direct link to high-stakes testing, is the dominant strategy to improve the quality of education at the present time. Indeed, high-stakes assessments of students, teachers, and school leaders currently are being used to judge the value of pre-K–12 schools and their school personnel, issue school rankings and report cards, determine which schools must provide their students other educational options, and make personnel decisions. Foster (2004) has urged scholars to problematize this metanarrative that is defining the story of how and why schools exist in terms of global competitiveness and economic dominance. School leaders and those preparing them must create counternarratives that emphasize social justice and provide a space for local initiatives and for reinventing democratic processes (Foster, 2004).

## Selection of Leaders

Who will lead schools may be one of the most critical challenges and one of the most important opportunities to influence social justice. Marshall (2004) characterized the current turnover in school administrators as "never a better time" to prepare new leaders for social justice (p. 10). She noted that by 2010 numerous surveys show that the profession will essentially be repopulated. This raises questions about who will fill the positions, what they will do, and how will they do it?

Faced with a short supply of qualified administrator candidates in the pipeline in many school systems as well as an interest in recruiting more minority and women applicants, states are exploring a range of strategies such as removing barriers for noneducators and recent retirees to assume these roles, establishing administrative internship programs for teachers, redesigning administrative positions, providing financial and other incentives, and recruiting administrators from other states. Florida, for example, has omitted the credentialing process for school administrators (see Herrington & Wills, 2005). California has considered a bill to expedite the credentialing process. The California fast-track program proposes to enable individuals to demonstrate their administrative skills through rigorous testing rather than by completing extensive university coursework. Little is known, however, about whether such expedited programs adequately prepare future administrators to identify systemic inequities and engage in their eradication (see Hess & Kelly, 2005).

Some school districts are establishing partnerships with universities to develop collaborative training programs for aspiring principals to increase the pool of qualified candidates and to ensure a stronger practitioner voice in the nature of the preparation (see Goldring & Sims, 2005). Often collaboration not only involves joint development of the courses and experiences but also shared delivery of the courses (see Cambron-McCabe, Cunningham, Harvey, & Koff, 2005). Such efforts offer the potential to confront embedded injustices that may exist in specific school sites. Collecting and analyzing data related to a particular school and school district enables educators to actually do equity-focused work (Skrla, Scheurich, Garcia, & Nolly, 2004). These collaborative programs, however, are not numerous and are found primarily in urban areas.

Central to the question of who will lead is what do we mean by leadership? If we accept that a school leader's role is developing and maintaining a clear focus on a core purpose embedded in student learning and that the leader engages directly in the improvement of teaching and learning, it is reasonable to posit that expertise in instructional practices and curriculum content must be central in our selection of leaders. Aggressive and intentional recruitment of teachers who possess demonstrated high-quality instructional skills can expand the candidate pool for administrative positions and provide greater potential for increasing the number of women and administrators of color in leadership positions.

Elmore (2000) asserted, "If public schools survive, leaders will look very different from the way they presently look, both in who leads and what these leaders do" (p. 3). The present ferment over this new conception of leadership provides an opportunity to reconsider within a social justice discourse what it means to lead in schools where student learning, rather than the management of daily operations, is the heart of the work. Thus far we have only tinkered around the edges of this dilemma by attempting to incorporate elements of instructional leadership into the traditional principal role. What if we start with inventing new roles directed at student learning (Boris-Schacter & Langer, 2002)? This would help us avoid the trap of responding to these new challenges with old approaches and traditional roles. Buchen (2000) has argued that it is time to give up on "trying to save or keep intact roles and institutions that no longer are fluid, aspirational, and future driven" (p. 35). If we desire to create learning organizations "where people continually expand their capacity to create the results they truly desire, where new and expansive patterns of thinking are nurtured, where collective aspiration is set free, and where people are continually learning how to learn together" (Senge, 1990, p. 3), radical action is required.

From a social justice perspective, the greatest challenge for the educational administration field may be to shift its mental model of what it means to be a school leader rather than a school administrator. Usdan (2002) has posed several questions that are helpful in reframing the roles and responsibilities of school leaders:

> If the criteria for success have changed in terms of our expectations of school administrators, how can we meaningfully reshape the substance and role of preparatory programs? If principals and superintendents are to be assessed on the basis of their ability to raise test scores, how can the jobs be constructively and realistically reconfigured? For example, could successful teachers begin to serve as instructional leaders enabling principals to discharge their important customary responsibilities as leaders who work with parents and the community on political and management issues that certainly cannot be ignored in schools? Is it time to rethink the assumption that one individual can or should handle such diverse administrative responsibilities? (p. 302)

Clearly, this reconceptualization of who will lead and what they will do reaches far beyond university administrator preparation programs to teacher preparation, school communities, and state policy makers as teachers' roles are also redefined. Goodlad (1990) has asserted that a critical moral dimension of schooling requires teachers as well as principals to provide responsible moral stewardship of schools. That is, if student learning and the school site are pivotal points for renewal, teachers play a central role in creating and sustaining school-wide change, not simply improving efforts in their own classrooms. This reconceptualization of roles involves more than improving current practice; it requires rethinking those practices and taking action to implement new ones within a more just, democratic context. Accordingly, it represents a significant shift regarding who will fill leadership roles and what they will do in those roles.

## The Achievement Gap

The focus on educational accountability has revealed the startlingly large performance gap between African American, Latino, and economically disadvantaged students and Caucasian students, particularly from middle-and upper-income families. For example, Haycock (2001) has noted that African American and Latino students' mean 12th-grade math and reading skills are comparable to those of Caucasian eighth graders. Substantial differences exist among groups not only in achievement but also in completion of high school and college. And, these gaps are wider than they were a decade ago (Fuller, 1998). Haycock has maintained that the gaps exist because "we take the students who have less to begin with and then systematically give them less in school" (p. 8). The differences show up in the curriculum taught, the resources spent, how teachers are assigned, and achievement expected.

Despite its critics, the school accountability movement has focused attention on the widening achievement gap among students and related equity concerns. It is no longer possible to conceal through aggregate data reports what we have known all along—achievement patterns vary markedly among different groups of students. The inability of schools to close this gap prompted Congress to pass the No Child Left Behind Act (2002). The Act tightens the assessment side of schooling and provides options for children stuck in failing schools. Under intense pressure from both the federal and state levels, school leaders are struggling with substantive and strategic approaches to achieve equity for poor and minority children.

Marshall (2001) noted in her North Carolina study of administrative licensure that state officials see the closing of the achievement gap as the way to address social justice. Some research has shown that illuminating the achievement gap is an important step in challenging the so-called deficit-thinking of school leaders by clearly showing that all children are not being served well (Reyes, Scribner, & Paredes Scribner, 1999; Skrla & Scheurich, 2001).[3] But critics assert that simply disaggregating test scores by race and class will not ensure a better education for poor and minority children. McNeil (2000), for example, cautioned that the intense emphasis on the achievement gap may actually worsen the current inequities for minority students as schools focus on test results and narrow educational opportunities. Anderson (2004) echoed this perspective, noting that if equity is locally lodged in classrooms and schools "we may end up legitimating the larger persistent social inequities [thereby] distracting attention and energy from the larger political movements needed to bring about real social change" (p. 255).

Confounding the social justice issues related to student achievement is a recent report showing that school districts educating the largest number of poor and minority children receive less state and local money than school districts educating the least number of poor and minority children (Orlofsky, 2002). At a time when it is imperative to provide a rigorous curriculum, quality teachers, intense professional development, and more instructional time, many school districts do not have adequate resources to meet the higher standards. The funding gap represents a major state-policy issue that cannot be separated from the efforts to close the achievement gap in school districts facing the greatest disparities (Dantley & Cambron-McCabe, 2001; Rusch, 2001).

In the face of the growing social inequality in the nation, how do we link educational equity and social equity? What skills do leaders need to engage the school and the community in confronting social justice issues? How do we avoid the trap of confusing gains in test scores with substantive educational improvement?

## Privatization of Education

Schools naturally are a place where values and ideas are transmitted to youth. The original intent of the American common school was to ensure an educated citizenry and to inculcate democratic values in its students. Although the promise of the common school has not been fully realized, political rhetoric has maintained a national commitment to safeguarding the collective welfare of our children through public education. In reality, however, the trend toward privatizing education poses a significant threat to the fulfillment of public education's promise. This recent shift toward privatization presents noteworthy challenges for schools, their leaders, and those preparing school leaders, and it has important social justice implications. Bauman (1996) has contended that greater consumer control of education entails a reduced governmental role in providing services and "a belief in efficiency and individuality over equity and community" (p. 627). Commenting that schools increasingly are seen as a private rather than public good, Giroux (2003) observed that schools, therefore, "are concerned less with demands of equity, justice, and social citizenship than with the imperatives of the marketplace, skill-based learning, and the needs of the individual" (p. 76).

Educational-choice strategies range from purely public models (e.g., theme-based magnet programs that remain public schools) to purely private models (e.g., state-supported vouchers available for private-school tuition). Regardless of the approach, each of these choice options has significant implications for the values and ideas that our schools transmit to students. School leaders and those preparing them need to understand these implications and be involved in policy discussions about strategies to open education to the marketplace.

Recent federal initiatives show increased support for a marketplace model of education, including public support for private schools. The federal government's current emphasis on providing educational options for families in the No Child Left Behind Act (2002) is based on the premise that competition, including private options, can improve educational opportunities and ultimately the academic performance of all children. Indeed, $77 million in the Bush administration's discretionary fund, which does not have to be approved by Congress, is channeled toward organizations that champion private education, including homeschooling (Merrow, 2004).

States have also shown an increased interest in providing greater education options for parents, particularly low-income parents, through various marketplace models of schooling. Murphy (1999) has argued that consumer-based control of education can be viewed as a logical next stage in the evolution of school governance. With confidence in public-sector educational monopolies dwindling, the public pressure for opening education to the marketplace is increasing (see Boyd & Miretzky, 2003; Hill, 2002; Lewis, 1993; Richards, Shore, & Sawicky, 1996). The marketplace is viewed by some as the only way to provide options for the poor that the rich traditionally have enjoyed. In fact, school-choice initiatives in some locales have created strange bedfellows in that conservative citizen groups have joined forces with parents of color to support efforts to open education to the marketplace.

Despite mounting public interest, critics of marketplace models of education argue that consumer choices should not drive the educational enterprise. More specifically, some fear that the privatization of education will hinder efforts to diversify and democratize American schools (Fowler, 1991). Because families will select schools with staff members and students who look like them and think as they do, this will decrease diversity within schools. Giroux (2003) has further argued that the corporatized model of education "cancels out the democratic ideals and practices of civil society by either devaluing or absorbing them within the logic of the market" (p. 79).

Substantial current attention focuses on various voucher proposals under which families would receive a state voucher of a designated amount per child that can be redeemed at a public or private school of their choice.[4] States may be reluctant to adopt voucher plans to fund all education because students currently supported by their families in private schools or home education programs would receive state support under a general voucher program. However, targeted voucher plans, focusing on disadvantaged students or those attending deficient public schools, are likely to increase and are currently being considered in about half of the states.

Unlike states' hesitation to adopt comprehensive voucher systems to fund education, most have enthusiastically enacted charter school legislation during the past few years. In 1992 only two states—Minnesota and California—had passed charter school legislation, but by December, 2003, charter school legislation had been passed in 40 states, Washington, D.C., and Puerto Rico (Education

Commission of the States, 2002; U.S. Charter Schools, 2003). Charter school laws vary greatly across states, but most relax state regulations for schools that are granted charters by state or local education agencies or state universities. Most charter school laws place a cap on the number of charters that will be awarded, and some place restrictions on the types of entities that can apply (e.g., non-sectarian and nonprofit groups).

Private companies presently manage about 10% of the charter schools nationally, and several virtual or online charter schools have been established. Critics of corporate involvement in schools contend that some important features of the school program, including the values and desires of the local community, may be neglected with so much riding on the companies' reaching their target objectives (McCarthy, 2002a).

School leaders, those preparing them, and policy makers need to understand the values guiding various models to privatize education because current decisions in this regard will affect the next generation of students and beyond. Consumer-driven education, with its focus on individual choice and advancement, differs greatly from the government-run common school that focuses on promoting the nation's general welfare. Moreover, these privatization strategies have important social justice implications for education as individual schools will become more homogeneous because they are designed to appeal to only a portion of the market. This could have a negative impact on efforts to promote diversity and respect for those with different backgrounds and beliefs. Clearly, each of these choice-based models provides a vision for our educational system; these competing visions must be questioned and carefully examined.

School leaders will face very different educational environments and challenges in the age of school privatization. Leadership preparation programs need to explore the potential for the school privatization movement to alter the purposes and basic structure of schooling in our nation. If school privatization becomes dominant, the change in the nature of education in our nation could be as momentous as the common school movement in the 1800s.

## Implications for the Preparation of School Leaders

As our field debates how school leaders should be prepared, attention often focuses primarily on the effectiveness and efficiency of schools. This narrow conversation results in the identification of specific skills and performances that potential administrators must exhibit—frequently ignoring knowledge that cannot be quantified. We are not contesting the importance of technical expertise; however, failure to prepare administrators to engage in difficult work that requires a shift in values, attitudes, and behaviors within the school community severely limits their ability to address fundamental social justice issues. Giroux (1993) has urged educational leadership faculty to create "a new language capable of asking new questions and generating more critical practices" (p. 37). He has noted that "such a language would have to reformulate traditional notions of authority, ethics, power, culture, and pedagogy" (p. 37). The emerging social justice discourse provides a means to create this language and to focus directly on concerns about equity, student achievement, diversity, privilege, and social responsibility.

For educational leadership preparation programs to promote a social justice orientation, they must develop in their students what McKenzie and Scheurich (2004) have called *practiced reflexivity*, where individuals consciously take responsibility for their actions—recognizing that all actions have an impact on the community. McKenzie and Scheurich further have noted that the school leader's job requires a constant, vigilant critical perspective that always asks these questions:

What are we doing? Why are we doing it? What do we value? Why do we value what we do? How are our values evident or not evident in our practice? How is what we're doing affecting all students? Is what we're doing privileging one group over another? Is what we're doing working for all students, why or why not? Are our practices transparent? Is our leadership transparent? (p. 3)

Such critical discourse calls for preparation experiences that are very different from traditional university programs. Pounder, Reitzug, and Young (2002) noted that this means that leaders must be provided with new analytical skills, knowledge, and dispositions to promote social justice in schools. Among their recommendations they suggested a range of ideas: participating in field-based inquiry focused on oppression and discrimination, analyzing empirical data regarding racism in schools, examining stereotypes related to oppression, facilitating the creation of a rigorous and inclusive curriculum, and developing socially just practices among all individuals within the school community.

The social justice leadership discourse means that administrative preparation programs must encourage future school leaders to think very differently about organizational structures and leadership roles. Instead of continuing with incremental reforms that simply add more layers to existing structures, it is imperative to reconstruct roles and relationships at the school level around a vibrant core purpose focused on social justice and directed at improving student learning. This cannot be accomplished without concentrated expertise in teaching and learning. School leaders must possess high-quality instructional skills, be able to support the learning of both students and adults in the school, raise critical issues concerning equity and privilege, and be able to provide leadership for collective responsibility for school improvement. A growing number of leadership preparation programs are attempting to meet these challenges with coursework and teaching strategies directed at educating leaders to do social justice work (see Hafner, 2009, for a rich discussion of teaching strategies, programs, and resources).

The interdependent nature of education requires all segments of the educational enterprise—local schools, state licensure boards, higher education, professional associations—to collaborate in the preparation of a new type of school leader who is strongly committed to achieving social justice, one who draws on wide-ranging fields including educational leadership, curriculum, instruction, learning theory, communication, political theory, cultural studies, early childhood education, and systems theory. A challenge at the forefront of the papers commissioned by the National Commission for the Advancement of Educational Leadership Preparation is the assertion that substantive change in leadership preparation requires collaboration among all segments of the schooling enterprise (Young, Petersen, & Short, 2002). New structures are needed to enable this deliberation. The disconnect among the groups that influence or are responsible for school leadership impedes thoughtful reconsideration of leadership preparation. At both state and federal levels, processes must be established to facilitate conversations leading to reconceptualizing leadership for social justice. At the state level, departments of education could begin the work by serving as conveners of such sessions. From ongoing dialogue, a broader vision could be forged for creating new leadership roles for social justice and the requisite preparation and licensure requirements.

At the preparation level, recognition of the inextricable link between practitioners and the academy signals the need for close collaboration in the design and delivery of leadership programs. This is particularly important because school leaders generally find the academy irrelevant to their work (Cambron-McCabe & Cunningham, 2002; Hess & Kelly, 2005). For the most part, the formal preparation of preservice administrators resides in the academy with minimal input from practice. These programs are developed and taught primarily by professors under the strong influence of state licensure requirements. A few districts, particularly urban districts, are forging new partnerships with higher education faculty to jointly design alternative preparation programs that meet their special needs. We think this form of collaboration can be paramount in redefining leadership roles if it is framed around an emphasis on social justice using a school district's own context. This could provide a means to develop the new analytical skills Pounder et al. (2002) identified.

Furthermore, higher education faculty must model the kinds of organizations they expect their graduates to create. This challenges faculty to reflect on their pedagogy and program content to determine if their efforts represent the social justice questions and actions that they urge practitioners to embrace. Modeling becomes particularly important in the context of the tremendous struggle school leaders confront in reforming their practice. Too often, the academy is viewed as incapable of altering its own programs and as having little potential for informing school reform. Kottkamp (2002) has cautioned that "the largest problem in changing our programs, making them more effective, lies in changing ourselves" (p. 3). Faculty cannot teach about creating and leading socially just schools with credibility if they are not modeling these principles in their own departments, which includes working with practitioners on the front lines to reform schools.

Perhaps it is most important for professors to undertake an advocacy role in influencing educational policy to achieve social justice (Cambron-McCabe & Cunningham, 2002). School leaders and those preparing them will need to be creative and proactive to address current challenges, drawing on the past as well as multiple disciplines for new perspectives to shift their thinking. Blaming school problems on children's characteristics, lack of resources, politics, societal conditions, and myriad other issues simply incapacitates our efforts to achieve substantive transformation of schools. Instead of simply responding to criticisms and calls for change, school leaders need to influence the direction of education in our nation. If graduates of educational administration programs are expected to take on new roles, faculty must be active participants in the political arena when state policies affect social justice issues; mentoring from a distance does not prepare educational leaders for this difficult work.

Social justice discourse in educational leadership is being defined by its inclusiveness and activism. Through a language of critique, public intellectuals are shaping a new discourse with profound implications for social justice and the education of school leaders. This new language may move us closer to Foster's (1986) dream of educating leaders "to develop, challenge, and liberate human souls" (p. 18).

## Notes

1. Numerous presentations have been made at annual meetings of the American Education Research Association, National Council for Professors of Educational Administration, and University Council of Educational Administration. *Leadership for Social Justice: Making Revolutions in Education* (Marshall and Oliva, 2009), has been created as a textbook for leadership preparation programs. Also, special issues of the *Journal of School Leadership* and *Educational Administration Quarterly* have been devoted to the social justice challenges facing educational administration.

2. See Furman and Gruenewald (2004) for an ecological critique of the current social justice discourse. They have argued that social justice must also consider the link between social and ecological systems and the impact on the future of humans, nonhumans, and habitats globally.

3. Deficit-thinking posits that students' academic failure results from the deficiencies they bring to school (i.e., poor, dysfunctional family, etc.). Consequently, this thinking leads to assignment in low-level classes, identification as special education, harsher discipline, and dropping out.

4. The Supreme Court found no federal constitutional barrier to voucher programs—under which state vouch-

ers can be redeemed at public or private schools—including religious schools (*Zelman v. Simmons-Harris*, 2002). However, such programs still may abridge stronger antiestablishment provisions in the constitutions of 36 states (see *Davey v. Locke*, 2004).

# References

Anderson, G. (2004). William Foster's legacy: Learning from the past and reconstructing the future. *Educational Administration Quarterly, 40*(2), 240–258.

Bauman, P. C. (1996). Governing education in an antigovernment environment. *Journal of School Leadership, 6*(6), 625–643.

Bogotch, I. E. (2002). Educational leadership and social justice: Practice into theory. *Journal of School Leadership, 12*(2), 138–156.

Bond, L. (1998). Disparate impact and teacher certification. *Journal of Personnel Evaluation in Education, 12*(2), 211–220.

Boris-Schacter, S., & Langer, S. (2002, February 6). Caught between nostalgia and utopia: The plight of the modern principal. *Education Week, 34*, 36–37.

Boyd, W. L., & Miretzky, D. (Eds.). (2003). *American educational governance on trial: Change and challenges*. Chicago: University of Chicago Press.

Bracey, G. (2000). *High stakes testing*. Retrieved from University of Wisconsin–Milwaukee, Education Policy Project, Center for Education Research, Analysis, and Innovation Web site: http://www.uwm.edu/Dept/CERAI/

Buchen, I. H. (2000, May 31). The myth of school leadership. *Education Week*, pp. 35–36.

Burrello, L. C., Lashley, C., & Beatty, E. E. (2001). *Educating all students together: How school leaders create unified systems*. Thousand Oaks, CA: Corwin Press.

Cambron-McCabe, N. (2009). Preparation and development of school leaders: Implications for social justice policies. In C. Marshall & M. Oliva (Eds.), *Leadership for social justice: Making revolutions in education*. Boston: Allyn & Bacon.

Cambron-McCabe, N., & Cunningham, L. (2002). National Commission for the Advancement of Educational Leadership: Opportunity for transformation. *Educational Administration Quarterly, 38*(2), 289–299.

Cambron-McCabe, N., Cunningham, L., Harvey, J., & Koff, R. (2005). *The superintendent's fieldbook: A guide for leaders of learning*. Thousand Oaks, CA: Corwin Press.

Cibulka, J. (2004, Spring). The case for academic program standards in educational administration: Toward a mature profession. *UCEA Review*, pp. 1–5.

Council of Chief State School Officers. (1996). *Interstate School Leaders Licensure Consortium: Standards for school leaders*. Washington, DC: Author.

Dantley, M. E. (2003). Principled, pragmatic, and purposive leadership: Reimagining educational leadership through prophetic spirituality. *Journal of School Leadership, 13*(2), 181–198.

Dantley, M., & Cambron-McCabe, N. (2001, April). *Administrative preparation and social justice concerns in Ohio*. Paper presented at the American Educational Research Association Annual Meeting, Seattle, WA.

Dantley, M. E., & Tillman, L. C. (2009). Social justice and moral/transformative leadership. In C. Marshall & M. Oliva (Eds.), *Leadership for social justice: Making revolutions in education*. Boston: Allyn & Bacon.

*Davey v. Locke*, 540 U.S. 712 (2004).

Delgado, R., & Stefancic, J. (2001). *Critical race theory: An introduction*. New York: New York University Press.

Donmoyer, R., Imber, M., & Scheurich, J. (1995). *The knowledge base in educational administration: Multiple perspectives*. Albany, NY: SUNY Press.

Education Commission of the States. (2002, August). *State notes on charter schools*. Retrieved from http://www.ecs.org/ecsmain.asp?page=/html/issues.asp?am=1

Elmore, R. (2000). *Building a new structure for school leadership*. Washington, DC: The Albert Shanker Institute and Consortium for Policy Research in Education.

English, F. (2000, April). *The ghostbusters search for Frederick Taylor in the ISLLC standards*. Paper presented at the American Educational Research Association Annual Meeting, New Orleans, LA.

English, F. (2004, Spring). Undoing the "done deal": Reductionism, ahistoricity, and pseudoscience in the knowledge base and standards for educational administration. *UCEA Review*, pp. 6–7.

Foster, W. (1986). *Paradigms and promises: New approaches to educational administration*. Buffalo, NY: Prometheus Books.

Foster, W. (2004). The decline of the local: A challenge to educational leadership. *Educational Administration Quarterly*, *40*(2), 176–191.

Fowler, F. C. (1991). The shocking ideological integrity of Chubb and Moe. *Journal of Education*, *173*, 119–129.

Fuller, H. (1998). Transforming learning: The struggle to save urban education. *UCEA Review*, pp. 1–3.

Furman, G. (2000, November). *The ISLLC rendition of community: Contradiction and control?* Paper presented at the annual convention of the University Council for Educational Administration, Albuquerque, NM.

Furman, G., & Gruenewald, D. (2004). Expanding the landscape of social justice: A critical ecological analysis. *Educational Administration Quarterly*, *40*(1), 49–78.

Giroux, H. A. (1993). Educational leadership and school administrators: Rethinking the meaning of democratic public cultures. In T. A. Mulkeen, N. Cambron-McCabe, & B. J. Anderson (Eds.), *Democratic leadership: The changing context of administrator preparation*. Norwood, NJ: Ablex.

Giroux, H. A. (1997). *Pedagogy and the politics of hope: Theory, culture, and schooling*. Boulder, CO: Westview Press.

Giroux, H. A. (2003). *The abandoned generation: Democracy beyond the culture of fear*. New York: Palgrave Macmillan.

Goldfarb, K. P., & Grinberg, J. (2002). Leadership for social justice. *Journal of School Leadership*, *12*(2), 157–173.

Goldring, E., & Sims, P. (2005). Modeling creative and courageous school leadership through district-community-university partnerships. *Educational Policy*, *19*, 223–249.

Goodlad, J. (1990). *Teachers for our nation's schools*. San Francisco: Jossey-Bass.

Grogan, M. (2004). Keeping a critical, postmodern eye on educational leadership in the United States: In appreciation of Bill Foster. *Educational Administration Quarterly*, *40*(2), 222–239.

Gronn, P. (2002). Designer leadership: The emerging global adoption of preparation standards. *Journal of School Leadership*, *12*(5), 552–578.

Gruenewald, D. (2003). Foundations of place: A multidisciplinary framework for place-conscious education. *American Educational Research Journal*, *40*(3), 619–654.

Hafner, M. M. (2009). Teaching strategies for developing leaders for social justice. In C. Marshall & M. Oliva (Eds.), *Leadership for social justice: Making revolutions in education*. Boston: Allyn & Bacon.

Haycock, K. (2001). Closing the achievement gap. *Educational Leadership*, *58*(6). Retrieved from http://www.ascd.org/readingroom/edlead/0103/haycock.html

Hedges, L. V., & Nowell, A. (1998). Black-white test score convergence since 1965. In C. Jencks and A. Phillips (Eds.), *The black-white test score gap* (pp. 149–181). Washington, DC: Brookings.

Herrington, C. D., & Wills, B. K. (2005). Decertifying the principalship: The politics of administrator preparation in Florida. *Educational Policy*, *19*, 181–200.

Hess, F., & Kelly, A. (2005). An innovative look, a recalcitrant reality: The politics of principal preparation reform. *Educational Policy*, *19*, 155–180.

Hill, P. T. (Ed.). (2002). *Choice and equity*. Stanford, CA: Hoover Institution Press.

Kottkamp, R. (2002). What makes a difference in developing effective school leaders? A challenge to the field. *TEA/SIG: Teaching in Educational Administration*, *9*(2), 1, 3.

Larson, C., & Murtadha, K. (2002). Leadership for social justice. In J. Murphy (Ed.), *The educational leadership challenge: Redefining leadership for the 21st century* (pp. 134–161). Chicago: National Society for the Study of Education.

Lewis, D. A. (1993). Deinstitutionalization and school decentralization: Making the same mistake twice. In J. Hannaway & M. Carnoy (Eds.), *Decentralization and school improvement* (pp. 84–101). San Francisco: Jossey-Bass.

Lopez, G. R. (2003). The (racially neutral) politics of education: A critical race theory perspective. *Educational Administration Quarterly*, *39*(1), 68–94.

Lugg, C. A. (2003). Sissies, faggots, lezzies, and dykes: Gender, sexual orientation, and a new politics of education. *Educational Administration Quarterly*, *39*(1), 95–134.

Marshall, C. (2001, April). *School administration licensure policy in North Carolina*. Paper presented at the American

Educational Research Association Annual Meeting, Seattle, WA.

Marshall, C. (2004). Social justice challenges to educational administration: Introduction to a special issue. *Educational Administration Quarterly, 40*(1), 5–15.

Marshall, C., & McCarthy, M. (2002). School leadership reforms: Filtering social justice through dominant discourses. *Journal of School Leadership, 12*(5), 480–502.

Marshall, C., & Oliva, M. (Eds.). (2009). *Leadership for social justice: Making it happen.* Boston: Allyn & Bacon.

Marshall, C., & Parker, L. (in press). Vignettes of leaders'social justice dilemmas. In C. Marshall & M. Oliva (Eds.), *Leadership for social justice: Making revolutions in education.* Boston: Allyn & Bacon.

Maxcy, S. (2000, November). *Leadership clones, copies and mutations: Scientific management and leadership philosophy in educational administration.* Paper presented at the American Educational Research Association Annual Meeting, New Orleans, LA.

McCarthy, M. (2002a). The changing environment for school leaders: Market forces. In G. Perreault & F. Lunenburg (Eds.), *The changing world of school administration* (pp. 91–108). Lanham, MD: Scarecrow Press.

McCarthy, M. (2002b). Educational leadership preparation programs: A glance at the past with an eye toward the future. *Leadership and Policy in Schools, 1,* 202–221.

McKenzie, K., & Scheurich, J. (2004, July). Position paper for Miami University Education Summit, Oxford, Ohio.

McNeil, L. (2000). *Contradictions of school reform: The educational costs of standardized testing.* New York: Routledge.

Merrow, J. (2001). Undermining standards. *Phi Delta Kappan, 82,* 653–659.

Merrow, J. (2004, March 26). *The Merrow report* [Television broadcast]. New York: Public Broadcasting Service.

Mitchell, K. J., Robinson, D. Z., Plake, B. S., & Knowles, K. T. (Eds.). (2001). *Testing teacher candidates.* Washington, DC: National Academy Press.

Murphy, J. (1999). New consumerism: Evolving market dynamics in the institutional dimension of schooling. In J. Murphy & K. Seashore-Lewis (Eds.), *The handbook of research on educational administration* (2nd ed., pp. 405–419). San Francisco: Jossey-Bass.

National Policy Board for Educational Administration. (2000). *Standards for advanced programs in educational leadership.* Arlington, VA: Author.

No Child Left Behind Act, 20 U.S.C. § 6301 *et seq.* (2002).

Oliva, M. (2001, April). *Texas educator certification and social justice.* Paper presented at the American Educational Research Association Annual Meeting, Seattle, WA.

Orlofsky, G. (2002). *The funding gap: Low-income and minority students receive fewer dollars.* Retrieved from http://www.edtrust.org/main/documents/investment.pdf

Paige, R. (2003, Fall). Under the microscope: Educational progress in Houston. *The Beacon: Journal of Special Education and Practice, 2*(2), 1–8.

Parker, L., Deyhle, D., & Villanas, S. (1999). *Race is…race isn't: Critical race theory and qualitative studies in education.* Boulder, CO: Westview.

Pounder, D., Reitzug, U., & Young, M. (2002). Preparing school leaders for school improvement, social justice, and community. In J. Murphy (Ed.), *The educational leadership challenge: Redefining leadership for the 21st century* (pp. 261–288). Chicago: University of Chicago Press.

Reyes, P., Scribner, J., & Paredes Scribner, A. (1999). *Lessons from high performing Hispanic schools: Creating learning communities.* New York: Teachers College Press.

Richards, C. E., Shore, R., & Sawicky, M. B. (1996). *Risky business: Private management of public schools.* Washington, DC: Economic Policy Institute.

Rusch, E. (2001, April). *Preparing leaders for social justice in New Jersey.* Paper presented at the American Educational Research Association Annual Meeting, Seattle, WA.

Senge, P. (1990). *The fifth discipline: The art and practice of the learning organization.* New York: Doubleday.

Skrla, L., & Scheurich, J. (2001). Displacing deficit thinking in superintendent leadership. *Education and Urban Society, 33*(3), 235–259.

Skrla, L., Scheurich, J., Garcia, J., & Nolly, G. (2004). Equity audits: A practical leadership tool for developing equitable and excellent schools. *Educational Administration Quarterly, 40*(1), 135–163.

U.S. Charter Schools. (2003). *State info.* Retrieved from http://www.uscharterschools.org/pub/ uscs_docs/sp/index.htm

Usdan, M. (2002). Reactions to articles commissioned by the National Commission for the Advancement of Education Leadership Preparation. *Educational Administration Quarterly*, *38*(2), 300–307.

Young, M., Petersen, G., & Short, P. (2002). The complexity of substantive reform: A call for interdependence among key stakeholders. *Educational Administration Quarterly*, *38*(2), 137–175.

*Zelman v. Simmons-Harris*, 536 U.S. 639 (2002).

# CHAPTER TWENTY-ONE

# Overcoming the Obstacles to Leadership

SUSAN MOORE JOHNSON & MORGAEN L. DONALDSON

LACEY'S HIGH SCHOOL NEEDED HER TALENT AND SKILLS. LOCATED IN AN URBAN, WORKING-CLASS community, the school was struggling to serve all students well and had failed to make Adequate Yearly Progress for two years running. As a social studies teacher, Lacey had developed considerable skill in teaching with a project-based format during her four years in the classroom, and her students were making steady progress as a result. But the reach of her expertise was limited by her classroom walls. Teachers in her school were dedicated to their students, but not to one another's growth. Whatever they had learned over time—how to do project-based learning, how to facilitate classroom discussions, how to effectively use technology—remained largely private. No one asked; no one told. As a result, the school's instructional capacity remained static, no more than the sum of individual teachers' strengths and deficits.

## Tempered Enthusiasm

The standards and accountability movement has placed extraordinary demands on schools like Lacey's to improve instructional outcomes. To meet these demands, principals are appointing increasing numbers of teacher leaders to work with colleagues in such roles as instructional coach, lead teacher, mentor coordinator, and data analyst. Because recent large-scale retirements have left a shrinking pool of veteran teachers, principals often ask teachers in the second stage of their career, with 4 to 10 years of experience, to take on these specialized roles.

Second-stage teachers may find this opportunity attractive for several reasons (Donaldson, 2005; Johnson & the Project on the Next Generation of Teachers, 2004). First, many of them feel increasingly competent and confident in their work, and they want to share their acquired expertise with others. Lacey acknowledged, "I'm pretty good" at teaching social studies. She said that over time she had developed "a wider repertoire for teaching students at many levels" and had become more comfortable in her classroom and her school. Research confirms Lacey's sense of increasing skill and effectiveness. On average, students of fourth-year teachers learn more than students of first-year teachers (Rockoff, 2004).

Second, becoming a teacher leader promises to reduce isolation. When they begin their career, many of today's new teachers expect to work in teams but are dismayed to find themselves working alone day after day. Lacey expressed regret about the lack of collegial interaction in her school: "It's just you alone in your classroom. You don't get into each other's classrooms very often."

Third, becoming a teacher leader offers an opportunity to vary one's responsibilities and expand one's influence. Many second-stage teachers want to have a hand in making decisions about how their school operates. Lacey criticized "the way it's set up right now. You don't move up. You do the same thing the whole time." She liked the idea of using her growing expertise to help "change the bigger picture."

Thus, competent and confident second-stage teachers like Lacey welcome opportunities to collaborate with colleagues, learn, grow, and expand their influence. Having taken on these roles, how do second-stage teachers fare?

With colleagues at the Project on the Next Generation of Teachers, we interviewed 20 second-stage teachers who had assumed roles as teacher leaders (Donaldson et al., in press). These teachers worked in a range of settings: elementary and secondary schools, urban and suburban communities, and several metropolitan areas across the United States. We found that, although these teachers were initially enthusiastic about their new roles, they encountered unforeseen challenges. The schools in which they worked remained largely unchanged, with an egg-crate structure that reinforced classroom boundaries and a professional culture that discouraged teacher leadership. These findings suggest that, to reap the full benefits of teacher leadership, school administrators need to provide formal support structures and build leadership roles into the structure of the school.

## Business as Usual

On the whole, few schools have reorganized to make the most of the expertise teacher leaders offer. Usually, the new roles are simply appended to a flat, compartmentalized school structure in which classroom teachers continue to work alone. Instructional coaches, for example, are expected to make periodic classroom visits and advise fellow teachers about their practice. But this model does little to change business as usual. The classroom teacher remains isolated and in charge, while the teacher leader arrives only occasionally as a visitor.

Teacher leaders' marginal status is underscored by the fact that their positions are typically funded with outside grants from year to year, rather than being built into a school's regular budget. Thus, the positions remain add-ons to the school program. When the funds run out, the school can eliminate these roles without seriously disrupting its operations.

In addition, teacher leaders' roles are seldom well defined. Principals often regard teacher leaders as a source of extra help in a school that is strapped for human resources. As a result, many teacher leaders spend their time as apprentices or assistants in administration—supervising the cafeteria, subbing for absent staff, or overseeing the logistics of testing—rather than using their instructional expertise to improve teaching at the school.

# A Triple Threat

Teacher leaders' efforts to share their expertise can also be undermined by the culture of teaching. In fact, the professional norms of teaching present a daunting challenge to teacher leaders who are asked to improve their colleagues' instruction. Our interviews suggested that colleagues often resist these teacher leaders' work because they see it as an inappropriate intrusion into their instructional space, an unwarranted claim that the teacher leader is more expert than they, and an unjustified promotion of a relative novice to a leadership role. Thus, the norms of autonomy, egalitarianism, and deference to seniority that have long characterized the work of teaching remain alive and well in schools.

## Protecting Autonomy

Teacher leaders said that they were often rebuffed when they offered to observe in colleagues' classrooms or made suggestions about teaching. Mai, a mathematics coach and fifth-year teacher, was responsible for organizing professional development meetings, demonstrating sample lessons for other teachers, and offering feedback on their teaching. She reported, "I can't even enter one teacher's room because he is not open to me coming to his room while he teaches." She explained further, "There are other teachers, especially teachers who have been teaching for a long time, who aren't comfortable with being observed, period." The school's teachers' union representative told Mai she could not "evaluate or make judgments, good or bad, on teachers or teaching practice. So I can't say, 'You did a great job with behavior management,' even though that's nice feedback to get." By denying her entrance to their classrooms and restricting the kind of feedback she could provide, Mai's colleagues asserted their right to decide what and how to teach.

## Ensuring Egalitarianism

Teachers also questioned the premise that a peer could possess expert knowledge or presume to act on it. Clark, a 10th-year elementary teacher, reported that his colleagues assumed that he and the other instructional facilitator felt superior and avoided him. Frustrated, Clark contrasted his current, strained interactions with the relaxed, collegial relationships that he had enjoyed before he became an instructional facilitator.

Others told of being criticized by peers because their role granted them unusual privileges or special access. Anna, a math consultant and fifth-year elementary teacher, taught full time and ran after-school classes on how to use the district's math curriculum. Several of her peers resented the fact that she could get substitutes to cover her classes so that she could observe and coach other teachers. Anna's role also required her to coordinate often with her principal, which seemed to create distrust and jealousy among her colleagues. It was, she said, "hard not to come off as the principal's pet."

## Reinforcing Seniority

Teacher leaders in the second stage of their career often said that their colleagues viewed them as too young or inexperienced to have such a role. When Mai, age 29, tried to assist a veteran teacher in using the district's math curriculum, she was asked confrontationally, "And *how* old are you?" Even those who were not so young and had entered teaching after another career were criticized for their inexperience. Dave, a 45-year-old who had been teaching for seven years, was supposed to help others implement a new math curriculum and analyze student test data in his elementary school. Some of his colleagues, although younger, still questioned his appointment, asking, "Why him? Why didn't I get that job? I've been doing this for 18 years."

## Teacher Leaders Cope

Such opposition was discouraging—sometimes demoralizing. To persist with their leadership work, the second-stage teachers devised strategies to minimize their colleagues' resistance and the emotional burden it placed on them. The following coping strategies often helped teacher leaders avoid provoking other teachers' fears, deflect opposition, and diminish tensions when they arose. But these strategies also tended to legitimize the traditional culture of teaching and its norms of autonomy, egalitarianism, and deference to seniority.

### Wait to Be Drafted

Although teacher leaders were supposedly chosen for their special expertise, few roles came with explicit qualifications or procedures for selection. When no established process existed for choosing teacher leaders, colleagues often saw appointments as acts of favoritism by the principal. They raised objections on the basis of claims of seniority, the default mechanism for distributing special rights and privileges among teachers.

Anticipating that veterans might criticize them for their inexperience or question their qualifications, many of the teacher leaders whom we interviewed refrained from volunteering for leadership positions until they were drafted. For example, Eric, a 6th grade instructional coach, anticipated the problem of "coming in as some sort of hotshot." Although he wanted the position, Eric hesitated when the principal first offered it; he waited until his more experienced colleagues expressed no interest in the role and encouraged him to take it. He reasoned that with this approach he could counter any opposition by arguing, "You're the ones who didn't want the role, so I'm expecting you guys to give me a little bit more support." This strategy, he thought, would oblige them "to be on board."

### Work with the Willing

Some teacher leaders who encountered resistance or opposition scaled back their efforts and worked only with their most willing colleagues. In doing so, they affirmed their colleagues' right to choose whether to accept their assistance. However, they also reduced their potential schoolwide influence.

Sarah had eight years of experience when she was appointed science curriculum coordinator for the two elementary schools in her district. In this role, she was supposed to help other teachers create and conduct inquiry-based science lessons. Other teachers had scant knowledge of her responsibilities, however, and administrators did little to help her gain access to classrooms and team meetings. Given this ambiguity and lack of support, Sarah chose to work with teachers who sought her out and ignore those who did not. She explained that she was on her own and limited by traditional boundaries: "I'm not an administrator, so I can't tell someone that they need to have me in their room." Therefore, she decided to help those who already welcomed her expertise. She found that working with these colleagues kept her busy, and she had little need to "drum up business" among other teachers.

Similarly, Lauren, an eighth-year teacher whose role as an elementary school literacy coordinator was also undefined and poorly supported, backed off from the challenges she encountered: "I've kind of given up the fight with the teachers who constantly cancel on me or don't want me in their room." Instead, she focused on improvements made by teachers who sought her help: "That's what inspires you and keeps you moving," she declared.

## Work Side by Side

Other teacher leaders tried to foster joint ownership of the reforms their roles were designed to champion and support. They cast themselves as sources of support, not supervisors, permitting their colleagues to decide how to incorporate proposed changes into their classrooms. In doing so, they often reinforced the belief that teacher leaders are no more expert than their peers.

Anna, for example, said she was advised by more senior colleagues not to present information "in a way that feels suffocating." Anna believed that by casting herself as a collaborator, rather than an authority, she enabled her veteran colleagues to take some ownership over changes to their practice.

Similarly, Kelly—an elementary school literacy coach and sixth-year teacher—described herself to her colleagues as a "facilitator" who connected them to resources that they could use to improve their practice rather than telling them how to teach. By allowing the teachers they worked with to determine how the reforms would play out in their classrooms, Anna and Kelly recognized and reinforced other teachers' autonomy. Their role was to support each teacher's approach to reform, not direct it.

In summary, the teacher leaders whom we interviewed coped with a traditional school organization and a teaching culture that prized and protected norms of egalitarianism, seniority, and autonomy. Because their roles were ill defined, these teacher leaders had to devise ways to be seen as legitimate and to gain access to teachers and classrooms without being rejected or becoming disheartened.

## Better Support for Teacher Leaders

Our interviews with teachers in the second stage of their career suggest that many want to vary their responsibilities, collaborate with peers, and influence teaching beyond their classrooms. In many ways, they are ideal candidates to provide the teacher leadership that schools urgently need. However, their accounts also reveal that their experience as teacher leaders often fails to fulfill their expectations and may do little to build their schools' instructional capacity.

Most teacher leaders we interviewed were left to define their own roles, which proved to be more of a burden than an opportunity. In the absence of any professional framework or established set of differentiated responsibilities to provide guidance or legitimacy for their roles, teacher leaders' offers of advice often strained their relationships with other teachers. No amount of skill, enthusiasm, or determination in these teacher leaders could fundamentally change the structure of schooling or culture of teaching.

We do not infer from this study that roles for teacher leaders are doomed. Rather, we conclude that the roles must be introduced deliberately and supported fully. Informal roles with unpredictable funding will never be taken seriously. To be viable, these roles must have well-defined qualifications, responsibilities, and selection processes.

In Peer Assistance and Review programs in districts such as Toledo, Ohio; Montgomery County, Maryland; and Rochester, New York, consulting teachers advise and evaluate all beginning teachers and some struggling veterans. The success and sustainability of these programs, the first of which was introduced in Toledo in 1981, suggests that school officials should focus on establishing and supporting a system of long-term, well-defined roles for teacher leaders.

Our interviews made it clear that the principal can make or break the role of teacher leader. It was not enough for the principal to be a passive supporter, as was the case for most of the teacher leaders we interviewed. Rather, he or she needed to anticipate the resistance that teacher leaders might encounter from colleagues and help them broker the relationships they would need to do their work.

A few teacher leaders said that their principals helped by having what one called a "big game plan," which explained to all the staff how teacher leaders would contribute to the school's effort to achieve its goals. Principals can build support for a teacher leader's role by explaining its purpose, establishing qualifications and responsibilities, encouraging applicants for the position, and running a fair selection process. They can work with the schedule and available resources to incorporate the work of teacher leaders into the structure of the school and provide common planning time, substitute coverage for peer observations, and use of faculty meetings for professional development. They can guarantee that teacher leaders are not diverted to take on administrative tasks. Because school culture is so crucial to the success of these roles, teachers must see the principal's practices and priorities as reinforcing a new set of norms that promote collaborative work, bridge classroom boundaries, and recognize expertise.

But principals' efforts alone will not enable teacher leaders to succeed. Fundamentally, the success or failure of teacher leaders will depend on their relationships with their colleagues. Teacher leaders need professional development that prepares them to respond to colleagues' resistance respectfully while helping these teachers improve their practice.

## Redefining the Norms of Teaching

The traditional norms of teaching—autonomy, egalitarianism, and seniority—exert a powerful and persistent influence on the work of teachers. They reinforce the privacy of the individual's classroom, limit the exchange of good ideas among colleagues, and suppress efforts to recognize expert teaching. Ultimately, they cap a school's instructional quality far below its potential.

If these norms remain dominant, many talented teachers who desire collaboration and expanded influence will become frustrated and leave education in search of another place to build a fulfilling career. Even more troubling—if these norms persist, they will continue to dissuade teachers from sharing vital knowledge about teaching and learning with their colleagues.

Schools cannot afford to lose promising teachers or squander opportunities to better serve students. It will take the efforts of all educators—district administrators, principals, teacher leaders, and teachers themselves—to redefine the norms of teaching and support teacher leaders in their work so that every school's instructional capacity expands to meet its students' needs.

# Note

This chapter is based in part on analysis and argument presented in "Angling for Access, Bartering for Change: How Second-Stage Teachers Experience Differentiated Roles in Schools," by M. Donaldson, S. Johnson, C. Kirkpatrick, W. Marinell, J. Steele, and S. Szczesiul, in press, *Teachers College Record*.

# References

Donaldson, M. L. (2005, April). *On barren ground: How urban high schools fail to support and retain newly tenured teachers*. Paper presented at the annual meeting of the American Educational Research Association, Montreal, Quebec, Canada.

Donaldson, M. L., Johnson, S. M., Kirkpatrick, C. L., Marinell, W. H., Steele, J. L., & Szczesiul, S. A. (in press). Angling for access, bartering for change: How second-stage teachers experience differentiated roles in schools. *Teachers College Record*.

Johnson, S. M., & the Project on the Next Generation of Teachers. (2004). *Finders and keepers: Helping new teachers survive and thrive in our schools*. San Francisco: Jossey-Bass.

Rockoff, J. (2004). The impact of individual teachers on student achievement: Evidence from panel data. *American Economic Review, 94*(2), 247–252.

# Teacher Leadership in the 21st Century

# CHAPTER TWENTY-TWO

# Preparing Teachers for Leadership Roles in the 21st Century

JULIE A. SHERRILL

THE MANY CALLS FOR EDUCATIONAL REFORM IN THE LAST 15 YEARS HAVE SHARED SEVERAL common themes, including increasing recognition of the importance of teacher quality and teacher leadership to school improvement efforts (The Holmes Group, 1986, 1990, 1995; National Commission on Excellence in Education, 1983; National Commission on Teaching and America's Future, 1996). New teacher leadership roles are emerging as educators and policymakers seek to improve the three major phases of the teaching career continuum: teacher preparation, induction, and ongoing professional development.

However, the new teacher leadership roles remain ill defined and unclear to both researchers and teacher leaders (see Conley & Muncey, this issue). The expectations attached to the new roles can be confusing, demanding, and overwhelming to teacher leaders, as well as to their colleagues and administrators (Collinson & Sherrill, 1997; Sherrill, 1993a; Wasley, 1991). Teacher leaders are literally forging their roles on site.

I have often desired a more clear and concise description of teacher leadership roles, coupled with a greater understanding of the foundational skills and knowledge teachers need to fulfill their roles successfully and of ways teachers are supposed to attain them. My desire for clarity stems from having studied emerging teacher leadership roles at the teacher preparation phase at a major research university (see Sherrill, 1993a), and having held positions of responsibility for induction and ongoing professional development programs for teachers in adjacent school districts. Universities and state are quickly adopting changes and altering requirements for teacher preparation, but they are not simultaneously developing and offering programs to prepare the teacher leaders who are expected to implement the changes. Teachers are expected to assume leadership roles with little or no preparation (Zimpher & Howey, 1992).

The complexity of the issues surrounding new roles for teachers cannot be ignored, but the development of common expectations of teacher leadership roles at the teacher preparation, induction, and ongoing professional development phases could prove helpful in setting high expectations, filling leadership positions with qualified individuals, and contributing to the continuous improvement efforts underway in many of today's schools.

Recognizing that any role assumed by a professional educator is influenced by local context, this article argues that basic expectations for teacher leadership roles can be drawn from existing research generated during the past decade. Like the teaching and learning standards initiated nationwide to provide common benchmarks and consistent expectations for teachers and students, similar guideposts for teacher leadership positions could enhance the reforms underway in teacher preparation programs and K-12 schools across the country. This chapter draws on existing research to outline common expectations for teacher leadership roles within three major phases of the teacher career continuum—teacher preparation, induction, and ongoing professional development.

## The Teacher Leadership Challenge

Wasley (1991) offers a generic definition of teacher leadership as "the ability to encourage colleagues to change, to do things they wouldn't ordinarily consider without the influence of the leader" (p. 170). However, as Wasley (1991) notes, the realities of practice for teacher leaders are much more challenging and complex than the rhetoric on reform suggests. Her case studies illustrate that teachers have been unresponsive to top-down efforts to improve their instruction through administratively created teacher leadership positions. Not only must teachers be full participants in any discussion about leadership roles, they must also feel supported and understood by administrators in order for any new leadership role to make a positive and lasting contribution to the improvement of teaching and learning in a given setting (Wasley, 1991).

Additionally, Zimpher and Howey (1992) note widespread acknowledgment that the expertise and the catalyst for change has to be embedded in a continuing way at the school site. However, the still common reality of staff development efforts in school districts reflects the notion that outside experts are best suited to encourage professional growth (Jilek, Loadman, & Derby, 1998). This deeply-rooted habit of thinking persists despite teacher reports that the best way to go about improving the quality of their professional practice is to spend more time learning from and working with colleagues (Bacharach, 1986; Wasley, 1991), and despite research indicating that collegial interactions are necessary to build the collaborative cultures associated with school improvement (Hargreaves, 1991; Little, 1990; Rosenholtz, 1989).

Studies that focus on school-university partnerships have underscored the many challenges in defining new leadership roles and responsibilities (Miller & Silvernail, 1994). Specific challenges include resolving conflicting fundamental interests (Snyder, 1994), establishing inter-institutional authority and fiscal responsibility (Neufeld, 1992), and providing long-term rewards for teacher leaders (Lieberman, 1992; Sandholtz & Merseth, 1992).

Many authors have pointed to the critical role of "boundary spanners" (Sandholtz & Finan, 1998), teacher leaders who have assumed roles created with the expectation that they will bridge the complex cultures of K-12 schools and higher education. The sheer diversity of titles illustrates the wide range of possibilities and expectations: Teacher leaders are referred to as clinical faculty, clinical educators, and clinical supervisors (Zimpher & Sherrill, 1996).

Zimpher and Howey (1992) point out that even the best of teachers are not prepared for such an assignment. Recent case studies have reported high levels of frustration from teachers piloting new leadership roles. The reported frustrations of these teachers and their lack of self-efficacy indicate that teacher leader roles called for in reform efforts need to have greater definition, and teachers need to have more purposeful preparation (Cornbleth & Ellsworth, 1994; Sandholtz & Finan, 1998; Sherrill, 1993a; Snyder, 1994).

Targeted selection and preparation for such roles may increase the visibility among colleagues and alleviate the types of feelings experienced by a clinical educator who stated:

> I don't think I should have to keep saying to the principal, "Aren't you at all interested in what I do half the day?" I mean, this district does share me with the university a half day. Most of the staff still don't know what I do. They know if I leave school it is somehow associated with the university and PDS (professional development school) work. They may not know I even have a title. More importantly, they don't recognize that I'm supposed to be doing things that should facilitate improvements in their own classroom and professional lives. I guess I just feel invisible. (Sherrill, 1993b)

The following section attempts to categorize the types of knowledge, responsibilities, and skills needed by teacher leaders as they assume leadership roles throughout the three major phases of the teacher career continuum: teacher preparation, induction, and ongoing professional development.

## The Teacher Career Continuum

### Teacher Preparation

In the report of the National Commission on Teaching and America's Future (1996), one of the five major recommendations is a reinventing of teacher preparation and professional development. The report recommends that teacher education and professional development programs be organized around standards for students and teachers. Additionally, the report suggests that extended, graduate-level teacher-preparation programs provide preservice students with a year-long internship in a professional development school.

Of the more than 1,200 schools of education in the nation, over 200 have created professional development schools. Each PDS is incorporating some variation of teacher leader roles for classroom teachers working with university faculty and preservice students (National Commission on Teaching and America's Future, 1996). The new roles require teacher leaders to link the experience of the school setting to university coursework for preservice students and to work with university faculty at school sites (Cornbleth & Ellsworth, 1994). Such "clinical faculty roles" are being interpreted more broadly than the traditional notion of cooperating teacher.

These new teacher leadership roles in a PDS are demanding. One clinical educator articulated her beliefs about her new role and the characteristics she modeled as follows:

> A clinical educator is a person who values collaboration generally and school-university collaboration specifically and has demonstrated an ability to work toward professional development and instructional improvement; demonstrates that he/she is an expert classroom practitioner who can articulate his/her beliefs about children, teaching and learning; takes risks and works at the edge of his/her knowledge; has a strong commitment to his/her own professional development and is willing to engage in continuing preparation for the role. And by the way, they must be able to tolerate a high degree of ambiguity too. (Sherrill, 1993a, p. 147)

Teachers assuming leadership roles that are integrally tied to the initial preparation of teachers will need training in collaborative planning and implementation as well as instructional and developmental supervision (Reiman & Thies-Sprinthall, 1998). Critical abilities for teacher leaders engaged in teacher preparation will include demonstrating expert classroom instruction and sound knowledge of effective teaching and learning strategies, facilitating conferences with preservice teachers in a differentiated and reciprocal manner, analyzing approaches to their work via adult learning theory, and providing feedback tied to theory and research.

## Induction

Research into the beginning years of teaching describes the transition years following preservice preparation as a period of chaos, often marked by a lack of support (Howey, 1988). In response to beginning teachers' concerns and high attrition rates in the first years of teaching (Heyns, 1988), entry year or induction programs for new teachers have evolved across the country. As a consequence, a number of teacher leadership roles, especially mentoring, focus specifically on emerging entry-year programs and other activities that support beginning teachers (Zimpher & Sherrill, 1996).

Teacher leaders cannot be expected to assume new mentoring roles armed with the skills necessary to work with peers. Teachers are not accustomed to "teaching" adults. However, their new roles can be enhanced through specific training. For example, Odell (1986) found that training clinical support teachers in supervision, relationship skills, and coaching techniques dramatically improved their effectiveness (see also Reiman & Thies-Sprinthall, 1998). The assignment of a well-trained support teacher or mentor to a beginning teacher was also found to be the most powerful and cost-effective intervention in an induction program (Huling-Austin, Putman, & Galvez-Hjornevik, 1986).

Classroom teachers assuming mentoring roles with entry-year teachers should have the opportunity, therefore, to acquire skills that enable them to develop relationships and nurture the growth and development of beginning teachers. They should learn how to systematically observe classroom instruction and coach beginning teachers, consulting as the need arises on classroom management, lesson development, and instructional strategies.

In addition to the skills required to work with beginning teachers individually and within cohorts, teacher leaders should also be adept at facilitating the conditions for mentoring. They need to know how to impact on the school building and district environments so that beginning teachers have opportunities to meet and talk with each other, observe other classrooms where outstanding teaching and learning is taking place, experiment with new instructional methods, and develop a sense of truth with their mentors and colleagues.

## Ongoing Professional Development

Rosenholtz's (1989) study of collaborative elementary schools indicated that "teachers from collaborative settings described their leaders as those who initiated new programs, tried new ideas, [and] motivated others to experiment and brainstorm solutions to teaching problems" (p. 24). Since teachers, in general, do not share a tradition of leadership or collaboration, Zimpher and Howey (1992) called for highly selected teachers to be prepared for a variety of school-focused leadership roles to meet the vision of school leadership described in the Rosenholtz study. Zimpher and Howey (1992) argue that these uniquely trained teachers should undertake a variety of leadership roles at the school site while maintaining some instructional responsibilities. As teachers, they would enjoy more peer credibility than "outsiders." As leaders on site, they could encourage and support more effective and job-embedded professional development than found in most traditional professional development programs.

Standard prerequisites for leadership roles that focus on the ongoing professional development of teachers in the school setting should include the following knowledge domains: knowledge of classroom processes and school effectiveness; knowledge of interpersonal and adult development; knowledge of instructional supervision, observation, and conferencing; knowledge of local district needs; and a disposition toward inquiry (Zimpher & Howey, 1992). Additionally, tangible examples of the skills and knowledge needed by teacher leaders assuming such roles would be demonstrated by: expanding and improving colleagues' basic teaching methods, modeling how to enable students to better monitor their learning and take greater responsibility for their actions in the classroom, improving the working climate of both individual classrooms and schools as a whole, and documenting in a more accountable fashion the effects of their teaching in order to provide parents and community with precise and relevant data about learning than standardized tests allow (Zimpher & Howey, 1992).

A particular challenge for individuals assuming this teacher leadership role is the relationship established with school administration. Ideally, school administrators would have the time and skills required to carry out much of the above, but the reality of school administration in today's schools makes it nearly impossible to devote the time and energy required to carry out these aspects of teacher professional development. As such, a relationship of trust, cooperation, and respect between identified teacher leaders and school administrators will be critical to the success of roles targeted at the ongoing professional development of teachers in a building or school district. The dynamics of these relationships could be the greatest facilitator, or barrier, to change.

Table 1 captures, in summary form, a core set of expectations for leadership roles across the teacher career continuum, combined with specific expectations for teacher leaders working with peers in leadership roles at the teacher preparation, induction, and ongoing professional development phases.

The table is not intended to be all-inclusive, but rather to be illustrative of the clarity necessary for better defining expectations for the new teacher leadership roles called for in today's education reform efforts. The mere attempt to compose such a categorization of expectations raised a number of questions for further consideration. Just who will be responsible for providing the prerequisite training needed for teachers to carry out these roles successfully? Who will pay for teacher leader training? What is being done relative to the preparation of school administrators to complement and enhance teacher leadership roles? Should there be prerequisites for leadership roles in certain phases (i.e., National Board Certification prior to assuming a leadership role in the ongoing professional development phase)?

## Conclusion

New teacher leadership roles are emerging as a result of educators and policymakers seeking to improve the three major phases of the teaching career continuum: teacher preparation, induction, and ongoing professional development. Data collected from Venture Capital schools in Ohio (Jilek, Loadman, & Derby, 1998) point to the fact that "previously prepared and newly prepared teachers and administrators are not and have not been prepared to take on the roles and functions which they are being asked to assume…both in preprofessional and professional development activities" (p. 16).

This article argues that basic expectations for teacher leadership roles at the teacher preparation, induction, and ongoing professional development phases can be drawn from existing research. By completing such a task, courageous educators attempting to improve their profession could begin with a common framework, a blueprint from which to embark on important work. Clearly identifying expectations for teacher leadership roles needed now and in the 21$^{st}$ century—and determining how educators will acquire the knowledge and skills needed to assume those roles successfully—are critical steps in the continuous reform efforts to improve public education in this country.

Table 1. Teacher Leader Expectations for Three Phases of the Career Continuum

**Core Expectations for All Phases:**
Demonstrate exemplary classroom instruction and sound knowledge of
    effective teaching and learning strategies.
Understand theories of adult development.
Demonstrate knowledge of clinical supervision models and processes that
    support effective descriptions of classroom practices.
Cultivate desired dispositions in teachers.
Guide colleagues by a reflective and inquiry-oriented posture.
Possess research based knowledge about teaching and learning.

| Teacher Preparation | Induction | Ongoing Professional Development |
|---|---|---|
| Articulate knowledge of the university teacher preparation curriculum. | Understand the unique needs and concerns of beginning teachers. | Demonstrate ability to assess, interpret, and prioritize local district and teacher needs and concerns. |
| Value collaboration generally and school-university collaboration specifically. | Demonstrate effective relationship skills and coaching techniques. | Recognize how to positively affect the broader culture of the school and establish positive relationships with administrators. |
| Facilitate conferences with preservice teachers and university faculty in a differentiated and reciprocal manner. | Develop relationships and nurture the growth and development of beginning teachers. | Understand action research and practice-centered inquiry. |
| Analyze their approach to work via adult learning theory. | Collect data related to classroom observations and provide constructive feedback. | Expand and improve colleagues' basic teaching methods. |
| Provide feedback tied to theory and research. | | Possess skills needed to facilitate effective workshops and presentations. |

# References

Bacharach, S. B. (1986). *The learning workplace: The conditions and resources of teaching*. Washington, DC: National Education Association.

Collinson, V., & Sherrill, J. (1997). Changing context for changing roles: Teachers as learners and leaders. *Teaching Education, 8*(2), 55–63.

Conley, S. & Muncey, D. E. (1999). Teachers talk about teaming and leadership in their work. *Theory into Practice, 38*(1), 46–55

Cornbleth, C., & Ellsworth, J. (1994). Clinical faculty in teaching education: Roles, relationships, and careers. In K. R. Howey & N. L. Zimpher (Eds.), *Informing faculty development for teacher educators* (pp. 213–248). Norwood, NJ: Ablex.

Hargreaves, A. (1991, April). *Restructuring restructuring: Postmodernity and the prospects for educational change*. Paper presented at the annual meeting of the American Educational Research Association, Chicago.

Heyns, B. (1988). Educational defectors: A first look at teacher attrition in the NLS-72. *Educational Researcher, 17*(3), 24–32.

The Holmes Group. (1986). *Tomorrow's teachers*. East Lansing, MI: Author.

The Holmes Group. (1990). *Tomorrow's schools: Principals for the design of professional development schools*. East Lansing, MI: Author.

The Holmes Group. (1995). *Tomorrow's schools of education*. East Lansing, MI: Author.

Howey, K. R. (1988). Why teacher leadership? *Journal of Teacher Education, 39*, 28–31.

Howey, K. R., & Zimpher, N. L. (1991). Patterns in prospective teachers: Guides for designing preservice programs. In F. B. Murray (Ed.), *The teacher educator's handbook* (pp. 465–503). San Francisco: Jossey-Bass.

Huling-Austin, L., Putman, S., & Galvez-Hjornevik, C. (1986). *Model teacher induction project study findings* (Report No. 7212). Austin: University of Texas at Austin, R&D Center for Teacher Education.

Jilek, J., Loadman, W., & Derby, L. (1998, February). *Ohio's P-12 systemic educational reform: Implications for the preparation of teachers and administrators*. Paper presented at the annual meeting of the American Association of Colleges for Teacher Education, New Orleans, LA.

Lieberman, A. (1992). School/university collaboration: A view from the inside. *Phi Delta Kappan, 74*, 147–155.

Little, J. W. (1990). The persistence of privacy: Autonomy and initiative in teachers' professional relations. *Teachers College Record, 91*, 509–536.

Miller, L., & Silvernail, D. (1994). Wells Junior High School: Evolution of a professional development school. In L. Darling-Hammond (Ed.), *Professional development schools: Schools for developing a profession*. (pp. 28–49). New York: Teachers College Press.

National Commission on Excellence in Education. (1983). *A nation at risk*. Washington, DC: U.S. Government Printing Office.

National Commission on Teaching and America's Future. (1996). *What matters most: Teaching for America's future*. New York: Teachers College Press.

Neufeld, B. (1992). Professional practice schools in context: New mixtures of institutional authority. In M. Levine (Ed.), *Professional practice schools: Linking teacher education and school reform* (pp. 133–168). New York: Teachers College Press.

Odell, S. (1986). Induction support of new teachers: A functional approach. *Journal of Teacher Education, 37*, 26–29.

Reiman, A. J., & Thies-Sprinthall, L. (1998). *Mentoring and supervision for teacher development*. New York: Addison Wesley Longman.

Rosenholtz, S. (1989). *Teachers' workplace: The social organization of schools*. New York: Teachers College Press.

Sandholtz, J. H., & Finan, E. (1998). Blurring the boundaries to promote school-university partnerships. *Journal of Teacher Education, 49*, 13–25.

Sandholtz J. H. & Merseth, K. K. (1992). Collaborating teachers in a professional development school: Inducements and contributions. *Journal of Teacher Education, 43*, 308–317.

Sherrill, A. (1993a). *A qualitative case study of the clinical educator role during a pilot year of implementation*. Unpublished doctoral dissertation, The Ohio State University, Columbus.

Sherrill, A. (1993b). {A qualitative case study of the clinical educator role during a pilot year of implementation}. Unpublished raw data.

Snyder, J. (1994). Perils and potentials: A tale of two professional development schools. In L. Darling-Hammond (Ed.), *Professional development schools: Schools for developing a profession* (pp. 98–125). New York: Teachers College Press.

Wasley, P. A. (1991). *Teachers who lead: The rhetoric of reform and the realities of practice.* New York: Teachers College Press.

Zimpher, N. L., & Howey, K. R. (1992). *Policy and practice toward the improvement of teacher education.* Oak Brook, IL: North Central Regional Educational Laboratory.

Zimpher, N. L., & Sherrill, J. A. (1996). Professionals, teachers, and leaders in schools, colleges, and departments of education. In J. Sikula, T. J. Buttery, & E. Guyton, (Eds.), *Handbook of research on teacher education* (pp. 279–305). New York: Macmillan.

# CHAPTER TWENTY-THREE

# Teachers as Leaders

## Collaborative Leadership for Learning Communities

PAMELA S. ANGELLE

*This We Believe Characteristics*
- Educators who value working with this age group and are prepared to do so
- Collaborative, courageous leadership
- A shared vision that guides decisions
- High expectations for every member of the learning community
- Organizational structures that support meaningful relationships and learning

THE IDEA OF LEADERSHIP IS RECOGNIZED THROUGHOUT THE SCHOOL REFORM LITERATURE AS critical to school improvement (Hallinger & Heck, 1996; Leithwood, Jantzi, Earl, Watson, Levin, & Fullan, 2004). Through increased understanding of the nature of leadership, the definition of this concept has expanded to include leadership at the teacher level. Given the scope of federal and district mandates that fall upon schools, schoolwide learning and the development of learning communities are essential. If schools are to operate as learning communities, then they cannot do so with the leadership of a single person or with a singular leadership strategy (Harris, 2002). Therefore, teacher leadership becomes imperative to the success of any school reform movement (Crowther, Kaagan, Ferguson, & Hann, 2002; Frost, Durrant, Head, & Holden, 2000; Katzenmeyer & Moller, 2001;Murphy, 2005). If mandates for accountability and improvement are not seen as valuable or are not implemented at the classroom level, they are doomed to mediocrity at best or complete failure at worst. Logically, embracing teacher leaders as part of a vision for improvement is a key to success.

The purpose of this article is to examine the role of teacher leadership in schools. To accomplish this end, areas which will be considered include:

- The concept of teacher leadership: definitions, roles, self-perceptions
- The relationship between principal leadership and teacher leadership
- The school culture necessary to support teacher leadership
- The organizational structures that support or challenge teacher leadership.

# The Concept of Teacher Leadership

A review of current literature reveals inconsistency in defining teacher leadership due to a myriad of concept variations, from leading by example to assuming a specific leadership position (Bowman, 2004; Crowther, Kaagan, Ferguson, Hann, 2002; Frost, Durrant, Head, & Holden, 2000; Katzenmeyer & Moller, 2001; Murphy, 2005; Wasley, 1991). Most teachers who take on leadership roles do not see themselves as leaders, reserving the term leader for those who take on formal roles, such as principals or district supervisors. Instead, they perceive that most of their work is done informally through collaboration (Moller, Childs-Bowen, & Scrivner, 2001). While definitions of teacher leadership differ, a commonly held notion is the expanded view of leadership beyond traditional classroom boundaries (Beachum & Dentith, 2004). Teacher leadership reflects teacher agency, through establishing relationships, breaking down barriers, and marshalling resources throughout the organization in an effort to improve students' educational experiences and outcomes (York-Barr & Duke, 2004).

## Definitions and Roles of Teacher Leadership

Teacher leaders are those teachers who maintain focus on student learning, seek lifelong learning for themselves, use facilitation and presentation skills, engage others in shared vision and meaning, develop and maintain relationships with other organization members, work with a sense of integrity, and plan and organize (Bowman, 2004; Moller, Childs-Bowen, & Scrivner, 2001). Snell and Swanson (2000) maintain, however, that expertise is the foundation of a respected teacher leader because the level of expertise establishes credibility with colleagues. The literature alternately suggests that teacher leaders are those who have the ability to "encourage colleagues to change" (Wasley, 1991, p. 23) and have the willingness to "lead beyond the classroom and contribute to the community of learners" (Katzenmeyer & Moller, 2001, p. 17). Teacher leadership has also been discussed as an issue of density where a larger number of people throughout the organization are involved in decision making and creating knowledge (Sergiovanni, 2001).

The duties of teacher leaders typically have more to do with a focus on teaching and learning, rather than a focus on the management of the school (Katzenmeyer & Moller, 2001). Specifically, teacher leaders may visit and observe other teachers, provide demonstrations and feedback to colleagues, attend conferences to re-deliver knowledge to their peers, and develop curriculum (Feiler, Heritage, & Gallimore, 2000). Collegiality, collaboration, and communication are skills listed as necessary for teacher leadership and are frequently found in the literature (Andrews & Lewis, 2002; Davidson & Dell, 2003; Fennell, 1999; Harris, 2002; Silins & Mulford, 2004; Thornton, Langrall, Jones, & Swafford, 2001). Hatch, White, and Faigenbaum (2005) examined teacher leadership beyond the school building level and found that teacher leaders can be effective at influencing policy outside of their school, including the district level and wider audiences through presentations and publications.

Just as the definition and duties of teacher leaders are ill-defined in the literature, so also are the roles, though Ogawa and Bossert (1995) argued that leadership is a quality embedded in relationships, not roles. Harris (2003) referred to both the informal roles and formal roles of the teacher leader. Informal roles encompass classroom-related functions such as planning, communicating goals, and regulating activities, while formal roles entail specific positions, including department head or subject coordinator—positions that remove the leader from the classroom. Teacher leadership roles are defined by Thornton, Langrall, Jones, and Swafford (2001) with a focus on change—in planning and initiating professional development, facilitating communication about the change, or in addressing curriculum development or problems.

The evolution of teacher leadership is discussed by Silva, Gimbert, and Nolan (2000) in terms of their roles. The development of the teacher leader role includes teacher as manager (e.g., department heads or master teachers), teacher as instructional leader (e.g., team leader and curriculum coordinator), and teacher as re-culture agent (e.g., reformers of goals and norms, proponents of collegiality) (Silva, Gimbert, & Nolan, 2000). Reform coaching is another role taken on by teacher leaders—a role that includes building capacity, serving as a bridge between administrators and teachers, and using knowledge to assist others in changing their practice (Coggins, Stoddard, & Cutler, 2003). Coaching roles, including reform coaches and content coaches, emphasize the traits of trust, determination, innovation, perseverance, and calm (Guiney, 2001).

## Self-perceptions of Teacher Leaders

A focused characterization of teacher leadership is further muddied by their self-perception, which often differs from the perceptions of their colleagues. Teacher leaders may alternately see themselves as reflective practitioners, action researchers, collaborators, mentors, instructional experts, or risk takers (Wynne, 2001). Teacher leaders, at times, perceive themselves as professional development trainers and curriculum innovators (Mimbs, 2002), while their colleagues may perceive them either in a positive light as teacher advocates (Beachum & Dentith, 2004) or in a negative light as elitists, harmful to teacher morale, or detrimental to accepted classroom practices (Smylie & Denny, 1990).

Allen (2004) examined teacher leadership in terms of their voice, pointing out that too often the teacher's voice focuses on everyday management issues rather than school renewal efforts. Moreover, teachers must believe that their voice will be respected, listened to, and acted upon. Otherwise, teachers will be unwilling to participate in any reform efforts. Allen categorized the types of voice in schools:

- Voting voice—which requires little time or risk
- Advisory voice—which requires time and some risk when the outcome is not a foregone conclusion
- Delegated voice—which may include teachers serving on a leadership team, thus requiring time and some risk in openly giving one's opinion
- Dialogical voice—which requires high levels of collegial interaction, a deep commitment, and a high level of risk.

Silva and associates (2000) noted that teachers' and principals' voices are missing from much of the literature advocating for teacher leadership, leading to the conclusion that teacher leadership has yet to be defined by those who actually practice the concept.

If teachers are the leaders, then what is the role of the principal? What are the conditions necessary for teacher leaders to flourish? What barriers might stand in the way of successfully encouraging teacher leaders at the school level? A reflection upon the National Middle School Association's beliefs (NMSA, 2003) provides a roadmap for the answers to these questions.

# Principal Leadership and Teacher Leadership

Schools that embrace teacher leadership are those "successful schools for young adolescents [which]are characterized by a culture that includes…courageous, collaborative leadership" (NMSA, 2003, p. 7). Collaborative leaders recognize that in today's schools, one person cannot adequately address the needs of all members of the school community. Empowering others to lead alongside the principal builds collegiality and shares opportunities for active participation in the improvement of the school. This sharing of power by the principal is critical to the success of teacher leadership but does not come without some risk and sacrifice from the school administration.

In schools that are improving in terms of student achievement, leadership is fluid and emerging, rather than fixed (Harris, 2002). This blurring of leadership between leader and follower is alternately termed as leadership that is distributed (Harris, 2003), invitational (Stoll & Fink, 1996), constructivist (Fennell, 1999), and parallel (Andrews & Lewis, 2002). By and large, leadership strategies that foster teacher leadership (Harris, 2002; Katzenmeyer & Moller, 2001; Silins & Mulford, 2004) parallel those strategies found in the school effectiveness literature (Edmonds, 1979; Hallinger & Murphy, 1986; Mortimore, Sammons, Stoll, Lewis, & Ecob, 1988; Sammons, 1999; Teddlie, Kirby, & Stringfield, 1989; Teddlie & Stringfield, 1993) and may include:

- Empowering others in the organization
- Promoting a shared vision and communicating it to all stakeholders
- Structuring an organization that promotes collaboration
- Exhibiting high expectations for innovation and effectiveness
- Providing adequate resources
- Trusting, supporting, and caring for others and expecting trust, support, and care in return.

Empowering schoolteachers as leaders requires that principals relinquish some of their power while still retaining ultimate responsibility and accountability (Harris, 2003). Thus, embracing the concept of teacher leadership may prove difficult for some school principals. Others may accept the concept in principle but not in practice. Acker-Hocever and Touchton (1999) studied the power relationships of teachers and principals and concluded that conditions for successful teacher leadership call for principals to give up power, to release control, to offer respect and trust, and to set up conditions for teachers to practice their leadership. However, a caveat to these obligations from the principal is that teachers must be willing to take the power and leadership when it is offered to them. Teachers must also be willing to cross the invisible boundaries from follower to leader.

Anderson (2004) extended the notion of power boundaries between principals and teachers with three models of influence. The buffered principal is surrounded by teacher leaders who act as foot soldiers protecting the principal from the other teachers. In this model, teacher leaders are the "powers that be" and exert pressure to carry out the decisions of the buffered principal. The *interactive principal* is involved with and works closely with all teachers and staff. This model is one of distributed, shared decision-making. The third model of influence is the contested principal. This principal is outside the loop and works against the teacher leaders. The teacher leaders, in turn, attempt to undermine the decision-making power of the principal. This is a model of conflict. Leadership practices that promote and empower teachers to contribute to school improvement through their leadership create an organization where all stakeholders can learn and grow. This type of learning organization is built upon collaboration, professional relationships, high expectations, and continual learning.

## School Culture and Teacher Leadership

The vision for middle schools encompasses learning, not only for adolescents, but for the adults in the school community as well. Schools that promote lifelong learning for all are "successful schools for young adolescents [which] are characterized by a culture that includes…high expectations for every member of the learning community…[with] students and teachers engaged in active learning" (NMSA, 2003, p. 7). Teachers who work in a culture of high expectations and continuous learning find that their leadership skills are actively called upon to contribute to the improvement of their school—leadership abilities that might otherwise wax stagnant in other environments.

The culture of continuous learning is sustained through ongoing, job-embedded professional development. Teacher leadership and learning are fostered through a teacher's role in planning and initiating professional development, where teachers work together to end professional isolation (Guiney, 2001). Through opportunities to model, share ideas for reform strategies, and participate in team-building activities, teacher confidence is boosted, increasing the likelihood that future teacher leadership opportunities will be accepted (Thornton, Langrall, Jones, & Swafford, 2001). Sustaining the initial enthusiasm and extending the learning of professional development can be achieved through interaction with colleagues. This is particularly true if implementation of the professional development is difficult (Feiler, Heritage, & Gallimore, 2000). In addition to professional development, teacher leadership promotes professional relationships and a participatory work environment through consensus building (Fennell, 1999; Ryan, 1999).

School cultures that support teacher leadership approach problem solving with enthusiasm, focusing on students as the cornerstone for all decisions. Moreover, these schools foster a high level of trust between teachers, principals, and the community. Teachers believe they are competent and effective, embracing opportunities for leadership (Ryan, 1999; Short, 1998). Schools with these cultures are referred to as learning organizations, characterized by collaboration, risk taking, and shared mission (Silins & Mulford, 2004).

The context in which a teacher works is particularly critical to the success of teacher leadership. A healthy work culture of trust and support where both principal and teachers share a purpose or set of goals will lead to a growth in teacher leadership (Moller, Childs-Bowen, & Scrivner, 2001). Work environments where teacher leadership thrives are those that emphasize collegiality, communication, and collaboration. School cultures built around these relationships find that teacher commitment to the job and loyalty to the organization are enhanced (Fennell, 1999).

## Organizational Structures and Teacher Leadership

### Aspects That Mediate the Leadership Process

Learning organizations with cultures where teacher leadership can flourish require "organizational structures that support meaningful relationships and learning" (NMSA, 2003, p. 7). In addition, factors in the school that hinder teacher leadership should be avoided. The following sections outline these success factors and barriers that extend across school levels, including the building-level principal, the teachers who participate in leadership, and the colleagues who work alongside the teacher leaders.

*Principals.* Clear communication with the teacher leaders is a vital component to the success of teacher leadership in a school. Principals must not only communicate their boundaries for decision making and power sharing but also their expectations for the role of teacher leader. While assisting the teacher leaders in developing their leadership skills, the principal should also hold them accountable for decisions made. Time release to work with other teachers and keeping administrative duties to a minimum provide a structure that encourages success for teacher leaders.

Principals can offer support for teacher leadership both overtly and covertly. Through empowering teachers, including them in decision making, recognizing their efforts, relinquishing control, sharing responsibility for failure, and giving credit for success, principals can send the message to the school community that teacher leadership is important and accepted in the school culture. Acknowledging and supporting teacher leaders can ultimately contribute to the success of the principal (Barth, 2001). As Barth notes, the success of "those at the front of the line depends on the support of those behind them" (p. 446).

While principal support is critical to the success of teacher leadership, school building leaders also must be cognizant of their own boundaries for power surrendering and communicate this to the teachers. Principals should take on the role of fostering expertise in the teachers, not promoting their own expertise (Short, 1998). Principals cannot really give empowerment to teachers. Principals can only create the environments and opportunities that lead to and support empowerment. As teachers take on empowering roles, principals must clearly communicate the responsibilities that accompany the roles and the goals the empowered teacher should work toward; that is, toward school-level goals rather than personal goals (Short, 1998).

Resources and time are repeatedly cited as barriers to teacher leadership (Harris, 2003; Ryan, 1999; Smylie & Denny, 1990; Wynne, 2001). While principals are often constrained by these factors as well, attempting to alleviate these barriers to teacher leadership sends a message of support to the teacher leaders.

*Teacher leaders.* Tapping teacher leaders to serve involves consideration of appropriateness and willingness. Most schools have limited resources and time capacity; therefore, teachers who can meet the greatest need should be selected. Fully supporting a few leaders is better than partially supporting many (Feiler, Heritage, & Gallimore, 2000). Expertise and leadership skills should be considered; however, just as critical, is the teacher's ability to influence colleagues and take risks. Teachers placed in leadership roles should be those for whom student learning is the first and last priority (Feiler, Heritage, & Gallimore, 2000).

Once given the opportunity to serve, teacher leaders receive intrinsic benefits from their position. Teacher leaders have the opportunity to be exposed to new ideas and to engage in nontraditional roles. Moreover, teacher leaders are able to collaborate with colleagues. Opportunities afforded to teacher leaders lead to greater feelings of professionalism (Wetig, 2002). As teachers grow in confidence and a self-perception of professionalism, their sense of agency within the organization may also increase; that is, teachers will naturally develop a perception that they have the means to accomplish goals and a shared purpose. Frost and Durrant (2002) contended that teachers do not need autonomy to restore a sense of agency but need a work culture that provides the capacity to exercise leadership, coupled with the satisfaction of having an impact on facets of the organization. These facets include an impact on teachers (e.g., personal, interpersonal, instructional practice), on the school (e.g., the processes, the culture, the capacity), beyond the school (e.g., knowledge), and on the students (e.g., metacognition, achievement).

Teachers who have the opportunity to pursue leadership roles in the school do not always have the willingness to serve. Barth (2001) noted that the Coalition of Essential Schools found that teacher leaders rarely comprise more than 25% of a school faculty. Why are more teachers not involved in this positive path to school improvement? Several factors may be responsible for this hesitancy. Some teachers are not prepared to confront hard issues or ask tough questions that may be required for decisions that must be made in the leadership role (Bowman, 2004). Teachers may lack the confidence and belief that they actually have the ability to lead others (Barth, 2001).

Teacher leaders may begin their work with high levels of enthusiasm; however, as the realities of balancing leadership roles with classroom obligations and personal lives set in, enthusiasm often wanes. In addition, personal discouragement at the slow wheels of change may lead to stress and burnout. Facing the constraints of time, resources, and flexibility also dampens the spirits of teacher leaders accustomed to excellence (Beattie, 2002; Lanting & Jolly, 2001). DiRanna and Loucks-Horsley (2001) found that burnout was common in teacher leaders because they are responsible for their classrooms as well as school-level leadership. Recommendations from these findings included the need for a leadership pipeline so that initiatives can continue if teacher leaders vacate their positions.

Ryan (1999) found that one of the greatest barriers to successful implementation of teacher leadership came from the types of situations in which teachers were asked to practice their leadership skills. All too often, teacher leaders are called upon to decide technical issues such as textbook choices and grade book packages rather than administrative decisions such as hiring teachers and budget development. Teachers who are asked to determine the individual work assignments of their instructional teams will feel more empowered by the shared decision-making capacity than those teacher leaders who vote on whether caps can be worn by students on Fridays. Teacher leaders who are deprived of the ability to make decisions on what they perceive are critical issues report greater dissatisfaction with their job, more stress, and less loyalty to their principal (Ryan, 1999).

*Colleagues and school environment.* A school environment that supports teacher leadership includes quality professional development for the teachers, a culture of collegiality and collaboration, and a respect for the autonomy and abilities of teachers (Katzenmeyer & Moller, 2001). Unfortunately, the greatest resistance to teacher leadership may come from colleagues. Fellow teachers do not always embrace their colleagues as leaders. When teacher leaders attempt leadership roles, fellow teachers may chastise them for being power hungry or wanting control (Bowman, 2004). Too few teachers take on leadership roles because of contentment with inertia and complacency in their current work of teaching. Moreover, insecure colleagues may take on an "us/them" mentality, separating the teacher leaders from the larger faculty (Barth, 2001). Colleagues can provide the greatest challenge to teacher leadership through active resistance to decisions made, initiatives advocated, or simply to the teacher leaders themselves (Barth, 2001). In these cases, without the principal's support, the concept of teacher leadership will likely fail in that environment.

## Conclusion

Teacher leadership is a phenomenon in which teachers daily walk on a balance beam, balancing their desire to influence and improve the school-wide organization with their calling to teach children and see them succeed. To ensure success for these teacher leaders, the school culture must value their work, the school principal must support their work, and their teacher colleagues must be willing to work alongside them as they strive for a more effective school. Collaboration, shared decision making, reflective practice, quality professional development, and shared goals are all part of an organizational culture that promotes the high expectations and school-wide learning necessary for successful teacher leadership. A courageous, collaborative leader willing to share power, extend boundaries, and provide support, respect, and appreciation is critical to a school embracing teacher leadership. Teachers who are willing to take risks, collaborate with colleagues, engage in nontraditional roles, and who are organized and committed to student learning will inspire excellence and contribute to school improvement as teacher leaders. Teacher leadership as a vehicle for implementing school reform requires a commitment from all members of the school community. Organizations that embrace leaders at all levels take the first step on the path to creating successful schools for young adolescents.

# References

Acker-Hocever, M., & Touchton, D. (1999, April). *A model of power as social relationships: Teacher leaders describe the phenomena of effective agency in practice*. Paper presented at the meeting of the American Educational Research Association, Montreal, Canada.

Allen, L. (2004). From votes to dialogues: Clarifying the role of teachers' voices in school renewal. *Phi Delta Kappan, 86*, 318–321.

Anderson, K. D. (2004). The nature of teacher leadership in schools as reciprocal influences between teacher leaders and principals. *School Effectiveness and School Improvement, 15*(1), 97–113.

Andrews, D., & Lewis, M. (2002). The experience of a professional community: Teachers developing a new image of themselves and their workplace. *Educational Research, 44*(3), 237–254.

Barth, R. (2001). Teacher leader. *Phi Delta Kappan, 82*, 443–449.

Beachum, F., & Dentith, A. (2004). Teacher leaders creating cultures of school renewal transformation. *The Educational Forum, 68*, 276–286.

Beattie, M. (2002). Educational leadership: Modeling, mentoring, making, and re-making a learning community. *European Journal of Teacher Education, 25*(2), 199–221.

Bowman, R. F. (2004). Teachers as leaders. *The Clearing House, 77*(5), 187–189.

Coggins, C. T., Stoddard, P., & Cutler, E. (2003, April). *Improving instructional capacity through school-based reform coaches*. Paper presented at the meeting of the American Educational Research Association, Chicago, IL.

Crowther, F., Kaagan, S. S., Ferguson, M., & Hann, L.(2002). *Developing teacher leaders*. Thousand Oaks, CA: Corwin Press.

Davidson, B. M., & Dell, G. L. (2003, April). *A school restructuring model: A toolkit for building teacher leadership*. Paper presented at the meeting of the American Educational Research Association, Chicago, IL.

DiRanna, K., & Loucks-Horsley, S. (2001). *Designing programs for teacher leaders: The case of the California science implementation network*. Columbus, OH: ERIC Clearinghouse for Science, Math, and Environmental Education. (ERIC Document Reproduction Service No. 465590)

Edmonds, R. R. (1979). *A discussion of the literature and issues related to effective schooling*. St. Louis, MO: Central Midwestern Regional Educational Laboratory.

Feiler, R., Heritage, M., & Gallimore, R. (2000). Teachers leading teachers. *Educational Leadership, 57*(7), 66–69.

Fennell, H. A. (1999, April). *Encouraging teacher leadership*. Paper presented at the meeting of the American Educational Research Association, Montreal, Canada.

Frost, D., Durrant, J., Head, M., & Holden, G. (2000). *Teacher-led school improvement*. New York: RoutledgeFalmer.

Frost, D., & Durrant, J. (2002). Teachers as leaders: Exploring the impact of teacher-led development work. *School Leadership and Management, 22*(2), 143–161.

Guiney, E. (2001). Coaching isn't just for athletes: The role of teacher leaders. *Phi Delta Kappan, 82*, 740–743.

Hallinger, P., & Heck, R. H. (1996). Reassessing the principal's role in school effectiveness: A review of empirical research, 1980–1995. *Educational Administration Quarterly, 32*(1), 5–44.

Hallinger, P., & Murphy, J. (1986). The social context of effective schools. *American Journal of Education, 94*, 328–355.

Harris, A. (2002, April). *Building the capacity for school improvement.* Paper presented at the meeting of the American Educational Research Association, New Orleans, LA.

Harris, A. (2003). Teacher leadership as distributed leadership: Heresy, fantasy, or possibility. *School Leadership & Management, 23*(30), 313–324.

Hatch, T., White, M. E., & Faigenbaum, D. (2005). Expertise, credibility, and influence: How teachers can influence policy, advance research and improve performance. *Teachers College Record, 197*, 1004–1035.

Katzenmeyer, M., & Moller, G. (2001). *Awakening the sleeping giant: Helping teachers develop as leaders.* Newbury Park, CA: Corwin Press.

Lanting, A., & Jolly, A. (2001, April). *Leadership transformations of two teachers and their principal: A case study.* Paper presented at the meeting of the American Educational Research Association, Seattle, WA.

Leithwood, K., Jantzi, D., Earl, L., Watson, N., Levin, B., & Fullan, M. (2004). Strategic leadership for large-scale reform: The case of England's national literacy and numeracy strategy. *School Leadership and Management, 24*(1), 57–79.

Mimbs, C. (2002). Leadership development as self-development: An integrated process. *Action in Teacher Education, 24*(3), 22–25.

Moller, G., Childs-Bowen, D., & Scrivner, J. (2001). *Teachers of the year speak out: Tapping into teacher leadership.* Greensboro, NC: South Eastern Regional Vision for Education.

Mortimore, P., Sammons, P., Stoll, L., Lewis, D., & Ecob, R. (1988). *School matters: The junior years.* Wells, UK: Open Books.

Murphy, J. (2005). *Connecting teacher leadership and school improvement.* Thousand Oaks, CA: Corwin Press.

National Middle School Association. (2003). *This We Believe: Successful Schools for Young Adolescents.* Westerville, OH: Author.

Ogawa, R. T., & Bossert, S. T. (1995). Leadership as an organizational quality. *Educational Administration Quarterly, 31*(2), 224–43.

Ryan, S. A. (1999, April). *Principals and teachers leading together.* Paper presented at the meeting of the American Educational Research Association, Montreal, Canada.

Sammons, P. (1999). *School effectiveness: Coming of age in the twenty-first century.* Lisse, The Netherlands: Swets-Zeitlinger.

Sergiovanni, T. (2001). *The principalship: A reflective practice perspective.* Needham Heights, MA: Allyn & Bacon.

Short, P. M. (1998). Empowering leadership. *Contemporary Education, 69*(2), 70–72.

Silins, H., & Mulford, B. (2004). Schools as learning organizations—effects on teacher leadership and student outcomes. *School Effectiveness and School Improvement Journal, 15*(3–4), 343–366.

Silva, D. Y., Gimbert, B., & Nolan, J. (2000). Sliding the doors: Locking and unlocking possibilities for teacher leadership. *Teachers College Record, 102*, 779–804.

Smylie, M. A., & Denny, J. E. (1990). Teacher leadership: Tensions and ambiguities in organizational perspective. *Educational Administration Quarterly, 26*, 235–259.

Snell, J., & Swanson, J. (2000, April). *The essential knowledge and skills of teacher leaders: A search for a conceptual framework.* Paper presented at the meeting of the American Educational Research Association, New Orleans, LA.

Stoll, L., & Fink, D. (1996). *Changing our schools: Linking school effectiveness and school improvement.* Buckingham, UK: Open University Press.

Teddlie, C., Kirby, P., & Stringfield, S. (1989). Effective versus ineffective schools: Observable differences in the classroom. *American Journal of Education, 97*, 221–36.

Teddlie, C., & Stringfield, S. (1993). *Schools make a difference.* New York: Teachers College Press.

Thornton, C. A., Langrall, C. W., Jones, G. A., & Swafford, J. O. (2001). *The emergence of teacher leaders through professional development.* Columbus, OH: ERIC Clearinghouse for Science, Math, and Environmental Education. (ERIC Document Reproduction Service N0.465594)

Wasley, P. A. (1991). *Teachers who lead: The rhetoric of reform and the realities of practice.* New York: Teachers College Press.

Wetig, S. L. (2002, April). *Step up or step out: Perspectives on teacher leadership.* Paper presented at the meeting of the American Educational Research Association, New Orleans, LA.

Wynne, J. (2001). *Teachers as leaders in education reform.* Washington, DC: ERIC Clearinghouse on Teaching and Teacher Education. (ERIC Document Reproduction Service No. ED 462376)

York-Barr, J., & Duke, K. (2004). What do we know about teacher leadership? Findings from two decades of scholarship. *Review of Educational Research, 74,* 255–316.

CHAPTER TWENTY-FOUR

# A Model of Power as Social Relationships

## Teacher Leaders Describe the Phenomena of Effective Agency in Practice

MICHELE ACKER-HOCEVAR & DEBRA TOUCHTON

FLORIDA'S *BLUEPRINT 2000: A SYSTEM OF SCHOOL IMPROVEMENT AND ACCOUNTABILITY* RAISED hopes in the early 1990s that implementing shared governance and participatory decision making structures at local school sites might better position teacher leaders in districts and schools to exercise their agency in some unique ways. Teacher leaders might be involved in designing learning environments and experiences to better meet the needs of each individual child (Florida Commission on Education and Reform, 1993). This study, conducted with six teacher leaders from representative parts of the state, however, shows how teacher leaders were constrained by a complex set of organizational arrangements: existing structures, cultures, and power relations, which impacted their levels and extent of participation and involvement to exercise agency freely at their schools. These teacher leaders were highly dependent on their school administrators' acceptance of their expertise and ability to work autonomously and collectively to get their jobs done. This study might use these teachers' struggles and successes to explore ways to better support school teacher leadership. Many of these struggles could serve as archetypes to examine the organizational arrangements that mitigate against teacher leadership efforts. Administrators must

(a) be supportive of teacher leaders;
(b) find ways to involve teachers in meaningful work;
(c) ensure teachers' contributions positively affect school-wide improvement efforts;
(d) buffer teacher leaders from conflicting system demands that potentially place them in harm's way.

Finding better ways to link leadership to supportive structures, cultures, and power relations is mandatory as federal, state, and district oversight increases, further jeopardizing these teacher leaders from exercising agency to improve teaching and learning in school-wide improvements efforts.

The references in this article reflect the thinking at the time this study was conducted. Interestingly, many of the ideas still resonate more than a decade later.

## Introduction

Teachers are regarded as key players in the restructuring of schools and education (Joyce, 1986; Schlechty, 1990). Past educational reforms, grounded in Taylorism, isolated teachers from decision making and viewed them as workers to be told what to do, and how to do it (Callahan, 1962). Based on a 19th-century industrial model, this hierarchical nature of public schools continues to promote an adversarial relationship between administrators as managers and teachers as laborers (Schlechty, 1990; Troen & Boles, 1994). The aim of restructuring schools is to re-culture schools from places of teacher isolation and adversarial relationships with administrators (Lortie, 1975) to school cultures that encourage collegiality and commitment (Lieberman et al., 1988). School change involves many key stakeholders in the decision making processes, chief among them current teachers (Schlechty, 1990; Sizer, 1984).

Two national reports, the Holmes Group's *Tomorrow's Teachers* (1990), and the Carnegie Task Force on Teaching as a Profession, *A Nation Prepared: Teachers for the 21st Century* (Carnegie Forum on Education and the Economy, 1986), called for empowering teachers. Recommendations include: restructuring teacher preparation programs; restructuring schools to provide a professional environment for teachers to work and learn; restructuring the teaching force to create new roles for teachers to provide active leadership in the redesign of their schools; and giving teachers a greater voice in the decision making that affects school governance (Carnegie, 1986, Holmes, 1990; Troen & Boles, 1994). The Carnegie Report (1986) specifically emphasizes "teachers should be provided the discretion and autonomy that are the hallmarks of professional work" with the "authority in making the key decisions about the services they render" (p. 56). Further, the authors of the Carnegie Report believe that, without teacher support, reforms will be short-lived, and substantial success in school reform will only come through creating a new profession of well-educated teachers, prepared to assume new power and responsibilities in redesigning schools for the 21st century (Carnegie, 1986).

In two separate in-depth studies of schooling, Sizer (1984) and Goodlad (1984) echo similar conclusions pertaining to school improvement and restructuring. Sizer posited that one imperative for better schools is for teachers and students to be given the opportunity to be involved in decision making that affects them. Goodlad proposed "genuine decentralization of authority and responsibility to the local school within a framework designed to assure school-to-school equity and a measure of accountability" (p. 275) and the "guiding principle being put forward is that the school must become largely self-directing" (p. 276). For schools to be self-directing, teachers' and administrators' power relationships must change. Teachers must be more involved in all facets of school decision making such as:

(1) developing and delivering curriculum;
(2) developing schools as learning communities;
(3) developing their own professional training programs;
(4) becoming self governing
     (Darling-Hammond, 1987; Darling-Hammond with Sclan, 1992; Darling-Hammond & Goodwin, 1993; Joyce, 1986; Rosenholtz, 1989; Schlechty, 1990; White, 1992).

This chapter examines how Florida teachers of the year (1996 and 1997) described the decision making structures, teacher culture, and power/micropolitics of their work. The authors were interested particularly in how teacher leaders use their agency to accomplish work and make decisions together under the educational reform taking place in Florida. To achieve this goal, we have examined the findings from six in-depth interviews with elementary teachers selected as teachers of the year during 1996 or 1997. We investigate their perspectives of site-based decision making structures within their work contexts and relationships. These six teacher leaders' perspectives were of interest to gain a better understanding of how they might exercise influence, which we call agency, in their practice, and how effective it is under Florida's educational reform efforts during this timeframe.

The framework for this chapter extends Bennett and Harris's (1997) "Three Dimensional Model of Organizational Operation" regarding the mutual interdependence of culture, power, and structure to stories told by the six teacher leaders. Additionally, we examine how the "Dimensions of Social Relationships: An Agency Model for Power" might appear in practice under this umbrella of structure, culture, and power (Acker-Hocevar & Bauch, 1998). We situate the six power dimensions of this agency model within the Bennett and Harris framework:

(1) *autonomy*,
(2) political efficacy and expertise,
(3) responsibility and accountability,
(4) collegiality and status,
(5) resources, and
(6) *hierarchical relations*

The "Dimensions of Social Relationships: An Agency Model for Power" rely on the ability of these teacher leaders to exercise effective agency through various power dimensions such as:

(a) freedom (choice) to make decisions and exercise independent reflection (autonomy);
(b) application of knowledge to exert influence as empowerment through their internal motivation to gain and use knowledge to affect changes in learning and teaching (political efficacy and expertise);
(c) use of informal relations to wield group influence as legitimate in the informal group through valued interpersonal skills (collegiality and status);
(d) access to rewards and sanctions to create possibilities for action (resources);
(e) and manipulation of the rules to attain preferred outcomes (hierarchical relations).

This study investigates the personal perspectives of teachers in relation to their use of effective agency in school organizations. It is thought that through these teacher voices, we can better understand how to assist teachers and principals in their work together to move beyond bureaucratic mandates and address substantive and cultural changes in schools. We are interested in how administrators use the full range of teacher expertise in making school improvements.

## Defining Agency

We examine several scholars' definitions that lend themselves to assessing agency in relation to the six power dimensions that comprise the Agency Model for Power. Giddens (1984) describes power as social relationships in which individuals have the necessary capabilities to intervene in events and alter their course. Bandura (1986, 1997) describes effective agency through efficacy derived from mastery or expertise, physiological and emotional states in the form of arousal which lower or add to performance, vicarious experience or the degree to which a person can identify with a person or model, and social persuasion, which relates to the trustworthiness of the persuader. From Hales (1995), we describe agency in terms of physical, normative, economic, and knowledge resources that afford greater influence and persuasion over events. Furthermore, from Haugaard (1997), we view agency as the ability to use "multiple interpretive horizons" (pp. 184–185) to transcend dominance and see things from many perspectives.

We suggest that responsibility and accountability may rest on the internal processes in the school to enable or "empower" teachers to take a legitimate role in their school's development. We use Kanungo's (1992) differentiation of empowerment from a relational and motivational dimension, and draw upon the recommendation that empowerment be viewed from the motivational dimension, rather than the relational one, as an antidote to powerlessness, as Kanungo suggests. In other words, empowerment is a cognitive response to work conditions that either increase one's sense of intrinsic motivation or decrease it. In terms of hierarchical relations, we view teachers' access to power relationships through applying the "rules of the game" to attain preferred outcomes. More specifically, by having a working knowledge of the system and how to get around certain obstacles in the formal power structures, these teachers might affect change (Clegg, 1989). We believe that teacher leaders may have the social capacity to gain group membership and leverage their membership in the school and beyond it to make changes (Barnes, 1988).

Next, we examine a brief history of Florida reform and its present foci.

## History of Florida's Reform

Florida's most recent history of reform runs parallel to several national trends over the last 10 to 15 years. These trends include raising academic standards, adopting decentralized authority structures, systemic redesign, standardized testing, increased parent involvement, and public accountability through the publication of individual school performance ratings (Florida Office of Program Policy Analysis and Government Accountability, 1997, p. 14). Taking their lead from national reports, Florida developed and approved *Blueprint 2000: A System of School Improvement and Accountability* in 1990 as the educational policy of the State. The intent of this legislation was to make the school the site of accountability by raising student and teaching standards and decentralizing the system so school districts, and schools were free to design learning environments and experiences to better meet the needs of each individual child (Florida Commission on Education and Reform, 1993). After almost a decade of creating new state programs accompanied by state regulations and categorical funding, the State returned to three central themes:

(a) school-based management,
(b) accountability through student assessment,
(c) fiscal deregulation.

This accountability legislation purportedly freed local educators from unnecessary state bureaucratic control while simultaneously institutionalizing a design for holding schools accountable for student performance at the local sites.

Elements of the Blueprint 2000 legislation mandated that all schools in Florida's 67 counties annually assess their schools' status in relation to the state's seven goals, set priorities, and develop school improvement plans (State of Florida Department of Education, 1992). A method for meeting this mandate was developed by the State and included the following requirements: each school was to create annually a School Advisory Council (SAC) comprised of teachers, students, parents, and local citizens representative of the ethnic and economic composition of the community; the SAC was approved and appointed by the school's District School Board for each new school year; schools conducted a needs assessment annually to determine their status on the mastery of the seven Blueprint goals; and the SAC developed a *School Improvement Plan* (SIP) based on the seven state goals. In addition to the state goals, school boards identified school goals and standards that reflected the needs of the local school community (State of Florida Office of the Auditor General, 1994). School Boards were responsible for approving and monitoring district schools' SIPs. The first school improvement plans were due at the end of the 1992–1993 school year and implemented during the 1993–1994 school year.

Much of the school improvement and restructuring literature is based on the premise that teacher empowerment, through participation in school-based decision making, will lead to educational reform and school improvement. With the passage of Blueprint 2000, now known as *Florida's System of School Improvement and Accountability*, the State of Florida implicitly mandated teacher involvement and participation in site-based decision making through the development and implementation of SIPs. The State of Florida continued its progress toward an integrated system of reform through the establishment of The Sunshine State Standards (SSS), which were developed and implemented in seven content areas: Language Arts, Mathematics, Science, Social Studies, Foreign Languages, Fine Arts, and Health. Districts began implementing The Sunshine State Standards during the 1997–98 school year. As many states turned to standards to improve student learning, Florida not only developed and implemented standards-driven reform but designed a performance-based criterion reference assessment instrument, the *Florida Comprehensive Assessment Test* (FCAT), that measured student progress in reading and math, based on the Language Arts and Mathematics SSS. It is important to note that Florida's standards-driven reform began well before the reauthorization of the Elementary and Secondary Act, known as No Child Left Behind legislation.

Despite this dramatic shift of authority from the state to the local site, established norms of organizational power arrangements seemed to thwart intended state changes. Specifically, many of these norms, embedded in power routines and relationships, lie beneath the surface within the day-to-day practices and structures of everyday school life (e.g., Bredeson, 1993; Lortie, 1975; Johnson, 1990; Mitchell & Beach, 1993). Analyzing how teachers negotiated these power routines is instrumental in understanding the norms of teachers' work lives, which might threaten or support the intended outcomes of recent reform efforts.

Since 1992, school-based accountability has been driving Florida's educational reform. Through the voices of these teachers, we find school-based decision making structures are in place in all of the schools, as dictated by law. How decision making is conducted, however, is quite another matter. The decision making structures are similar in the teachers' schools based on the mandates from the state, school advisory councils (SACs) and school improvement plans (SIPs). Additionally, grade level teams and other committees are organized when needed in areas such as discipline, technology, and communication.

# Teacher Leaders

Based on study results, we gleaned insights into the work context of teachers of the year and their day-to-day practices, which fostered or decreased conditions for increased involvement. Like other states, Florida annually designates an "outstanding" teacher from each of its 67 diverse school systems defined by county boundaries. Teacher award criteria include:

(a) demonstrated leadership at the school, district, and/or state and national levels;
(b) possession of a superior ability to foster excellence in education; demonstrated exemplary interpersonal skills (e.g., with parents and the community);
(c) evidence of collaboration with other professionals;
(d) and a strong commitment to effective teaching and learning.

Generally, we might assume, then, that these select teachers have mastered political power arrangements in a way that allows them to be seen as highly successful practitioners with influence. Their status and expanded roles within school-wide improvement might suggest that these teachers would exemplify changing beliefs about power, particularly because they represent the "ideal" teacher and are held up as models for other teachers by the State. On the other hand, these teachers could be the most compliant of teachers, politically selected by their counties to make them look good. Drawing from the work of Acker-Hocevar and Bauch (1998), we knew that overall, teachers of the year felt *less powerless* than their non-award counterparts; we wondered why this might be true.

## Teacher Leaders and Their School Demographics

We identified elementary teachers from six different regions of the state and intentionally selected teachers who had earned higher academic credentials than the bachelor's degree. These teachers represent small, medium, and large school districts, where there is a wide disparity in the range of socio-economic levels of students, numbers of students on free and reduced-price lunch, English as Second Language Learners (ESOL), and students with disabilities (see Table 1 below). These teachers have witnessed firsthand the impact of Florida's school improvement and accountability movement on schools, administrators, teachers, students, and parents. As such, they offer a unique perspective over time to "reading" the changes in structures, culture, and power relationships.

June is a nineteen-year veteran who is African American. She holds a Master's degree and is from a suburban PreK-5 school in a small to medium school district in north Florida. The student enrollment, 808, is the largest of the six teachers. The mobility rate of this school is the lowest of the six schools at 11.7%. The majority of the students are from professional educated families. June is in her first year of serving on the Education Standards Commission, a commission appointed by the education commissioner.

Nan's K-5 school is located in a large school district in central Florida. She has 14 years of experience, has an Educational Specialist degree, and is Euro-American. The student enrollment of her school is 710, the second largest school of the six teachers. Nan came to this school after serving in a district level position where she helped teachers with reading and writing programs.

Lynn's K-5 school is in a small to medium school district in west central Florida. She has 16 years of experience and a Master's degree; she too is Euro-American. The student enrollment of her school is 651. The administrator has been the principal of this school for many years.

Table 1. Teacher and School Demographics

| Teacher and School Demographics | Teachers | | | | | |
|---|---|---|---|---|---|---|
| | June | Nan | Lynn | Maria | Tim | Grace |
| **Teacher Demographics** | | | | | | |
| *Years of Experience* | 19 | 14 | 16 | 13 | 16 | 11 |
| *Year Teacher of the Year* | 1997 | 1997 | 1996 | 1997 | 1997 | 1996 |
| *Highest Degree* | M. Ed. | Ed. S. | MA | M. Ed. | Ed. D. | M. Ed. |
| **School Demographics** | | | | | | |
| *Student Population* | 808 | 710 | 651 | 648 | 612 | 550 |
| *% Mobility Rate* | 11.7 | 40.2 | 30.5 | 55 | 64.5 | 35.2 |
| *% on Free/Reduced Lunch* | 3.1 | 59.3 | 50.5 | 64.8 | 99.7 | 50.5 |
| *% in ESOL (ELL today)* | 6 | 5.8 | .4 | 10.5 | 28.5 | 1.5 |
| *% Students with Disabilities* | 25.3 | 14.7 | 22.7 | 15.2 | 6.7 | 21.4 |
| *% Gifted* | 9 | 1.8 | 0 | 1.2 | 5 | 2 |

Maria's K-2 school is in a small rural district in east central Florida. She has a Master's degree, is Euro-American, and has 13 years of experience. The school has a new administrator this year who is quite different from the previous administrator. The first-year principal, as described by Maria, is "by the book."

Tim's K-5, Title I school is located in a large south Florida school district. He has a doctoral degree and 16 years of experience; he is Euro-American. The percentage of students receiving either free or reduced-price lunches is the highest of the six schools, 99.7%. The mobility rate of this school is high at 64.5%. This school was identified as a Critically Low School for two years, 1996–97 and 1997–98, but has risen since then to a Level 2 school (at this time, critically low was the lowest rating for a school). Tim was at this school as a Teacher of the Year during the time it was identified as critically low. He moved to a high school in the same school district this year to head up a new program for students at risk. Tim's story is an interesting one in that he was able also to contrast elementary school culture with high school culture. Tim has participated as a member of the Florida League of Teachers for three years, a select group of outstanding teachers, who shape policy at the State level. He is also on the State Title I Task Force.

Grace's K-5, Title I school is located in a large school district in south Florida. She has a master's degree, 11 years of experience, and is Euro-American. The student enrollment is 550, reflecting the smallest student population of the six schools in this assessment. Grace was not at this school when she was a Teacher of the Year. Her previous school had a higher mobility rate of 87.6%, and the percentage of students receiving free and reduced lunch was 74.1%.

# Data Collection and Analysis

Teachers of the year were contacted in 1998 and asked to participate in an hour or longer phone interview that took place over a three-month period. The conversations were recorded, and both Acker-Hocevar and Touchton participated in the phone interviews through use of the conference call technique. All interviews were taped and transcribed.

Prior to the scheduled interview, each teacher was faxed or mailed the questionnaire that guided the interview. The points of discussion were:

- Describe the formal and informal work processes that lead to decision making in your school. (What roles do teachers play? Administrators? How are people held responsible/accountable for implementing decisions? What role do you play in decision making? How is this similar to or different from other teachers?)
- How do you define teacher expertise? What is the teacher culture at your school for teachers to use their knowledge and expertise? (How are various levels of expertise utilized? How does expertise afford your involvement in decision making?)
- Describe the power relationships within your school between different groups such as teachers and administrators? Probes for this question are: What do the teachers say about these relationships? How do you think about these relationships?
- Tell us a story about how you use your personal power in school? Help us gain "insights" into how or what you value and why it may be similar or different from other teachers? Administrators?

We used a phenomenological approach, meaning that the everyday experience of the teacher was the starting point to discover the themes in participant language. We established trustworthiness through individual member checks with all participants, researcher debriefing after each phone interview, and arriving at agreement on all the codes and categories. The authors discussed each interview after the first coding. Following the steps outlined in Lincoln and Guba (1985) and Miles and Huberman (1994), we

(1) identified the units of information in the transcripts,
(2) agreed upon several working categories to locate the specific units,
(3) grouped the categories together to identify major subthemes across all the interviews;
(4) combined subthemes into four major themes. The themes were:

- decision making structures,
- teacher culture,
- personal narratives,
- power/micropolitics.

The actual words of the teachers are used. The actual intent of the teachers' words was never changed.

# Decision Making Structures Theme

The first theme, decision making structures, has three subthemes:

(1) Teachers' perceptions of voice;
(2) Role of the administrator;
(3) Accountability and teacher surveillance.

## Teachers' Perceptions of Voice

The differences in responses to the decision making structures theme are based on how teachers perceive school-based decision making, not whether it is present. Considering only the decision making structures gives us little information on the power relationships within schools, and whether these teachers are granted a voice to make and implement decisions. Their stories, however, do provide us with insights into how they perceive their own power within decision making structures. Many of these teachers describe their colleagues as powerless, even though the structures are in place to empower them. In many situations, this is a result of administrative control over the structures in place.

The following quote from Grace illustrates her initial optimism and how willing she was to participate in shared decision making.

> Our school advisory council was a big thing for me and was definitely a decision making group made up of teachers, at least one teacher from each grade and parents…and within [the structure] no one individual had more decision making power in the council. How much participation and involvement and vision you have and wanted to have in that particular group was up to the individual. I felt like I had a role in the direction of the school.

Nan and June speak positively of their experiences in decision making. Lynn, in contrast, tells a very different story of her experiences. Nan states:

> So when I think about decision making in the team, we made decisions about our instruction, about the way we grouped children, about the whole—we were able to start from scratch and create it all, including who would be involved in it, meaning teachers, parents and children [talking about a creating a multi-age instructional program].

June worked on a team where they made decisions together, also. The team was central to decision making structures in the school. The teams were in close physical proximity, which enhanced their ability to work together. These teachers displayed their practice, actively learning from each other.

> The way our school is designed, four teachers have a common planning room where our desks are in the same place, and we have the same planning time, so we have time together. We have grade level meetings. We plan together and share materials.

Lynn's comments represent her frustration with labels ascribed to teachers who were not seen as "players."

Teachers simply go now through the motions of decision making, but no one takes it seriously. Teachers simply want to avoid being labeled as a person who is not in appearance of moving in the direction of the district. You go to committee meetings anymore, and everyone there sits stone silent and they wait to be told what to do. That's how it works. People refuse to do things anymore. We don't really have collaborative decision making. It's simply not there. You appear to have all kinds of stuff. People will do the work. They will produce documents. They will have something in writing that says, thus and so and such is happening, but they will do the bare minimum to meet the requirements. The idea of decision making is we will all get together at the end of the year and we'll go through the SIP and we'll get everyone to agree on a sentence and write it on the overhead and in the document. When it is finished, no one is really buying into things, or has a part in how things go. Because in the first place, somebody above the principal has already made that decision.

Each of the teachers expresses how they see themselves and others in their decision making structures. Some of the teachers feel as if they were exercising agency through their voice in the process, others express very little impact. Where teachers make a difference, they are involved and actively committed. Where there is little or no impact, there is silence and withdrawal.

## Role of the Administrator

When looking at decision making structures, it is necessary to take a close look at the role the administration plays. Often, what they do and what they do not do has a significant impact on decision making. We found that these teachers of the year recognized the role of the administrator in supporting and fostering teacher empowerment. They reflected on how different principals influence the decision making processes by freeing people to make and implement decisions. Administrators have a direct influence on power relationships within their schools. Several of the teachers told stories about changing principals, going from an empowering principal to a non-empowering one. Others talked about administrators' leadership styles, which either enhanced or detracted from their participation in shared decision making.

June comes from a school where a school-based decision making model was in place for 10 years. This model was the result of design teams. There were clear lines of authority and school-based decision making was done to change or implement a school-wide policy, adopt a new program, or alter an existing one, and/or add or modify school improvement goals. The teachers voted every year as to whether they wanted to retain this model. June explains how their previous administrator trusted and supported them in their decisions.

We had an administrator who was very willing to provide teachers with decision making power…our administrator actually relinquished his veto power so that his vote and his assistant principal's vote was equal to the other members. Now we are into our second year of a new administrator and things are different. You have different personalities in administrative positions. We're trying to keep this model going. What we've discovered is that the first administrator empowered us, left the reins loose in allowing teachers to make decisions and implement decisions more so than our new administrator. So that's what we're dealing with now. The shared decision making model still works, but it's different when teachers have been allowed to have certain administrative powers, I'd guess I'll call them. And then when those powers are reeled in, it's like you feel like there's something that has been taken away, that you were never supposed to have that type of power anyway. There is a strong power play right now because the teachers were empowered and now they feel that they are not empowered.

Maria describes how decision making seems to occur outside her school at the district level. With a new administrator, the principal appears to follow the book and district directives. Maria, too, has experienced changes in how she sees her role in relation to the new administrator.

> Since we have [had] a new administrator, I think she is very by the book and trying to do everything. Which is fine, I mean that's what she's got to do. But for us, there has been very little decision making. And currently most of the decisions that have been made this year, that have affected us, have been county-level decisions—well we're told they're county-level decisions that are just handed down. In fact, last year, we had changed math series and we had a county committee and the committee could not reach a consensus, so the county office just decided that none of the texts that we chose would suffice and chose a different one. And it's been a lot of that kind of thing—mostly handed down decisions. There's been very little discussion.

Maria's experience of powerlessness is more pervasive than the other participants. She sees the problem as a district and school problem. Tim, on the other hand, experienced a change in principals, too. His new principal, however, recognizes and uses teacher leadership as she learns about the school and her role.

> We thought with the change of principals, because one was very into, you know, building teacher leadership, but the other one was just really, initially, a very wonderful person, just getting her feet wet as a principal. She was so busy trying to find out how to be a principal that she relied on all of us who already had experience. Our school was one of the worst schools in the county, but we changed dramatically over six years.

Tim now compares his high school experiences this year and sees very little teacher input in decision making. He sees the size of the school and the power that is delegated to assistant principals as problematic. The lack of communication among administrators leads to misconceptions about what is taking place by the principal. This scenario places teachers in a precarious position, being in the middle between the principal and another administrator.

Grace tells a story about her involvement in a school committee at her present school. At the end of the year, the committee members were eager to discuss their recommendations with the administrators. All their efforts and hard work for an entire year were dismissed in one sentence. Nothing was implemented. She said of another committee incident:

> I suppose we felt let down as professionals that we had done a lot of good work and it didn't go anywhere. I think there are teachers who really want to move mountains here [the school], but because they have had the same type of situations in their committees, you know, it stops with this administrator, it seems like their morale to want to do anything is "yeah, but its gonna stop here and we're never going to see any action."

The role of the administrator seems to influence the degree and extent to which teachers feel their efforts are valued. Motivation is either increased or decreased based on how the administration recognizes the efforts of teachers. The new principal at Tim's school is different from the one at Maria's or June's schools. This administrator acknowledges teacher leaders and uses them to learn about her role.

## Accountability and Teacher Surveillance

With empowerment comes added responsibility and accountability. In all of the stories told by these teachers, the subject of raising scores and teacher accountability seems to be the most pressing. A sense of surveillance over their work implies that monitoring teachers' work will improve test scores. Maria's frustration is obvious.

> But there is a bigger emphasis on test scores at the county level. The evaluation process has changed drastically at our school…instead of two observations (a year) and an evaluation, we are getting two observations per week and an evaluation every 6 weeks. So I think the stress level has increased because of that.…I feel very accountable and I'm sure that test scores will be an issue as soon as they are in.

Lynn shares the same concerns as Maria about the pressure put on teachers.

> Somebody has to be accountable. They are making the teachers feel awfully accountable.…And if you [administrator] don't recognize the expertise of your teachers, and continually lord over them, treating them like children and being flat out mean to them, you know then I guess you do have a lot to fear (laughs) because when the boom lowers, you are not going to have people backing you as an administrator.

Tim too is upset at how teacher evaluations are centering on tests children take.

> You know, teachers' evaluations are going to start centering on how well your students are doing on a test. And so I think what's going to happen is that we are going to start focusing on how to get high scores and get away from some of the good fundamental practices that help improve education. It's not going to be on how am I going to help you improve, it's going to be, I'm monitoring you to see whether or not your kids are scoring well because that's how you are going to be evaluated. Not to say that we shouldn't be held accountable for the academic achievement of our students, but we have to look at more than just test scores.

The subthemes of decision making structures, perception of voice, role of administrator, and teacher accountability and surveillance appear to suggest that schools like June's, which institutionalized a decision making structure, were more successful in socializing a new principal to her role. The teachers exerted a collective agency and shared a common model for how to include their voice. In the other schools, the involvement and participation of the teachers were influenced greatly by the administrator. How teachers viewed their roles in decision making affected their perceptions of their empowerment or non-empowerment.

## Teacher Culture

The teachers' opinions reflect a sense and an understanding of the varying teacher cultures existing in their schools. To understand these various forms that teacher culture can take; we turn to Hargreaves's (1994) typology of teacher culture. Teacher cultures provide the context for teacher work. Hargreaves identifies two important dimensions of teacher culture: content and form. The content of teacher cultures is comprised of attitudes, beliefs, values, habits, and ways of doing things that are shared within a particular group, or among the teacher community within a school. The form that teacher cultures take represents the patterns of relationships and associations between members of the culture. Hargreaves identifies five broad forms of teacher culture: *individualism, collaboration, contrived collegiality, balkanization,* and the *moving mosaic.* He posits that the success or failure of educational change can be attributed to these different forms (relationships) of teacher culture in the school. Like Hargreaves, Sarason (1990) believes that through altering power relationships within schools, educational change will occur. He argues, "Schools will remain intractable to desired reform as long as we avoid confronting these existing power relationships" (Sarason, 1990, p. 5). These relationships are between teachers and administrators, teachers and teachers, teachers and parents, and teachers and students. Teachers' responses seem to indicate that the teacher cultures contribute greatly to teachers' feelings of empowerment or disempowerment.

## Individualism

The nature of teaching is a state of professional isolation, of working alone, separate from colleagues (Lortie, 1975; Fullan & Hargreaves, 1996); this dynamic contributes to the individualism teacher culture. The individualism teacher culture isolates teachers from their colleagues and focuses their attentions on their classrooms. Individualism, in itself, is not a negative condition; however, some researchers (Lortie, 1975; Rosenholtz, 1989) have focused on individualism as a psychological characteristic of teachers rather than as a result of workplace conditions. Hargreaves (1994) argues that individualism is a consequence of complex organizational conditions and constraints that need to be attended to if individualism teacher cultures are to be removed. He identified three determinants of individualism teacher culture: *constrained, strategic,* and *elective.* Constrained individualism occurs when teachers teach, plan, and generally work alone because of administrative or other situational constraints, such as non-involving styles of administration, school architectural structures, scarcity of planning space, shortage of teachers, and/or scheduling difficulties. Strategic individualism refers to the ways teachers actively construct and create individualistic patterns of work as a response to daily responsibilities of their work. Lastly, elective individualism, a preferred form of professional action for all or part of one's work, refers to a teacher's choice to work alone all or some of the time when there are opportunities to work collaboratively with colleagues. It is only when a majority of teachers isolate themselves, creating a negative individualism teacher culture that one could suspect a systemic problem where teachers might be withdrawing from threatening, unpleasant, or unrewarding working relationships.

Constrained individualism appears to be the case in two of the teachers' stories. They describe work situations where the administration has created a disempowering rather than empowering atmosphere. Because administrators have created a workplace where teachers are not valued, teachers consider staying in their rooms a safe option. The following comments are examples of what Hargreaves calls constrained individualism.

Maria discusses how she views teachers trying to negotiate agency around the rigidity and behavior of the new principal. These teachers resist covertly the control of this principal by exercising decision making within their classrooms in terms of materials they think are best for students.

> I do think we feel very isolated and that we don't; maybe, use our expertise as in areas of strengths and weaknesses as we should. Yes, we do make decisions, but they're more or less behind closed doors and we're not going to make it known. It's not an open thing. In other words, if I choose to do supplemental whatever, I'm not going to make it widely known because I don't know if that's going to be acceptable.

Lynn describes her response to the conditions that surround working in her school:

> Teachers practice avoidance and enter the silence of their classrooms. I immerse myself in my own world. I know what I have to say is not welcome, so I keep my mouth shut. Most people take the kind of apathetic attitude that I am going down to my room, close the door, and I am not going to have anything to do with it [school]. It is very common to hear people say, "I just stay away from the front office; I never go down there. As long as I do my thing down here and put it on paper so it looks like everything is going just as planned, I spend my day, and I get out of here."

Grace relates how she stays in her room. The differences between the principal and assistant principal make the working conditions difficult for teachers. Many teachers are avoiding the administrator they view as negative.

> You know I try to keep in my room and do the best job that I can for the 22 students that I have. I think it's a particular administrator to be honest with you. I don't think it's both administrators because one is positive and one wants to make sure that she has the final word. I don't know whether that's a power kind of issue or if she's really a hard worker and wants the best for the teachers, students, and parents. But it seems like that's where the buck stops.

Isolation from administration and the activities of the school is a result of the administration not valuing the teachers' input. Teachers reflected feelings of disillusionment in participating in daily school activities. To save themselves from disempowering feelings, they stayed in their classrooms, away from the administration.

## Collaboration Teacher Culture

The collaboration teacher culture supports the professional empowerment of teachers and fosters and builds upon qualities of openness, trust, and support between teachers and their colleagues. Within this culture, collaborative working relationships between teachers are spontaneous, emerging from the teachers themselves; voluntary because of the perceived value of working together; development-oriented, to meet the need, not the mandate of their own professional confidence and expertise as a community; pervasive across time and space, it is not a scheduled activity; and outcomes are unpredictable because discretion and control over what will be developed are within the control of the teacher, not the mandate. Collaborative teacher cultures are generally incompatible with centralized school systems and can cause difficulty for the administrator in providing the environment for a collaborative culture. This culture builds collective agency where teachers are able to interact knowledgably and assertively with the mandates of reform and accountability; able and willing to select which innovations to adopt, alter, and ignore as best benefits their purposes and circumstances (Hargreaves, 1994). Two examples of this culture are June's and Tim's schools.

June was in a school, as you may remember, that had site-based decision making long before it was mandated in Florida. The maturity of the teachers in wanting to work together was a valued norm in her school.

> Well as I explained, we are really going through a change with the new administrator and the communication before; we felt, was more open. The communication now, we feel, is more closed, and so what we have done, several times we've had informal faculty sessions, which the teachers called for. They said, we have to talk to administration. And out of the faculty meetings came a group called the communication committee…once a week, every week one team member from every section every grade level meets with the administration.

Tim relates a story about how he spear-headed a grant that focused on inter-agency collaboration. The intent of the grant was to work collaboratively across agencies to address the needs of the students in the school. Remarkably, no new programs were instituted. The focus of the grant was to work on collaboration among partners.

> We wrote a lot of grants…the Foundation had a whole different focus and they really wanted us to look at holistic improvement.…We tackled our full-service school problem [it wasn't working]. I was given leeway with this [the money], and I structured it. The grant was based on the input from teachers…whatever the committee wanted, we did as long as it was approved by the advisory council.

For June, because there was a collaboration teacher culture in place, a change of administration did not totally disrupt the teachers' collective agency. They found a way to stay empowered by using their collective voices. Tim's school also showed the resilience of a collaboration teacher culture by working together to bring their school from a state designation of "Critically Low" to a district designation of a demonstration site school where the district "sent other schools to see us and we were one of the seven schools in the county designated as a site for other schools to come and visit." Like June, Tim's school also changed administration. It was apparent in both of these cases that the strong collaboration teacher culture was the glue that maintained the teachers' sense of empowerment through the change.

## Contrived Collegiality Teacher Culture

Contrived collegiality teacher culture is seen as the antithesis of collaboration teacher culture. Collaboration among teachers is not spontaneous, but it is regulated by administration; it is compulsory, not voluntary; it is fixed in time and space—scheduled by the administration; it is implementation- rather than development-oriented—teachers are told what to implement; and outcomes are predictable rather than unpredictable. This culture replaces spontaneous, unpredictable, and difficult-to-control forms of teacher-generated collaboration with forms of collaboration that are captured, contained, and contrived by the administration, giving the impression that there is a collegial culture in place when in fact there is none. Systems must give schools and teachers the responsibility for development as well as implementation of state reform initiatives, providing teachers the flexibility to work with one another in developing programs of their own. This approach is empowering teachers rather than "cosmetically empowering teachers" (Hargreaves, 1994) through contrived collegial cultures. Grace's response is a good example of schools that look like they are collaborative when they are not.

> And each year teachers are assigned and sometimes signed up for, if they don't actually participate, to be on the subcommittee of the plan. At each meeting we are responsible for keeping notes and an agenda. We have, I guess, something like a record sheet that basically has what the expectations are, how we go about meeting those expectations, and who is responsible for meeting those expectations as well as the time frame. And when we meet each month we review these and take these to the advisory committee. But I think the perception is that most teachers feel they are not going to get any further than the one administrator. So after we exhaust all our ideas, typically, no action is taken.

Examples of contrived collegiality teacher culture may be an unintentional outcome of Florida's educational reform and accountability movement. Teachers are expected to be involved and included in the decision making process. Therefore, administrators are forced to "make the process look good," causing teachers to feel that the process is a sham.

## Balkanization Teacher Culture

In the balkanization culture, teachers work in separate and sometimes territorial groups that give them identity and provide the basis for power, status, and resources. Balkanized teacher culture is defined by the pattern of interrelationships among teachers. Teachers work neither in isolation nor with most of their colleagues as a whole school, but in small sub-groups within the school. Low permeability, high permanence, personal identification, and a political complexion characterize this form of teacher culture. The political complexion often causes divisiveness in the school because of the imbalances of power and status. These kinds of power relationships are evident in several of the teachers' stories.

Although June's school has aspects of a collaborative teaching culture, there is also evidence that balkanization is present.

> We are pretty much separated by grade level, because all of us teach the same things and we work and we share with each other. The different grade levels know who is good and who is not. I don't know if this is a power play, but sometimes I hear comments in my group. I know our third grade team is strong. In 10 years, we have had a [school] teacher of the year every year, and in our third grade team now, four teachers have been teachers of the year.

Nan's view of balkanization is based less on physical structures and more on philosophical differences among the faculty:

> There is a group of us who meet together and are like-minded, but we sought each other out. We feel supported by the principal—she has allowed us opportunities to do whatever we wanted to do. Another group of teachers feel blocked by the principal—they don't think philosophically about teaching and learning the same way the principal wanted to move. Then there is a group who doesn't care about it [where the principal was moving the school].

## Mosaic Teacher Culture

The fifth teacher culture is what Hargreaves (1994) calls the moving mosaic, similar to Senge's "learning organization" (Senge, 1990). In this teacher culture, the school is committed to continuous improvement; teachers work together closely as colleagues in planning, decision making, and classroom practice; all or most teachers are leaders at some point or another; the principal is the leading learner. This culture, described by Hargreaves as emergent, is flexible, responsive, dynamic, and has blurred boundaries. Hargreaves cautions that the moving mosaic, although it sounds like Utopia, can easily become the manipulative mosaic, with teachers and schools having responsibilities without the power, as the center retains control over the essentials of curriculum and testing, over the basic products, which teachers must turn out. Much of the future of teachers' work and the degrees of empowerment contained within it will be settled by how this emerging context of organizational flexibility is determined and defined (p. 69).

Of the six teachers interviewed, Tim's school was the closest to this description of teacher culture. The school had been identified as one of the worst in the county, a Critically Low School. Through grants written by teachers, and teachers working for the students, the school became a district demonstration school. However, this school is beginning to have its problems because it is getting larger, as described by Tim. "Our former principal was up for principal of the year and we started getting credibility for the school through a lot of things we were doing. And then we started the Resource Room (for teachers) because there wasn't a place in the school for teachers to come together collaboratively and work."

## Personal Narratives

The third theme, personal narratives, emerged from the stories that teachers told us. We found that each teacher had a personal narrative that was woven throughout the interview. We share these with you now. We tell these stories to inform what shapes our relationships with others and informs our institutional commitments (Johnson, 1993, p. 150). These narratives, woven into the historical fabrics we are a part of, are responses to circumstances confronted in our lives, circumstances we interpret often through our behaviors-in-action. Johnson (1993) refers to these behaviors as actions possessing "imaginative synthetic unity" (p. 152). Thus, we write and rewrite our stories into meaningful and purposeful accounts through a process that ultimately renders our stories coherent. Our accounts, consequently, lend themselves to self-understandings and offer us the potential for self-transformation. Through our reflections, learning, and imaginings, we can engage in the daily and ongoing processes of construction and reconstruction of self to consciously and unconsciously shape who we are. Teachers face numerous challenges and problems in their work lives. These stories suggest how teachers construct their roles as teachers, make sense of their worlds, and determine what is meaningful to them. These narratives are calls for action which motivate and enable teachers to exercise agency within moral understandings. These moral understandings involve a "broad range of imaginative structures, such as image schemas, various types of prototype structure, metonymy, and metaphors. As a result, they do not simply mirror some objective reality or category rather; they define that reality by means of imaginative structure" (Johnson, 1993, p. 192).

To understand how the teachers in this study chose to exercise agency, we use metaphors, roles, scripts, frames, and models, as suggested by Johnson (1993) in his book, *Moral Imagination*. By using these structures we explore insights, raise questions, and view how certain moral issues are generated through these various lenses. For example, how did the teachers choose to use their agency to make an impact with parents, students, colleagues, and also within the larger professional and political arenas of their work? Responses that underlie these scripts, frames, and models call often for action, in difficult circumstances. We expand Johnson's concept to include the actions contextualized within organizational structures, power relationships, and cultural norms of teachers' work that add meaning to these teachers' work and stories.

This study defines how these teachers use their definitions of psychological empowerment around four task-related cognitions—meaning, competence, choice, and impact (Kane & Montgomery, 1998). We begin with Tim's narrative around the metaphor of *advocate*, examine June's script for *fairness*, Lynn's frame for *enabling others*, Nan's model of *teacher professionalism*, Maria's role in her *relationships with the administration*, and Grace's frame of *innovation*. These teachers construct and reconstruct their stories within particular cognitive frames.

### Advocacy

Advocacy was Tim's personal metaphor. He chose to be an advocate for other teachers, and this choice consistently brings him back to his role and identification with other teachers. "I can't forget that I am a teacher and that is where I am coming from. What is good for teachers is good for kids. I mean, that's been my whole philosophy. If I am going to be an advocate for teachers, it is because I want to make them better advocates for students." The metaphor of advocacy for Tim generates persistence. He explains he learned how to stand up for what he wanted even in the face of defeat. Tim saw many teachers get knocked down and give up. He explains often to other teachers that you may lose some battles and win others, but you "can't let the fact that you lose the battle mean you can't move forward with what you are trying to do." Tim's advocacy role includes articulating the basic needs of teachers. "Until you take care of basic needs, you can't move to higher levels of performance. The lack of supplies, materials, information, and administrative directives which entrenches teachers in non-productive work eats away at their professionalism." Tim complains about the lack of time in schools, particularly larger secondary schools. Teachers don't have time to dialogue and reflect on their professional practices together. He strives to find ways for teachers to have opportunities for dialogue, reflection, teacher leadership, mentoring, and feedback for improvement and growth.

## Fairness

June is motivated by an intrinsic set of rules around fairness formed by her race, religion, and concern for people. She relates how as an African American growing up in Washington, DC, she confronted unfairness when her father was transferred to Nebraska; she was the only Black in her college classes at the university. She describes herself as a combination of what she knows and who she is as a person. "I'm a person. When there is a problem, I can look for the positives and see a way to find the possibilities of a solution. I am seen as being very fair. I've had people tell me that. That's why people select me to be a facilitator. Colleagues feel that I won't represent any one group at the expense of another." Later June says, "Plus, I am a Christian, so it's important that I do things the way I'm taught to do….If I hear something, I don't repeat it to anybody. And, if I am in group and I'm hearing a rumor, I will go to my room. Or, if I stay, I will find another point of view and share it." June censors her actions in terms of what she views as fair, often taking risks to be a spokesperson for the group. She relates an incident where teachers and the new administration met in a faculty meeting; the meeting was tense. "…[N]obody would talk. I was a nervous wreck, but I thought this is ridiculous." June felt that if the teachers' complaints were to be understood, someone had to voice these complaints. "So in the most positive way that I could, I started talking and then other people started talking, getting things going."

## Enabling Others

Lynn's reference for action is to enable others through her emotional support. "I am very much in [support] that we don't keep doing things for people. We open up opportunities for people and we teach them how to run with it…I am not here to cripple people." Lynn said she felt the pain of other teachers and saw her role as helping teachers who could turn around and help kids. She referenced her actions against her code of personal responsibility for enabling others to help themselves, particularly in viewing problems from the source of the problem "Don't make it yours. Making it yours is not going to make it any better." Lynn believes that being able to separate oneself from the problem takes a lot of self-discipline and putting aside one's own needs and seeing the bigger picture. "The first thing we want to do is righteously defend ourselves and sometimes righteously defending ourselves is not it. You have to know how to pick your battles….It is knowing how to stand there and not become a victim."

## Teacher Professionalism

Nan is a take-charge person, a self-motivated learner, who identifies areas for her professional development and pursues those areas. Her model of professionalism involves teachers in roles of examining their own practices and constantly improving them. Nan is most comfortable doing workshops that she has lived in her classroom. She uses her teacher expertise to befriend like-minded teachers who, like herself, see improvement as a moving target, take charge of their professionalism, to study and reflect on their practice. She sees herself as able to translate teachers' professional needs into meaningful actions through listening. "Listening to other people, knowing what teachers want to do, what they don't want to do, as well as insight, and a direction to move in terms of best practices is important." Nan is respectful of other teachers and feels strongly that teachers need ongoing challenges for professional growth. Her schema for professionalism affects how she sees other teachers as learners. Some teachers are willing and open to learning new teaching techniques that are philosophically aligned with their beliefs. Other teachers are resistant to any change, and the last group of teachers gives the appearance of change, but nothing substantive occurs to their beliefs and practices.

## Relationships

Maria's agency is defined by her relationships with the administration. She worked under three different types of administrators we categorize as laissez-faire, charismatic, and authoritarian. Her description of the laissez-faire administrator is "He was very laid back and whatever you want to do was okay, as long as everything is going along fine." The second administrator was creative and innovative and "student achievement improved." Presently, with the third administrator, Maria sees herself as isolated. She relates how the present administrator took away the keys from all the teachers, changed the way they did their plan books, and instituted a policy regarding teachers' children coming to the school.

> You know we have always had access to our classrooms; we've always had keys and things and that's changed. We can't go and come as we please anymore—we had to turn in our keys—and the way we've done our plan books has changed and for a lot us change is not an issue. It's the way the change [occurred]—it's more of the reason for the change, or the way the change was bought about. Even child care [laughs]....our children could be bused here after school, or if they were here, stay with us until we left....Now they can't; they have to go to daycare.

Maria sees her agency for action diminished with the current administrator. She contrasts this administrator with the charismatic administrator who was at the school the year before as the "best teaching year I have ever had....He could walk in with an idea and we would think 'Oh my goodness, we can't do that, and by the end of the meeting, we were sold and ready to go." Three different types of administrators evoked different actions and perspectives for how Maria thought about her role as a teacher. The most recent change in administration was drastic and stressful. Maria feels resentful that every teacher is treated the same and her administrator "goes by the book." Low morale at the school is a problem. Maria is trying hard to understand this administrator's actions.

## Innovation

Grace sees herself helping other teachers devise creative ways to help students learn. She contrasts her present school with her previous one.

I just don't see a lot of progress being made. I came from a very progressive school with a principal who really believed in giving people the freedom to try out new things she thought were beneficial. I see this school as very rigid, and this is what you can do and this is what you cannot....We are far behind times at this school. I've tried to tell teachers some of the things we're doing at my other school; they can't believe it....I have tried to share at this school but nothing happens.

Grace sees the inability of teachers to picture something different as blocking their openness to possibilities and innovation. This lack of imagination, coupled with an administrative team that blocks teachers' recommendations, perpetuates a cycle of no action, a lack of experimentation, little dialogue, and fosters teacher withdrawal from participation. Grace confides she is leaving this school at the end of the year. She has been there for two years and does not picture herself in a "school like this where nothing happens."

All of these teachers' narratives have certain common denominators. Teachers talk about their need to make a difference in their profession. They view their choices and impact in relation to the freedom given by the administration. Lynn talks about her need to be involved and make an impact where she can. She sees her ability to engage honestly as limited. She withdraws in silence and works outside of her school to impact education. She confides, "I am very involved politically outside of school, but no one knows this."

Other teachers like Nan see their influence as a choice. "I felt like I had a whole lot of influence....It was up to me. The administrator trusted me and was philosophically similar to me in how she thought about teaching and learning." Tim too speaks of how he worked "side-by-side" with the principal and had much power granted to him.

Maria observes that her principal "felt so pressured and held so accountable that pressure was put on her." She was puzzled at the principal's request that any ideas be submitted formally in written proposals, and the twice a week classroom observations for "time on task" to raise test scores, which kept teachers busy preparing for the next observation. Maria was not sure that the request for written proposals was authentic, and not a cover-up and delay tactic for the principal not to make any decisions.

Administrators affected the extent of agency exercised by teachers individually and collectively. June notes, "We had an administrator who was very willing to provide the teachers with decision making power." Our present administrator is "someone who is learning and does not have much experience. It's hard because if we work in the manner that we are used to working, we are [seen as] usurping the administrator's power. . . ."

Grace saw much of what teachers wanted to happen at her school stopped by one of the administrators who "controlled" everything. She bemoans the fact that she does not see the children at her school being prepared for the 21st century. Her influence can extend only so far. "We're stopped. We have no one there for us a lot of the time." Grace reflects on her failure to make change. "I just say well maybe I need to try another aspect. Maybe I didn't present it in a way that seemed appealing. 1 try not to let it—even though it does—get me down."

Their positive attitudes, willingness to see the big picture, ability to examine alternative views, and insights about their roles, framed their personal narratives. These narratives were around advocacy, fairness, enabling others, relationships, professional development, and innovation. This openness furthers our understandings of what drives agency in these teacher leaders. Now we turn to the fourth theme, power/micropolitics of the school.

# Power/Micropolitics

Institutions, such as schools, are defined by their broader organizational purpose, functioning, and value-systems, though these may be loosely linked. Devolved authority has the potential to "decouple" (Weick, 1969) or strengthen these bonds depending on how power is exercised. Individual teachers bring their own socially conditioned beliefs, values, and perspectives into a school and therefore have views, or at least assumptions, about the curriculum, teaching practices and other processes and technologies of schooling.

Power/micropolitics takes into account that not all teachers have the same capacity to persuade others to adopt their views. Moreover, self-interest is involved, since some practices may serve the interests of a particular individual, or groups, but not those of others. There are therefore, direct and indirect incentives for teachers to bargain or negotiate with one another and with the administrators of their schools, although much of this activity may be implicit (Ball, 1987; Hoyle, 1986), while other activities such as teacher governing bodies or alliances with other teachers and administrators may be more explicit.

Throughout the teachers' interviews, we see evidence of how the underlying power/micropolitics of the schools and their districts impact the agency these teachers influence. Often, the knowledge of how to work around hierarchical relations is beneficial, but only in larger districts where there is less chance of being stopped in one's actions. In Tim's case, he desperately wanted to keep the resource room where teachers met to work collaboratively. When the new principal came, he orchestrated an event, which made it difficult for the new principal to take away the resource room and use it for overcrowding in the school. Tim relates this story:

> You know we had this resource room—I don't know if I explained this to you. That was one of the things that I did right. I worked with a reading teacher and we realized that there wasn't a place in the school for teachers to come together collaboratively and work together because you can't do it in the lounge and you can't do it in your room. So we took half of our classroom, which was an old portable at the time, and we partitioned it off and we changed it into a teacher resource room. We brought all the resources in there, all the reading books, the Xerox machine, the book binder, and everything was accessible to the teachers. Nothing was "fill out a form and we'll get it to you in two days." Everything was right there for the teachers. We put computers in there….I was afraid that the new principal was going to take it away because we started running into some space problems with over-population with the migrant kids we picked up. So, not knowing if she would or not, we did something kind of weird. We dedicated the room to our old principal. We got this huge brass plaque and named it after her. We had a big dedication ceremony. So we invited everybody from the region to come in and said "now, how can you take it away from us?"

The distribution of power within an institution is as much a part or a reflection of its culture as it is of its structures. Structure, culture, and power interpenetrate one another.

Micropolitical theory seeks to identify the overt and covert ways groups devise to influence certain rules, both in private and public ways. Furthermore, it tries to reveal who maintains control over what issues, and who acquires and exercises control and power over others (Hoyle, 1986; Malen, 1995). Often, these rules are explicated in the everyday practices within the context and relationships in teachers' work-lives. These rules become part of their tacit knowledge about the culture and micropolitics of the school (Ball 1987; Beare & Slaughter, 1993; Rosenholtz, 1989). The stories told by Grace and Lynn illustrate how, in Grace's school, teacher expertise was not valued, while in Lynn's school, the principal controlled too much.

Grace wrote grants for herself but could not engage others in the process with her. She reframed problems to brainstorm different strategies to make an impact. She felt others resented her status as teacher of the year when she changed schools. "At this school I have had to contend with, 'Oh, you know more than the rest of us.' Or when I've made mistakes, 'Oh, I'm glad you made a mistake, I didn't think you made any mistakes." Grace tried to keep a sense of humor about this projected sense of animosity, but she was hurt. She worked with her team as the leader, and her principal complimented her on her ability to bring cohesion and direction to her team. She was able to get support for a Parent's Math Night from other teachers at the school, but she felt her impact was limited.

Lynn exerted influence outside of the system through her political involvement on State task forces. She had to see a way to make a difference. If she could not do so in her school, she would do so outside of it. She talks about how she would plant ideas with the principal so that the principal would think that it was her idea and give permission to Lynn to go ahead.

Tim relates how teachers can team up with administrators and form alliances which can be damaging to a school. "If you have teachers who are into power, you can have teachers make an alliance with administration that can be very detrimental to the school." June speaks of something similar when she says, "…[T] here are certain individuals that want their way—you don't talk to this person because what you say will go straight to the principal. Or, whatever you say will be turned around and it will hit the ears of so and so. And you can see that this person does and says certain things to be in the 'in-group."

Three of the teachers told stories around the power/micropolitics of parental support and involvement. In June's school, parents were very active. They met together away from the school to discuss new programs that they wanted implemented at the school. June talks about how the site council is implementing a policy to restrict parents from dictating curriculum changes at the school.

> So formally, we've got site-based decision making, the school advisory council, then we also have decisions that are kind of made through the PTO, but we've had to try to control that through our site-based. Actually, we have an item going through site-based now to control parents trying to tell teachers what to teach. So we are working on that now. If we have a policy in place with the guidelines then we don't have the butting heads. We have such high parent involvement. We have been like the number one school in the whole district that puts in the most parent volunteer hours. It's always been that way. Parents come to PTO meetings; they go to board meetings; they go to school zoning meetings; these parents know everything. The school advisory council incorporates parents. They know what levels students are supposed to be achieving, so they want programs instituted that they have read about or heard about or observed in other schools that work. And so they want to make the decisions to put them in our school. But, you know, it just can't work that way. So that's why right now we're just putting into place some guidelines that the parent group has to follow.

Nan has observed that teachers' perceptions of parents were often tied to their working relationship with the principal. The group of teachers who worked well with the principal saw parents as partners, whereas the group who did not work well with the principal viewed parents as the enemy. The last group, who did the minimum required of teachers, involved parents only to the extent that the principal required.

Maria who was the least able to exercise agency of all the teachers sees parents as having far more power than teachers. She sounds angry at the fact that parents can see the superintendent and get what they want, whereas she could talk to the superintendent, but it would not have any impact on the day-to-day rhythm in her district.

The influence of teachers in the system is a combination of how well they know how to work the system, their perceived expertise, the influence afforded them, the collective agency of the group, and the norms within the school and district. However, there is yet another issue. Tim relates how shocked he was to find out that in his district, one that ostensibly supports site-based decision making, principals are told to make the decisions. He expresses his concern about the disconnect between what teachers are told and what administrators are told and wonders how new administrators joining the ranks, often young and inexperienced, might make sense of this dynamic and involve teachers.

We have presented four themes from the teacher interviews. In qualitative research, the links to theory emerge after the data are analyzed. The findings suggest that teacher cultures, decision making structures, and power/micropolitics are intertwined. Some teachers are afforded power, whereas others are not. There is evidence that something else, namely, actions that are an affront to the teacher's dignity and respect create negative conditions for teachers' work in schools.

## Conclusions

The teachers interviewed in this study are different in many ways. Nevertheless, they share many traits such as being perceptive about the politics of their work, articulating viewpoints about an issue, focusing on continual growth and development, and expressing an overall concern about their involvement in decision making that impacts improved teaching and learning. The teachers' stories lead to vivid experiences learned from their observations and experiences, personally, with other teachers, and organizationally (Bandura, 1986). These experiences, for example, are sometimes felt vicariously, as when Lynn tells about the pain she feels for other teachers. She is expressing her anger at what she witnesses because she identifies with these teachers. She is distraught by the actions of the administration and relates how teachers who have differing opinions receive disrespectful labels below.

> Teachers are talked down to something terrible. If you have the nerve to speak out, to have a suggestion, to think of a better way, and it does not go along with what is being pushed, then you need to be re-educated or ignored. And if you keep opening your mouth, you are put down…begin to acquire labels such as 'rigid' and 'not-flexible enough.' So you wear these labels—you get branded; it is extremely unfair.

Maria tells the story about how the keys to teachers' classrooms are taken from them—very unfair. Grace shares a story about her principal withholding praise from her for receiving two grants and how the work of a committee for an entire year is dismissed hastily. On the other hand, June talks about the relationships at her school with a positive tone. "I am in the kind of school that is nurturing. I am treated with respect, and people encourage me to be a facilitator and a leader."

The loss of commitment because of poor leadership is hard to measure on an achievement test. Principals can choose to develop supportive teacher cultures that engender responsiveness, innovation, and respectful ways of being. They can encourage meaningful involvement, recognize teacher expertise and utilize it, and be a cheerleader for the teachers in the school. Alternatively, they can provide no time for reflection, dialogue, and ignore teacher knowledge and expertise, take no action on decisions, discount the work and suggestions of teachers, and create a culture of disrespect, where as Lynn says, "people feel crucified."

This research suggests that teacher-leaders are able to understand the "big picture" and envision the broader impact of decisions made by administration as well as teachers. Teachers who exert the most agency in this study have the most empowering principals and the least disempowering work contexts. They are treated with respect and valued by their colleagues and principals. They work within and across school structures and boundaries to establish social linkages and networks among their peers and within the community.

The stories illustrate how the six empowerment/power dimensions: autonomy, political efficacy and expertise, responsibility and accountability, collegiality and status, resources, and hierarchical relations were seen throughout the four themes and tied to the framework of structure, power, and culture. Tim, Nan, and June exhibited the most agency overall of the six teachers. They used their autonomy to reflect, dialogue with other teachers, and make decisions that were supported by their administrators. Through autonomy, other opportunities for creative ways to address challenges in the schools and build collective agency were demonstrated among the teachers.

We saw that political efficacy and expertise impact learning. June states, "It's knowing the group of students you are teaching and the best way to get knowledge to them. Knowledge reflects what I know about my students, their individual learning styles, the content, and what you know and share with other teachers."

Tim, after moving from an elementary to a high school, expressed feeling like a beginning teacher. His principal wanted him to begin immediately to work with other teachers that can be "salvaged," but Tim said "no," stating that he had no credibility yet with his peers. Tim's decision represents collegiality and status as teacher leaders, like Tim, know that for this dynamic to occur, relationships must be established first. This awareness of how to treat other teachers as professionals depicts how all these teachers work as colleagues with other teachers.

The issue of responsibility and accountability was expressed through the teachers' concerns about the state's accountability measures (e.g., The Sunshine State Standards and the FCAT). Teachers feel responsible for their students' achieving the State standards and doing well on tests. They are concerned; however, that the push for increased test scores will be detrimental to students in the end because innovative and creative teaching and learning practices might be sacrificed to the test.

In all cases, the teachers spoke of writing grants, both for their own classrooms and the school. They recognized that they are resources to other teachers by opening their classrooms to their colleagues to observe their instructional practice as well as to talk about it. They reflect on the knowledge and skills of how to work within the system to the benefit of students and their colleagues. Their keen sense of the formal structure and hierarchical relationships helps them find ways to work around the bureaucratic rules, without losing sight of their values, or engaging in unethical activities.

Power relationships, critical to the change process, can transform or maintain the culture and structures of schools. The interdependence of structure, power, and culture is corroborated by these teachers' stories over and over again, no matter what the situation—empowering or disempowering. Teachers cannot be given power (empowered) without accepting it. Teachers need to develop this sense of empowerment. On the other hand, administrators must know how to create conditions that foster empowerment and release their control over teachers, alter their roles, and engender commitment, trust, and respect.

Florida's intent was to transfer power to teachers through Florida's System of School Improvement and Accountability legislative educational policy. However, what was not anticipated was that this transfer and sharing of power could get stuck because principals do not know how to share power, or want to give up control. The structures, culture, and power relationships in many of these schools did not reflect the intent of the Florida legislation primarily because changes in the practices of how principals traditionally have been held responsible for their schools was at odds with school-based accountability. The teachers recognized, in all cases, the difficult position of administrators during this time of increasing school accountability and raising test scores. Several of the teachers remarked that principals are not taught how to empower their faculty and staff. Administrators need to "know different types of personalities and how people interact and interrelate with each," as June points out. Further she says, "They have to feel comfortable that they are not less of an administrator because they are empowering teachers."

Finally, it appears to us, as the pressure on all educators continues to increase, principals must find authentic ways to support teachers, not to increase their stress through surveillance and micromanagement techniques. These administrative actions neither build professional teacher cultures, nor improve practice. Rather, principals should err on the side of promoting risk-taking, seeking to address teacher and student needs that focus on teaching and learning. Principals might play a buffering role in protecting teachers from unnecessary pressures from their districts and the state. They could seek to build collective agency, reflective practice, and common planning times for teacher dialogue. Principals can foster development by focusing on the internal strengths of their staffs, negotiate external demands that are stressful, and provide opportunities for growth. By providing an open-minded stance that enables teachers and administrators to listen to each other, educators can learn together. Evaluating the effects of programs, policies, and services across different client groups to assess their impact is critical. Knowing what works and what does not, how to work with people, how to manage conflict, and how not to be afraid of taking risks are essential for today's school leaders who wish to develop teacher leaders and build empowering teacher cultures.

# References

Acker-Hocevar, M., & Bauch, P. A. (1998). *Florida award perspectives on empowerment and their involvement with parents under recent school reform efforts. Organizational, Theory, Dialogue.* Bloomington, IN: Indiana University Press.

Ball, S. J. (1987). *The micro-politics of the school: Towards a theory of school organization.* New York, NY: Methuen & Co.

Bandura, A. (1986). *Social foundations of thought and action. A social cognitive* view. Englewood Cliffs, NJ: Prentice-Hall.

Bandura, A. (1997). *Self-efficacy: The exercise of control.* New York, NY: W. H. Freeman.

Barnes, B. (1988). *The nature of power.* Cambridge, UK: Polity Press.

Beare H., & Slaughter, R. (1993). *Education in the twenty-first century.* New York, NY: Routledge.

Bennett, N., & Harris, A. (1997). *Hearing truth from power? Organization theory: School effectiveness and school improvement.* Paper presented at the annual meeting of the American Educational Research Association, Chicago.

Bredeson, P. V. (1993). Letting go of outlived professional identities: A study of role transition and role strain for principals in restructured schools. *Educational Administration Quarterly, 29*(1), 34–68.

Callahan, R. (1962). *Education and the cult of efficiency.* Chicago, IL: University of Chicago Press.

Carnegie Forum on Education and the Economy. (1986). *A nation prepared: Teachers for the 21st century.* Washington, DC: Carnegie Forum on Education and the Economy.

Clegg, S. R. (1989). *Frameworks of power.* Newbury Park, CA: Sage Publications.

Darling-Hammond, L. (1987). Policy and professionalism. In A. Lieberman (Ed.), *Building a professional culture in schools* (148–166). New York, NY: Teachers College Press.

Darling-Hammond, L., & Goodwin, A. L. (1993). Progress toward professionalism in teaching. In G. Cawelti (Ed.), *Challenges and achievement of American education: The 1993 ASCD yearbook.* Alexandria, VA: ASCD.

Darling-Hammond, L., with Sclan, E. (1992). Policy and supervision. In C. D. Glickman (Ed.), *Supervision in transition: The 1992 ASCD yearbook.* Alexandria, VA: ASCD.

Florida Commission on Education and Reform. (1993). *Blueprint 2000: A system of school improvement and account-ability: For 1994–95 school improvement plans.* Tallahassee, FL: Florida Commission of Education Reform and Accountability.

Florida Office of Program Policy Analysis and Government Accountability. (1997). *Improving student performance in high-poverty schools.* Tallahassee, FL: OPPAGA Report Production.

Fullan, M., & Hargreaves, A. (1996). *What's worth fighting for in your school?* New York, NY: Teachers College Press.

Gannon, M. (1996). *The new history of Florida.* Gainesville, FL: University Press of Florida.

Giddens, A. (1984). *The constitution of society.* Cambridge, MA: Polity Press.

Goodlad, J. L. (1984). *Educational Renewal: Better teachers, better schools.* San Francisco, CA: Jossey-Bass.

Hales, C. (1995). *Managing through organizations: The management process, forms of organization and the work of man-agers.* New York, NY: Routledge.

Hargreaves, A. (1994). *Changing teachers, changing times: Teachers' work and culture in the postmodern age.* New York, NY: Cassell.

Haugaard, M. (1997). *The constitution of power: A theoretical analysis of power, knowledge and structure.* New York, NY: Manchester University Press.

Holmes Group, (1986). *Tomorrow's teachers.* East Lansing, MI: Holmes Group.

Hoyle, E. (1986). *The politics of school management.* London, UK: Hodder and Stoughton.

Johnson, M. (1993). *Moral imagination.* Chicago, IL: The University of Chicago Press.

Johnson, S. M. (1990). *Teachers at work.* New York, NY: Basic Books, Inc.

Joyce, B. (1986). *Improving America's schools.* New York, NY: Longman.

Kane, K., & Montgomery, K. (1998). A framework for understanding disempowerment in organizations. *Human Resource Management 37*(3 & 4), 263–275.

Kanungo, R. (1992). Alienation and empowerment: Some ethical imperatives in business. *Journal of Business Ethics, 11,* 413–422.

Lieberman, A., Saxl, E. R., & Miles, M. (1988). Teacher leadership: Ideology and practice. In A. Lieberman (Ed.), *Building a professional culture in schools* (pp. 148–166). New York, NY: Teachers College Press.

Lincoln, Y., & Guba, E. (1985). *Naturalistic inquiry.* Newbury Park, CA: Sage.

Lortie, D. C. (1975). *School-teacher: A sociological study.* Chicago, IL: University of Chicago Press.

Lukes, S. (1974). *Power: A radical view.* London, UK: Macmillan.

Malen, B. (1995). The micropolitics of education: Mapping the multiple dimensions of power relations in school pol-itics. In J. D. Scribner & D. H. Layton (Eds.), *The study of educational politics* (pp. 147–168). Bristol, PA: The Falmer Press.

Miles, M., & Huberman, A. M. (1994). *Qualitative data analysis: A sourcebook of new methods.* Thousand Oaks, CA: Sage.

Mitchell, D. E., & Beach, S. A. (1993). School restructuring: The superintendent's view. *Educational Administration Quarterly, 29*(2), 249–274.

Rosenholtz, S. (1989). *Teacher's workplace: The social organization of schools.* New York, NY: Longman.

Sarason, S. B. (1990). *The predictable failure of educational reform: Can we change the course before it's too late?* San Francisco, CA: Jossey-Bass, Inc.

Schlechty, P. C. (1990). *Schools of the twenty-first century.* San Francisco: Jossey-Bass.

Senge, P. M. (1990). *The fifth dimension: The art and practice of the learning organization.* New York, NY: Doubleday.

Sizer, T. R. (1984). *Horace's compromise.* Boston: Houghton Mifflin.

State of Florida Department of Education. (1992). *Blueprint 2000.* Tallahassee, FL: Department of Education.

State of Florida Office of the Auditor General. (1994). *Overview of the implementation of a system of school improve-ment and accountability (Blueprint 2000).* Tallahassee, FL: Office of the Auditor General.

Tebeau, C. W. (1971). *A history of Florida.* Coral Gables, FL: University of Miami Press.

Troen, V., & Boles, K. (1994, February). A time to lead. *Teacher,* 40–41.

Weick, K. (1969). *The social psychology of organizing.* Reading, MA: Addison-Wesley.

White, P. (1992). Teacher empowerment under "ideal" school-site autonomy. *Educational Evaluation and Policy Analysis, 14*(1), 69–82.

# CHAPTER TWENTY-FIVE

# Exploring New Approaches to Teacher Leadership for School Improvement

MARK A. SMYLIE, SHARON CONLEY, & HELEN M. MARKS

DURING THE PAST 20 YEARS TEACHER LEADERSHIP HAS BECOME AN ESTABLISHED FEATURE OF educational reform in the United States. In the mid-1980s, arguments began to appear in the scholarly and professional literatures asserting that teacher leadership was a crucial element of school improvement and the development and "professionalization" of the teacher work force. To some observers, it would be impossible to improve schools, attract and retain talented teachers, or make sensible demands upon school administrators without promoting teacher leadership (e.g., Little, 1988; Wasley, 1991). To others, creating opportunities for teacher leadership was a moral imperative, to give teachers their professional due and to provide all children with the quality of education they deserve (e.g., Barth, 2001; Maeroff, 1958).

It was not always seen this way. The planned change literature of the 1970s and early 1980s emphasized the importance of strong leadership for school improvement, but most of it focused on the principal or the superintendent (Fullan, 2001). More often than not, teachers were considered impediments to rather than leaders of improvement (Little, 1988). Even today, the subject of teacher leadership is cloaked in ambivalence. We look to teachers and their leadership to help solve today's educational problems, yet we consider teachers a primary cause of the problems that we call on their leadership to solve.

Of course, teacher leadership is not the product of 'recent educational reform. The literature has long recognized teachers' informal leadership in schools and classrooms (Smylie, 1997). For years, teachers have also assumed various formal leadership roles in union activity, as department chairs, and as members of advisory committees. Weise and Murphy (1995) remind us that the idea of teacher leadership as a means of reform dates back at least to the early 1900s, to progressive educators' calls to reshape schools as democratic communities.

Even though the idea of teacher leadership has been around for quite some time, our thinking about its form; its function, and its role in school improvement has evolved considerably. In the past 10 years several new approaches to teacher leadership have emerged. In this chapter, we explore three of these new approaches. We begin with a brief historical review describing the evolution of teacher leadership since the early 1900s. Then we examine teacher research as a form of teacher leadership. We explore several models of distributive school leadership. Finally we consider self-managed teams as means of teacher leadership and substitutes for administrative leadership. These new approaches depart from the individual empowerment, role-based models of teacher leadership that dominated the 1980s and early 1990s. They reframe teacher leadership as a more collective, task-oriented, and organizational enterprise. Are these new approaches more effective forms of leadership for promoting schoolwide improvement? We entertain this question and its implications for teacher leadership development at the end of the chapter.

## Teacher Leadership in Historical Perspective

It is difficult to think about the one-room schoolhouse of the 19th century and not also think about the teacher as an organizational leader (Fuller, 1989). It was not until the beginning of the 20th century, however, that we began to hear about teachers as leaders and the importance of teacher leadership to school reform. With the advent of the "professional" school administrator, the growth of centralized control, and the scientific management of schools in the early and mid-1900s, teacher leadership became an issue of workplace democracy. According to Weise and Murphy (1995), critics of these reforms argued that it would be virtually impossible for schools to promote a democratic society if they were not democratic communities themselves. Dewey (1903) argued, for example, that until public education was organized in such a way that "every teacher had some regular and representative way to register judgment upon matters of educational importance, with assurance that this judgment would somehow affect the school system, the assertion that the present system is not, from the internal standpoint, democratic seems to be justified" (p. 195).

Such critiques formed the foundation for the teacher council movement of the 1910s and 1920s and the democratic administration movement of the 1930s and 1940s (Weise & Murphy, 1995). These movements established new opportunities for teachers to participate in school- and district-level policy making (Conley, 1991). While these opportunities were not widespread, their aim was to "make all [teachers] students of the problems of the schools and proficient helpers in solving those problems" (Ortman, 1923, p. 11). Beyond organizing teachers to help solve specific educational problems, the driving force behind these efforts was to "democratize" schools and increase their capacity to promote democratic society. In this regard, teacher participation in policy making was an expression of key democratic principles—self-determinism of teachers in their work and the "enfranchisement" of teachers in educational administration (Weise & Murphy).

Efforts to develop teacher leadership faded in the shadow of community control initiatives of the 1960s and 1970s, but they were renewed in the mid-1980s in response to the regulatory, bureaucratic reforms of the late 1970s and early 1980s (Murphy, 1990). By the late 1980s, nearly every American state had adopted or was studying some form of teacher leadership program or policy (Smylie, 1997). District-level initiatives abounded. Opportunities for teacher leadership came in the form of career ladder and mentor teacher programs, the appointment of master and lead teachers, and policies to decentralize and involve teachers in school- and district-level decision making,

While their association with workplace democracy was not completely lost, these teacher leadership initiatives followed from a different set of assumptions and objectives. First, teacher leadership was seen more specifically as an instrument of school improvement and of improvement of student academic learning. These initiatives would place teachers in positions of influence and decision-making authority, thereby increasing the human resources available for school improvement. Teacher leaders would break down "a backbreaking educational bureaucracy" that impeded reform and restricted teachers' ability to work according to their own notions of best practice (Lichtenstein, McLaughlin, & Knudsen, 1992, p. 37). This objective was consistent with literature of the late 1970s and 1980s that argued that educational improvement was best pursued at the school level, at the point closest to the problems to be solved (Bacharach & Conley, 1989; Firestone & Bader, 1992). It was also consistent with the logic that made paramount the involvement of people most instrumental to the solution of those problems—teachers.

Second, these teacher leadership initiatives were considered important means of "empowering" individual teachers, "professionalizing" the teacher workforce, and improving teacher performance (Lichtenstein et al., 1992). The teacher leadership initiatives of this period were closely associated with role-based theories and models of individual work redesign and job enhancement (Hart, 1990; Pounder, 1999). In general, they followed a logic that variation and expansion of teachers' work, including increased leadership responsibilities with commensurate recognition and compensation, would increase teachers' motivation, job commitment, satisfaction, and performance. New leadership roles would provide more effective incentives to attract and retain the best teachers in the profession. Moreover, these new roles would benefit not only the individual teachers who performed them, but also others in the school community, as teacher leaders applied their expertise to program development, decision making, and the professional development of their colleagues.

Today our thinking about teacher leadership is changing again. Since the mid-1990s there has been a shift away from individual empowerment and role-based initiatives toward more collective, task-oriented, and organizational approaches to teacher leadership. According to Leithwood and Jantzi (2000), many of the more ambitious role-based teacher leadership initiatives of the late 1980s and early 1990s have been abandoned. Indeed, one is hard pressed to find more than a few entries about these earlier forms of teacher leadership in scholarly and professional education literature published after the mid-1990s.

The reasons for this shift are not clear, but there are at least two possible explanations. First, the evidence on the effectiveness of the individual empowerment, role-based teacher leadership initiatives of the 1980s and early 1990s is equivocal at best. Much of what counted for teacher leadership at that time was the "appointment and anointment" of individual teachers to new "quasi-administrative" positions—rungs on career ladders, lead and mentor teachers, and membership on decision-making bodies—to share in managerial work (Bacharach, Conley, & Shedd, 1986; Pounder, 1999; Yendol Silva, Gimbert, & Nolan, 2000). Following the image of the "great man" in the principal's office, these positions embodied a "heroic" model of individual leadership. It was not always clear how teacher leaders were to perform their new roles. Moreover, these roles were not always focused on things that matter most to teachers—curriculum, instruction, and student learning (Little, 1988). These initiatives typically brought teachers into the "hierarchy" of administrative leadership. At the same time, ironically, they often failed to consider adequately the implications for principals and other school administrative leaders.

According to Smylie (1997), the research found that these initiatives produced mixed outcomes. Despite their tendency to focus on noncurricular and noninstructional matters, teacher leaders generally found that these roles provided new opportunities for professional learning and development. These roles were also associated with the development and adoption of innovations at the school and district levels, but they did little to promote the implementation of these innovations, particularly innovations aimed at promoting other teachers' professional development, improving classroom instruction, and increasing student learning. Overall, the research indicates that these teacher leadership initiatives did little to support school-level improvement.

The research was clear, however, that, these teacher leadership initiatives could cause serious problems (Smylie, 1997). They could create work overload, stress, role ambiguity, and role conflict for teacher leaders as they tried to balance their new school-level responsibilities with their classroom responsibilities. The introduction of new teacher leadership roles could also create tension and conflict among teacher leaders, administrators, and other teachers. The research demonstrated that the organizational contexts of schools could exert substantial influence, often negative, on the performance and outcomes of these leadership roles. This evidence signaled clearly that it was not enough to think about teacher leadership solely in terms of roles and the individuals who occupy them. One also had to think about the organizational conditions necessary for teacher leadership to function effectively.

A second possible reason for the shift away from individual empowerment and role-based leadership is that we have learned a great deal about leadership and school improvement in the past 10 years, and these lessons point to potentially better ways to think about teacher leadership (Fullan, 2001). We understand that administrative leadership is crucial to school improvement, but we also understand that principals alone cannot provide all the leadership necessary to promote and sustain improvement over time (Donaldson, 2001). We have learned that school improvement and the improvement of teaching and student learning depend fundamentally on the development of teachers' knowledge, abilities, and commitments—their "will and skill" (Newmann & Wehlage, 1995). Moreover, we have come to understand that "restructuring" schools is not sufficient to improve them. The reform literature strongly suggests that improving teaching and student learning has less to do with structural changes in schools than with changes in what occurs within those structures (Elmore, Peterson, & McCarthey, 1996; Smylie & Hart, 1999). Structure certainly matters; however, changing structures is not synonymous with changing the social organization and cultures of schools (Fullan). These lessons and the research on the teacher leadership initiatives of the 1980s and early 1990s prompt us to expand our thinking about teacher leadership and school improvement.

## New Approaches to Teacher Leadership

We now examine three new approaches to teacher leadership that have emerged during the past 10 years—teacher research as a form of teacher leadership; models of distributive leadership; and self-managed teams as sources of teacher leadership and substitutes for administrative leadership. Each of these new approaches has deep theoretical and philosophical roots. Each moves past the idea of leadership as manifested in individuals occupying formal positions to more dynamic, organizational views of leadership.

There is little empirical research to date that examines these new approaches "in action." Nevertheless, there is some initial evidence that these new approaches take us in positive directions. While the evidence is not conclusive, there are reasons to believe that these new approaches to teacher leadership are more conducive to school improvement than earlier ones.

It should be noted that it is difficult to discuss teacher leadership without saying something about leadership itself. Leadership has defied commonly accepted definition (Immegart, 1988). However, the new approaches to teacher leadership that we explore in this chapter are consistent with recent literature that defines leadership as a social influence process aimed at achieving some collective or organizational end (Bass, 1990; Yukl, 1998). As a social influence process, leadership permeates organizations rather than residing in particular people or formal positions of authority. As a result, leadership can come from and be exercised by a wide range of organizational participants. In schools, therefore, teachers, parents, and students, as well as administrators and others in formal positions, have potential for leadership in their relationships with others and through various aspects of their respective work. The first approach to teacher leadership sees leadership in teachers' efforts to develop new knowledge from inquiry into their own schools and classrooms.

## Teacher Research as Leadership

The idea of teacher as researcher is almost a century old. In his brief historical account, Henson (1996) tells us that as early as 1908 concerted efforts were made to involve teachers in research. In 1910 the subject of teacher research appeared in the *Journal of Educational Psychology*. By the early 1900s teachers were recognized as the people best able to identify problems pertinent to teaching. They were charged with investigating solutions to those problems, although, according to Olson (1990)) this work was never called research. Calls for teacher research to support school- and district-level curriculum development increased in the 1920s (Henson, 1996). In the 1950s teachers were urged to become researchers of their own classrooms. The most recent efforts to promote teacher research began in the late 1980s with a number of inquiry projects in the United States and Great Britain (Cochran-Smith & Lytle, 1999b). In 1994, the National Society for the Study of Education acknowledged the importance of teacher research by publishing a yearbook on the subject (Hollingsworth & Sockett, 1994).

Teacher research has been defined in many ways. We follow Cochran-Smith and Lytle (1999b) and adopt a broad definition of teacher research that encompasses all forms of teacher inquiry involving any systematic, intentional, and self-critical study of one's work, including inquiry referred to as action research, practitioner inquiry, teacher inquiry, and so on. For the most part, teacher research has been considered an individual activity geared toward teachers' personal professional development and improvement (Henson, 1996). In the past 10 years teacher research has also been viewed as a form of teacher leadership and a way to promote school improvement (Cochran-Smith & Lytle, 1998). Advocates of teacher research contend that it not only provides useful knowledge for teachers themselves; it also is an important source of knowledge about teaching for the larger educational community (Pappas, 1977). According to Cochran-Smith and Lytle (1999b), "the concept of teacher research carries with it an enlarged view of the teacher's role—as decision maker, consultant, curriculum developer, analyst, activist, school leader" (p. 17).

Central to the notion of teacher research as teacher leadership is the issue of influence. Advocates argue that teacher research can "challenge the hegemony of a university-generated knowledge base for teaching" (Cochran-Smith & Lytle, 1999a, p. 282). As a source of "learning through doing" it can influence individual teachers' classroom practices. Moreover, because of its local nature and its close relationship to practice, teacher research may be a potentially powerful source of influence in efforts to improve schools (Cochran-Smith & Lytle, 1999a). By conducting research teachers may increase their sense of efficacy, enabling them to feel that they are better able to promote change (Henson, 1996). Teachers who are involved in research may become more reflective, critical, and analytical not just of their own teaching but of schooling practices around them.

Most studies of teacher research examine how it is conducted, factors that support or constrain its practice, and its implications for learning and change for teacher researchers themselves (see Henson, 1996; Zeichner, 1994). Relatively little has been written about teacher research as a form of teacher leadership or a means to promote change at the school level; however, the literature that has examined these functions of teacher research generally reports positive outcomes. Zeichner points to the work of the Boston Women's Teachers' Group and to other lesser-known cases in which teacher research has helped to shape schoolwide programs and policies. Tikunoff, Ward, and Griffin (1979) describe a model of school-based collaborative action research in which a researcher, a staff developer, and a group of teachers in a school worked together to identify a problem within the school, conducted research on it, and implemented a staff development program to address the problem. They found that this process led to considerable change in teacher practice schoolwide (see also Griffin, Lieberman, & Jacullo-Noto, 1983).

In another study Harris and Drake (1997) examined a high school that used schoolwide teacher research teams to develop teachers as change agents and to promote a more collaborative, reflective faculty culture. These teams were linked to a participative school-level decision-making structure that was to develop programs and policies from teacher research findings. Harris and Drake found that for the most part teachers perceived individual and organizational benefits from their work They saw the group research experience as a source for their own professional development. Moreover, they believed that the research experience enhanced their ability to promote change at the school level. It is interesting to note that even though these teachers performed various leadership tasks as part of their work, and even though they considered themselves better able to promote school-level change, they did not see themselves as leaders. Instead, they reserved the concept of leadership for principals and others in formal administrative positions.

Additional evidence concerning teacher research and leadership comes from a study by Clift, Veal, Holland, Johnson, and McCarthy (1995) of a collaborative leadership project for school improvement. This project involved a partnership among five public schools and a team of university teacher education researchers, Clift and her colleagues describe the project not as action research where teachers and administrators jointly collected and analyzed data but as "action science," where university researchers took primary responsibility for data collection and analysis and teachers and administrators worked together to identify problems in their schools, set research agendas, and engaged in "public reflection" of findings. According to Clift and her colleagues, the project resulted in individual learning and growth among all project: participants, teachers, administrators, and university faculty alike. Most notable for this discussion, they found that the project helped teachers develop a greater sense of individual and collective efficacy for leadership and a stronger ability to initiate and influence school-level improvement planning. As the project progressed and as participants studied the evidence that had been collected, teachers and administrators began "planning, arguing, and negotiating" desired changes in their respective schools (p. 23). Their joint deliberation around evidence resulted in new improvement plans in each school.

One of the more recent systemic studies of teacher research for leadership development and school improvement is the five-year evaluation of the Bay Area School Reform Collaborative (BASRC) (Center for Research on the Contest of Teaching, 2000; Copland, 2001). BASRC was formed in the San Francisco Bay Area in 1995 as one of six initial local Annenberg Challenge projects. It provides grants to 86 Leadership Schools to implement a six-stage school-based Cycle of Inquiry for school improvement. The cycle begins with identifying a broad problem statement and proceeds to reformulating the problem statement and focusing effort, identifying measurable goals for student learning, building a concrete action plan, putting that plan into place, and collecting data and analyzing the results. The results should suggest new problems to investigate, and the cycle repeats. BASRC expects that this cycle will inform and motivate local school change through evidence and analysis

(Center for Research on the Context of Teaching). It provides a vehicle for sharing leadership functions among teachers and administrators and building leadership capacity throughout the school, as teachers are called upon to be leaders and authoritative decision makers. BASRC and its Cycle of Inquiry suggest a model of leadership defined less by the actions of single leaders than by a set of leadership tasks shared across a broad segment of a school community.

Longitudinal case studies and surveys of principals provide some evidence that the BASRC Cycle of Inquiry has helped to promote teacher leadership and school improvement. According to the principal survey data, teacher leadership had developed in 90% of the Leadership Schools (Copland, 2001). Case studies of 10 Leadership Schools show that the Cycle of Inquiry established a process that enabled teachers to assume leadership roles typically performed by administrators (Center for Research on the Context of Teaching, 2000). Across these cases, teachers worked on teams to develop goals for schoolwide improvement and to delegate problem solving to other groups within the school. They shared best practices with fellow teachers and, in some schools, led searches for new administrators. A number of these schools developed new leadership structures to support improvement activity, including a rotating system of lead teachers to replace the principal, the appointment of teachers to serve as co-principals, and new interschool partnerships that supported shared leadership. These and other examples of teacher leadership brought new expectations for principals to work more as professional colleagues of teachers than as their administrative superiors.

The cases suggest that BASRC's Cycle of Inquiry led to significant changes in school culture and core practices. They show that where strong cycles of inquiry developed, teacher professional community and professional development were strengthened. Teachers collaborated to evaluate student work, to develop new curricula and student assessments, to experiment with new teaching practices, and to solve classroom and school-level problems, The cycle helped teachers to develop shared knowledge, a common language, and a collective sense of efficacy that moved them deeper into school improvement efforts.

In summary, this literature suggests that teacher research can serve as a form of teacher leadership and as a source of influence for school improvement. It suggests that inquiry, particularly inquiry in collaborative contexts or "inquiry communities," can create new opportunities for teachers to learn and lead efforts to improve their schools (Cochran-Smith & Lytle, 1999a; Fullan, 2001). Moreover, the evidence suggests that the products of teacher research—the knowledge, the findings of inquiry—can provide an impetus and a direction for improvement planning and other organizational changes at the school level.

## Models of Distributive Leadership

Another approach to teacher leadership comes through several emerging models of distributive leadership. In the mid-1990s the education literature began to discuss leadership that was exercised not only by people in formal positions of authority but also by people outside those positions. The literature stressed the importance to school improvement of leadership that was distributed and performed across roles. It called us to shift our attention away from individual and role- based conceptions of leadership and toward organizational and task-oriented conceptions of leadership.

Ogawa and Bossert (1995) traced these notions of distributive leadership back to ideas that were developed in the 1950s and 1960s. At that time, organizational and administration theorists were beginning to think of leadership not simply as a role-specific phenomenon but as an organization-wide phenomenon. For example, Barnard (1968) observed that the "authority of leadership" is not limited to those in executive positions. He implied that leadership might be exercised by any member of an organization. Similarly, Thompson (1967) argued that leadership flows throughout organizations, spanning levels and flowing both up and down organizational hierarchies. Others argued that leadership should be thought of as an organizational quality that could be measured and assessed organization-wide (e.g., Tannenbaum, 1962). Beginning in the 1970s, Griffiths (1979) and later others writing in the education literature (e.g., Haller & Knapp, 1985) began to direct our attention away from "leadership" ro the acts of "leading." This distinction refocused attention beyond the person and the role to leadership tasks, behaviors, and functions.

Three related models of distributive leadership have emerged in the education literature since the mid-1990s. One model, articulated by William Firestone and his colleagues, views leadership as the performance of key tasks or functions rather than as the work of people in formal leadership roles (Firestone, 1996; Heller & Firestone, 1995). According to this view, leadership tasks in schools can be and often are performed by people outside of formal administrative positions, including teachers, parents, and students. When leadership is defined as certain kinds of work, it is more important that the work be done well than that it be performed by a particular individual.

In a series of studies, Firestone and his colleagues associated the success of complex innovations with the distributed performance of several key leadership functions: (a) providing and selling a vision; (b) obtaining resources; (c) providing encouragement and recognition; (d) adapting rules and procedures to support the innovation; (e) monitoring improvement; and (f) handling internal and external disturbances. In a study of elementary schools that had successfully institutionalized a new curriculum designed to help students develop and apply critical thinking and problem-solving skills, Heller and Firestone (1995) found these leadership functions well performed in each school. They also found that these functions were performed not by any "heroic" leader, such as the principal, but by a number of different people in a variety of overlapping roles, including principals, teachers, central office personnel, and outside consultants. In addition, they found that the same functions were often performed by people in different roles. This complementary redundancy enhanced the effectiveness of the functions and provided some insurance that the functions would be performed if there were turnover in personnel or if particular individuals failed to do their part. In a companion study of the inclusion of special education students in general education classrooms, Mayrowetz and Weinstein (1999) offered similar findings. In schools where special education inclusion had taken root, each leadership function was carried out by multiple individuals in different roles in a redundant, mutually reinforcing manner. As Heller and Firestone found in their study, these individuals included school and central office administrators, teachers, aides, and parents.

Another model of distributive leadership has been described by Ogawa, Pounder, and their colleagues (Ogawa & Bossert, 1995; Pounder, Ogawa, & Adams, 1995). Rather than viewing leadership as the distributed performance of specific tasks or functions, they describe leadership as an organization-wide resource of power and influence. Drawing upon institutional perspectives of organizations, Ogawa and Bossert argue that leadership occurs not through the actions of individuals but through interaction among individuals. Because it occurs through interaction, influence that is exerted through leadership cannot be assumed to be unidirectional; it can flow up and down levels and between units of organizations. Ogawa and Bossert describe leadership as the multidirectional flow of influence through networks of roles that constitute organizations. Thus, as the flow of power and influence, leadership is not confined to certain roles but is distributed across roles, with different roles having access to different levels and types of power and influence. Drawing upon institutional perspectives of organizations, Ogawa and Bossert argue that leadership occurs not through the actions of individuals but through interaction among individuals. Because it occurs through interaction, influence that is exerted through leadership cannot be assumed to be unidirectional; it can flow up and down levels and between units of organizations. Ogawa and Bossert describe leadership as the multidirectional flow of influence through networks of roles that constitute organizations. Thus, as the flow of power and influence, leadership is not confined to certain roles but is distributed across roles, with different roles having access to different levels and types of power and influence. This view of leadership is consistent with political theory concerning power and influence among "lower" participants and the politics of upward influence in complex organizations (e.g., Mechanic, 1962–1963; Porter, Allen, & Angel, 1981).

As distributed across networks of roles, leadership can be considered an organization-wide phenomenon or an organizational quality. Pounder, Ogawa, and Adams (1995) examined the relationship of the leadership exercised by different individuals and groups in schools to four functions of effective organizations: (a) goal achievement; (b) ability to control relationships with the environment; (c) commitment among members to the organization; and (d) social solidarity among members. They also examined the relationship of leadership from different sources to several measures of school performance: (a) perceived organizational effectiveness; (b) student absenteeism; (c) academic achievement; and (d) faculty and staff turnover. Pounder and her colleagues defined leadership as the "amount of raw social influence" held by different individuals and groups in schools. They examined the amount of influence held separately by principals, teachers, secretaries, and parents and the sum of separately held influence as a measure of total leadership influence in a school.

This study found that total leadership influence in schools was associated with school performance through its effect on several organizational functions. Total leadership was directly and positively related to the level of goal achievement and commitment. High goal achievement was associated with low student absenteeism and higher achievement. Commitment was associated positively with members' perceptions of school effectiveness and was associated with low faculty and staff turnover. Rather than all actors possessing similar amounts of influence over the same things, Pounder and her colleagues found that individuals in different roles exerted influence on different organizational outcomes. For example, the leadership influence of principals and groups of teachers was positively related to organizational commitment, while parent leadership was associated with low student absenteeism and higher achievement. The study concluded that people in many different roles can lead and affect the performance of their schools in different ways.

Leithwood and Jantzi (2000) adopted a similar perspective to study the effects of principal and teacher leadership, separately and together, on school organizational conditions and student engagement with school. They examined the effects of leadership on (a) the clarity and awareness of school mission and goals; (b) collaborative school culture; (c) the perceived effectiveness of school planning processes; (d) the school's instructional program; (e) structure and organization that support school mission and goals; (f) information collection and decision making; and (g) policies and procedures that support instruction, student learning, and teacher professional growth. They examined the effects of leadership on student engagement, taking into consideration as mediating factors these organizational conditions and "family educational culture" (i.e., assumptions, norms, values, and beliefs held by the family about intellectual work in general, school work in particular, and the conditions that foster both). Leithwood and Jantzi found that principal influence and teacher influence were both separately and positively related to school organizational conditions, Principal and teacher influence had an indirect relationship to student engagement through school organizational conditions.

Leithwood and Jantzi (2000) found that total leadership influence had a significant positive relationship to school organizational conditions, although this relationship was not as strong as the independent effects of principal influence and teacher influence. Like Pounder and her colleagues (1995), Leithwood and Jantzi conclude that both teacher leadership and principal leadership matter to school organizational functions and, through those functions, to student outcomes. And like Pounder and her colleagues, Leithwood and Jantzi contend that total leadership influence, as an indicator of the distribution of leadership influence across roles in a school, has a positive relationship to the quality and effectiveness of school organization.

A third model of distributive leadership, described by Spillane, Halverson, and Diamond (2000, 2001), builds upon task-oriented views of leadership and views of leadership as an organizational property. Drawing upon activity theory and theories of distributed cognition, Spillane and his colleagues argue that leadership practice is constituted in the interaction of school leaders, followers, and situations. The social distribution of leadership means more than the division or duplication of leadership tasks among formal and informal leaders. In their view, leadership is "stretched over" the practice of two or more leaders in their interactions with followers. As performed in the interactions among multiple leaders and followers, leadership practice occurs 'in between" people (see also Donaldson, 2001). Leadership influence may therefore be multiplicative rather than additive because the interactions among two or more leaders in carrying out a particular leadership task may amount to more than the sum of the leaders' practices.

Previous research underscores the relational nature of leadership. It indicates that leaders not only influence followers but are also influenced by them and that leaders are dependent on those they lead (Dunlap & Goldman, 1991; Hollander, 1978). From a distributive perspective, the role of followers in leadership practice involves more than influencing the actions taken by formal leaders. Followers are an essential constituting element of the social interaction that is leadership activity.

Finally, Spillane and his colleagues argue that leadership is distributed in the dynamic web of people, interactions, and situations. Situation is not external to leadership activity but one of its core constituting elements. Leadership cannot be extracted from its organizational, structural, and social-cultural contexts. Thus, aspects of the situation can enable or constrain leadership activity at the same time that leadership activity can transform aspects of the situation over time. Situation is both constitutive and constituted of leadership practice.

To date, there are few reports of research that illustrates this third model of distributive leadership in action. In a preliminary report of their study of 13 Chicago elementary schools, Spillane, Halverson, and Diamond (2001) indicate that the performance of leadership tasks is often distributed among multiple leaders, including principals, teachers, assistant principals, counselors, and curriculum coordinators. Citing examples from case studies of these schools, they describe the co-enactment of leadership tasks by multiple leaders. These examples also illustrate how different areas of knowledge and expertise brought by different leaders can work interdependently in leadership task performance and can contribute to the effectiveness of leadership task performance in a way that is greater than the contribution any one leader might make alone. These findings are consistent with research related to the other two models of distributive leadership.

These three models of distributive leadership have several implications for teacher leadership. First, they indicate that teachers can and do perform important leadership tasks inside and outside formal positions of authority. The research suggests that school improvement is promoted by the distribution and the coordinated and redundant performance of leadership functions across roles, including teachers along with other members of school organizations. Distributed leadership requires mutual reliance among all school personnel even though, by virtue of their positions or knowledge and skills, different personnel might perform some leadership tasks better than others (Thurston, Kenz, Schacht, & Clift, 1995). Different teachers may lead from different strengths and lead in different ways (Wasley, 1991). Distributing leadership tasks among a number of people is important because the principal cannot "do it all." And while it is true that the division and distribution of labor may be important given the scope and fragmentation of principals' work (Fullan, 2001), the logic of distribution indicates that school leadership overall is ultimately enhanced by the different knowledge and skills brought by a variety of people and by the commitments that are developed among those who perform leadership tasks together.

Second, these models of distributive leadership suggest that teacher leadership may make both independent and, with leadership from other sources, additive or multiplicative contributions to school improvement and outcomes for students. Teacher leadership has "added value" to administrative leadership in schools. Depending on how one conceptualizes it, that "added value" may be equal to or greater than the sum of the parts.

Third, the argument that leadership is an organizational property reminds us that teacher leadership as a social influence process is a "given" in schools. Whether or not they occupy leadership roles, whether or not they perform particular leadership functions, teachers can exert influence by simply being part of the "webs" of relationships that define school organizations. We are reminded that influence in schools is exercised in all directions and among all participants. We are also reminded that relationships among leaders and followers are mutually influential and co-dependent. Even as "followers," teachers shape at the same time that they are shaped by other sources of leadership in their schools. Because leadership exists and functions in the relationships between leaders and followers, teachers as followers are by definition a constituting part of school leadership. Teachers are also key actors who shape the situations in which leadership relationships develop and are exercised.

In recent years there has been growing emphasis on self-managed teams for promoting teacher collaboration, improving teaching and student learning, and addressing problems of school organization (Fullan & Hargreaves, 1992; Pounder, 1998). Teams are small task groups in which members have a common purpose, interdependent roles, and complementary skills (Yukl, 1998). Self-managed teams are accorded considerable responsibility and discretion in how to perform their work. These work groups can be considered "intact social systems" whose members have the authority to handle internal processes as they see fit in order to perform their work (Hackman & Oldham, 1980, p. 164). In schools, teams may be created to increase teacher responsibility for group performance and outcomes and to expand opportunities for self-direction and management (Pounder, 1999). The logic of teams is that teachers' commitment, knowledge, and skills will be developed as they assume collective responsibility and as they work together to design their own methods for pursuing group objectives (Hackman, 1998).

In at least two ways, self-managed teams can be considered sources of teacher leadership. First, it is possible that these social units and the products of their work may promote improvement at the school level. Second, well-composed and well-functioning teams can exert substantial social and normative influence over their members, shaping their thinking, beliefs, and behaviors (Hackman, 1990; Yukl, 1998). Through their relationships and the work they perform together, teacher members can influence and lead one another. Group processes and the influence teachers may exert over one another in teams can provide some substitute for external administrative leadership, reducing the need for administrative initiative, guidance, and control (Bass, 1990; Kerr & Jermier, 1978; see also Pitner, 1988).

The management literature suggests that teams can improve organizational effectiveness; however, the evidence is mixed and much of it is based on weak research (Yukl, 1998). Hackman (1998) contends that what differentiates teams that "go into orbit and achieve real synergy from those that crash and burn" (p. 235) has much more to do with how teams are structured and supported than with any inherent virtues or liabilities of teaming itself (see also Yukl). His research found that teams benefit from being "set up right in the first place" (Hackman, 1990, p. 10). They require an organizational context that supports team performance through appropriate rewards, makes available relevant training and consultation, provides clear work requirements, and removes constraints on the team's work. Additional conditions of effectiveness include group composition appropriate to the task and work that is motivating to team members. Teams benefit from healthy interpersonal processes that increase the synergistic gains and reduce what Hackman calls "process losses" that result from lack of motivation and problems with coordination of activity.

Teams also require strong internal leadership to be effective (Hackman, 1990). This is another way that teams provide opportunities for teacher leadership. In a study of interdisciplinary teacher teams at the middle school level, Crow and Pounder (2000) found that teacher leadership skills and expertise were important aspects of "group composition" that enhanced team effectiveness. Teams with designated leaders generally functioned better than leaderless teams. Teams that exercised the greatest leadership in their schools were those that had strong leaders and a significant amount of member experience working in that particular school setting as well as in other team settings. These experiences gave teams expertise in "how things are done," helped them judge the implications of decision choices, and gave them confidence to *try* new ways of doing work.

In addition, teams require strong external leadership and support to be effective (Hackman, 1998). Crow and Pounder's study (2000) found that lack of support from other teachers and administrators eroded team members' sense of efficacy, discretion, and autonomy. Lack of clarity from school administrators about what teams were to achieve also diminished members' sense that their teams were actually self-managing and compromised teams' work. Bauer and Bogotch (2001) also found that district administrative support and support from the building principal and building staff strongly influenced measures of team effectiveness and/or satisfaction with "site council" teams composed of teachers and others connected with the schools. We take up the issue of external leadership again in the conclusion of this chapter.

Given these conditions of effectiveness, what contributions can the leadership of teacher teams make to school-level improvement? Much like the management literature, the education research provides mixed answers. The education literature suggests that self-managed teams may be an effective way to accomplish particular tasks and promote collaboration and development of team members (Witziers, Sleegers, & Imants, 1999). In a comparative study of teachers on teams and in non-team work arrangements, Pounder (1999) found that teachers on teams reported significantly greater work motivation, job satisfaction, work efficacy, and professional commitment than their non-teaming counterparts. The research Pounder reviewed for that study reached similar conclusions. Erb's studies (1987, 1995) of interdisciplinary teacher teams found that teaming reduces teacher isolation and focuses teachers' attention and coordinated action on student learning. Erb found that teachers on teams were more likely than their non-team counterparts to develop coordinated curricular and instruction plans. Teachers on teams tended to address student problems earlier and more systematically. They communicated earlier and more frequently with parents. They were more proactive in changing their classroom practice to address problems. Teamed teachers spent more time talking about curricular and co-curricular issues, and they were generally more knowledgeable about curricular and instructional matters than their non-teamed counterparts. In addition, teamed teachers were more likely than non-teamed teachers to integrate their instruction across subject areas. Other studies have demonstrated that in comparison with non-teamed teachers, teamed teachers tend to experience greater work satisfaction, sense of professionalism, and professional efficacy (Pounder, 1999). Teamed teachers also tend to have more knowledge of one another's work (Ashton & Webb, 1986) and provide more intellectual assistance and support to one another. Finally, teaming provides considerably more opportunities for direct and indirect involvement of teachers in decision making, including greater access to information (Kruse & Louis, 1997).

Studies of the effects of teacher teams on whole school improvement are not as encouraging (Donaldson, 2001; Witziers et al., 1999). In their study of high school departments as teams, for example, Herriot and Firestone (1984) found that departmental structure created barriers that hindered communication, collaboration, and curricular coherence across the larger school community. Interdisciplinary teams fared no better in promoting collaboration and collective decision making at the school level (Witziers et al., 1999). Kruse and Louis (1997) found that interdisciplinary teams undermined schools' ability to address schoolwide issues. In the middle schools they studied, the demands on teachers to deal with issues at the team level—from the management of team work to performing the work itself—minimized the opportunities that teachers had for engaging issues of teaching, student learning, and school organization across teams. Teaming appeared to inhibit the development of school-level reform agendas. Chrispeels' (1992) case studies of elementary schools also documented inconsistent influences of teams at the school level.

These findings are consistent with Yukl's (1998) assessment of the management literature that large organizations with many self-directed teams can experience serious problems coordinating activities and reaching agreement on strategic issues at the organizational level. This evidence does not necessarily mean that teacher teams cannot promote improvement at the school level. As Muncey and Conley (1999) pointed out, a shift to thinking, organizing, and planning around teaming may potentially provoke rethinking and experimentation about school structure, teaching strategies, and student learning—the central goals of educational reform (see Friedman, 1998). However, it may mean that strong external leadership is needed to set the direction for and to coordinate team work at the school level and to avoid organizational fragmentation (see Hackman, 1998). This conclusion is supported by the investigations of collective teacher research discussed earlier in the chapter.

## Conclusion

In this chapter we explored three new approaches to teacher leadership. We began with a brief historical overview of the evolution of teacher leadership since the early 1900s, ending with a discussion of the individual empowerment, role-based initiatives of the late 1980s and early 1990s. We discussed teacher research as a form of teacher leadership, different models of distributive leadership, and the leadership of self-managed teacher teams. We argued that these new approaches to teacher leadership represent a substantial shift from earlier initiatives. Looking across these new approaches, we see that they emphasize the importance of collective versus individual leadership; leadership aimed at the level of the school, not just at the level of the classroom; leadership focused on developing important aspects of school organization, curriculum, and instruction, not simply on administrative tasks; and leadership organized around important functions, not simply people and positions. The evidence from research to date, while not fully developed, suggests that these new approaches to teacher leadership can promote school improvement and that they appear to be more effective in this regard than previous models. Our experiences with teacher leadership initiatives of the 1980s and early 1990s reveal the limitations of the teacher as "heroic leader." However, we see in these new approaches the greater capacity of teachers to influence. We see that school improvement may be better served by teacher leadership that does not act alone but is part of a broad system of leadership influences and tasks performed by multiple actors.

What are the implications for teacher leadership development, or for that matter, school leadership development more generally? First, the fact that these new approaches to teacher leadership appear to be more effective than formal leadership roles for individual teachers in promoting school improvement does not mean that the latter should necessarily be abandoned. Recent research on school improvement in Chicago elementary schools documented the important contributions that teachers hired in instructional coordinator positions made in promoting curricular, instructional, and organizational improvement in their schools (Smylie, Wenzel, & Fendt, in press). At the same time, this research showed that these coordinators were much more effective when they worked as members of a broader constellation of school leaders, including principals, other teachers, and sometimes parents, each performing complementary task aimed at school-level improvement. These findings suggest that although it may be very useful to develop formal teacher leadership roles, these roles should not be relied upon as the primary means for promoting school improvement. Instead, they might best be developed as part of a schoolwide network of leadership.

This leads to a second implication, that the development of school leadership should not be aimed primarily at individual leaders but at leaders collectively. It is no less the case with these new approaches that the performance and outcomes of teacher leadership hinge on teachers' capacity to perform their tasks well. The capacity to lead is a function of knowledge relevant to the task, knowledge of the context, and process knowledge and skills (Little, 1988). If school leadership functions as a system of work performed by multiple actors, it makes little sense to develop that leadership by focusing on knowledge and skills of individual leaders outside the context of that system, Instead, we need to consider ways to develop the collective capacity of teachers, principals, and others who perform tasks of leadership together at the organizational level.

That said, it is clear that principals play a crucial role in the performance and outcomes of teacher leadership, whether it is exercised individually or in a collective context (Barth, 2001; Bizar & Barr, 2001). It is a paradox of teacher leadership that it requires administrative leadership to be effective, even those forms of teacher leadership, such as self-managed teams, that serve as substitutes for administrative leadership (Bass, 1990). For teacher leadership to work well, principals may be required to provide examples, incentives, guidance, and support, as well as the means of accountability (Smylie & Hart, 1999). It may fall to them to keep teacher leadership focused on meaningful work (Little, 1988). Principals need to know how to develop, support, and rnanage these new forms of leadership. Their unique position in the school organization gives them the resources, the ability, and the authority to do this leadership management work well. It is the principal who may best be able to direct the work of self-managed teams toward broader organizational objectives. It is the principal who may best be able to support teacher research and link it to school-level improvement planning and decision making and to teacher professional development activity. It is the principal who may be needed to coordinate and manage the performance of distributed leadership tasks. It is the principal and/or district administrator who can clarify the goals and processes of teacher teams, participate in defining the parameters of their work, and set the goals for which they will be held accountable (Bauer & Bogotch, 2001). We cannot assume that principals and district administrators know how to do these things particularly well. So while it makes sense to develop school leadership collectively, the importance of developing administrators' capacity for supporting these new approaches to leadership cannot be overlooked.

Finally, as with previous initiatives, it is unlikely that these new approaches to teacher leadership will be effective if they are not supported by the broader organizational and institutional contexts in which they develop and function. In writing for the 89th NSSE yearbook on teacher professionalism, school restructuring, and leadership, Rallis (1990) argued that the challenge of school leadership generally, and teacher leadership in particular, is not to find "super" leaders but "to discover and to promote the conditions that allow the process of leadership to flourish" (p. 186). There is no reason to believe that the lessons from research on individual role-based models of teacher leadership are not applicable to new task-oriented, organizational forms of leadership. Lack of leadership precedent will constrain the development and exercise of any form of teacher leadership (Little, 1988). So will hostility or resistance from other teachers (Lieberman, Sad, & Miles, 1992) And of course, there is the principal and the central office.

Donaldson (2001) describes the problems this way, He argues that schools have leadership-resistant architectures. There is no time to convene people to plan, organize, and follow through. Contact and the transaction of business are usually "on the fly" and communication is often haphazard, The culture and social norms of schools conspire against leadership development, Teacher rewards tend to be intrinsic and student-focused. Norms of individualism, autonomy, and privacy are pervasive. Teacher isolation and individualism and the history of hierarchical relationships in schools may doom collaborative effort. Donaldson concludes that school conditions can paralyze "action-in- common" because work is generally not conceived as interdependent, feedback on practice is scarce, and schools cannot stop the action long enough to understand the central adaptive challenges well enough to meet them. These are the very organizational problems that bedeviled previous efforts to develop teacher leadership (Smylie, 1997). Individual role-based models of teacher leadership were simply not strong enough to overcome them. However, the new forms of collective, task-oriented, organizational approaches to leadership we discussed in this chapter hold greater promise for overcoming these seemingly intractable problems. The initial evidence is encouraging, but more work needs to be done to experiment with these new approaches over an extended period of time and to study their implementation and outcomes systematically. Then we will have a much better idea whether these new approaches can fulfill their initial promise of promoting meaningful school-level improvement.

# References

Ashton, P. T., & Webb, R. B. (1986). *Making a difference: Teachers' sense of efficacy and student achievement.* New York: Longman.

Bacharach, S. B., & Conley, S. C. (1989). Uncertainty and decision-making in teaching: Implications for managing line professionals. In T. Sergiovanni and J. H. Moore (Eds.), *Schooling for tomorrow: Directing reform to issues that count* (pp. 311–329). Boston: Allyn & Bacon.

Bacharach, S. B., Conley, S., & Shedd, J. (1986). Beyond career ladders: Structuring teacher career development systems. *Teachers College Record, 87,* 563–574.

Barnard, C. I. (1968). Functions of the executive. Cambridge, MA: Harvard University Press.

Barth, R. (2001). Teacher leader. *Phi Delta Kappan, 82,*443–449.

Bass, B. M. (1990). *Bass & Stogdill's handbook of leadership* (3rd ed.). New York: Free Press.

Bauer, S., & Bogotch, I. E. (2001). Analysis of the relationships among site council resources, council practices, and outcomes. *Journal of School Leadership, 11,* 98–119.

Bizar, M., & Barr, R. (2001). *School leadership in times of urban reform.* Mahwah, NJ: Lawrence Erlbaum Associates.

Center for Research on the Context of Teaching. (2000, May). *Assessing results: Bay Area School Reform Collaborative-Year 4.* Stanford, CA: Center for Research on the Context of Teaching, Stanford University.

Chrispeels, J. H. (1992). *Purposeful restructuring: Creating a culture for learning and achievement in elementary schools.* Washington, DC: Falmer.

Clift, R. T., Veal, M. L., Holland, P., Johnson, M., & McCarthy, J. (1995). *Collaborative leadership and shared decision making: Teachers, principals, and university professors.* New York: Teachers College Press.

Cochran-Smith, M., & Lytle, S. L. (1998). Teacher research: The question that persists. *International Journal of Leadership in Education, 1,* 19–36.

Cochran-Smith, M., & Lytle, S. L. (1999a). Relationships of knowledge and practice: Teacher learning in communities. In A. Iran-Nejad & P. D. Pearson (Eds.), *Review of Research in Education, 24* (pp. 249–305). Washington, DC: American Educational Research Association.

Cochran-Smith, M., & Lytle, S. L. (1999b). The teacher research movement: A decade later. *Educational Researcher, 28*(7), 15–2 5.

Conley, S. (1991). Review of research on teacher participation in school decision making. In G. Grant (Ed.), *Review of research in education, 17* (pp. 225–266). Washington, DC: American Educational Research Association.

Copland, M. A. (2001, April). *Shared school leadership: Moving from role to function in an inquiry-based model of school reform.* Paper presented at the annual meeting of the American Educational Research Association, Seattle, WA.

Crow, G. M., & Pounder, D. G. (2000). Interdisciplinary teacher teams: Context, design, and process. *Educational Administration Quarterly, 36,* 216–254.

Dewey, J. (1903). Democracy in education. *Elementary School Teacher 4*(4), 193–204.

Donaldson, G. A. (2001). *Cultivating leadership in schools: Connecting people, purpose, and practice.* New York: Teachers College Press.

Dunlap, D. M., & Goldman, P. (1991). Rethinking power in schools. *Educational Administration Quarterly, 27,* 5–2 9.

Elmore, R. F., Peterson, P. L., & McCarthey, S. J. (1996). *Restructuring in the classroom: Teaching, learning, and school organization.* San Francisco: Jossey-Bass.

Erb, T. O. (1987). What team organization can do for teachers. *Middle School Journal, 18*(4), 3–6.

Erb, T. O. (1995). Teamwork in middle school education. In H. G. Garner (Ed.), *Teamwork models and experience in education* (pp. 175–198). Boston: Allyn & Bacon.

Firestone, W. A. (1996). Leadership roles or functions? In K. Leithwood, J. Chapman, D. Corson, P. Hallinger, & A. Hart (Eds.), *International handbook of educational leadership and administration* (Vol. 2, pp. 395–418). Dordrecht, The Netherlands: Kluwer.

Firestone, W. A., & Bader, B. D. (1992). *Redesigning teaching: Professionalism or bureaucracy?* Albany, NY: SUNY Press.

Friedman, V. J.,(1998). Making schools safe for uncertainty: Teams, teaching, and school reform. *Teachers College Record, 99*(2), 335–370.

Fullan, M. (2001). *The new meaning of educational change* (3rd ed.). New York: Teachers College Press.

Fullan, M., & Hargreaves, A. (1992). Teacher development and educational change. In M. Fullan & A. Hargreaves (Eds.), *Teacher development and educational change.* London: Falmer Press.

Fuller, W. E. (1989). The teacher in the country school. In D. Warren (Ed.), *American teachers: Histories of a profession at work* (pp. 98–117). New York: Macmillan.

Griffin, G. A., Lieberman, A., & Jacullo-Noto, J . (1983). *Interactive research and development on schooling: Executive Summary of final report.* Austin: University of Texas, Research and Development for Teacher Education.

Griffiths, D. (1979). Intellectual turmoil in educational administration. *Educational Administration Quarterly. 13*(3), 43–65.

Hackman, J. R. (1990). *Groups that work (and those that don't).* San Francisco: Jossey-Bass.

Hackman, J. R. (1998). Why teams don't work. In R. S. Tinsdale et al. (Eds.), *Theory and research on small groups* (pp. 245–267) New York: Plenum.

Hackman, J. R., & Oldham, G. R. (1980). *Work redesign.* Reading, MA: Addison-Wesley.

Haller, E., & Knapp, T. (1985). Problems and methodology in educational administration. *Educational Administration Quarterly, 21*(3), 15 7–168.

Harris, E., & Drake, S. M. (1997). Implementing high school reform through school-wide action research teams: A three year case study. *Action in Teacher Education, 19*(3), 15–31.

Hart, A. W. (1990). Work redesign: A review of literature for education reform. In S. B. Bacharach (Ed.), *Advances in research and theories of school management and educational policy* (Vol. 1, pp. 3 1–69). Greenwich, CT: JAI Press.

Heller, M. F., & Firestone, W. A. (1995). Who's in charge here? Sources of leadership for change. *Elementary School Journal. 96*, 65–86.

Henson, K.T.(1996). Teachers as researchers. In J. Sikula, T.J. Buttery, & E. Guyton (Eds.), *Handbook of research on teacher education* (pp. 53–64). New York: Macmillan.

Herriott, R. E., & Firestone, W. A. (1984). Two images of schools as organizations: A refinement and elaboration. *Educational Administration Quarterly, 20*(4), 41–57.

Hollander, E. P. (1978). *Leadership dynamics.* New York: Free Press.

Hollingsworth, S. & Sockett, H. (Eds.) (1994). *Teacher Research & Educational Reform.* National Society for the Study of Education Yearbooks.

Immegart, G. L. (1988). Leadership and leader behavior. In N.J. Boyan (Ed.), *Handbook of research on educational administration* (pp. 259–277). New York: Longman.

Kerr, S., & Jermier, J. (1978). Substitutes for leadership: Their meaning and measurement. *Organizational Behavior and Human Performance 22*, 374–403.

Kruse, S. D., & Louis, K. S. (1997). Teaching teaming in middle schools: Dilemmas for a school-wide community. *Educational Administration Quarterly, 33*, 261–289.

Leithwood, K., & Jantzi. D. (2000). The effects of different sources of leadership on student engagement in school. In K. A. Kiley & K. S. Louis (Eds.), *Leadership for change and school reform: International Perspectives* (pp. 50–66). New York: RoutledgeFalmer.

Lichtenstein, G., McLaughlin, M. W., & Knudsen, J. (1992). Teacher empowerment and professional knowledge. In A. Lieberman (Ed.), *The changing contexts of teaching. Ninety-first yearbook of. the National Society for the study of Education, Part I* (pp. 37–58). Chicago: National Society for the Study of Education.

Lieberman, A., Saxl, E. K., & Miles, M. B. (1992). Teacher leadership: Ideology and practice. In A. Lieberman (Ed.), *Building a professional culture in schools* (pp. 148–166). New York: Teachers College Press.

Little, J. W (1988). Assessing the prospects for teacher leadership. In A. Lieberman (Ed.), *Building a professional in schools* (pp. 78–106*).* New York: Teachers College Press.

Maeroff, G. I. (1988). *The empowerment of teachers: Overcoming the crisis of confidence.* New York: Teachers College Press.

Mayrowetz, D., & Weinstein, C. S. (1999). Sources of leadership for inclusive education: Creating schools for all children. *Educational Administration Quarterly, 35*, 423–449.

Mechanic, D. (1962–63). Sources of power of lower participants in complex organizations. *Administrative Science Quarterly, 7*, 349–364.

Muncey, D. E., & Conley, S. (1999). Teacher compensation and teacher teaming: Sketching the terrain. *Journal of Personnel Evaluation in Education, 12*(4), 365–385.

Murphy, J. (1990). The educational reform movement of the 1980s: A comprehensive analysis. In J. Murphy (Ed.), *The educational reform movement of the 1980s: Perspectives and cases* (pp. 3–55). Berkeley, CA: McCutchan.

Newmann, F. M., & Wehlage, G. G. (1995). *Successful School Restructuring.* Madison: Center on Organization and Restructuring of Schools, University of Wisconsin.

Ogawa, R. T., & Bossert, S. T. (1995). Leadership as an organizational quality. *Educational Administration Quarterly, 31*, 224–243.

Olson, M. W. (1990). The teacher as researcher: A historical perspective. In M. W. Olson (Ed.), *Opening the door to classroom research.* Newark, NJ: International Reading Association.

Ortman, E. J. (1 92 3). *Teacher councils: The organized means for securing the co-operation of all workers in the school.* Montpelier, VT: Capital City Press.

Pappas, C. (1997). Making "collaboration" problematic in collaborative school-university research: Studying with urban teacher researchers to transform literacy curriculum genres. In J. Flood, S. B. Heath, & D. Lapp (Eds.), *Handbook of research on teaching literacy through the communicative and visual arts* (pp. 215–231). New York: Macmillan.

Pitner, N. J. (1988). Leadership substitutes: Their factorial validity in educational organizations. *Educational and Psychological Measurement, 48*, 307–3 15.

Porter, L. W., Allen, R. W., & Angel, H. L. (1981). The politics of upward influence in organizations. In L. L. Cummings & B. W. Staw (Eds.), *Research in organizational behavior* (Vol. 3, pp. 109–149). Greenwich, CT: JAI.

Pounder, D. G. (1998). Teacher teams: Redesigning teachers' work for collaboration. In D. G. Pounder (Ed.), *Restructuring schools for collaboration: Promises and pitfalls* (pp. 65–88). Albany, NY: SUNY Press.

Pounder, D. G. (1999). Teacher teams: Exploring job characteristics and work related outcomes of work group enhancement. *Educational Administration Quarterly, 35,* 317–348.

Pounder, D. G., Ogawa, R. T., & Adams, E. A. (1995). Leadership as an organization-wide phenomenon: Its impact on school performance. *Educational Administration Quarterly, 31,* 564–588.

Rallis, S. (1990). Professional teachers and restructured schools: Leadership challenges. In B. Mitchell & L. L. Cunningham (Eds.), *Educational leadership and changing contexts of families, communities, and schools. Eighty-ninth yearbook of the National Society for the Study of Education, Part II* (pp. 184–209). Chicago: National Society for the Study of Education.

Smylie, M. A. (1997). Research on teacher leadership: Assessing the state of the art. In B. J. Biddle et al. (Eds.), *International handbook of teachers and teaching* (pp. 521–592). Dordrecht, The Netherlands: Kluwer.

Smylie, M. A., & Hart, A. W. (1999). School leadership for teacher learning and change: A human and social capital development perspective. In J. Murphy & K. S. Louis (Eds.), *Handbook of research on educational administration* (2nd ed., pp. 421–441). San Francisco: Jossey-Bass.

Smylie, M. A., Wenzel, S. A., & Fendt, C. R. (in press). The Chicago Annenberg Challenge: Lessons on leadership for school development. In J. Murphy & A. Datnow (Eds.), *Leadership for school reform: Lessons from comprehensive school reform designs.* Thousand Oaks, CA: Corwin.

Spillane, J., Halverson, R., & Diamond, J. R. (2000). *Towards a theory of leadership practice: A distributed perspective.* Evanston, IL: Northwestern University, Institute for Policy Research.

Spillane, J., Halverson, R., & Diamond, J. B. (2001). Investigating school leadership practice: A distributed perspective. *Educational Researcher, 30*(3), 23–28.

Tannenbaum, A. S. (1962). Control in organizations: Individual adjustment and organizational performance. *Administrative Science Quarterly, 7,* 236–257.

Thompson, J. D. (1967). *Organizations in action.* New York: McGraw-Hill.

Thurston, P. W., Kenz, K., Schacht, M., & Clift, R. T. (1995). Exploring leadership. In R. T. Clift & P. W. Thurston (Eds.), *Distributed leadership: School improvements through collaboration* (pp. 155–1 77). Greenwich, CT: JAI.

Tikunoff, W. J., Ward, E., & Griffin, G. A. (1979). *Interactive research and development on teaching study: Final report.* San Francisco: Far West Laboratory for Educational Research and Development.

Wasley, P. A. (1991). *Teachers who lead: The rhetoric of reform and the realities of practice.* New York: Teachers College Press.

Weise, R., & Murphy, J. (1995). SBM in historical perspective, 1900–1950. In J. Murphy & L. Beck, *School-based management and school reform: Taking stock* (pp. 93 –115). Thousand Oaks, CA: Corwin.

Witziers, B., Sleegers, P., & Imants, J. (1999). Departments as teams: Functioning, variations and alternatives. *School Leadership and Management, 19,* 293–304.

Yendol Silva, D., Gimbert, B., & Nolan, J. (2000). Sliding the doors: Locking and unlocking possibilities for teacher leadership. *Teachers College Record, 102,* 779–804.

Yukl, G. (1998). *Leadership in organizations* (4th ed.). Upper Saddle River, NJ: Prentice Hall.

Zeichner, K. M. (1994). Personal renewal and social construction through teacher research. In S. Hollingsworth & H. Sockett (Eds.), *Teacher research and educational reform. Ninety-third yearbook of the International Society for the Study of Education, Part I* (pp. 66–84). Chicago: National Society for the Study of Education.

# Conclusion: "Leading Against the Grain"

## Redefining Teacher Leadership in the 21st Century

ELEANOR BLAIR HILTY

---

Teaching is not what I expected. When I grew up in rural West Virginia and went to school. I remember what teachers did and I remember the role that they played. There was pride in teaching. High school teachers were looked at as leaders in the community and people that you looked up to. Those days are gone. People feel, and I didn't realize this until I was teaching, that it's kind of degrading to say, "I'm a high school teacher." You have to say it under your breath. I used to think people had a lot of respect for high school teachers, but I feel that they don't anymore. It's just a guy who wants to teach school is just the attitude I get now. That is kind of an embarrassment to me because I do enjoy I . . .—High School Teacher

TEACHING HAS TRADITIONALLY ATTRACTED INDIVIDUALS WHO COME TO THE PROFESSION FOR THE right reasons but find the public schools are the wrong institutions for their dreams and aspirations. Teachers express dissatisfaction with the profession for many reasons, but most focus on the dissatisfactions associated with a low salary and limited autonomy. Attempts to improve the status of the profession have generally focused on increasing the educational requirements for entry into the profession, raising salaries, and encouraging collaboration and shared decision-making among major stakeholders. These efforts to recognize the various levels of skill, education, and expertise of teachers often "open the door" to opportunities for teachers to assume important leadership roles beyond the classroom. More specifically, better trained teachers assume roles that challenge traditional notions of school leadership, and higher qualifications ultimately provide opportunities for teacher leaders to practice independent decision-making. A renewed interest in teacher leadership as a cornerstone of most teacher education programs in the 21st century is an important indicator that the public is ready to put teachers on the front-line of school reform efforts and acknowledge the essential knowledge and skills that they bring to schools and communities.

Teachers have always played one of the most important roles in schools and in the educational histories of most adults. I am frequently besieged with stories of the best or worst teachers that individuals had as students in K-12 schools. Adults may remember little about their educational histories, but it is seldom that I encounter someone who does not remember their favorite/worst teacher. These teachers have shaped our views of education and had a powerful influence on who we ultimately became as adults. However, any discussion of teachers is always fraught with a consideration of the difficulties faced by individuals who choose teaching as a career—issues related to low salary and status, difficult students, even more difficult parents, and so on. Questions regarding why anyone would want to be a teacher are always front and center in these discussions. Efforts to promote teacher leadership in the schools recognize the important roles that teachers play in the lives of children and adults and highlight the relationship that exists between teachers and the communities that they serve. Teachers possess an understanding of the values, beliefs, and attitudes that shape the lives of their constituents, and they are often able to do that in a way that combines both personal and professional expertise.

Historically, issues surrounding the "feminization" of the profession limited a serious consideration of teaching as a profession, and the notion of teachers as leaders was considered a moot issue. Throughout most of the twentieth century, teaching was seen as a semi-profession with few opportunities for advancement, increased levels of responsibilities or pay; a profession that allowed for easy entry and even easier reentry after extended periods of unemployment (Lortie, 1975). Even so, in earlier times, schools were small, and teachers often assumed the roles of both teacher and principal. Even today, as secondary programs consolidate and expand, teachers are given opportunities to assume the roles of department head or lead teacher in various curricular or program areas. Thus, teachers have a tradition of leading in informal ways or in positions with limited formal authority. These shifting responsibilities have seldom been explored or considered phenomena worthy of discussion. However, as teacher leaders gain prominence at local and regional levels, there must simultaneously be efforts to grant them formal authority in their positions as teacher leaders; it is necessary to recognize the value of their contributions and honor the authority that they must have in their decision-making. At this point, teacher leadership will cease to be merely "lip-service" to increased professional status, and it will become a true measure of the seriousness when we embrace the idea of teacher leaders in the schools. If we truly want to meet the challenge of public schools for this still new century, teachers acting as teacher leaders must guide our vision of where we are going, and most importantly, how we can get there. Teacher leaders will not take the place of traditional leadership positions in the schools, but more importantly, they will complement those efforts.

Since the 1980s, numerous national reports have called for the reform of American education with increased accountability for student achievement. These reports continue to reflect the depth of public dissatisfaction with the schools. Public schools are perceived as institutions with little accountability and a limited ability to respond to changing demographics and the demands of failing economic and political systems; schools don't "work" anymore. Unfortunately, a significant portion of young people fail or drop out of school each year, and good teachers either leave the profession early or simply "burn out." Critics of American education argue that the welfare of the nation is in jeopardy if the public schools do not commit to meaningful change in the 21st century. Once again, however, efforts to talk about *all* schools or *all* communities are inherently flawed. The structure and organization of schools in the United States grant tremendous autonomy to how local education agencies operate. Opportunities for school *leaders* (teachers and administrators) to explore the possibilities of multi-layered leadership opportunities that engage ALL major stakeholders are possible, but often discouraged through the formal organization of the school bureaucracy. The literature in education is full of recommendations for the establishment of professional learning communities, school improvement teams and ideas regarding the sustainability of distributed leadership and leadership capacity building. The most exciting aspect of these proposals is that they put teachers "front and center" in efforts to reform schools by recognizing the unique skills and expertise that teachers bring to the "table." While questions about curriculum, tests, and equity issues are central to attempts to make the public schools amenable to the needs of society, central to a consideration of these issues is a cadre of individuals with a knowledge base and skills in both pedagogy and leadership as well as a commitment to an ideology that espouses a belief in equity and social justice. Teacher leaders must be a key component of any solution to the problems that we face in 21st century schools; they are our most valuable resource, and currently they are underappreciated and underutilized.

## "Making the Familiar Strange and the Strange Familiar": Teacher Leaders in "New" Territory

Noted educational anthropologists George and Louise Spindler coined the phrase, "making the familiar strange and the strange familiar" in their discussions of education in cultures other than the United States. Their perspective was that it is hard for us to look at schools with a critical eye because they are too familiar. Schools have been a part of most people's lives since they were very young. It is difficult to step back and truly examine them as someone foreign to this culture might see them. There are too many deeply embedded "taken-for-granted-assumptions" about how to "do" schools, and this makes it extremely difficult to get individuals to question the integrity of these institutions or the motives of those who work within the confines of these public spaces. How do we explain the lack of differentiated leadership roles for women in the schools? Is it simply a coincidence that the vast majority of individuals in leadership positions in the schools are male? Yes, these numbers are changing, but as Katzenmeyer and Moller (2009) discuss, "Within every school there is a *sleeping giant* of teacher leadership that can be a strong catalyst for making changes to improve student learning" (p. 2). As *teachers as* leaders becomes a metaphor to guide our thinking about how schools are structured and run on a daily basis, it also becomes a metaphor that challenges our thinking about the familiar roles and responsibilities of teachers and their relationships to power and authority.

*Teachers as* leaders is by necessity also a gender issue that forces us to confront institutional forces that limit the choices available to women teachers or that refuse to affirm and reward styles of leadership that vary from the traditional. This conflict is evident in the daily, and all too familiar, struggles surrounding power and authority. In Weiler's (1988) study of women teachers and administrators she found that "they inherit positions in already existing, highly complex institutions....Feminist and antiracist teachers and administrators who seek to redefine curriculum and social relationships inside and outside the classroom find themselves in conflict with existing patriarchal ideology and hierarchical relationships" (p. 101). Teachers have traditionally played subordinate roles in the schools, and attempts to change that scenario are frequently met with resistance from both teachers and administrators. Teacher leaders often complain that their worst critics are other teachers who do not want to change the status quo. Central to any effort to reinvent school in a new image is a reconsideration of the role of teacher leadership in these schools and a visualization of broad-based leadership capacity building in the form of distributed leadership, professional learning communities and/or school improvement teams. A period of re-education and skill building will be a key part of any substantive and meaningful change efforts. Essential to these efforts will be the support and involvement of school administrators. Teacher leaders will need their support as they attempt to renegotiate their relationships within the educational bureaucracy. Furthermore, if the movement to make the voices of teacher leaders a central part of the reform and re-envisioning of school programs, teachers must be seen as essential conduits between the schools and the community. Their understanding of the chasm between the values, beliefs, and attitudes of the school and those of the community will be important to any serious efforts to produce a critical examination of schools and "make the familiar strange, and the strange familiar." These kinds of efforts are fundamental to changing the schools, and once it begins, it has the potential to become a revolution where a quality education for ALL children in ALL schools is the only acceptable victory.

## "Leading Against the Grain"

Seeing teachers as leaders in schools requires confronting the obstacles that have prevented them from assuming these roles in the past. Some of these obstacles are related to gender bias, but others are more personal, related to narrow definitions of leadership roles and responsibilities within schools and communities. It is imperative that teachers be prepared in their teacher education programs to work as leaders in all types of schools, regardless of geography, demographics and/or socioeconomic levels. Teachers are accustomed to viewing the teaching process as both an art and a skill. Thus, it is perhaps easier for them to recognize that leadership is also a creative endeavor, an effort that is by necessity both fluid and dynamic. Cochran-Smith (1991) conceptualized the notion of "teaching against the grain." She described this skill in the following way:

> Teaching against the grain stems from, but also generates, critical perspectives on the macro-level relationships of power, labor, and ideology—relationships that are perhaps best examined at the university, where sustained and systematic study is possible. But teaching against the grain is also deeply embedded in the culture and history of teaching at individual schools and in the biographies of particular teachers and their individual or collaborative efforts to alter curricula, raise questions about common practices, and resist inappropriate decisions. These relationships can only be explored in schools in the company of experienced teachers who are themselves engaged in complex situation-specific, and sometimes losing struggles to work against the grain. (p. 280)

For teachers acting as leaders the tasks are not easy. Teacher leaders are not the norm, and the effort requires a combination of skill and courage to "lead against the grain" both within and beyond the school. At a minimum, teachers "leading against the grain" demonstrate the following qualities in their professional work:

- A willingness to challenge the political and bureaucratic forces that support the inertia and mediocrity that dominate schools;
- a rigorous and critical examination of the values, beliefs and attitudes that inform and shape the curriculum as well as the organizational/technical policies and procedures that guide school improvement and professional development efforts;
- a commitment to leadership capacity building as the cornerstone of all serious and substantive work in the school;
- a focus of all educational initiatives on the growth and development of children;
- ongoing efforts to acquire and develop the knowledge, skills, and dispositions that are prerequisite to becoming an effective teacher leader, as well as an ongoing commitment to providing multiple roles and opportunities for the growth of future teacher leaders.

The list of qualities could be quite long, and I encourage students to generate a list of additional qualities that they believe a teacher "leading against the grain" must possess. However, in effect, a teacher
leader must see herself as an agent of change, not just in the classroom, but in many different venues
associated with the role of teacher. Teachers must challenge current thinking about schools and "push"
to get major stakeholders to "make the familiar strange, and the strange familiar" in the examination
of *how* change occurs, *who* takes responsibility for making it happen and the knowledge that will
inform the changes that occur; knowledge is not neutral, and there is very little objectivity evident
in most decision-making. Our schools have the opportunity, resources, knowledge, and skills to create a model system of education, and yet, we have grown accustomed to routinely accepting a pervasive mediocrity that does nothing to mediate the rising levels of school failure and dropouts.
Teachers who "lead against the grain" will demand a rethinking and reorganization of the "school culture" that facilitates (and expects) the creation of schools where teaching and learning are shaped by
a clearly articulated knowledge base regarding what works and what does not work, as well as a consideration of the many "voices" that must contribute to the meaningful reform of schools. In collaboration with teachers, administrators, school staff, parents, students, and community members,
schools can be a place for dialogue and a mutual sharing of wants, needs, and desires as a prerequisite for the creation of better schools, better teachers, and better students.

The concept of "scaffolding" has often been used to describe the social relations and reciprocity inherent in the teaching and learning process (Erickson, 1984; Ladson-Billings, 1994; Wood,
Bruner, & Ross, 1976). The value of this metaphor lies in its emphasis upon the interconnectedness
of the teaching/learning process. This metaphor is equally descriptive of the work of teachers acting
as leaders in schools, classrooms, and communities. Borrowing from the ideas of Ladson-Billings
(1994),

> I can see teachers as leaders providing "scaffolding" for other teachers. In this way, they are helping teach-
> ers "move from what they know to what they need to know" as both teachers and learners....to build upon
> their own experiences, knowledge, and skills to move into more difficult knowledge and skills. Rather than
> chastise them for what they do not know, these teachers find ways to use the knowledge and skills...as a
> foundation for learning and leading." (p. 124)

Bondy and Ross (1992) suggest that "Changing the status quo in schools requires the collective efforts
of teachers. Teachers need to learn how to gain power and influence....[a need to] help teachers develop the micro-political awareness and competence needs to foster collaborative action among teachers and improve the school experiences of students" (p. 13). Similarly, according to hooks (1994),
"Changing the status quo" is not easy, and it is important to remember that "teachers are rewarded
when [they] do not teach or attempt to teach against the grain. The choice to work against the grain,
to challenge the status quo, often has negative consequences" (p. 203). Teachers acting as leaders in
schools will help their colleagues (and students) better understand the purpose of a vision guided by
the democratic principles that shaped our nation while simultaneously questioning practices that lead
to the inequitable distribution of knowledge, power and resources (Giroux, 1989; Greene, 1985). Good
teachers will become good leaders in their schools when the bureaucracy (and its leaders) expands
the hierarchical structure of schools to accommodate new roles and responsibilities for teachers.
Teachers must seek out these "new" roles and responsibilities and support those individuals who
attempt to move the schools in this direction, but prerequisite to all of this is an acknowledgment
and affirmation of the unique skills and insights that teachers bring to schools. Alongside a recon-

ceptualization of teacher roles must be a realization that administrators should be acting as colleagues to these teachers, not bosses or supervisors, and sharing equal responsibility for designing successful schools and programs that meet the needs of students and families. The unequal distribution of power in schools has unfortunately contributed to the mediocre performance of teachers and students. Once again, teacher leaders represent the most likely candidates to lead schools toward a renewed vision of effective schools that are able to articulate and work proactively to achieve the aims and purposes of 21st-century schools. Teacher leadership must become the norm, and new teachers must enter these schools as competent professionals trained to both teach AND lead in tomorrow's schools.

## Note

Small sections of this paper were modified and revised from a previous publication by the author: Hilty, E. B. (1999). Southern schools, southern teachers: Redefining leadership in rural communities. In D. Chalker, & R. Haynes. (1999). *Leadership for rural schools: Lessons for all educators.* Lancaster, PA: Technomic Publishing Company, Inc.

## References

Bondy, E., & Ross, D. (1992). Micro-political competence: How teachers can change the status quo. *The Clearing House,* September/October, pp. 10–14.

Cochran-Smith, M. (1991). Learning to teach against the grain. *Harvard Educational Review, 61*(3), 279–307.

Erickson, R. E. (1984). School literacy, reasoning, and civility: An anthropologist's perspective. *Review of Educational Research, 54*(4), 525–546.

Giroux, H. (1989). Rethinking education reform in the age of George Bush. *Phi Delta Kappan, 71*(8), 728–730.

Greene, M. (1985). The role of education in a democracy. *Educational Horizons, 63,* 3–9.

hooks, b. (1994). *Teaching to transgress: Education as the practice of freedom.* New York, NY: Routledge.

Katzenmeyer, M., & Moller, G. (2009). *Awakening the sleeping giant* (3rd ed. ). Thousand Oaks, CA: Corwin.

Ladson-Billings, G. (1994). *The dreamkeepers: Successful teachers of African American children.* San Francisco, CA: Jossey-Bass Publishers.

Lortie, D. C. (2002). *Schoolteacher: A sociological study* (2nd ed.). Chicago: University of Chicago Press.

Spindler, G., & Spindler, L. (2000). *Fifty years of anthropology and education: 1950–2000: A Spindler anthology.* New York, NY: Routledge.

Weiler, K. (1988). *Women teaching for change: Gender, class & Power.* South Hadley, MA: Bergin & Garvey Publishers, Inc.

Wood, B., Bruner, J., & Ross, G. (1976). The role of tutoring in problem solving. *Journal of Child Psychology and Psychiatry, 17,* 89–100.

# Suggested Resources and References for Further Study

## Capacity Building

Harris, A., & Lambert, L. (2003). *Building leadership capacity for school improvement*. Berkshire, England: Open University Press.

Lambert, L. (2003). *Leadership capacity for lasting school improvement*. Alexandria, VA: Association for Supervision and Curriculum Development.

Senge, P., Cambron-McCabe, N., Lucas, T., Smith, B., Dutton, J., & Kleiner, A. (2000). *Schools that learn: A fifth discipline fieldbook for educators, parents, and everyone who cares about education*. New York, NY: Doubleday.

## Distributed Leadership

Chrispeels, J. H. (Ed.). (2004). *Learning to lead together: The promise and challenge of sharing leadership*. Thousand Oaks, CA: Sage.

## Professional Development

Drago-Severson, E. (2004). *Helping teachers learn: Principal leadership for adult growth and development*. Thousand Oaks, CA: Corwin.

Sparks, D., & Hirsh, S. (1997). A *new vision for staff development*. Alexandria, VA: Association for Supervision and Curriculum Development.

## Professional Learning Communities

DuFour, R. (2002). The learning-centered principal. *Educational Leadership, 59*(8), 12–15.

DuFour, R., & Eaker, R. (1998). *Professional learning communities at work: Best practices for enhancing student achievement.* Alexandria, VA: Association for Supervision and Curriculum Development.

DuFour, R., Eaker, R., & DuFour, R. (Eds.). (2005). *On common ground: The power of professional learning communities.* Bloomington, IN: National Educational Service.

Roberts, S. M., & Pruitt, E. Z. (2003). *Schools as professional learning communities.* Thousand Oaks, CA: Corwin Press.

Smith, S. S., & Scott, J. J. (1990). *The collaborative school: A work environment for effective instruction.* Reston, VA: National Association of Secondary School Principals.

# School Improvement

Marzano, R. J. (2003). *What works in schools: Translating research into action.* Alexandria, VA: Association for Supervision and Curriculum Development.

Reeves, D. B. (2004). *Accountability for learning: How teachers and school leaders can take charge.* Alexandria, VA: Association for Supervision and Curriculum Development.

Reeves, D. B. (2006). *The learning leader: How to focus school improvement for better results.* Alexandria, VA: Association for Supervision and Curriculum Development.

Schmoker, M. (1999). *Results: The key to continuous school improvement* (2nd ed.) Alexandria, VA.: Association for Supervision and Curriculum Development.

Schmoker, M. (2001). *The results fieldbook: Practical strategies from dramatically improved schools.* Alexandria, VA: Association for Supervision and Curriculum Development.

# Teacher Leadership

Ackerman, R. H., & Mackenzie, S.V. (Eds.). (2007). *Uncovering teacher leadership: Essays and voices from the field.* Thousand Oaks, CA: Corwin.

Crowther, F., with Ferguson, M., & Hann, L. (2008). *Developing teacher leaders: How teacher leadership enhances school success* (2nd ed.). Thousand Oaks, CA: Corwin.

Danielson, C. (2006). *Teacher leadership that strengthens professional practice.* Alexandria, VA: Association for Supervision and Curriculum Development.

Elmore, R. F. (2001). *Building a new structure for school leadership.* Washington, DC: The Albert Shanker Institute.

Gabriel, J. G. (2005). *How to thrive as a teacher leader.* Alexandria, VA: Association for Supervision and Curriculum Development.

Harris, A., & Muijs, D. (2004). *Improving schools through teacher leadership.* Maidenhead, Berkshire, UK: Open University Press.

Katzenmeyer, M., & Moller, G. (2009). *Awakening the sleeping giant* (3rd ed.). Thousand Oaks, CA: Corwin.

Killion, J., & Harrison, C. (2006). *Taking the lead: New roles for teachers and school-based coaches.* Oxford, OH: National Staff Development Council.

Kouzes, J., & Posner, B. (1995). *The leadership challenge: How to get extraordinary things done in organizations.* San Francisco, CA: Jossey-Bass.

Lieberman, A., & Miller, L. (2004). *Teacher leadership.* San Francisco, CA: Jossey-Bass.

Mangin, M. M., & Stoelinga, S. R. (2008). *Effective teacher leadership: Using research to inform and reform.* New York: Teachers College Press.

Marzano, R. L., Waters, T., & McNulty, B. A. (2005). *School leadership that works: From research to results.* Alexandria, VA: Association for Supervision and Curriculum Development.

Moller, G., & Pankake, A. (2006). *Lead with me: A principal's guide to teacher leadership.* Larchmont, NY: Eye on Education.

Reeves, D. B. (2008). *Reframing teacher leadership to improve your school.* Alexandria, VA: Association for Supervision and Curriculum Development.

Thompson, S. C. (2004). *Developing teacher leaders: The principal's role.* Westerville, OH: National Middle School Association.

Troen, V., & Boles, K. (2003). *Who's teaching your children? Why the teacher crisis is worse than you think and what can be done about it.* New Haven, CT: Yale University Press.

## Miscellaneous Resources and Web Sites

http://cstp-wa.org/sites/default/files/CSTP-leadership_2007.pdf
(Teacher to Leader: Dilemmas in Teacher Leadership)

http://www.cstp-wa.org/sites/default/files/teacher_leadership_skills_framework.pdf
(Teacher Leadership Skills Framework)

http://www.cstp-wa.org/sites/default/files/self%20assessments_all_web.pdf
(Teacher Leader Self-Assessment)

http://www.ctl.vcu.edu/
(Center for Teacher Leadership)

http://www.leadershipteacher.org/
(Leadership Teacher: Creating Real World Classroom Connections)

http://www.teacherleaders.org/
(Teacher Leaders Network)

http://www.teacherscount.org/
(Teachers Count)

# Contributors

**Emily Brumley Abernathy** is a native of Western North Carolina and an alumna of the University of North Carolina at Asheville with a Bachelor of Arts degree in Literature. She is currently pursuing a Master of Arts in Teaching English through Western Carolina University.

**Michele Acker-Hocevar** is an Associate Professor in the Educational Leadership and Counseling Psychology Department at Washington State University, Tri-Cities. Her work on leadership and school development addresses power issues and inclusion of various organizational members as legitimate partners in building more participatory workplaces.

**Ann S. Allen** is Assistant Professor in Educational Leadership and Foundations at Western Carolina University. A graduate of the University of Kentucky, she has experience as an elementary teacher, junior high teacher, and elementary principal. Her doctoral degree is from the University of Cincinnati in Urban Educational Leadership. Her research agenda includes public schools and leadership preparation.

**Pamela S. Angelle** is Assistant Professor in Educational Leadership and Policy Studies at The University of Tennessee, Knoxville. Her research interests include distributed leadership and teacher leadership, with a focus on organizational conditions which contribute to a collegial school community.

**Roland S. Barth is** founding director of the Harvard Principals' Center and is a consultant to schools, school systems, state departments of education, universities, foundations, and businesses in the United States and abroad.

**Nelda Cambron-McCabe** is a Professor, Department of Educational Leadership, Miami University, Ohio. She was an advisory board member and a coordinator of the Danforth Foundation Forum for the *American School Superintendent*.

**Sharon Conley** is Professor of Education at the University of California at Santa Barbara. Research interests are in the general areas of organizational behavior in education and the administrative and managerial work environments of teachers.

**Monica Coyle** is an English teacher at North Bergen High School, North Bergen, New Jersey.

**Terrence E. Deal** is as the Irving R. Melbo Professor Emeritus at the University of Southern California's Rossier School. He is a lecturer and author whose research interests focus on leadership and organizations.

**Morgaen L. Donaldson** is an Assistant Professor of Educational Leadership at the University of Connecticut, a Research Associate at the Center for Policy Analysis, and a Research Affiliate of the Project on the Next Generation of Teachers at Harvard University. She is currently conducting studies on principals' approaches to human capital development within their schools; teacher leadership in deregulated urban schools; and the effects of state policy on secondary school practices in four New England states.

**Terry K. Dozier** is Associate Professor and Director of the Center for Teacher Leadership at Virginia Commonwealth University School of Education. Her work focuses on promoting and supporting teacher leadership that enhances the quality of teaching and the teaching profession.

**Richard DuFour** recently retired as Superintendent of Adlai Stevenson High School in Lincolnshire, Illinois. He currently resides in Moneta, Virginia.

**William A. Firestone** Associate Dean of Academic Affairs; Professor of Educational Leadership and Policy at Rutgers Graduate School of Education, New Brunswick, NJ. He is interested in educational leadership and educational policy. More recently he has examined how leadership is distributed in districts and how different patterns of leadership can help schools improve.

**David Gabbard** is Professor in the Department of Curriculum and Instruction at East Carolina University. His research focuses on critical education policy studies. He has edited or co-edited several books, including *Knowledge and Power in the Global Economy: The Effects of School Reform in a Neoliberal/Neoconservative Age* and *Education as Enforcement: The Militarization and Corporatization of Schools* (w/Kenneth J. Saltman).

**Marjorie F. Heller** is a retired Superintendent of the Little Silver School District, Little Silver, NJ.

**Mary Jean Ronan Herzog** is a Professor in the Department of Educational Leadership & Foundations at Western Carolina University, Cullowhee, North Carolina. Her research and writing have focused on issues and concerns in rural education and cultural studies.

**Eleanor Blair Hilty** is an Associate Professor in the Department of Educational Leadership & Foundations at Western Carolina University (WCU), Cullowhee, North Carolina. Through her work at WCU, she teaches educational foundations courses (F2F and Online) to both undergraduate and graduate students in the United States and Jamaica. Her research and writing focus on teacher's work and teacher leadership.

**Institute for Educational Leadership, Inc.** For more than thirty-five years, the Institute for Educational Leadership (IEL)—a non-profit, nonpartisan organization based in Washington, D.C.—has worked to achieve better results for children and youth. IEL has created and continued to nurture diverse networks across the country. Their efforts are focused through five programs of work: *Developing Leaders; Strengthening School-Family-Community Connections; Governing; Connecting and Improving Systems That Serve Children and Youth; Improving Preparation for Work.*

**Susan Moore Johnson** is Carl H. Pforzheimer Jr. Professor of Teaching and Learning, Harvard Graduate School of Education, Cambridge, Massachusetts.

**Joseph Kahne** is currently the John and Martha Davidson Professor of Education and Dean, School of Education at Mills College, Oakland, CA. His research focuses on ways school practices and new media may be influencing youth civic and political development. He also studies urban school reform.

**Marilyn Katzenmeyer** is president of Professional Development Center, Inc., and she currently engages in consultation, instructional design, and professional writing. She most recently served as a faculty administrator at the University of South Florida, where she was responsible for the development and implementation of the Executive Leaders Program, a leadership development opportunity for school-based administrators and teacher leaders who were transitioning into district-level leadership roles, and for the coordination of a Transition to Teaching project with a local school district.

**Linda Lambert** is founder of the Center for Educational Leadership at California State University, Hayward where she is professor emeritus. She is a major contributor to the field of teacher leadership.

**Ann Lieberman** is an Professor Emerita from Teachers College, Columbia University. She was a Senior Scholar at the Carnegie Foundation for the Advancement of Teaching for 10 years. She is now a senior scholar at Stanford University. She is widely known for her work in the areas of teacher leadership and development, collaborative research, networks and school–university partnerships, and the problems and prospects for understanding educational change.

**Helen M. Marks** is an Associate Professor Educational Policy and Leadership at The Ohio State University. Her interests include school leadership and its distribution, school restructuring, civic engagement, community service learning, and student outcomes of schooling.

**Martha M. McCarthy** is Professor and Chair of the Department of Educational Leadership and Policy Studies at Indiana University at Bloomington in the School of Education. Primary research interests pertain to church/state relations involving schools, free expression rights, equity concerns, privatization of education, curriculum censorship, and leadership preparation.

**Gayle Moller** is Associate Professor Emerita in the Department of Educational Leadership and Foundations in the College of Education and Allied Professions at Western Carolina University in Cullowhee, North Carolina. She was formerly Executive Director of the South Florida Center for Educational Leaders. The Center served large urban school districts in South Florida. Teacher leadership, professional learning communities, and professional development have been interests of Gayle's for the past twenty years.

**Donna E. Muncey** is an adjunct faculty member at St. Mary's College of Maryland.

**Kent D. Peterson** is Professor at the University of Wisconsin-Madison, Department of Educational Administration, Madison, WI. Research interests include work on principals, school culture, school reform.

**Linda Searby** is an Assistant Professor and Program Chair in Educational Leadership at the University of Alabama, Birmingham. Her research interests include women and leadership, mentoring, and reflective practice. Dr. Searby does consulting for schools and has recently started a program called Coaching New Principals, designed to assist principals in goal setting and monitoring, developing a positive school culture and climate, facilitating school leadership teams, public relations and communication, and instructional leadership.

**Phillip C. Schlechty** is one of the nation's foremost authors and speakers on school reform and is the founder and chief executive officer of the Schlechty Center. His intensive work—promoting the Schlechty Center's vision for public education—is a reflection of his dedication and commitment to public education.

**Lisa Shaddix** was a participant in the Teachers as Leaders program of the Mountain Brook, Alabama School system which represented an attempt to facilitate the empowering of teachers to utilize their leadership skills and contribute to the system as it fulfills its mission to offer education to its students that is effective, challenging, and engaging.

**Julie A. Sherrill** is an educational administrator at Upper Arlington High School, Upper Arlington, Ohio.

**Mark A. Smylie** is a Professor and Chair of Educational Policy Studies at the University of Illinois at Chicago. Research and teaching interests include school organization, leadership, and change, urban school improvement, teacher leadership, learning, and professional development.

**Kathleen Topolka-Jorissen** is Assistant Professor in Educational Leadership and Foundations at Western Carolina University. Her research and teaching disciplines focus on policy and practice related to educator quality, including the preparation, evaluation and professional development of principals and teachers. Dr. Topolka-Jorissen earned her B.S., M.A., and Ph.D. from the University of Minnesota.

**Debra Touchton** is an Associate Professor and Program Director for Educational Leadership Graduate Programs at Stetson University. Her work focuses on school development, educational change, and women in leadership.

**Joel Westheimer** is a Professor and member of the Faculty of Education, University of Ottawa, Ottawa, Canada. His research and teaching interests are in the areas of politics and education, citizenship education.

**Sherry Willis** is currently serving as Principal of Southwest Elementary School in Hickory, North Carolina. She has been a school administrator with Hickory City Schools for 17 years after serving 19 years as a classroom teacher in the primary grades.

**Meena Wilson** is a Research Associate with the Center for Creative Leadership, Greensboro, NC.

## Studies in the Postmodern Theory of Education

*General Editor*
*Shirley R. Steinberg*

Counterpoints publishes the most compelling and imaginative books being written in education today. Grounded on the theoretical advances in criticalism, feminism, and postmodernism in the last two decades of the twentieth century, Counterpoints engages the meaning of these innovations in various forms of educational expression. Committed to the proposition that theoretical literature should be accessible to a variety of audiences, the series insists that its authors avoid esoteric and jargonistic languages that transform educational scholarship into an elite discourse for the initiated. Scholarly work matters only to the degree it affects consciousness and practice at multiple sites. Counterpoints' editorial policy is based on these principles and the ability of scholars to break new ground, to open new conversations, to go where educators have never gone before.

For additional information about this series or for the submission of manuscripts, please contact:

Shirley R. Steinberg
c/o Peter Lang Publishing, Inc.
29 Broadway, 18th floor
New York, New York 10006

To order other books in this series, please contact our Customer Service Department:
(800) 770-LANG (within the U.S.)
(212) 647-7706 (outside the U.S.)
(212) 647-7707 FAX

Or browse online by series:
www.peterlang.com